D0250414

Introducing the Reformed Faith

San Diego Christian College
Library
Santee, CA

Other Books by Donald K. McKim

The Church: Its Early Life

The Authority and Interpretation of the Bible:
  An Historical Approach (with Jack B. Rogers)

The Authoritative Word: Essays on the Nature of Scripture (editor)

Readings in Calvin's Theology (editor)

What Christians Believe About the Bible

A Guide to Contemporary Hermeneutics:
  Major Trends in Biblical Interpretation (editor)

How Karl Barth Changed My Mind (editor)

Ramism in William Perkins' Theology

Theological Turning Points: Major Issues in Christian Thought

Major Themes in the Reformed Tradition (editor)

Encyclopedia of the Reformed Faith (editor)

Kerygma: The Bible and Theology (4 volumes)

The Bible in Theology and Preaching

Westminster Dictionary of Theological Terms

God Never Forgets: Faith, Hope, and Alzheimer's Disease (editor)

Historical Handbook of Major Biblical Interpreters (editor)

Historical Dictionary of Reformed Churches
  (with Robert Benedetto and Darrell L. Guder)

Calvin's Institutes: *Abridged Edition* (editor)

284.2
MJ58i

Introducing the Reformed Faith

Biblical Revelation, Christian Tradition,
Contemporary Significance

Donald K. McKim

Westminster John Knox Press
LOUISVILLE
LONDON • LEIDEN

© 2001 Donald K. McKim

All rights reserved. No part of this book may be reproduced or transmitted in any form or by any means, electronic or mechanical, including photocopying, recording, or by any information storage or retrieval system, without permission in writing from the publisher. For information, address Westminster John Knox Press, 100 Witherspoon Street, Louisville, Kentucky 40202-1396.

Scripture quotations from the New Revised Standard Version of the Bible are copyright © 1989 by the Division of Christian Education of the National Council of the Churches of Christ in the U.S.A. and are used by permission.

Book design by Sharon Adams
Cover design by Night & Day Design

First edition

Published by Westminster John Knox Press
Louisville, Kentucky

This book is printed on acid-free paper that meets the American National Standards Institute Z39.48 standard.⊗

PRINTED IN THE UNITED STATES OF AMERICA

01 02 03 04 05 06 07 08 09 10 — 10 9 8 7 6 5 4 3 2 1

Library of Congress Cataloging-in-Publication Data is on file at the Library of Congress, Washington D.C.

ISBN 0-664-25644-9

To my family
LindaJo, Stephen, and Karl
whose sustaining love means everything to me.
This book is for you with my deepest love and gratitude.

Contents

Preface

Many people have helped to shape this book over a number of years. Important teachers at Westminster College (Pa.) and Pittsburgh Theological Seminary who conveyed their knowledge of Reformed theology and helped to instill a love for the Reformed faith include Jack Rogers, Thomas Gregory, John Gerstner, Ford Lewis Battles, Robert Paul, and Arthur Cochrane. I could not have asked for a better array of Reformed scholars and persons of faith with whom to study. For their care for me, I will always be grateful.

Westminster John Knox Press and my editor for this project, Stephanie Egnotovich, have been wonderful to work with once again. They graciously permitted me extra time to finish this manuscript. I am honored to have this work published with this venerable press of the Reformed tradition.

This book is dedicated to my family, LindaJo, Stephen, and Karl. Words cannot express my gratefulness to them for all their love, support, and the joys they have brought to my life. I can never give back to them all that they have given to me. For the precious treasure of their love, I give thanks to God.

Donald K. McKim

Germantown, Tennessee
St. Valentine's Day, 2000

Introduction

I hope this book will open doors. It is written for people who want to explore. It is written to provide perspectives, raise questions, and suggest ways in which a particular theological understanding—the Reformed faith—has approached a number of important Christian doctrines.

I wrote this book from a need. My years of teaching and writing as a theologian and serving as a pastor in churches have convinced me of the need for an introductory guide for laity and students. Laypersons in churches of the Reformed tradition often find themselves in these churches for a variety of reasons, including convenience and friendship. This is fine. But as they move around in the church—unite with it as members, perhaps—they also need to acquaint themselves with what the church believes. The task of educating new members (and current members) is carried out in differing fashions among the various Reformed denominations. Sometimes a long period of study is required. That's good. Other times, a quick review of some major doctrines is combined with introducing the particular life of the individual congregation. That's fine. In other places, unfortunately, the educative task is not carried out at all. That's bad.

For a long time I have wanted to provide an introductory guide that can help Reformed Christians gain an understanding of their faith. As a theologian, my approach naturally gravitated to surveying important Christian doctrines or teachings. Thus, *Introducing the Reformed Faith* was conceived.

Though I have spent my life in one branch of Reformed churches (Presbyterian) and in one denomination (Presbyterian Church [USA]), I have tried to write with a broad Reformed perspective that keeps in mind the varieties of views within the Reformed family. Some of my own theological interests and perspectives as a Reformed theologian will clearly emerge through the way I work with the materials. This is unavoidable, of course. But I hope I've given a fair rendering of various views. I have leaned more heavily on some writers than on others—John Calvin's work is cited most.[1] But I hope that as one reads, some familiarity with other theologians and documents will be apparent.

Each of the words in the title of this book—*Introducing the Reformed Faith*—is important. The book is an "introduction." Over the years, I have written a number of more technical resources on Reformed theology that have been useful to scholars, pastors, seminary students, and some inquisitive laypersons.[2] But the Reformed faith needs to be understood by more than just a select ("elect"!) few. It is a faith for all persons, and I keenly feel the need for laity in our churches, as well as seminarians and pastors, to have access to a primer to open the first doors for further study. Here I want to introduce the Reformed faith by sharing some of its perspectives and theological perceptions on doctrinal issues. No other book for nonspecialists approaches the Reformed faith in this way.

Because it is an "Introduction," several disclaimers are needed. First, this work is not a full theological treatment of each of the doctrines presented. Whole books can be and have been written on each topic here. Trained theologians will be frustrated with the brevity of the chapters. But my goal is to discuss main elements, not all the intricate details.

Second, this treatment of the topics is selective. The full range of Reformed thought is not presented on each doctrine. I've chosen perspectives that I consider important in the Reformed tradition, but I'm well aware that a whole host of worthy Reformed thinkers and documents are not mentioned. Some readers will wish I had steered more into other writers. But open doors can lead those interested to the joy of discovering new theologians!

Third, this book is not meant to be technical theology. I hope it is intellectually challenging and accurate. But I have written for those with no previous theological background. All the intricacies of the questions and the complexities of the arguments are not presented here. Theological scholars will not find much new here; nor will they think I have dealt adequately with all the issues and questions. I know this book can only scratch the surface in the most cursory way when it deals with the component parts of each chapter: Biblical Bases, Christian Tradition, Reformed Emphases, Contemporary Significance. I want the materials here to be a springboard for more theological study and reflection. I hope to tantalize Reformed folks to dive into deeper waters. The endnotes and other segments of the book introduce more sources for exploration.

Yet I do not apologize for the fact that this is a theology book. Christian theology, like every discipline, has a specialized language and vocabulary. Words are the building blocks of theological thought, and understanding the basic vocabulary is important. My *Westminster Dictionary of Theological Terms* (Louisville, Ky.: Westminster John Knox Press, 1996) can be a helpful companion in providing snapshot definitions of many terms. Theological terms have long histories and varied usages. Opening the pages of a theological book requires learning new language, pondering issues in new ways, and engaging in forms of thought that may not be exactly familiar. Newness is part of the adventure of theological study. I hope that in a small way this book will draw us to lifelong theological learning—particularly about the Reformed faith.

The second word in the title, "Reformed," is significant too. Reformed Christians have long contemplated what exactly it is that makes them "Reformed."[3] Reformed theologians also wrestle with this question. Is it a certain history or tradition? Is it a certain set of doctrinal beliefs? Is it a form of polity or church government, such as the presbyterian or congregational systems? Can a church simply call itself "reformed" because it wants to?

The question of "What is 'Reformed'?" has elicited a number of answers. In chapter 1 I mention some of the main historical developments of Reformed churches and Reformed thought as they emerged out of the sixteenth-century Swiss Reformation. Venerable theologians of that time such as Huldrych Zwingli, John Calvin, and Heinrich Bullinger shaped theological understandings in unique ways that distinguished them from other church reform movements of the era—particularly the Lutheran and the Anabaptists. The Reformed "tradition" spread through Europe and beyond so that today Reformed churches are found throughout the world.[4] Each church or groups of churches, perhaps, has its own definition of what it means to be "Reformed."[5]

So what I present here is not a full discussion of Reformed theology. I've named one recurring section "Reformed Emphases" to indicate that, over time, *some* of the Reformed tradition and *some* Reformed theologians have emphasized focus on a doctrine in a particular way. Several names and some documents appear more frequently than others; other scholars could have written each section in much different ways. My intent is to show what some of the most important Reformed emphases have been as they have developed from a variety of perspectives. Reformed theology is not monolithic, but within the Reformed family and in the Reformed stream of theological thought some distinctive contributions and clear trajectories are obvious. No absolute "Reformed formulation" took place at any point. The tradition has been enriched by its varieties and diversities of expression.[6] Yet these varieties have maintained distinctiveness as Reformed expressions over against those of other traditions and perspectives.[7]

Also, Reformed Christians—and Reformed theology—have always recognized that "Reformed expressions" are understandings of Christian faith that emerge from and are in dialogue with the whole Christian church and Christian tradition as a whole. We are first of all members of the universal Christian church before we are members of our specific denominations. We are "Christians" (noun) before we are "Reformed Christians" (adjective).

Partially for this reason I have structured each of the doctrinal chapters the same way. Reformed Christians begin with the biblical revelation as our source for doing theology. Thus, "Biblical Bases" are considered for each doctrine. I've used a number of biblical references in the text, and I hope that readers will take the time to consult them. Scripture is the foundation on which our theological understandings are built. In the midst of Hitler's attempt to take over church and state in 1934, the Confessing Church in Germany met and produced the Theological Declaration of Barmen. This document, primarily authored by Karl Barth, became an influential "Reformed confession" for its courageous witness in dangerous times. The synod of Barmen asked that the words of their Declaration be judged by their fidelity: "See whether they agree with Holy Scripture and with the Confessions of the Fathers. If you find that we are speaking contrary to Scripture, then do not listen to us! But if you find that we are taking our stand upon Scripture, then let no fear or temptation keep you from treading with us the path of faith and obedience to the Word of God. . . ."[8]

Reformed Christians want to understand what the Christian church through the centuries has understood biblical teachings to be on each topic and the ways the church has formulated theological understandings of what became Christian doctrines. Thus, "Christian Tradition" is considered throughout. This book should show that our faith is part of the mainstream of Christian tradition. This segment of each chapter conveys our wider Christian heritage.

"Reformed Emphases" have emerged as people who consider themselves "Reformed" have wrestled with the Christian tradition, shaped and reshaped it, and then confessed their own understandings of its import. In this way, Reformed thought is both catholic and ecumenical—"catholic" in that it emerges from dialogue with the whole Christian tradition, and ecumenical in its dialogue with Christian communions today. The different Reformed responses to doctrines have sometimes thoroughly affirmed what the church and Christian tradition have considered to be orthodox or "right belief." At points, Reformed theologians have chosen to emphasize one of the streams within the broad Christian tradition—often the stream that emerges from the work of St. Augustine in the fifth century. At other times the Reformed have modified the tradition itself and moved in new directions in light of what Reformed Christians have heard God saying by the power of the Holy Spirit through the Scriptures. These varieties are seen in the chapters that follow.

The "Reformed Emphases" segment of each chapter displays, I trust, the ongoing dialogue of Reformed theology and confessional statements with Holy Scripture and with the inherited Christian tradition of doctrinal understandings.

This dialogue will continue into the future. One of the "mottoes" of Reformed churches has been: "The church reformed and always being reformed according to Scripture." As Reformed Christians continue to listen to God's word in Scripture and be open to the leading of the Holy Spirit, new insights can emerge. The Christian tradition of the past is not yet finished, and Reformed theology is part of this ongoing flow of faith. Jane D. Douglass rightly noted that "Reformed theology is still in the making, still unfinished, and will be till the end of time."[9] This book is a very modest mile marker along the way.

Each chapter concludes with a brief segment on "Contemporary Significance" that presents short suggestions of the ways that each particular doctrine has relevance and meaning for today's church and Christian persons. Contemporary relevance is an important dimension of Reformed theology itself. Doctrine should be clearly understood and meaningfully articulated, and it should lead to a deeper devotion to God and service in God's reign. John Calvin set the tradition in this direction when he wrote that "we are called to a knowledge of God: not that knowledge which, content with empty speculation, merely flits in the brain, but that which will be sound and fruitful if we duly perceive it, and if it takes root in the heart."[10] The Heidelberg Catechism always asks what "advantage" or "benefit" it is to know a specific doctrine.[11] The "Contemporary Significance" of each doctrine is a key part of our theological understanding—to realize in what ways doctrinal teaching can and does impact our lives in this world.

This brings us to "faith," the third main word in the title, *Introducing the Reformed Faith*. In an earlier work, I wrote that "the Reformed faith is the faith of Christian people. It is a living, vital stream of faith providing a basis for the lives of millions throughout the world."[12] I will be grateful if this book captures not only the important intellectual features of the faith, but also the vitality of what this faith can mean for our living. The title of the book is not *Introducing Reformed Theology* or *Introducing the Reformed Tradition*. *Introducing the Reformed Faith* calls us to realize that what we believe theologically does impact the ways we live. Christian sermons seek to turn the "nouns" of theology into "verbs"—for the living of our lives under God. But as we look at a number of "nouns" here—in the form of Christian doctrines or teachings—I hope they will become more than simply pages to be read. I hope the doctrines become living, vital ways of understanding Christian faith so they will not merely "flit in the brain," but will "take root in the heart." The Reformed faith is a faith of *living people*.[13]

The question here is the same one that God asked the prophet Ezekiel in the valley of the dry bones: "Mortal, can these bones live?" (Ezek. 37:3). Can the "bones" of theology—of Christian doctrine—"live" today? Can theology be meaningful for us? Can what we believe so shape and form our lives that we will have joy in the knowledge of God?

I believe the Reformed faith can enhance and deepen our Christian faith. Reformed faith is one way of understanding what it means to be a Christian person. It is not the only way, of course. What I present here is not meant to argue for a "Reformed exclusivity" or that this is the only right and proper way of understanding Christian doctrine. But I do write from the conviction that the Reformed faith does give us biblically faithful and theologically responsible ways of understanding the Christian faith and Christian theology. These understandings shape and transform our lives to greater knowledge and service of God.

I wrote my doctoral dissertation on William Perkins (1558–1602), an English Reformed theologian and Puritan of the sixteenth century. He defined theology this way: "Theology is the science of living blessedly for ever."[14] Theology itself will not save us. Reformed theology will not save us. But our theology can convey the riches of God's Word and God's divine self-communication to us in Jesus Christ through the Scriptures by the power of the Holy Spirit. May *Introducing the Reformed Faith* open doors to further understanding and invite you to "live blessedly for ever."*

---

*A note on language. I am committed to the use of inclusive language and have tried to follow that commitment throughout this book. Quoted texts, however, have been left as they appear for the most part. So also, the term "kingdom" of God has been used in its traditional sense along with the term "reign of God."

Ways to Use This Book

This book can be used in several ways. It is written primarily for laity and students who want to find out something about the Reformed faith as it has come to us in the Reformed theological tradition. Each chapter is structured the same way: Introduction, Biblical Bases, Christian Tradition, Reformed Emphases, Contemporary Significance, and Questions for Reflection and Discussion.

Individual/Group Study. This book can be read by people individually or as part of a group in a church school, new members class, or adult study class.

Ways to Use the Book. Several ways to use this book include:

1. Read the book straight through as you study each doctrine.

2. Read a specific segment in each of the chapters. You could study the biblical materials, the Christian tradition, or Reformed emphases in each of the chapters to gain a biblical, historical, or a Reformed view of all the doctrinal topics.

Levels of Engagement. This book can be read at two general levels of engagement.

1. Read only the text. It is written as simply as possible to introduce the study of theology and the Reformed faith.

2. Read the text and study the endnotes. The notes for each chapter give references for further study. Many of the works cited are available in theological libraries or through interlibrary loan programs of public libraries.

1

Believing in God:
Confessing Our Faith

The whole "household of God" (1 Tim. 3:15) known as the Christian church has many members. We are spread across the globe in every nation of the world. We are all members of the same family, even as we are divided into numerous groups or denominations.

The Reformed Family

The "Reformed" family is one of the groups within the Christian church. We have a family history. We belong with those Christians whose early ancestors came from the continent of Europe in the sixteenth century. The most important and well known of these ancestors was the theologian John Calvin (1509–1564), who lived in Geneva and became one of the most significant thinkers in western Europe.[1] Calvin was a student of Holy Scripture, a teacher, writer, church and community leader, and one of the most brilliant theologians in the history of the Christian church. His understandings of Scripture and his theological writings were key in forming a tradition that emerged through his followers after his death. This tradition, with leaders such as Heinrich Bullinger (1504–1575), Theodore Beza (1519–1605), and John Knox (1514–1572), became known as the "Reformed" tradition,[2] primarily because it emphasized the reform of the church according to the Word of God.[3]

The Reformed tradition spread throughout Europe as people joined together in Reformed churches.[4] Calvin and his earlier contemporary Huldrych Zwingli (1484–1531), who was also an important theologian, allied themselves with the emerging Protestantism associated with the church reforms of Martin Luther (1484–1546). This broad movement of religious reform became known as the Protestant Reformation. Luther and his followers believed that many of the teachings and practices of the prevailing Roman

Catholic church were contrary to Scripture. The Protestant movement, originating from Luther's protests against Rome, was a major revolution throughout Europe. Eventually, three main streams or traditions of Protestantism took shape: Lutheran, Anabaptist, and Reformed. The Lutheran tradition followed the teachings of Luther; the Anabaptist tradition rejected both Roman Catholicism and also many of the teachings of Luther, particularly regarding infant baptism. The Reformed tradition emerged from Zwingli and Calvin.

The Reformed tradition is also sometimes referred to as Calvinism. Calvin's followers built on his work to address issues of their own times and places. Though Calvin himself had a brilliant systematic mind, his successors in the seventeenth century systematized theology even further. It became more detailed and cast in the mold called scholasticism, which had been the method of teaching in the schools of the Middle Ages. Calvinism spread from central Europe into the Netherlands and to the British Isles in Scotland and England, becoming associated with Puritanism in the seventeenth century. Calvinism also spread to the Americas by emigration. In the eighteenth and nineteenth centuries through the work of missionaries, important Reformed bodies of churches were established in Africa and also in Latin America, Asia, and the Near East. Many of these churches continue to thrive today through indigenous leadership, and in these areas the highest growth rates of new Reformed churches are found.

The Reformed faith, then, has its family tree. Though diversities abound, important common ingredients mark us as brothers and sisters in the Reformed family. These "family resemblances" are discovered in the ways in which we find that our faith is best nourished, our understandings of the Scriptures and theology best articulated, and our Christian lives best focused.

One common characteristic is that we are a confessional people; we frequently profess or confess what we believe. We believe in God, we celebrate God's gracious love in Jesus Christ, and we confess that faith, often through formal written statements called "confessions." Like Peter and John of old, "we cannot keep from speaking about what we have seen and heard" (Acts 4:20). The history of the Reformed tradition is filled with confessions of faith by Reformed Christians written at different times and places.[5] As Reformed Christians, we believe that confessing our faith is one of the most important things we can do. This practice of confessing faith has a long history.

Confessions and Creeds
Biblical Confessions

The psalmist proclaims: "Let the redeemed of the LORD say so" (Ps. 107:2). From early days, people of faith have spoken of their faith. The psalmist was individually proclaiming what the nation of Israel frequently did (see Deut. 6:4–9; 26:5–9).[6] At times of great importance, the people paused to speak their faith. They summarized and declared what they believed most deeply. These confessions were passed along to later generations as a witness to belief in God and God's actions in their lives and in the life of the nation.

New Testament Christians also confessed faith. The apostle Peter, in the midst of Jesus' ministry, was asked by his master: "Who do you say that I am?" Peter answered, "You are the Messiah, the Son of the living God" (see Matt. 16:13–18; Mark 8:29). The earliest and briefest Christian creed is simply, "Jesus is Lord" (1 Cor. 12:3). The apostle Paul passed along several summary statements of what early Christians believed about Jesus Christ—his life, death, and resurrection (Rom. 1:3–4; 1 Cor. 15:3–4). He called on others to say so—to confess their faith (Rom. 10:9; 1 Cor. 12:3). As the Christian church expanded its mission and ministry throughout the Mediterranean world, the Christian communities found it important to establish a common body of belief and affirm their faith as witnesses to their Lord and Savior. Confessional statements, in varying amounts of detail, emerged.

Early Christian Creeds

Early Christians confessed their faith at baptism.[7] Candidates for baptism, called "catechumens," learned about the Christian faith and after this time of instruction were ready to profess their own Christian faith. Their profession consisted of reciting a "creed" (from the Latin word *credo*, "I believe") that summarized what the church believed and what they believed.

The basic formula of baptism "in the name of the Father, Son, and Holy Spirit" came to be expanded in the early Christian centuries. By the end of the second century, the Old Roman Symbol ("symbol" was a common name for a creed) was taking shape. The Apostles' Creed eventually developed from the Old Roman Symbol between the fifth and eighth centuries in southern France. Charlemagne, the Holy Roman Emperor, ordered the Apostles' Creed to be used for instruction in the faith. When Christians confessed their faith, they were saying what they believed about God the Father, Son, and Holy Spirit.

The theological conflicts of the fourth century led to two important church councils, the Councils of Nicaea (A.D. 325) and Constantinople (A.D. 381). These two councils were crucial in establishing official church teaching on the doctrines of who God is (the Trinity), who Jesus Christ is (Christology), and who the Holy Spirit is (Pneumatology). The Nicene Creed as we know it today was written to witness to the church's faith, to identify orthodox or "right" Christian belief over against "heresy" (the choosing of "another way"), and to bring the different churches of the Christian community into solidarity with each other. The Nicene Creed begins by proclaiming, "We believe. . . ."

Summaries of belief, confessions of faith, and creeds played a crucial role in the early church period. They passed along Christian tradition and the emerging beliefs of the church about its faith. They capsulized Christian experience by putting into words what Christians found to be true in their lives of faith. They unified the church and gave it identity. They were used for the worship and praise of God. They became norms for teaching and preaching. Creeds also conveyed a way of reading and interpreting the Scriptures that showed how the church was understanding its authoritative writings. Creeds and confessions defined right Christian belief or orthodoxy in the midst of various other views.

Church Confessions

The practices of the early church regarding church confessions set the direction for later Christian creeds and confessions as well. A confession of faith can be defined as "a public declaration before God and the world of what a church believes."[8] Individuals can and do confess their own personal faith, which is important, but church confessions take on a communal character when individuals join with others in the household of faith and say, "We believe."

Confessional Directions

Church confessions are important statements and extend in three directions.

1. Churches confess their faith to convey their gratitude to *God*. They respond in thankfulness to God's self-communication in Scripture and supremely in Jesus Christ. Confessing our faith shows our acceptance of responsibility in trying to be faithful and obedient servants of God.

2. Churches also confess their faith to convey to *themselves* what they are committed to believing and doing as God's people. A confession of faith is a type of mission statement—a declaration of what is believed and the implications of those beliefs for daily life.

3. Churches confess their faith to convey to the *world* whom they serve and what they believe. Through their confessions, churches can speak to the world in a more unified way. They declare their self-understanding—their understanding of who God is and what God has done—and they affirm what they believe to be true and what they deny. In this way, social and political dimensions, as well as theological and church perspectives, are part of the confessing act.

Times for Confessions

Church confessions arise from needs to proclaim or confess the Christian faith. Often in the history of the church, a particularly pressing problem led churches to affirm what they believed in the face of temptation or danger. Confessions may emerge from the church's need to correct a distortion of the gospel. Some political or cultural movement may be attacking the church or subtly tempting it into idolatry. In the face of these challenges, churches may issue a confession of faith. Urgent situations can call forth the church's affirmation of its faith.

Types of Confessions

Several types of confessions have been part of the Christian church's witness through the centuries.

1. *Short Summaries.* Some confessions present short summaries of Christian belief. Used for teaching or liturgical purposes, they say succinctly what the church believes. The best-known example is the Apostles' Creed. A contemporary example is A Brief Statement of Faith (1991) of the Presbyterian Church (U.S.A.).

2. *Comprehensive Statements.* A number of church confessions, particularly those written during the Protestant Reformation in the sixteenth century, are comprehensive statements of what Christians believe. They cover many doctrinal teachings and are detailed expositions of faith. Examples are the Augsburg Confession (1530) in the Lutheran tradition and the Second Helvetic Confession (1566) in the Reformed tradition.

3. *Specific Issues.* Sometimes the church must confess its faith in the midst of teachings regarded as false or heretical. Confessional statements focused on specific issues are needed to proclaim the positive witness of the gospel and to combat error. Examples are the Nicene Creed (A.D. 325, A.D. 381) and Chalcedonian Formula (A.D. 451) from the early church and the Theological Declaration of Barmen (1934) from contemporary times.

Functions of Confessions

These differing types of confessions may also serve varying functions for the church's witness and ministry.

1. *Worship.* Confessional statements in Christian worship and liturgy help to familiarize a wide array of people with a document. Sometimes whole creeds are used (Apostles' and Nicene), and at other times, portions suffice. Another form of confession—the catechism—may also be used. When employed in worship, congregations are reminded that confessions of faith are acts of gratitude and praise.

2. *Instruction*. Confessions of faith are also teaching documents. They assist in interpreting Scripture, in understanding church traditions, and in keeping the broader faith of the church in view so that one's own faith does not become narrow or biased. Catechisms can function to prepare children and adults for professing personal faith in Jesus Christ and for church membership.

3. *Defense of Orthodoxy*. As positive statements of how a church understands the gospel, confessional statements witness to the common beliefs of a confessional community. They affirm certain understandings and actions while rejecting others. Confessions can serve as a means of passing on church tradition and of preserving the church's conception of its faith.

4. *Help in Danger*. When the church faces temptation and danger, confessions can strengthen the community toward fidelity to the gospel. The seductions of racism, sexism, warfare, and social or economic injustice can be corrosive and thus must be met by clear statements of the church's faith.

5. *Church Discipline*. Confessional standards also function in churches when they become required confessions for ordination of ministers and church officers. Thus church leaders must be in agreement with the theological standards of the church as they lead congregations.

Church confessions can serve a variety of purposes, none of which are exclusive purposes in themselves. Confessional documents function on these different levels to provide ways of expressing the church's faith and life.

Limitations of Confessions

Though church confessions serve necessary purposes and emerge at critical periods in the church's life as normative statements of belief, they are also limited in a number of ways. They may be written at a time of danger or problem in a specific historical setting, and as such may address certain issues in very direct and significant ways. The particular time and place of a confessional writing will cause limitations when it is read by later generations. All such documents face the limitations of their own historical circumstances in terms of the language and thought forms in which they are expressed. The church's formulations about the Trinity and Christology in its early centuries were written under the influence of then-current philosophical ideas as well as understandings about the nature of the world and its natural processes. Social, cultural, and political assumptions are inevitably expressed in confessional writings. All are historically conditioned, even the great, classical statements of Christian belief.

For this reason, developing appropriate guidelines for interpreting confessional statements is important, just as such guidelines are developed for interpreting the Bible. As Christians study confessional writings, we must be guided by historical sensitivities and use the best resources available to hear what the confession is affirming or denying in terms of its own historical circumstances, before we seek to transfer its insights into our own settings.[9]

Reformed Confessions

Reformed Christians frequently confess their faith. As Reformed thought spread across western Europe in the sixteenth and seventeenth centuries, new church communities produced a number of confessions of faith.[10] These confessions functioned well for their own historical times and places.

In this earlier period, Reformed confessions emerged from six streams or traditions.[11] The first flowed from the work of Huldrych Zwingli in Zurich and spread through German-speaking Switzerland. The second phase was the Genevan tradition associated with John Calvin and his followers. The spread of Calvinism into eastern and western Europe marks a third stream. The German Reformed confessional tradition emerged to constitute a fourth type of confessional writing. A fifth phase is found with the teachings of the Synod of Dort in the Netherlands (1619), which codified Calvinism against the teachings of James Arminius and the Arminianism of his followers. The sixth phase of the Reformed confessional tradition is found in the Helvetic Consensus Formula (1675) and controversies with the School of Saumur. Each of these streams produced important confessional documents that served the needs of Reformed Christians in their various settings.

A distinctive mark of the Reformed tradition historically has been this propensity to create new confessions as new occasions and situations arise.[12] The result is a whole body of Reformed confessional writings from the sixteenth century to the current day.[13] In new contexts, Reformed Christians have felt the need to "say so," as redeemed people of the Lord (Ps. 107:2).

Ecumenical Impulses

The Reformed faith impels persons to confess their faith as part of the ecumenical church, the whole people of God. The movement here is first from what Christians believe to what Reformed Christians believe. Reformed churches are a portion of the full household of faith. As such, Reformed theology and Reformed faith are open to hearing, dialoguing with, and learning from other theological viewpoints and Christian communions. Though some Reformed bodies have tended to become more narrow and almost assume that their formulations are the only means of expressing God's truth, this impulse runs counter to the genuine heartbeat of Reformed faith. Reformed faith is open to God's Spirit, who may encounter us at any time in any place.

Reformed Christians should seek and listen to other voices since perhaps through them an essential theological insight will be given.

Confessional Authority

Confessions of faith have authority. They gain their authority as expressions of Christians' beliefs in a certain time and place. These beliefs are appropriate expressions of the biblical message, the claims of Jesus Christ, and what the Spirit is leading the churches to confess. The fact that there are so many Reformed confessions and that Reformed Christians have invariably produced confessional statements at key points in the lives of their communities indicates that the confessional task is taken seriously.

No one formulation of Christian truth or confessional utterance is completely normative or binding on all other Reformed Christians. "New occasions teach new duties," and even venerable and important Reformed confessions of the past must be supplemented by expressions of faith in new, contemporary contexts. While confessions speak authoritatively to the churches and with great power, their authority is ultimately *relative, temporary,* and *provisional.* These characteristics do not diminish a confession's importance, but they warn against absolutizing any one particular document (or one theologian!) and considering the task and joy of confessing faith anew to be ended. Confessing our faith is an ongoing responsibility of the people of God.

1. *Relative.* Our confessions are always "relative" in their authority in that they look beyond themselves to the authority of Scripture as the guideline for Christian theology and the means of understanding Christian experience. A confession of faith is, in effect, a commentary on Holy Scripture.[14]

2. *Temporary.* Confessions are "temporary" in that they are open-ended. They look forward to the future and to what new ways the Spirit of God may lead the church to confess a new understanding or perspective. The question is always: "What is God calling us to do in Jesus Christ through the power of the Holy Spirit right here and now?"

3. *Provisional.* To recognize that confessions are "provisional" means that they are written by limited, sinful, and fallible Christians who are shaped and influenced by their own cultural settings and assumptions. As we read older confessional documents, we can see clearly points at which such assumptions strongly molded the way theological matters were understood and articulated. In a real sense, we must seek the intentions of confessional documents and not read them in a literalistic manner in which we simply transfer what they say into our own times.[15]

New Confessions

A new confession "does not seek to replace the older Confessions but to clarify and to explain them in the face of new questions."[16] The church must always keep a listening and obedient ear open for God's word to come in new and fresh ways. When that word is spoken and heard, it must also be proclaimed. Confessional writings are one form by which Christian proclamation ("preaching") is carried out. In a real sense, "the Confession occurs not when we think we have discovered the truth, but when the truth has found us."[17] For this reason, delegates to the Synod of Barmen exclaimed in the midst of the rising Nazi power that "with gratitude to God, they are convinced that they have been given a common word to utter."[18] The Holy Spirit in sovereign freedom uses a specific occasion as the opportunity for the church to confess its faith in Jesus Christ who is "the one Word of God which we have to hear and which we have to trust and obey in life and in death."[19] The church listens, hears, and proclaims that which is a witness to Jesus Christ. As the apostle Paul wrote, "we also believe, and so we speak" (2 Cor. 4:13).

A new confession of faith provides the freedom for Christian persons to decide to act and obey. Profound new meanings from older confessional documents may emerge in difficult times. Reformed Christians are also sustained by the profound profession in the Heidelberg Catechism that our only comfort in life and in death is that "I belong—body and soul, in life and in death—not to myself but to my faithful Savior, Jesus Christ"; or the answer to the first question of the Westminster Shorter Catechism, that our "chief end" or main purpose in life is "to glorify God and to enjoy [God] forever."[20] These enduring words ring true to Christian faith and Reformed experience in every era. Believers will always be nurtured by these words, even if centuries old.

But new confessional statements provide vital opportunities for Christians to profess their faith and witness in their own contexts. A new confession is an important moment, a chance to confess Jesus Christ today. No matter what form or type of confession is composed, the Reformed Christian is faced with deciding whether in and through that statement the true voice of God in Jesus Christ is heard by the work of the Holy Spirit. Does this statement say what needs to be said, confess what needs to be confessed, and urge action in ways that actions are needed—in light of the Scriptures, the other confessions of the church, and supremely, in light of Jesus Christ? For "a confession does not tyrannize or coerce." It does not "force itself" upon people. It does not "extort subscription." A confession grants women and men "the freedom to prove its words and then to respond in obedience."[21] This authority and freedom characterize a new confession.

Confessing Our Faith

The Reformed faith expresses itself in confessions of faith. In the first 150 years of their existence, Reformed communities produced at least fifty confessions of faith. Yet, "no one can provide an official list of Reformed confessions, as no one has the authority to set boundaries."[22]

The renowned theologian Karl Barth defined a Reformed creed as:

> a statement, spontaneously and publicly formulated by a Christian community within a geographically limited area which, until further actions, defines its character for outsiders; and which, until further action, gives guidance for its own doctrine and life; it is a formulation of the insight currently given to the whole Christian church by the revelation of God in Jesus Christ, witnessed to by Holy Scriptures alone.[23]

Reformed Christians live by the insights God has given in Jesus Christ. We "confess" this faith, and we probe what our confession means for Christian action in the life of the church and in our own lives. In confessing, we bear witness to God's grace, and we respond in gratitude. We "say so"—to the world, to the church, and to ourselves.

We live our lives as God's people in the midst of culture and history. We write and speak of our faith because our faith itself compels us to do so. We cannot keep silent about the Gospel! As we witness here and now in the service of God, however, we look to the future and live in hope (Rom. 5:2). We eagerly anticipate the day when "at the name of Jesus every knee should bend, in heaven and on earth and under the earth, and every tongue should *confess* that Jesus Christ is Lord, to the glory of God the Father" (Phil. 2:10–11).

Questions for Reflection

1. What Reformed churches have you been a part of or do you know about? (See the list of Reformed churches in Canada and the United States on page 193.) Have these churches been primarily similar to each other or different? In what ways?

2. From your knowledge of history, recount instances where it would have been dangerous for a church body to produce a confession of faith. Do you think that could ever be the case in this country?

3. In what ways do the creeds and confessions of the church nurture your faith? What are some ways in which these documents can be integrated more fully into the church's life and work?

4. With what church creed or confession are you most familiar? What are its strengths? Its weaknesses?

5. If you were to compose a confession of faith, what type would it be? What elements would you include? In what ways would you like to see it used?

2

Scripture: The Word of God

The Reformed faith takes theology seriously. We believe that God has given us minds to know God and hearts to love God. But the big question is: How do we "know God"?

In one sense our quest for the knowledge of God is the most important issue we can deal with in life. We need to know God, just as we need to know ourselves. We need to know both who God is and who God is in relation to who we are. That's why John Calvin began his *Institutes of the Christian Religion* with the famous sentence: "Nearly all the wisdom we possess, that is to say, true and sound wisdom, consists of two parts: the knowledge of God and of ourselves."[1]

The Reformed faith has always emphasized that God is made known to us in and through the Holy Scriptures. We turn to the Bible to gain knowledge of God. Supremely, that knowledge of God is found in Jesus Christ, for "Christian doctrine affirms that God is essentially as he is shown to be by Jesus."[2] Only through the Scriptures do we know anything of Jesus Christ. So the Bible is the basic source both for our coming to a knowledge of God and for our theological understandings of the whole Christian faith. We are able to do our theological thinking on the basis of one source of knowledge: the Bible.

Why do we turn to the Bible? Why have the Scriptures of the Old and New Testaments been so central to Christian theology and to the Reformed faith?

The simple answer is that Christians believe the Scriptures are the revelation of God.[3] The Scriptures uniquely convey a knowledge of God. They provide a knowledge of God that we can gain in no other way, through no other source. The Christian church turns to the Scriptures for understanding and guidance. Individual Christians find in the Scriptures the comfort and challenge they need as they seek to be followers of Jesus Christ. In the Bible, we encounter God, so the Scriptures are commonly referred to as the "Word of God." They are the self-expression of God. They have come to us in the words of human beings, like us, who lived in their own settings and cultures, yet who have conveyed—by the power of God's Holy Spirit—the knowledge of God and knowledge of God's will that the church and every Christian need in order to live as God desires.

Biblical Bases

The Bible presents a God who "in the beginning" created "the heavens and the earth" (Gen. 1:1). This God is great and sovereign over all things. This God is hidden from human perceptions since humans are God's creatures and separated from God by the limits of their own selves and—in a theological sense—by their behavior, or sin.

Yet the astounding message of the Bible is that this God has not stayed in the heavens and let the creatures who live on Earth go their own ways. Instead, God communicates with the creation and has been revealed to human beings.

The revelation of God's self comes in different ways. The Bible tells us of a number of covenants that God made with individuals and groups. In the Old Testament, God calls Abram and Sarai to leave their homeland and go forth so that God could bless them and make of them a great nation (Gen. 12:1–3). God made covenants with Noah (Genesis 6), Moses and the people of Israel (Exodus 20), David (2 Chron. 21:7), and others. Through these covenants, God was made known to the people and a special relationship established with them. In the New Testament, God's supreme covenant was made in Jesus Christ (1 Cor. 11:23–26).

These covenants are astounding because God is revealed in them! Who God is, what God does, and what God wants humans beings to be and do can all be known. The Bible portrays a God who is revealed and who seeks a relationship of love, peace, and justice with humanity. This activity of God was not required. God could have created the cosmos and then stepped away forever, letting all the processes of nature and all the actions of billions of people go along without any interference or intervention. But the biblical picture is far different. In the Bible we meet a God who communicates with humans, who calls, speaks, and shows us who God is. God has been revealed to the world, and the Bible is our source for knowing this God.

This self-communication or revelation is depicted in the Bible in many ways. In the Old Testament, the Hebrew term *gelah* literally means "to uncover." It takes on a particularly theological meaning when God is the subject, or the one who "reveals" (1 Sam. 2:27; cf. 3:7). Other Old Testament terms associated with "seeing" (Amos 1:1), "showing" (Amos 7:1; Ezek. 39:13), and "appearing" (Gen. 26:2; Lev. 9:6) give the fuller picture—that God is making God's self known to people in a variety of ways. In the New Testament, the Greek work *apokaluptō* has the same sense, that which has been "hidden" has now been "revealed" (Rom. 1:17–18; Eph. 3:5). Words such as "declare" (Col. 4:3), "make known," and "show" again point to the same reality: God is revealed.[4]

The Bible recognizes God as revealed in nature, as when the Psalmist proclaims, "The heavens are telling the glory of God; and the firmament proclaims his handiwork" (Ps. 19:1). Gaze into the heavens and ask yourself, "Who created these?" (Isa. 40:26). For those who know God, the incomparable wonder of creation leads us to worship and praise (Psalm 104).

But a more major theme in the Hebrew Scriptures is that God is known by what God does. Specifically, God is revealed through what are perceived to be God's actions in history. In the Old Testament, the people of Israel believed that God made the divine self known to them in the midst of their slavery in Egypt and by bringing them liberation in the exodus from Egypt (Ezek. 20:5, 9). A refrain throughout the Hebrew Scriptures is God saying, "I am the LORD your God, who brought you out of the land of Egypt, out of the house of slavery" (Deut. 5:6; cf. Ex. 20:1). Some see the whole theology of the Old Testament as developing from the exodus event when the people of Israel experienced God's "mighty hand and . . . outstretched arm" (Deut. 4:34; 26:8). God is revealed in history, particularly in the nation-saving event of bringing slaves into freedom.

In the biblical materials several dimensions of God's self-communication and revelation stand out. God clearly has taken the initiative in revelation. Humans cannot possibly ascend to the heavens, peel back the clouds, and look into the face of God. No limited (and sinful) human being can do that! But astonishingly, we don't have to try. God has made the first move by speaking and acting to make God known. God is portrayed as "calling" to people, inviting them into relationship with the Lord. In the story of Adam and Eve, while they were hiding from God in the Garden of Eden (because of their sin), God "called" to them (Gen. 3:9f.). God called Abram and Sarai from Haran to begin a new people (Gen. 12:1–3). God acted to reveal the divine "name" to Moses at the burning bush (Ex. 3:1–6), and God is revealed to the prophets who are called to proclaim God's word (Isaiah 6; Jer. 1:4–19; Hos. 1:1f.). God declares who God is and what God wants people to do by revealing the divine self to them.

Second, God's revelation is eminently personal. The Scriptures proclaim many things about God: God is holy, just, loving, and righteous. But the goal of these revelations of God's character is not merely to impart correct infor-

mation about the Almighty. Instead, God's purpose in revelation is to recon-
nect with humanity, to reestablish the fellowship relationship marked by trust,
love, and obedience, a relationship that sin has disrupted and destroyed. God
restores this relationship by revealing God's own self. It is God who "speaks"
in the Scriptures. God's word comes to women and men, and that word is the
communication of God's self. God speaks to Abraham and makes him God's
friend (James 2:23). God spoke with Moses "face to face, as one speaks to a
friend" (Ex. 33:11). God's people were said to be "the apple" of God's eye
(Deut. 32:10). Supremely, God's own self is revealed in a human person: in
Jesus Christ (John 1:1; 2 Cor. 5:19). God's own person is revealed and made
known to humans.

Also, in the Bible, God's revelation often takes a written form. The Scriptures are full of the expression, "Thus says the Lord" (Obad. 1:1; Nahum
1:12). God reveals God's divine purpose and plan to those who will proclaim
God's word. Frequently, this word proclaimed is put into written form. The
Ten Commandments were written (Ex. 24:12), as were the words of a
covenant (Josh. 24:26), and prophets were often commanded to speak and to
write (Jer. 30:2; Ezek. 43:11; Hab. 2:2). The Gospels initially circulated in
communities of faith as oral traditions, but they were later edited and written.
Paul's letters were circulated as written documents to early churches.[5] The
visionary prophet John was told to "Write in a book what you see and send it
to the seven churches . . ." (Rev. 1:11). These written words form the story of
God's revealing work in the history of the people. The story is an ongoing revelation of God to all who hear and read, even in the present day. The written
form is not a hindrance to God's revelation of God's own self and God's will.
It is the means by which God communicates and continues to do so.

One other dimension is important in considering God's self-revelation in
written form. Two New Testament texts point to what is often referred to as
the "inspiration" of Scripture. In 2 Timothy 3:16–17, the verses read: "All
scripture is inspired by God and is useful for teaching, for reproof, for correction, and for training in righteousness, so that everyone who belongs to
God may be proficient, equipped for every good work." While the original
biblical writer did not have in mind the full range of biblical writings—Old
and New Testaments—that the church has today, the church has understood
this passage to mean that the scriptural writings all share a "God-breathed"
character. God has worked in and through the biblical writers and editors to
inspire them and to assure that the message they convey is what God wants
communicated. These verses indicate that Scripture originates with God, that
it is "God-breathed" or "inspired" (Gr. *theopneustos*).[6] God originates the
divine message. The Scriptures are "from God."

Notice too the purpose of this "inspiration." The Scriptures may be "useful" for teaching, reproof, correction, and training in righteousness—in short, for the purposes of divine salvation. The Bible is inspired by God to convey God's divine message of salvation so that women and men will know how to be in relationship with God and to live in obedience to God's will and purposes.[7] The purpose of inspiration is to "equip" those who read the Scriptures in the ways God wants. The Bible has a very functional authority.[8]

A second passage of importance is 2 Peter 1:21: ". . . no prophecy ever came by human will, but men and women moved by the Holy Spirit spoke from God." This verse emphasizes the means God uses to convey God's divine message. By the power of God's Holy Spirit, human beings speak and proclaim God's message. The Spirit "moves" the biblical speakers and writers. The fact that the Scriptures originate with God does not exclude the human. Rather, through the human writers the divine message is conveyed.[9] No biblical verses provide any explanation of this method of transmission, any "theory of inspiration." It is a mystery. God is able to use humans—with all their personalities, limitations, and cultural conditionings—to convey God's word in written form.[10]

The Christian Bible is composed of two major parts: the Old Testament and the New Testament. The Old Testament is the Hebrew Scriptures, writings that the Christian church shares in common with Judaism. The Old Testament was written in the Hebrew language and encompasses thirty-nine books written by many people over a long period of time. These writings embrace a number of different literary forms: narrative, poetry, history, wisdom, etc.[11] They were written by people who wrote as people of their own times; their writings reflecting their worldviews, religious ideas, and cultural customs.

The Hebrew Scriptures are those writings that the people of Israel regarded as authoritative for their lives of faith as the covenant people of God. The faith traditions of Israel were communicated orally through the generations and also put in written form and regarded as divine writings or "scripture." Through time, several types of Hebrew Scriptures emerged:

- Torah—the five books of God's "law" or "instruction" detailing the ordering of life for the people of Israel
- Historical works—the story of the nation's history from the death of Moses
- Prophetic writings—the sayings and writings of Israel's prophets
- Psalms—the songs Israel used in worship
- Wisdom literature—writings to indicate the way of life for the people of God to follow.

Gradually, three main divisions of Hebrew Scriptures appeared that were considered as "canon." "Canon" literally means a measuring rod. The term came to be used of religious writings as they became a norm or rule for faith. Theological understandings in both Judaism and Christianity were passed on through the body of authoritative writings that the religious communities recognized as providing guidance. Through several stages, three main groups of Hebrew writings became canonized

- The Torah or Pentateuch (Genesis to Deuteronomy; around 400 B.C.)
- the Prophets (including historical works, around 200 B.C.)
- the Writings (remaining books, around A.D. 90).

By the time of Jesus, the main features of the Hebrew canon were set. Jesus referred to these writings and regarded them as authoritative. He frequently quoted Scripture with the introductory phrase, "It is written" (Matt. 4:4; Mark 14:27; Luke 4:4). At other points he asked, "Have you not read . . . ?" (Matt. 12:3; Mark 12:10; Luke 6:3). Jesus recognized that the Scriptures were inspired by God as when he said, "David himself, by the Holy Spirit, declared, 'The Lord said to my Lord, "Sit at my right hand, until I put your enemies under your feet"'" (Mark 12:36). In an important passage, Jesus reaffirmed the centrality of loving God and loving neighbors as crucial to what God desires, when he said of the great commandment in Deuteronomy 6:4–5: "There is no other commandment greater than these" (Mark 12:31; cf. Matt. 22:40, where Jesus says, "On these two commandments hang all the law and the prophets"). The Hebrew Scriptures were Jesus' Bible, and he regarded the Old Testament writings as having authority in matters of faith and action.

Throughout the New Testament the writers quoted from various Old Testament passages and interpreted them in light of their emerging faith that Jesus of Nazareth was God's messiah. Early Christians regarded Jesus as the promised "coming One" who would save the people (see Acts 7; cf. 1 Peter 2:1–10). New Testament writers saw the Hebrew Scriptures as predicting the life, death, and resurrection of Jesus Christ (Isa. 7:14 and Matt. 1:23; Ps. 16:8–11 and Acts 2:25–28) as well as other events such as the gift of the Holy Spirit (Joel 2:28–32 and Acts 2:16).

Christian Tradition

The early Christian church began to regard certain writings as authoritative and eventually as canonical. These writings included the Gospels that tell the story of the life of Jesus, the writings of apostles including the letters of Paul, and other writings as well. During the third and fourth centuries, elements of the New Testament canon became more precise. But not until the Easter letter of Bishop Athanasius in A.D. 367 was the list of twenty-seven books that are today regarded as the New Testament given official church status. This list was ratified by church councils in the years A.D. 393 and 397. Thus, it took several centuries for an agreed-upon list of authoritative writings or "scriptures" to be officially sanctioned by the church. Along with the Old Testament, these writings became authoritative for the Christian church's beliefs and practices.[12]

The "authoritative word" of Scripture began to be described in many ways by the church's theologians.[13] In the third century, Origen said that the Scriptures "were written by inspiration of the Holy Spirit at the will of the Father of All, through Jesus Christ."[14] St. Augustine said, "All that is in these Scriptures, believe me, is profound and divine."[15] Martin Luther said of the Scriptures: "Here you will find the swaddling-clothes and the manger in which Christ lies. Simple and little are the swaddling clothes, but dear is the treasure, Christ, that lies in them."[16] All of these statements, and many more, by the church's theologians and in its credal statements affirm the Bible's authority for the church's life and for the lives of all Christians.

The church has believed that it is the work of the Holy Spirit who brings the gift of faith in Jesus Christ to persons and who also "testifies" or "persuades" them that the Scriptures are God's divine revelation. John Calvin indicated that we know Scripture is the Word of God, not on the basis of human reason, but by "the secret testimony of the Spirit." The "testimony of the Spirit," said Calvin, is "more excellent than all reason."[17] We experience Scripture as God's divine revelation in this way. Calvin wrote that "the same Spirit . . . who has spoken through the mouths of the prophets must penetrate into our hearts to persuade us that they faithfully proclaimed what had been divinely commanded."[18]

With the rise of science, advances in historical thinking, biblical criticism, and emerging philosophical questions in the seventeenth century and later, the view that the Bible was God's divine revelation and an authoritative word from God was severely challenged.[19] To meet the intellectual challenges, some Protestant theologians developed a view of the "inerrancy" of Scripture.[20] In this view, God has directly inspired the biblical writers to ensure that each word they wrote was the exact word God wanted and that what they wrote was free from error of all kinds. This includes historical and scientific teachings as well as theological truths. To admit even the smallest error or mistake in biblical teachings would mean that God was not perfect. The theory of inerrancy assumed that God wanted the Bible to be without error of any kind and that to ensure this kind of book, God directly inspired each and every word of all the biblical writers. A further dimension of this view was that this inspiration and inerrancy applied to the original "autographs" or original writings of Scripture. Later transmissions and translations may have minor inaccuracies, but the original texts of Scripture were inspired and inerrant.[21]

By the early twentieth century, other views about the nature of the Bible had also emerged.[22] "Liberal theology," associated with the German theologians including Adolf von Harnack, believed the best way to understand the Bible was not as a book of inerrant facts but as a record of ancient religious experiences. God's true revelation is found in Jesus Christ. The other parts of the Bible may be "revelation" insofar as their writers were open to God and genuinely reflected their encounter with the true God. The Bible was written by human, fallible authors who recorded their religious experiences. These writers were "religious geniuses" whose natural powers were elevated to a high degree, and thus they may be said to be "inspired."[23] In this view, the Bible does not have to be without error to have validity and importance as a religious document.

A well-known clash between these two views of the Bible occurred in the fundamentalist/modernist controversy of the 1920s,[24] which climaxed in the famous Scopes trial, or "monkey trial," in Dayton, Tennessee, in 1925 over the issue of evolution. People who identified with "fundamentalism" argued that the Bible presents a historically and scientifically accurate account of the creation of the world and the creation of human beings. They rejected the theory of evolution to explain human origins because they believed it contradicted the literal, biblical teachings. The "modernist" side represented the view that scientific theories that contradict the Bible may be true in themselves and that the Bible is not a textbook of inerrant information.[25]

These two viewpoints about the nature of the Bible are not the only alternatives in the Christian tradition. Other contemporary views associated with theological movements have other ways of understanding what the Bible is and important issues relating to it.[26] Each view approaches the Scriptures from its own perspectives and is marked by certain emphases or accents.

Despite the diversities, it may be affirmed that in the Christian tradition, the Scriptures of the Old and New Testament are unique. They are the revelation of God, or, as some say, they are "witnesses to" the word of God. The Scriptures have authority for the church and for the Christian's life of faith.

Reformed Emphases

The Reformed tradition has highly emphasized the importance of the Scriptures as the means by which God's will and purposes are made known. Scripture is the source of our knowledge of Jesus Christ, who is made known by preaching the gospel message.[27] The Holy Spirit gives the illumination of faith by which we experience the power of Scripture and God's revelation of the divine self within our own lives. The Scriptures are authoritative for Christian belief and the life of faith.

Three Views

Reformed theologians hold a number of contemporary views about the Bible. Historically, three main positions have been important in the Reformed tradition.

1. *The Bible as a Book of Inerrant Facts.* Francis Turretin (1623–1687) and the "Old Princeton Theology," associated with professors Archibald Alexander (1772–1851), Charles Hodge (1823–1886), and B. B. Warfield (1841–1913), defended this view, which holds that the Bible must be completely accurate in all it teaches—both "scientifically" and "theologically." Since God is perfect and cannot lie, and since Scripture is the "word of God," they concluded that Scripture must be perfect and without error in its original (and now lost) autographs. The words of Scripture convey the truth of God without error.[28]

2. *Scripture as a Witness to Revelation.* This view is associated with the Swiss Reformed theologian Karl Barth (1886–1968).[29] Barth believed Scripture becomes authoritative as it "witnesses" to God's revelation in Jesus Christ. The Bible itself is not the revelation; Jesus Christ is the true revelation of God. The Holy Spirit brings the words of Scripture "alive" so that they become revelatory of who God is and what God has done. Scripture was written by fallible, human authors. Scripture is "inspired" in that it witnesses to its special content—God's revelation in Jesus Christ, who is the Word of God.

3. *A Divine Message in Human Thought Forms.* A third stream of Reformed thought can be seen as associated with Calvin, Abraham Kuyper (1837–1920), Herman Bavinck (1854–1921), and G. C. Berkouwer (1903–1996).[30] Here, the emphasis is on Scripture as the Word of God in that it presents God's divine message of salvation through the words of human writers. These writers were "inspired" by God but fully shared in the human limitations of their own cultures and time periods.[31] The purpose of the Bible is not to present inerrant facts, but to tell the story of salvation. In this view, Scripture does not need to be inerrant, since the truth of the biblical message does not depend on completely accurate facts. The Bible may be said to be "infallible" in the sense that it will not deceive or lead its readers astray on its central purpose: to proclaim the gospel of Jesus Christ.[32]

Reformed Confessions

Early Reformed confessions usually began with a formal article on Holy Scripture that frequently lists the canonical books of Scripture.[33] They agree that the ultimate authority for the church and for Christian life is Jesus Christ, who is known through the Holy Scriptures. Scripture is the Word of God and a certain authority for the church.[34] One comes to acknowledge Scripture's authority by the work of the Holy Spirit.[35] Scripture is inspired by God.

Yet none of the Reformed confessions provide any section on the intricacies of inspiration and "no suggestion was anywhere given that Scripture addressed matters of science, or that it provided technically inerrant information on world matters. In these confessions the authority of Scripture resided in its saving function, not in the form of words used."[36] Heinrich Bullinger wrote:

> We know very well that the Scripture is not called the Word of God because of the human voice, the ink and paper, or the printed letters (which all can be comprehended by the flesh), but because the meaning, which speaks through the human voice or is written with pen and ink on paper, is not originally from men, but is God's word, will, and meaning.[37]

So Reformed Christians look to the Scriptures as God's authoritative word, even though they may differ in their understandings of how the Scriptures relate to God's revelation and on issues of biblical interpretation.[38] Scripture has authority since it comes from God and is therefore to be "believed and obeyed" as "the rule of faith and life."[39]

Contemporary Significance

People at the beginning of the twenty-first century may wonder how a collection of ancient books can be significant for life today. Through its history, the Christian church has affirmed that the Bible can and does have a continuing power and importance for life—in whatever time period or culture we find ourselves.

The Bible addresses our most basic questions: Who is God? Who are we? How are we to live? In and through the Scriptures, Christians have found God's revelation and have found that God speaks to them in new and ongoing ways. The Bible is the story of God's relationship with the world. God has reached out to the world in love, to bring salvation and a new way of living to those who have faith in Jesus Christ. The Bible is authoritative because it is God's self-revelation and because it proclaims a unique message—a message not found in any other place. No other discipline or approach to life addresses our basic human condition the way the Bible does. The Holy Spirit of God brings us this faith and certainty. Those who study the Scriptures can use the best contemporary methods and tools to understand better what the biblical texts mean. In our time and in every time, God's message will come to us, through the words of human writers. God will continue to be revealed, to reach for us in love with the story of salvation in Jesus Christ, and to guide us in the way God would have us live in this world.

Questions for Reflection

1. In what ways is it helpful for Christians to have an understanding of how the Scriptures developed and were drawn together into a canon?

2. What implications does one's view about the nature of Scripture hold for issues such as the Bible and science, or the Bible and cultural issues?

3. Which of the three views mentioned above as having marked Reformed theology is closest to your own view of the nature of Scripture?

4. What are appropriate guidelines for interpreting the Scriptures?

5. If you were discussing the Bible with a friend, what reasons would you give for believing that Scripture is the Word of God?

3

Trinity: Who Is God?

One of the most basic Christian beliefs is that we believe God is "one God in three persons." This is the doctrine of the Trinity—mysterious and difficult to comprehend. Since we are dealing with God, we recognize that we can never comprehend God totally. All our ways of speaking and understanding are limited. Nowhere do we experience this more than when we describe our faith in God as "trinity" or "triune"—one God in three persons.

Biblical Bases

The word "trinity" does not occur in the Bible. The term was developed by the church and its theologians through the course of several centuries to describe realities found in Scripture. These realities evolved around two convictions of the early Christians: God is "one" and God is "three."[1]

The early church shared a belief in "one God" in common with Judaism. Christianity emerged out of Judaism, which had for centuries confessed its faith in one God. This distinguished the Jewish faith from neighboring religious faiths which worshiped "many gods" (polytheism). The people of Israel proclaimed: "Hear, O Israel: The LORD is our God, the LORD alone" (Deut. 6:4). There are no "other gods," no rivals to the one Lord, the one God (monotheism). The Lord is God, there is no other beside this God (Deut. 4:35).

The early church confessed its faith in the God of Israel, but with a difference. The church had experienced Jesus of Nazareth. In him, people experienced God in a special sense. In his life, death by crucifixion, and resurrection from the dead, Christians believed that God was present.

The church also experienced the day of Pentecost (Acts 2). God's holy Spirit came upon the church in a special way. The Spirit led people to be baptized and to proclaim Jesus Christ as God's promised Messiah (Acts 2:36). As

23

early churches began to grow up around the Mediterranean world, Christians
sensed God's ongoing presence with the church by God's Spirit.

As New Testament writings took shape, the conviction grew that God was
specially present in the person of Jesus and that God was specially present with
the church through God's Holy Spirit.[2] This Spirit continued the work of wit-
nessing to Jesus Christ, and empowering the church for ministry. The risen
Christ, who is ascended into heaven (Acts 1:6–11) continues to be present in
the church's mission and ministries. In short, the earliest Christians began to
recognize that they were experiencing God in three unique yet related ways:
as the God of Israel—who is creator and sustainer of the world; as Jesus
Christ—who conveyed God's loving presence uniquely; and as the Holy
Spirit—who is not an impersonal force, but a personality who empowers the
church to be the people of God and followers of Jesus Christ in this world.

In various New Testament writings, the "Father," "Son," and "Holy
Spirit" are mentioned and thus linked together. These important points
include the baptism of Jesus (Matt. 3:16–17), at the Great Commission (Matt.
28:19), in Paul's benediction to the Corinthian church (2 Cor. 13:13), in Paul's
description of spiritual gifts in the church (1 Cor. 12:4–6), and in Peter's
account of God's work of salvation (1 Peter 1:2). These "triadic formulas"
point toward a distinctive relationship among Father, Son, and Holy Spirit.[3]

Yet other biblical descriptions also highlight the "oneness" of God in the
church, as God is present as Father, Son, and Holy Spirit. Thus Paul wrote:
"There is one body and one Spirit, just as you were called to the one hope of
your calling, one Lord, one faith, one baptism, one God and Father of all, who
is above all and through all and in all" (Eph. 4:4–6). While linking the three
together points to their distinctiveness and special relationship, so recognizing their common work points to their oneness.[4]

Thus, the New Testament writings portray a common faith in the earliest
churches in one God. But they also point to this one God being known in
three distinct ways: as Father, Son, and Holy Spirit. Each of these, in the New
Testament, has particular characteristics and is operative or acts in the world
in differing ways. This understanding, however, led to a number of other
important questions: What is the meaning of the "three" and of the "one"?
What is the nature of the relationships among Father, Son, and Holy Spirit?

Christian Tradition

It took the church several centuries to find the best way to articulate
answers to these issues and others relating to the question, "Who is God?"
Intertwined with this discussion were the related issues of "Who is Jesus
Christ?" and "Who is the Holy Spirit?"[5]

At a number of points, the church rejected ways of answering these questions. Basic to the discussion were two main problems: In what ways is God "one"—even as God is known as Father, Son, and Holy Spirit? And, in what way is God distinctly Father, Son, and Holy Spirit so that a unique relationship exists among these three?

In addition, as Christianity spread through the Mediterranean world, Christian theologians found it necessary to use the thought-forms and concepts of Greek and Roman philosophy to give exactness to what they were trying to say. On one hand, this development was most helpful. It provided a precise vocabulary that could be understood by many people, since the Greek and Latin languages were so prominent. On the other hand, however, using Greek and Roman philosophy moved the language of Christian theology away from the biblical thought-forms and expressions. As new and important questions were raised, church theologians had to respond in ways that their contemporaries could understand and also in ways that were consistent with and derived from the biblical materials which they considered to be their primary sources of authority. All these dimensions presented many challenges.

One rejected option was to consider God as one, and Jesus and the Holy Spirit as "lesser gods." A group called the "Monarchians" wanted to stress the one divine source or principle for all things. This approach meant that the Jesus as the Son and the Holy Spirit would have to be "subordinate" to God the Father. The church rejected this view.

The third-century theologian Tertullian introduced the term "trinity" into theological discourse as well as the Latin terms *substantia* ("substance") and *persona* ("person"). Tertullian said that the three members of the Trinity were distinct numerically. In God's work in the world, each has different functions or roles to play. But the three persons are united in their "essence" or "substance" (literally: "that which stands under"). They all share the same "Godness," even as they are unique as well. Thus there is both a unity and a trinity in God. While each of the members of the Godhead are distinct from the others, they are not fundamentally or basically separated or divided from each other. The Godhead—Father, Son, and Holy Spirit—share one substance while being three persons.

The problem of the "unity" and "diversity" in the Godhead also implied questions about how the three persons of the Trinity were related. A fourth-century theologian named Arius raised the issue of how the Son was related to the Father. His view was that there is only one God. This God cannot change or share or communicate anything of the divine being to any other entity or person. To do so would mean that God is divisible and that the deity would be turned into two Gods. Arius taught that before God created the heavens and the earth, God created a being who is superior to all subsequent creation.

This is the Logos, the Son, who became God's agent in creation and helped in creating the world. The Logos is in an intermediate position between God and the created world. The Son or Logos is not eternal, since only God is eternal. Since the Logos was created by God, Arius's slogan became: "There was [a time] when he was not." Since the Son was created, and not eternal, the Son is a creature. Thus the Son does not share the same "essence" or "substance" with God the Father.

The first of the church's ecumenical councils to settle the issues raised by Arius was called by the Emperor Constantine and met at the city of Nicaea in Asia Minor in June 325. Nearly three hundred bishops were present. The creed or confession of faith that resulted from the council stressed the real and essential relationship between the Father and the Son. It confessed faith in "one Lord Jesus Christ, the Son of God, begotten from the Father as only-begotten, that is, from the substance of the Father, God from God, light from light, true God from true God, begotten, not made, *homoousios* ["of the same substance"] with the Father. . . ." The emphasis is on the real and substantial relationship between the two. The term *homoousios*, meaning "of the same substance," became an important way of affirming that the Father and the Son shared the same reality or are both "God." In this, the creed countered Arius's views. The Council of Nicaea settled the issue of the relationship of the Father and Son by saying they are coeternal.

Yet the Nicene statement only barely mentioned the Holy Spirit. A strong defender of the Nicene Creed, Bishop Athanasius (d. 373) developed a more detailed view of the Spirit. A group called the "Tropici" were teaching that the Spirit is "the greatest of the angels" and thus not fully divine. Athanasius countered that the Holy Spirit is "not a creature" but is fully divine and belongs in the "holy Triad." Athanasius believed Scripture teaches that the Holy Spirit is fully divine and also *homoousios* with the Father and the Son. The Spirit and the Son are intimately related—and share the same substance with God the Father. If the Holy Spirit unites men and women with the divine Son of God, the Spirit must also be divine.[6] Thus Athanasius stressed the unity of the Trinity and the full participation of each member in the divine essence.

While Athanasius stressed the oneness of the Godhead, other theologians from the eastern region of Cappadocia emphasized the trinity of the divine persons. These theologians, Basil the Great, Gregory of Nyssa, and Gregory of Nazianzus, sought to answer some of the questions Athanasius had not addressed on these matters. They explained how one substance could be present in the three members of the Godhead at one time. The Cappadocians emphasized the distinguishing characteristics of each of the members of the Trinity. Each has particular functions to carry out. Thus, while each member is set apart from the others by virtues of these functions, Father, Son, and

Holy Spirit still share an essential unity as coequal members of the Godhead. The Cappadocians also affirmed the full divinity of the Holy Spirit. The Son and Spirit are not subordinate to the Father, but share the same substance.[7]

Despite these developments after the Council of Nicaea, there were still disruptions in the church over the "Who is God?" issue. In A.D. 381, the Emperor Theodosius I called a church council at Constantinople. The creed that emerged (called today the Nicene Creed because it expanded on the earlier credal statement of the Council of Nicaea, A.D. 325) elaborated statements about the Son and also added a long section on the Holy Spirit. This creed affirms the Holy Spirit as "the Lord, the Giver of life, who proceeds from the Father. Who, with the Father and the Son is worshiped and glorified." Here the Spirit's full divinity is affirmed as the Holy Spirit is worshiped and glorified along with the Father and the Son.

The great fifth-century theologian Augustine most fully developed the doctrine of the Trinity. He emphasized God's absolute unity in the Trinity. All three members are fully and equally God. While these three are identical in their substance, they are distinguished by their relationships. In the Trinity, there are distinct persons. The Holy Spirit is the Spirit of the Father and of the Son. Later, this view was to cause a split between the Western and Eastern churches. Eastern churches thought it was more theologically correct to say that the Holy Spirit proceeds from the Father, as was originally indicated in the Nicene Creed (A.D. 381). Western churches believed it is more biblically and theologically correct to say that the Spirit proceeds from the Father and the Son (Lat. *filioque*)—indicating the Spirit is the Spirit of both. This view had been incorporated into the Nicene Creed by the Third Council of Toledo in A.D. 589.

Augustine was also important because of his use of analogies to describe the Trinity. He recognized that the Trinity was mysterious and that no analogies can perfectly explain it. But in his interpretation of Scripture, Augustine often saw "references" to the Trinity wherever he encountered the number "three." An analogy he used was the experience of love. The experience of love demonstrates a lover, an object loved, and a bond between them—the love that unites them. This, said Augustine, was analogous to the Father, Son, and Holy Spirit. The Spirit is the bond of love that unites Father and Son in the divine Trinity. Thus, "God is love" (1 John 4:8, 16).[8]

Since the days of the early church, theologians have distinguished between the "immanent" Trinity and the "economic" Trinity. The immanent Trinity refers to God within God's own self. That is, it is a way of speaking of the divine being as Father, Son, and Holy Spirit—without any reference to creation or humans. The economic Trinity refers to God in relation to the Trinity's work in the world. God, as God carries out various actions in the

world—as Father, Son, and Holy Spirit in relation to humans—is referred to
as the economic Trinity. These distinctions enable us to understand and say
certain things about God. God is eternal and separate from creation. God also
acts within creation and human history. God is known as Father, Son, and
Holy Spirit.[9]

Reformed Emphases

Reformed theologians and the early Reformed confessions maintained a
thoroughly "orthodox" doctrine of the Trinity. They accepted the teachings
of the early church councils and also the *filioque* clause of the Western church
that affirms the Holy Spirit proceeds "from the Father and the Son."[10] Typical is the Belgic Confession (1561), which says

> We believe in one only God, who is one single essence, in which are
> three persons, really, truly, and eternally distinct, according in their
> incommunicable properties; namely, the Father, and the Son, and the
> Holy Ghost. The Father is the cause, origin, and beginning of all
> things, visible and invisible; the Son is the Word, Wisdom, and Image
> of the Father; the Holy Ghost is the eternal Power and Might, pro-
> ceeding from the Father and the Son.[11]

Then, it is noted that

> nevertheless God is not by this distinction divided into three, since the
> Holy Scriptures teach us that the Father, and the Son, and the Holy
> Ghost have each his personality, distinguished by their properties; but
> in such wise that these three persons are but one only God.[12]

Thus, God as triune, "one God in three persons," is affirmed.

The Reformed theologian Friedrich Schleiermacher (1768–1834) ended
his large work *The Christian Faith* (750 pages of English text) with a "Conclusion: The Divine Trinity," a discussion of only fourteen pages.[13] Schleiermacher did not believe that this doctrine is "an immediate utterance concerning
the Christian self-consciousness, but only a combination of several such utter-
ances"—meaning that it was a doctrine that goes beyond the boundaries of the
proper religious field of knowledge.[14]

Karl Barth, in the twentieth century, made the Trinity a major emphasis in
the whole structuring of his theological work. The revelation of God as the
triune God stands as a kind of preview of Barth's treatment of Christian dogmatics or theology as a whole. God's revelation is the foundation of all theology. In Holy Scripture, God is revealed in a divine self-disclosure as Revealer,

Revelation, and Revealedness—corresponding to God as Father, Son, and Holy Spirit.[15] Thus, for Barth, the doctrine of the Trinity is "not an exercise in abstract theological speculation. It is the church's reflection on its experience of God who makes God's self known in the revelation that both *is* and is contained *in* the Bible."[16]

Barth does not use the language of "person" in describing the Trinity, but rather the term "mode of being" (Ger. *Seinsweisen*). He wrote that "by the doctrine of the Trinity we understand the Church doctrine of the unity of God in the three modes of being of Father, Son, and Holy Ghost, or of the threefold otherness of the one God in the three modes of being of Father, Son, and Holy Ghost."[17] God eternally intends to relate to the creation God has made and to all humanity within the cosmos. The triune God elects to reconcile and redeem the world in Jesus Christ by the power of the Holy Spirit. Thus God can "meet us and unite" God's self to us, because God is God in "three modes of being as Father, Son, and Spirit."[18] There is no subordination of the Son and the Spirit to the Father but all accomplish the work of the triune God in salvation.

For Jürgen Moltmann, the whole Godhead suffers with humanity in the sufferings and death of Jesus Christ on the cross. God's love is at the heart of the divine being and experience. The cross and suffering of Christ are thus shared by the triune God.[19] In this sharing, and God's compassionate, self-giving love we find in the Trinity an important model for human community. The three persons of the Trinity exist in and for each other, as Father, Son, and Holy Spirit. This "indwelling" (Gr. *perichoresis*) and circulation of the divine life among the members of the Godhead is their unity and their diversity. The Trinity is eminently a "social trinity" in that the three are united by the "bond of love" and are a "living fellowship of the three Persons who are related to one another and exist in one another."[20] God's ultimate kingdom is where the full community of God's free love for the consummated creation will be freely shared. If this is the end toward which history moves, then the Christian church should model this inner-trinitarian life in the present age. It should be passionately involved in struggles for liberation, justice, and freedom. For "the triune God, who realizes the kingdom of his glory in a history of creation, liberation and glorification, wants human freedom, justifies human freedom and unceasingly makes men and women free for freedom."[21]

Letty Russell, a contemporary feminist theologian in the Reformed tradition, has used the image of "partnership" in relation to the Trinity and the human community to suggest that the Trinity can help us understand the true nature of partnership. Christian faith proclaims that God sets us free for mutuality, reciprocity, and a totally shared life in community, in partnership with one another. This partnership is marked by "fellowship" (Gr. *koinonia*) with its characteristics being discovered in "their perfection in the Trinity, where there is a focus of relationship in mutual love between the persons and toward creation."[22] If we take this seriously, then, we will recognize that "our relationship with God is ultimate, and therefore all other social roles and hierarchies are no longer of ultimate importance. This does not mean that such human relationships do not matter, but rather that they are refocused because of Christ's gift of freedom (Gal. 5:1)."[23] In this way, the Trinity informs and shapes our human community and human actions.

Contemporary Significance

A number of contemporary theologians continue to probe issues related to the doctrine of the Trinity.[24]

Trinitarian Language

The "language" of the Trinity is one concern. "Father, Son, and Holy Spirit" can give the impression that the first member of the Trinity is male. "Father" as a term for God is biblically based (Matt. 6:9; John 17:5, etc.) and some insist that it should be recognized as a divinely revealed name for God that must not be neglected or modified. Others recognize the term "Father" to point to God's parental nature, as a personal God—over-against the impersonal gods worshiped in the biblical and early church periods. So the use of "Father" by Jesus and the early creeds is to indicate the intimate, personal nature of God as a parent—not as a male "father."[25]

Some have suggested that the use of masculine language to describe "Father, Son, and Holy Spirit" reinforces patriarchy and the wrong notion that God is male.[26] A number of formulae have emerged as proposed alternatives to the church's use of the "trinitarian formula" ("Father, Son, and Holy Spirit") for liturgy, including baptisms. These suggestions include Creator, Redeemer, and Sustainer; or Creator, Christ, and Spirit. Resistance to this approach often centers on the concern that to define God in terms of what God does (function)—as creator, redeemer, and sustainer—instead of who God is (Father, Son, Holy Spirit) will lead to the heresy of modalism, which saw God as having three different modes of appearance or as revealed at different times in different ways, rather than being eternally "one God in three persons."[27]

A further concern about trinitarian language relates to the ancient categories of "essence," "substance," and "person" found in doctrinal descriptions of the Trinity. The concern is that these categories may reflect philosophical or psychological understandings of those who used them centuries ago, but that they are no longer the language of contemporary persons nor do they reflect the views we hold.[28]

For example, trinitarian thought says that the "Son is generated from the Father" and that the Spirit "proceeds from the Father and the Son." "Generation" is a term to indicate a difference between the Father and the Son. "Procession" indicates the difference of the Spirit from the Father and the Son. Thus, the "first member generates, the second is generated, and the third proceeds."[29] Some today would say that this language is too abstract and philosophically dense to be meaningful.

A clearer example may be with the word "person." To speak of "one God in three persons" can be seen as problematic if the term "person" is taken, as we usually take it today, as meaning an isolated individual with a self-consciousness.[30] We speak of "being one's own person," as being "self-sufficient" as a person. Our contemporary, Western-world use of the term tends to individualize "person" so that we do not think of the term in a communal context. The communal, social setting was what was intended by the use of the Greek term *prosopon* and the Latin term *persona* for "person," found in the work of early church theologians. A person is a "person" in relation to others; we recognize a person by his or her face, as distinguished from all other "persons."[31] So, also with God. Contemporary theologians who emphasize the relational nature of personhood stress that the "three persons" of the Trinity relate to each other fully, equally, and with love.[32] As one theologian has written:

> Theologically, however, we must say that Father, Son, and Holy Spirit are not three distinct, divine, rational beings, three subjects, or three separate selves. Nor are they distinct parts of a single divine self, which, in its oneness, hovers unseen behind or above the separate faces. There are not three personalities in God, although we certainly might speak of a personality of God. The one God is fully present and active in each and all modes of being and action; yet God is not distinguishable except in one or another of these modes of being and action. One or another of the faces is required to identify the one God.[33]

It has been suggested that the term "face" or "identity" be used as a supplement to the traditional "person" to help clarify this concern. Thus, we might say that "there is only one divine reality, but it has three distinguishable and interrelatable identities."[34]

Implications

While seemingly abstract and theoretical, the doctrine of the Trinity is actually quite practical and essential for describing who God is and what God does.[35]

1. *Indivisible Trinity*. One basic conviction is that "no member of the Trinity acts without the cooperation of the others."[36] To put it another way, "*all* of God is involved in *everything* God does."[37] While different works may be attributed to different members of the Trinity (the "economic" trinity), these cannot be separated from the full work of the "one" God (the "immanent" trinity). Thus, the works of the Trinity are not divisible. Thus, we will never find two "faces" of God that are in opposition to each other. What we believe that God the Spirit is leading us toward in our lives will not be contrary to what God the Father has revealed or God the Son has shown us. We can trust the full biblical revelation of God. God will not contradict God's own self.

2. *Community*. If the divine trinity shows a community of Father, Son, and Holy Spirit bonded by love, then humans created in God's image find their truest life and fulfillment in human community and not in isolation. The Christian church is the community where our lives can find joy in the fellowship of those who share in the trinitarian life of God as God's people. The "social trinity" points us to the recognition that because God is "a plurality in unity, the ideal for humankind does not focus on solitary persons, but on persons-in-community."[38] God intends that we reflect the divine nature in our human lives. This draws us into life-in-relationship and life-in-community. Supremely, these relationships—in the church and in the whole of life—will be marked by love, which is of the very essence of who God is as Father, Son, and Holy Spirit (1 John 4:8, 16).

3. *Model of Love*. If love is of the essence of God and is to be the mark of those who live reflecting the divine image, then this love will be shared in the human community and in all our relationships. For "if in the divine community there is no above and below, superior and inferior, but only the free society of equals who are different from each other but live together in mutual openness, respect, and self-giving love, so it is in a truly human society of people who are sexually, racially, socially, politically, and religiously different from each other."[39] We share love with others.

We extend our care as well to our environment and all nature around us, as stewards of God's good creation. We human beings are "to be concerned for the welfare of creation in the way that God is."[40] As the triune God reaches out to the world and permeates the world with the divine reality of Father, Son, and Holy Spirit, so humans may witness to the Trinity by our efforts to tend to the earth and the cosmos, to care for the earth as our home.

4. *Efforts for Justice*. The love of the Trinity will also express itself in efforts for justice as the triune God is concerned in Scripture to take up the cause of the powerless and those in need. We are concerned with the just distribution of the earth's resources; with relationships that are liberating and not oppressive; with honor and respect, freedom and dignity as ways of living life both

personally and in society. We seek justice, because the triune God is just. For "the Trinity understood in human terms as a communion of Persons lays the foundations for a society of brothers and sisters, of equals, in which dialogue and consensus are the basic constituents of living together in both the world and the church."[41] In praying the prayer Jesus taught, through the power of the Holy Spirit, we are praying for God's just reign to come "on earth as it is in heaven"—in the fullness of the life of the triune God. On earth, we pray, and we anticipate now, the full, shared life of the Trinity. We look forward to the day when we will join with the saints in proclaiming: "Great and amazing are your deeds, Lord God the Almighty! Just and true are your ways . . ." (Rev. 15:3; cf. 16:7).

Questions for Reflection

1. Are you able to distinguish the actions of God as Father, Son, or Holy Spirit in your life? In what ways?

2. For what reasons was it important for the early church to develop as complete an understanding of the Trinity as possible?

3. If you were trying to explain the Trinity to a friend, what points would you stress?

4. What implications are there for your church in seeing the Trinity as the model of community that God intends? What implications are there for your own life?

5. Do you believe that the traditional language of the Trinity should be supplemented by other terminology? Why or why not?

4

Creation: What Has God Done?

At one time or other, every thoughtful person looks at the world, nature, and other people, and wonders, "Where did all this come from?" Many questions arise: Did all this emerge out of nothing? Is there a scientific explanation for it all? Is there a meaning to all we see around us? Who am I? Why am I here? How do we explain the fact that there is "something" rather than "nothing"?

The Christian faith answers these questions with one word: God. God is the source of all we see and experience, of the whole world, and of the universe. God is the creator of "all things seen and unseen," as the Nicene Creed says. God is the source of meaning for human history and for individual lives.

The Christian doctrine of creation affirms God's work as the creator of all things, the "maker of heaven and earth" (Apostles' Creed). In many ways, this is a primary Christian confession of faith. It is the first thing affirmed about God in both the Nicene and the Apostles' Creed. But as these creeds make clear, and as Christian tradition indicates, God's action of creation is the action of the triune God, of God the Father, God the Son, and God the Holy Spirit. The triune God who has acted in history in Jesus Christ and who is at work in history by the Holy Spirit is the God who has created all things. The God who knows us and loves us in Jesus Christ and who is present with us by the Holy Spirit is also our creator. The God of power, the God who is able to bring into existence all that is . . . this God is the God we know as revealed in Jesus Christ, and who through the Holy Spirit is intimately with us. Our knowledge of God the creator is not a detached knowledge, something we recognize in a casual way. Our knowledge of God the creator is a knowledge of a God who is related to us. The God who is beyond us in power and glory has freely and graciously come to us in Jesus Christ and is with us by the Spirit.

Biblical Bases

The opening sentence in the Bible makes it clear that God is the creator: "In the beginning . . . God created the heavens and the earth" (Gen. 1:1). The affirmation is echoed in other parts of the Old Testament: "Have you not known? Have you not heard? The LORD is the everlasting God, the Creator of the ends of the earth" (Isa. 40:28); "Thus says God, the LORD, who created the heavens and stretched them out, who spread out the earth and what comes from it, who gives breath to the people upon it and spirit to those who walk in it" (Isa. 42:5; cf. 45:18). The Psalms are full of praise to the God who commands and creates (Ps. 148:5; cf. Ps. 89:11; Ps. 104).[1] God is the creator of life. All vegetation, animals, and ultimately humans themselves owe their existence to the loving power of the creator (Genesis 1; 2). God is the creator of humans (Gen. 1:27; 5:2; Mal. 2:10), of Israel (Isa. 43:15), and of "all things" (Eph. 3:9; Rev. 4:11; Ex. 20:11). When people in the Hebrew scriptures confessed their faith, they remembered God as the "maker of heaven and earth" (Gen. 14:18–22; cf. Jer. 32:17; Neh. 9:6; Psalm 136). The wisdom literature of the Hebrew Bible extols the God who creates (Prov. 3:19–20; 8:22–31). The miracles of God's creation are proclaimed poetically in Job (38–41). The prophet Isaiah exults in the creator God (Isa. 40:12–26; 42:5; 43:1; 44:24–28; 48:13; 51:9–10; 54:5), while Jeremiah speaks for the one who is the creator of the land (Jer. 4:23–28; 5:21–25) as well as creator of world history (Jer. 18:1–12; 27:5–6). In the prophet Amos, we find short hymns of creation (Amos 4:13; 5:8; 9:5–6; cf. Isa. 37:16; Jer. 51:15–19).[2]

Creation occurs by God's "word" (Gen. 1:3). When God speaks, all things come into being (Genesis 1, 3, 6, 9, etc.; Ps. 33:9; 148:5). God's "Word" is also identified in the New Testament with Jesus Christ who existed eternally with God (John 1:1). Some New Testament passages indicate that in, through, and for Christ all things were created (John 1:3; Col. 1:15–16; Heb. 1:1–2). Jesus Christ is the Word who "became flesh and lived among us" (John 1:14). God's Spirit, as well, plays a role in creation (Gen. 1:2; Job 33:4; Ps. 104:30). So creation in the Scriptures is portrayed as the work of the triune God, initiated by God the Father and carried out by God the Son and the Holy Spirit.[3]

Christian Tradition

Early Christians soon became vitally aware that it was important to confess their faith in God as creator. They lived in a context where many different philosophies and worldviews had their own teachings about the origins of the world.[4]

Philosophical Views

The philosopher Plato used a myth to explain the origin of the world. He spoke of the production of all things by the work of a "Demiurge"—a kind of master celestial crafter—who shaped the world out of chaos as he viewed "eternal ideas" above him. The Demiurge imposed an order on materials that already existed, the earth's elements: air, fire, and water. The crafter works like a human crafter, forming the world out of materials that have existed eternally according to patterns ("ideas") that have also existed eternally. Thus a dualism, or two principles—the spiritual ("ideas") and the material ("forms")—are the foundational elements for creation of the world.

The philosophy of Gnosticism was also common in the world in which early Christians lived. Gnosticism taught that matter was evil and that "God" is good. A good God, they reasoned, could not create an evil, material world. So they speculated that God did not create the world directly. The material world was created by a "Demiurge" who was a being distinct from God. From the true God there emanated "aeons" which are like sparks of light, falling into the dark chaos of matter. The Demiurge was the creation of a fallen aeon and is thus neither "God" nor "matter." The Demiurge brings the visible, material world into existence and rules over it. The Demiurge was an inferior, "second-string" deity who was an intermediary between the supreme God and the material world.

Both Platonism and Gnosticism were dualistic philosophical systems in that they recognized two equal principles of power: the spiritual and the material. Both were involved in the creation of the world. On the other end of the spectrum, a philosophy later called "pantheism" was monistic. That is, it said there was only one principle or power in the universe and that is called "God." God and the world are identical in this view. Platonism and Gnosticism kept God away from the world, not wanting the "spiritual" to be defiled by the "physical." Pantheism, on the other hand, merged God and the world into one, so the world is divinized. The term "pantheism" comes from two Greek words (*pan* and *theos*) and means "all is God" (or "God is all").

God the Creator

The early Christian church rejected these philosophical views by affirming that God created all things (except God) by a free willing and choice. God chose to create the world. God did so and pronounced it "good" (Gen. 1:25, 31). There was no other equal principle or power who was involved in creation (vs. dualism). To say there is would be to believe in the existence of two rival "gods," each with equal power. There was no implication that the physical or material world was evil—the good God created it, and it was "good." To say that the material world was evil would set God against or at odds with the creation. The Scriptures that speak of God's care, love, and delight in the creation could never support such a view.

Nor, on the other hand, is the world a "part" of God in the sense of the world being divine, like God (vs. monism). The world is not "God's double." The world does not emerge from God in the way that an oak tree grows from a seed, so that they fuse together as one. Instead, the Christian God is the creator who stands distinct from the creation. God is portrayed in Scripture as the transcendent "Lord" of all things, including the created order. God is "different from" the creation, in that God is God. In the Christian view, the creation is dependent on its creator. The creation is distinct from its creator.

Creation Out of Nothing

Early Christian theologians in rejecting these alternatives taught that God created the world out of nothing (the Latin phrase is *ex nihilo*). God called the world into being by God's word (Ps. 33:6, 9), and all things were created. God did not form the universe out of something that already existed. God created out of nothing. Early theologians recognized that nothing is coeternal with God. God alone is free and sovereign over all, and no other principle or power apart from God can be a competing being. God brought the universe into existence by a free, purposeful act of the divine will. As the fourth-century theologian Basil of Caesarea put it: "The Maker of the universe needed only the impulse of his will to bring the immensities of the visible world into being."[5] In the beginning, there was only God and God's will or desire to create.

God Creates in Freedom

Regardless of the ways or means that God used to create, God did so in freedom. God's will is subject to no other will or power. God is sovereign. There was no "necessity" for God to create. Creation is "a free act not only of the Father but of the trinitarian God."[6] God's decision to create the cosmos was an act of divine freedom "done solely because of the divine purpose of love."[7]

Implications

This view of God as creator has a number of important implications. While it is not found explicitly in Scripture, it has been the clear view of the Christian church that God's creation of all things "out of nothing" is implied by the biblical materials.[8] Only God is eternal. God was the creator "in the beginning." It is only God who has always existed. All matter and all creation had a beginning; only God existed before "the mountains were brought forth" or God had "formed the earth and the world." From "everlasting to everlasting," God is God (Ps. 90:2).

1. *God Is the Source of All.* Clearly as well, God is the source of all things. The Christian confession rejects dualism and monism. Positively it asserts that God as the sovereign Lord of all is the one on whom every aspect of existence depends. All things gain their existence and their life from God. No other source is ultimate. No other principle, force, or being is coeternal with God and so no other source than God can be the creator. God did not organize that which previously existed; God brought into existence as creator all things out of nothing. As the third-century theologian Tertullian put it, "there was no power, no material, no nature of another substance which assisted [God]."[9]

2. *Evil Is an Intrusion.* If all things exist from God's will, then, say Christian theologians, nothing is evil in and of itself. The problem of the existence of evil in a world created by God is an important and complicated one.[10] If all things exist by virtue of their creation by God out of nothing, then all things share in the essential goodness that is God's. That which is created bears the marks of its creator. If, as Christian theology maintains, God is love; God is gracious; God is faithful, compassionate, and perfect in and of God's self, then God's creation as an expression of God's will is rightly characterized—as in the Genesis creation accounts—as being "good" (Gen. 1:4, 10, 12, 18, 21, 25, 31). Augustine in answer to the dualism of the Manichees wrote: "Evil is not a substance; it is the perversion of a nature that is essentially good."[11] For "since an original perfection is ascribed to creation, the evil that is present in the world had to come later."[12] Evil is an intrusion into the good creation and does not originate in God.

3. *There Is Meaning and Purpose.* Another implication of God as creator of all things out of nothing is that there is purpose for the world and for individual lives. All creation is an expression of the will and purposes of God. There is meaning to our human existence and to human history. Our human existence is "intelligible and purposive in its essential nature because its source and origin lie in the will of God."[13] The God who is active in history and in our lives today is the same God who has created all things. The Christian story is the story of the creator God who is also the redeemer God and who has come into this world in Jesus Christ. In him, God seeks to restore the original goodness of creation and the relationship God created women and men to have in the primal "garden of Eden" (Genesis 1–2). God's purposeful will is exercised throughout all creation and within the course of human events as well. God's

purposes will triumph throughout the cosmos, which has been "groaning in labor pains until now," awaiting the day when "the creation itself will be set free from its bondage to decay and will obtain the freedom of the glory of the children of God" (see Rom. 8:19–23). The meaning and purpose of all human existence will be revealed on that day when God is "all in all" (1 Cor. 15:28).

4. *All Is Dependent on God.* The Psalmist exclaimed, "Know that the LORD is God! It is he that made us" (Ps. 100:3). The universe and all that dwells therein—"all creatures great and small"—owe existence to the free, creative, and loving purpose of God to create. We are radically dependent on God for this life as well as for the "new life" promised through Jesus Christ in his death and resurrection, as well as for the "life everlasting" in eternal life. Our human finitude and contingency means we are limited in many ways. Every moment of our experience is punctuated with the recognition of this reality. All that God created depends on God. It is good, in itself. It may exist in freedom and experience the fullness of existence or of human life itself. But all depends on God as creator for its being. As one theologian put it:

> Among the many activities of God, His creative activity is surely the one most essential for our existence. It is through this activity that we are brought into being, and it is this activity, therefore, that establishes our deepest, because our most essential, relation to God: He is our Creator and thus our Lord. Correspondingly, the doctrine of God as Creator is, perhaps, the most fundamental conception we can have of God.[14]

To be totally dependent on God our creator liberates us from dependencies on any person or object that is less than God. Our whole lives are to be devoted to serving the one who made us, for God made us and we belong to God (Ps. 100:3).

5. *Creation Is Interdependent.* Many contemporary theologians are acutely aware of the mutual interdependence of all the created order. Concerns over ecology and destructive forces within the earth's environment have heightened the recognition that there is a unifying oneness to creation in that all elements coexist and are interdependent on all others. This leads to a theological examination of our views of nature and the environment, as well as the whole ecosystem.[15] If the triune God is both "unity" and "diversity" ("one God in three persons"), with the communion of love binding all together, so the cosmos itself reflects this same unity and diversity as the expression of the creative act of the triune God.[16]

Reformed Emphases

Reformed faith shares these common Christian convictions about creation with the broad Christian tradition. The Scots Confession proclaims God has created "all things in heaven and earth, visible and invisible" while the French Confession indicates God also created "invisible spirits, some of whom have fallen away and gone into perdition, while others have continued in obedience"—a reference to angels.[17] These remind that God's creation is not identical with the world we see around us—the earth and sky; it is also the creation of that which is "invisible" and beyond our sense perceptions.

Triune God Creates

Confessions in the Reformed tradition convey the majesty and greatness of God as they proclaim God as creator. The triune God as creator is affirmed by the Westminster Confession of Faith, which says that "it pleased God the Father, Son, and Holy Ghost, for the manifestation of the glory of his eternal power, wisdom, and goodness, in the beginning, to create or make of nothing the world, and all things therein, whether visible or invisible, in the space of six days, and all very good."[18] The Belgic Confession highlights the role of the Son in creation: "We believe that the Father, by the Word—that is, by his Son—created of nothing the heaven, the earth, and all creatures, as it seemed good unto him, giving unto every creature its being, shape, form, and several offices to serve its Creator."[19] The Second Helvetic Confession declares that "this good and almighty God created all things, both visible and invisible, by his coeternal Word, and preserves them by his coeternal Spirit (Ps. 33:6)." While God the Father is considered to be the "source" of creation, the creation of all things is a trinitarian activity. Thus, the Reformed tradition has emphasized that

> the Christian doctrine of creation takes its impress from the revelation of Christ and the experience of the Spirit. The One who sends the Son and the Spirit is the Creator—the Father. The One who gathers the world under his liberating lordship, and redeems it, is the Word of creation—the Son. The One who gives life to the world and allows it to participate in God's eternal life is the creative Energy—the Spirit. The Father is the creating origin of creation, the Son its shaping origin, and the Spirit its life-giving origin. Creation exists in the Spirit, is molded by the Son and is created by the Father. It is therefore from God, through God and in God.[20]

It is God as Father, Son, and Holy Spirit who creates.

Identity of Creator and Redeemer

If God as Father, Son, and Holy Spirit is the divine creator, it is clear that the God who creates is also the God who redeems the creation in Jesus Christ.

The simplest assertion is that there is an "identity of God the Creator and God the Redeemer."[21] There is no wedge or gap between the God who created "all things" and the God who will ultimately redeem the cosmos and be "all in all" (1 Cor. 15:28). The God who created is the same God who redeems in Jesus Christ. For "Christian doctrine affirms that God is essentially as he is shown to be by Jesus."[22] Jesus Christ is "the image of the invisible God, the firstborn of all creation; for in him all things in heaven and on earth were created, things visible and invisible, whether thrones or dominions or rulers or powers—all things have been created through him and for him" (Col. 1:15–16). This Jesus Christ is the one who became a human for the sake of our salvation. In Jesus Christ we see a human person in whom "creation stands before us in reality and becomes recognizable."[23] The "mystery" of God's creation is "open to us in Jesus Christ."[24] God did not have to create the world. As Barth noted, "God has no need of us, He has no need of the world and heaven and earth at all. He is rich in Himself. He has fullness of life; all glory, all beauty, all goodness and holiness reside in Him. He is sufficient unto Himself, He is God, blessed in Himself. To what end, then, the world?"[25] This is the riddle or mystery of creation: why did God create? The answer is, according to Barth, that "creation is grace." Creation is God's gift. It is God's gift of free love. The creator God is also the reconciling, redeeming God who creates in order to convey divine grace and have fellowship with the creation and the humans who are created. This love of the creator for the creation became concrete in the person of the redeemer, Jesus Christ.[26] In this way, Jesus Christ is both the beginning and the goal of creation. As the New Testament's most famous verse puts it, "For God so loved the world that he gave his only Son, so that everyone who believes in him may not perish but may have eternal life" (John 3:16). The God we know and love in Jesus Christ is also the divine creator. The creator God is the redeemer God.

Purpose of Creation

The Belgic Confession indicates that God gives each creature its "being, shape, form, and several offices" in order to "serve its Creator." God continues to uphold and govern the creation through divine providence "for the service of mankind" to the end that humans may serve God.[27] The Westminster Shorter Catechism, in its first question, asks what is humanity's "chief end" or purpose. The answer is that our chief end is "to glorify God, and to enjoy [God] forever."[28] These responses show the Reformed conviction that the cosmos was created for a purpose, that human existence has a purpose—and that we are not an "accidental collocation of atoms" that came together in a blind process of evolution or by pure "chance." God created for a purpose:

that humanity and all creation will know the Creator and be in fellowship with the Creator.[29] In Jesus Christ, this purpose of creation finds its fulfillment, and humans are freed from the power of sin to give praise and love and worship to their Creator.[30] The divine creation has as its goal "the revelation of the glory of God."[31] Humans may look on the created order as the "theater of God's glory," said Calvin, and this leads us to praise.[32] The psalmist proclaimed, "The heavens are telling the glory of God; and the firmament proclaims his handiwork" (Ps. 19:1). The creation is good; humans may praise and glorify their creator as they gaze upon God's works. Because we know God is the creator, we may see in the creation God's "wisdom, power, justice, and goodness."[33] To realize that God has created the universe and has called humans to participate in it as "God's children" by serving God and serving others within it, is to recognize the "great benefits" God has "conferred upon us." It leads us to "trust, invoke, praise, and love" God.[34]

Contemporary Significance

The doctrine of creation has great contemporary significance, especially in an era so influenced and dominated by science and technology. Questions about *how* the word was created have abounded in every age. In earlier times, the biblical accounts in Genesis were taken as what today we would call a "scientific" explanation for the "how" of creation: God created all things, by God's word, in a space of "six days," exactly and literally as the Genesis accounts state. With the rise of modern science and cosmological theories—especially the theory of evolution—scientists and many Christians saw that a literal reading of the biblical texts was not appropriate. Historical-critical studies of the Bible pointed to the Genesis accounts as being stories with an intentional theological, rather than "scientific," meaning. The Bible's purpose was to tell "why" God created; not "how."[35] Science and Christian theology use two different types of "languages"—for different purposes. They need not conflict with each other.[36] This means that "there is nothing inherently inconsistent in holding both to evolutionary theory and to faith in God the creator." Whatever our assumptions about the stages, processes, or time spans involved in the world's creation by God, these do not "substantively affect the central claim of faith in God the creator." We can explore the ways in which "scientific" and "theological" understandings come together "without insisting on a proof or disproof of the one by the other."[37] Mutual enrichment of science and theology—not warfare—should be the goal.

The doctrine of creation is also a strong warning against idolatry. Creation is the free act of the sovereign God. Idolatry is the attempt to gain control over God by substituting some power, thought, or object in God's place. The

Heidelberg Catechism defines idolatry in relation to the first commandment (Ex. 20:3) as "to imagine or possess something in which to put one's trust in place of or beside the one true God who has revealed himself in his Word." Instead we are to "acknowledge the only true God, trust in him alone, in humility and patience expect all good from him only, and love, fear and honor him with my whole heart. In short, I should rather turn my back on all creatures than do the least thing against his will."[38]

When we "abolutize" or "trust in" or "idolize" any creature or any part of God's created order, rather than trusting in God alone, we sin. Idolatries today come in many forms, many "shapes and sizes." They emerge out of our ideologies, our addictions, our destruction of creation, our neglect of God and neighbors. We may idolize ourselves, our heritage, our achievements or status, our "securities." But all of these turn us away from the worship and praise of our Creator who created us for fellowship and a relationship of trust and love, to "glorify God and enjoy God forever." To devote ourselves to lesser purposes or spend our lives in pursuits that we ourselves decide are in "our best interests" is to idolize and serve that which is not God. In an acquisitive society, where possessions and wealth are such visible badges of "power," the temptations to idolatry are real, and being seduced into idolatry is difficult to escape.

But if the Creator/creature relationship is our most essential relationship to God, then our whole lives are to be devoted to God's service, to the service of others, and to giving glory to our Creator who has loved us and redeemed us in Jesus Christ. To abolutize any "proximate good" or any lesser goal than giving glory to God is to plunge into idolatry.[39] The doctrine of God the Creator keeps us focused on the One to whom all glory, honor, and power are due (Rev. 4:11) and on our own grateful response as we seek to "do everything for the glory of God" (1 Cor. 10:31).

Questions for Reflection

1. What is the significance of affirming that God created "all things out of nothing"?

2. What implications are there in the Christian affirmation that "God created all things good"?

3. Why is it important to affirm that God is both "transcendent" (over and beyond the creation) and "immanent" (in and with the creation)?

4. In what ways do you understand how evil can be present in God's good creation?

5. Does the theory of evolution affect your view of "God the Creator"?

5

Providence: What Is God Doing?

What is God's relationship with this world? Is God detached from this world? Is God active in this world? These issues confront us daily.

We wonder when we look around us in this world. There is much beauty in nature and joy in human relationships. It is easy to attribute those "nice things" to God. But that is not the whole story of our world or our existence, for this is also a world in which disasters occur, people die from dreaded diseases such as cancer or the AIDS virus, where violence is a fact of life, and where people do not always treat us in love and justice. Where is God in all of this? Perhaps God is merely a detached spectator—if God even exists at all! It is hard to listen to Christians who speak of a loving and just God. As someone asked, "How can you believe in a 'good God' in a 'hell of a world'?"

Biblical Bases

Both the Old and New Testaments show us a God who is thoroughly involved in creation. The God who created all things is also the God who continues to uphold all things by divine power and love while working within creation to carry out what God wants accomplished. This theme is expressed in the Scriptures in a number of ways.

Old Testament

God sustains the physical creation—the universe and all within it. The book of Psalms is a rich source of praise to the God who has created and who continues to care for the world. Psalm 104, for example, celebrates God creating the world and providing for it. The Psalmist praises the God who makes "springs gush forth in the valleys; they flow between the hills, giving drink to every wild animal; the wild asses quench their thirst. By the streams the birds of the air have their habitation; they sing among the branches. From your lofty abode you water the mountains; the earth is satisfied with the fruit of your work" (Ps. 104:10–13).

This is the God who causes "the grass to grow for the cattle, and plants for people to use, to bring forth food from the earth, and wine to gladden the human heart, oil to make the face shine, and bread to strengthen the human heart" (vv. 14–15). The earth and all within it look to God "to give them their food in due season," for "when you give to them, they gather it up; when you open your hand, they are filled with good things. When you hide your face, they are dismayed; when you take away their breath, they die and return to their dust. When you send forth your spirit, they are created; and you renew the face of the ground" (vv. 27–30). This leads the Psalmist to praise God: "May the glory of the LORD endure forever; may the LORD rejoice in his works—who looks on the earth and it trembles, who touches the mountains and they smoke. I will sing to the LORD as long as I live; I will sing praise to my God while I have being. May my meditation be pleasing to him, for I rejoice in the LORD" (vv. 31–34).

God also sustains humans within the creation. In the story of Adam and Eve, God provided for the ongoing continuation of the human race by blessing Adam and Eve and commanding them to "be fruitful and multiply" (Gen. 1:28). God also provided clothing for the couple before they were expelled from the Garden of Eden (Gen. 3:21). In the history of Israel, God provided for the needs of the people as they were liberated from Egypt and spent forty years in the wilderness. They received food (Ex. 16:1–36; Num. 11:4–35) and drink (Ex. 17:1–7; Num. 20:2–13). The lives of persons are also preserved—as when Elijah was miraculously fed by ravens (1 Kings 17:6). More generally is the promise that "The LORD is your keeper; the LORD is your shade at your right hand" (Ps. 121:5; cf. Psalm 91).

Yet God not only sustains and upholds, God also guides. God guides both individuals and, in the Old Testament particularly, the nation of Israel.

The story of Joseph is a prime example. After facing the hatred of his brothers and slavery in Egypt, Joseph rose to a position of prominence. When he met his brothers after his father's death, he was able to say: "Even though you intended to do harm to me, God intended it for good" (Gen. 50:20). Joseph was conscious of God's guiding and directing his life to carry out God's purposes.

In an earlier episode in the book of Genesis, in the story of God's command to Abraham to sacrifice his son Isaac, when Isaac asked his father, ". . . where is the lamb for a burnt offering," Abraham answered: "God himself will provide the lamb for a burnt offering, my son" (Gen. 22:7–8)—which is precisely what happened (Gen. 22:9–14). This guidance in providing for what was needed led Abraham to call the place "The Lord will provide" [traditionally: Heb. *Jehovah Jireh*; Gen. 22:14].

In a broader sense, God's purposes were being carried out in the calling of Abraham and Sarah to be God's people and to enter into a covenant relationship with God (Genesis 12; 17). God was with the descendants of Abraham and Sarah as they were slaves in Egypt and worked mighty deeds in their behalf (Ex. 6:5–8), so that the people of Israel could be liberated from slavery. This led to a song of praise: "Who is like you, O LORD, among the gods? Who is like you, majestic in holiness, awesome in splendor, doing wonders? You stretched out your right hand, the earth swallowed them. In your steadfast love you led the people whom you redeemed; you guided them by your strength to your holy abode" (Ex. 15:11–13). This sense of God's guidance was strong through Israel's history as God's mighty "deeds" were remembered:

> I will call to mind the deeds of the LORD;
> I will remember your wonders of old.
> I will meditate on all your work,
> and muse on your mighty deeds.
> Your way, O God, is holy.
> What god is so great as our God?
> You are the God who works wonders;
> you have displayed your might among the peoples.
> With your strong arm you redeemed your people,
> the descendants of Jacob and Joseph. . . .
> Your way was through the sea,
> your path, through the mighty waters;
> yet your footprints were unseen.
> You led your people like a flock
> by the hand of Moses and Aaron.
>   (Ps. 77:11–15, 19–20)

God's guiding purposes were recalled by Israel's prophets when through them, God reminded the nation of God's mighty acts: "For I brought you up from the land of Egypt, and redeemed you from the house of slavery; and I sent before you Moses, Aaron, and Miriam" (Micah 6:4; cf. Isa. 43:15–17). This is the God who is "God of the whole earth" (Isa. 54:5).

God's purposes are carried out in individual lives (Ps. 57:2; 138:8; Prov. 19:21) and in history to accomplish God's will (Isa. 46:10; 55:11). These purposes are God's plan (Isa. 5:19; 19:17; Jer. 49:20) which nothing can thwart (Jer. 32:27) and which leads ultimately to God's eternal reign (Ps. 146:10).

New Testament

The same emphasis on God's gracious providing for creation and humans is found in the New Testament as well. Jesus assured his disciples that God's care is real and personal, and that nothing is too small to be of concern to God—even the "hairs of your head" (Matt. 10:29–31). God is at work in this world (John 5:17) through God's Son to sustain "all things" (Heb. 1:3) and to care for persons (1 Peter 5:7).[1] God is "not far from each one of us" (Acts 17:27) and cares for even the "birds of the air" and the "lilies of the field" (Matt. 6:26–28). God supplies our needs (Phil. 4:19).

According to the New Testament, God's plan and purposes find their fulfillment in Jesus Christ. God has brought salvation in Jesus Christ, according to the divine plan (Acts 2:23; 4:28). In Jesus Christ, God has made known the "mystery" of the divine will according to God's "good pleasure" which is set forth in Christ (Eph. 1:9). In Christ there is redemption and forgiveness of sins (Eph. 1:7). This is God's "plan for the fullness of time, to gather up all things in him, things in heaven and things on earth. In Christ we have also obtained an inheritance, having been destined according to the purpose of him who accomplishes all things according to his counsel and will" (Eph. 1:10–11; 3:11; 2 Tim. 1:9). God's purposes are for salvation (Rom. 8:28–39; 9:11, 17) and lead to the ultimate divine reign (Rev. 11:15).

Christian Tradition

The biblical materials have led Christian theologians to understand God's continuing involvement and care for the world as well as God's government of the world as the doctrine of providence.[2] "Providence" comes from the Latin verb *provideō* meaning "to provide for" or "to foresee."[3] Most broadly, it refers to God's divine plan through which the whole creation will eventually come to God's ultimate goal. It describes God's working within human history, sustaining creation, and accomplishing God's purposes in and through history. This understanding of God's work is perceived by faith, as historical events and the events within the lives of believers are seen as expressions of God's guidance and direction.[4]

Parts of Providence

Christian theology has typically seen the doctrine of providence as having three parts. God *preserves* the creation; God *cooperates* with all created beings; and God *governs* or *guides* all things toward the accomplishment of God's ultimate purposes.[5]

1. *Preservation.* God preserves the creation.[6] If God had simply brought all things into being by an act of creation and then stopped, what would have happened? If this were so, then everything that was created would instantly have ceased to exist. Without an upholding, sustaining, and preserving power of God, the created order would have collapsed into nothingness—into the chaos there at the beginning (Gen. 1:2). God's care for the world is to preserve that which has been created as it has been created and to sustain all things so that they can continue to exist.

In this respect, all things continue to depend on God. All things depend on God for their ultimate creation as well as for their ongoing life. God preserves the creation by sustaining it. God continues to exercise a divine energy to see that the creation is maintained, upheld, and preserved.[7] Order prevails and life can continue to develop because there is the sustaining power of God. This was recognized by ancient philosophers who were quoted by the apostle Paul: "In him [God] we live and move and have our being" (Acts 17:28). No part of creation is self-sufficient. All that exists depends on God for ongoing life.

2. Also, God *cooperates* with all created beings.[8] It is important to realize that humans choose freely to carry out their decisions and move in various directions in life in relation to God's divine purposes. This is the theological issue of God's divine sovereignty as creator and ruler of the universe and humanity's own freedom to make choices and exercise their own wills in relation to their decisions.[9] Many have seen a great tension or even a contradiction here. How can God accomplish the divine purposes in history if humans can exercise their own choices, which may or may not be consistent with God's desires? Much debate in the history of Christian theology has occurred over these issues.

The best understanding is to recognize that the Scriptures affirm both dimensions. God is active; humans are active. God is at work in the world to sustain and care for the world and to carry out God's divine will. Humans make their choices, live their lives, and move in their directions according to their own understandings and decisions. They act in accord with their own impulses and judgments. God is able to work in a cooperative way with all "lesser powers" or persons to accomplish the divine purposes. God works with us and in us and through us to do what God wants done in this world. We ourselves cannot tell the difference between "God's work" within us and "our own work." In one sense, we do not act solely by ourselves, because God's power is at work within us (Eph. 3:20; Phil. 2:13). Yet we do act—we *really* act—because we use the powers that God has created within us to use. We act according to our minds, our intuitions, our wills, our hearts. We act freely. But at the same time, we can believe that God's will is cooperating with our wills to carry out God's ultimate divine purposes. In Scripture we find that God's character is "so great and majestic that it can embrace human freedom and responsibility within itself without being thereby assaulted or even limited."[10] God could ascribe to us no "higher honor" or treat us "more seriously" than to acknowledge that in the face of God's great lordship over us as creator, God also "makes the activity of the creature the means of [God's] own operation. This is the depth of His mercy."[11] How all this works is a mystery. It is difficult to comprehend completely *how* this is possible from a purely intellectual view. But both factors—God's will and human actions—are present in Scripture and in the Christian tradition. Though we cannot explain it, we can still confess by faith as a reality.[12] There is "a Divine activity over and in the creaturely activity of [humans]."[13]

3. A third aspect of God's providence is God's *guidance* or *governance*.[14] God is portrayed in Scripture as the "King of kings and Lord of lords" (1 Tim. 6:15; Rev. 19:6) who reigns over all (Ps. 22:28, 29), eternally (1 Tim. 1:17). The whole universe was created by God, it is sustained by God, and God is at work within it. God works in the world, in human history, and in individual lives to guide all things to God's final ends or purposes. God carries out both divine grace and divine judgment among peoples. God's purposes are being carried out through all God's activities. These purposes are for the whole world as well as for those who believe in God and have faith in Jesus Christ. Another way to put it is to say that not only is the eye of God *over* history, but that the hand of God is *in* history. There is an end toward which all things move: the final reign of God. What God is doing in human history and in individual lives is guiding all things and persons toward that final reign.[15]

Aspects of Providence

Another way to look at the doctrine of God's providence is to distinguish between two aspects. God's *general providence* is God's overall rule in the universe as a whole. God upholds the order of the universe and maintains its operation.[16]

A concept that has been central to this understanding is natural law. Natural law has a long historical and philosophical tradition and means that God has established certain principles or "laws of nature" that are the means by which God's sustaining and governing of the universe are carried out. An example is the law of gravity. When fruit falls from a tree, we say it does so not directly because of God, but because of the law of gravity at work on the fruit. God has established this means of working in the world. Other laws of nature enable the universe to continue to exist in an orderly way. They are the ways by which God is at work in a general way in the world.[17]

A second aspect of providence is God's *special providence*. Each part of the cosmos is part of the whole creation over which God stands as "Lord" or "ruler." God cares for, guides, and governs each part in relation to the whole creation. In this respect, God may be said to be personally involved in acting within the created order and especially with human beings. As humans cooperate with God's purposes, they discover God's presence and direction in their personal lives. Their needs are met, and they find that even the smallest details of their lives are of concern to God. Some speak of "special providence" to describe finding that certain events, answers to prayer, or deliverance from difficulties are part of God's personal care. They experience God's sustaining and guiding through the help that comes at times of special need.

God's "general" and "special" providence are not two different providences. They are the same providence of God, but carried out and experienced in two different relationships. One is the "big picture"—God's general, overall sustaining and guiding. The other is the "personal"—God's intimate involvement with all levels of creation, "all creatures great and small," especially God's direct activities in the lives of persons. Belief in God's special providence is "love's answer of confidence that in God's revelation love is both possible and meaningful. It is not, as it may at first seem, a projection of pride which sees the believer lifted above all others as a 'special' object of Providence. Rather, it is ventured as a formulation of thankfulness and humility in the face of this gift of confidence."[18]

Oppositions to Providence

The Christian doctrine of providence has sought to maintain a fidelity to the teachings of Scripture over and against some opposing viewpoints and tendencies.

1. *God Is remote.* Some have seen God as a being who is totally removed from creation and thus not involved in creation. This was the view of an eighteenth-century philosophy known as Deism. In Deism, God created the world, but then moved away from the creation. At creation, God established certain properties within creatures, constructed various laws of nature, and then let creation move in its own directions. God is not directly involved in it. God is a remote God who is detached, aloof, and distanced from the creation. In the wake of Isaac Newton's discoveries about motion and mechanics, philosophers and theologians began to view the universe as a great machine with perfectly functioning components. The image is of a watchmaker making a watch and then leaving it to function solely on its own, or a wind-up toy top that has been put in motion and then left to go on its own until it finally stops. This viewpoint emphasized God's transcendence as over and beyond creation to such a degree that all connections between God and the creation are severed.

2. *God Is All/All Is God.* An opposite tendency is to emphasize God's immanence or God's "nearness" to the creation to such a degree that God is absorbed into the creation, or else the creation is absorbed into God. This is the viewpoint called Pantheism. Its very simple tenet was that "God is all" and "all is God." The principle of "God" is identified with the creation itself and becomes completely identical with it. To speak of "providence" from a pantheistic view is to speak simply of the "course of nature." The "natural" and the "supernatural" are identified as identical.

3. *Determinism/Fate.* Another form of opposition to the Christian doctrine of providence is Determinism. This concept is found in the ancient Stoic philosophers who believed that the whole universe was determined by the principle of blind fate. There is a universal, eternal law that rules all things so that nothing happens in the world by "chance." One must accept one's fate, which has decreed all things, and simply acquiesce in whatever occurs to one in life.

Each of these three viewpoints is at odds with the Christian doctrine of providence. The Christian view upholds God as transcendent, but also affirms that God is intimately involved in the creation (vs. Deism). The Christian view upholds God as involved in the creation, but not absorbed by it or in it. God is still separate from the creation as its Lord and ruler (vs. Pantheism). The God of the Bible is a just, wise, and powerful person—not a blind principle of causality or fate (vs. Determinism). These elements distinguish the Christian doctrine of providence from other philosophical viewpoints.

Reformed Emphases

While Christian theologians have affirmed that God is personally involved in sustaining, caring for, and guiding the creation, certain aspects of the doctrine of providence have been understood in differing ways.[19]

Reformed faith has been distinctive in emphasizing the relationship between providence and other aspects of salvation. Some traditions (including those stemming from John Wesley) have emphasized human freedom and choice in making decisions that God then weaves into the divine plan. Technically, this is called God's "foreknowledge." God, being God, foreknows or foresees all that will come to pass, including what all humans will decide to do in their individual decision making—as well, whether or not they will accept salvation through faith in Jesus Christ. God's "providence" is God's helping them in their decisions—through grace, through use of their powers of reason, through many means. The emphasis is on human freedom: the liberty to choose and make decisions in life.

Reformed faith has typically emphasized God's governing providence and the conviction that God's divine plan and purposes guide the creation, human history, and human lives.[20] The God who *knows* all things also *wills* all things.[21] The Reformed have seen an inevitable connection between God's "willing" and God's "knowing." Since God is not limited by time or by the sequence of events and is in what we might call the "eternal present," many Reformed theologians have contended that what God knows, God wills. Whatever knowledge of events or persons God has, for example, is knowledge that is real because of what God has willed about those events or persons. What God wills, God does. God does not have to "wait," as we do, to see what others will do. God knows from all eternity what events and actions will be, because these are all expressions of God's will and purposes.[22]

This emphasis in Reformed theology has drawn criticism and raised questions. Three of these frequently occur.

The Question of Evil

If God governs all things, then what of the evil in the world? Does God ordain terrible sufferings and tragedies, especially for those who seem innocent victims? Why should such evils befall them? This is the issue of "theodicy"— of justifying God's justice and goodness in the face of suffering and evil.[23]

No form of Christian theology affirms that God is the "author of evil" in the sense of having created evil.[24] Evil is that which opposes God and God's will. It stands against God and is that which God does not will to do. The origin of evil in the universe is a mystery. We do not know why it is present or why it occurs. Reformed faith recognizes that God is against evil. The purposes of God in this world are purposes that we see most clearly in Jesus Christ, who withstood all that was evil and that was in opposition to God. Jesus' way was to overcome evil by doing good.

So we do not speak of God "sending" evil upon us or causing those things in our lives that are against the purposes of God's gracious love and justice as we know these in Jesus Christ. Natural disasters and tragedies often occur for unexplainable reasons. They are not expressions of God's direct will since they bring sufferings and consequences that we believe are not what God seeks or intends for the creation or for humans. The answer of Christian faith to the problem of evil is that God can bring good out of evil and has the power to do so. The clearest example of this power is God's action in overcoming the world's great evil—the death of Jesus—by his resurrection. God can overcome the worst suffering and evil, and God has done so by raising Jesus Christ from the dead.

Human evil is caused by humans and the actions they take. We are responsible for those things we do that are in opposition to God's will and purposes. In that sense, we share in the evil of the world. God does not create that which is in opposition to the divine will, but as humans we often enact that which opposes God. In this respect, we cannot blame our evil on God. We must confess that we ourselves are accountable.

The Question of Suffering

This question is complicated and one for which no rational answer ultimately exists. We cannot and will not ever know why people suffer. In the book of Job, the righteous Job questioned why calamities befell him when he had not committed terrible sins to deserve these evils. His only comfort came from his experience of God and the recognition God did not abandon him, but was with him through his sufferings. His experience was that God's presence had become real. Job said, "I had heard of you by the hearing of the ear, but now my eye sees you" (Job 42:5). Job did not receive an answer to his questions; he received God's presence to sustain him.

Likewise, neither the Scriptures nor the Reformed faith seeks to assign a direct correlation between specific sufferings and specific actions (though sometimes we suffer directly because of certain actions we have carried out). No one can say to another, "You are suffering because. . . ." To paraphrase a current saying: Bad things *do* happen to good people. But in God's providential purposes, when evil and suffering come upon us, we can believe that God is still with us and that God's loving grace and power will see us through. This is the comfort of the apostle Paul's affirmation: "We know that all things work together for good for those who love God, who are called according to his purpose" (Rom. 8:28).

The Question of Prayer

The Reformed understanding of providence may also lead to the question: Why pray? If God sustains and governs all things according to God's divine plan and purposes, then of what value is prayer? Why should Christians pray if God's will is eternal? Does prayer "change God's mind" about certain things?

An insight from the thought of John Calvin is helpful here. In writing about providence, Calvin indicates that God's providence "sometimes works through an intermediary, sometimes without an intermediary, sometimes contrary to every intermediary."[25] This means that sometimes God may work in this world directly ("without an intermediary"), sometimes "contrary to every intermediary" (as in what are commonly regarded as "miracles" where apparent "laws of nature" do not function as they normally do), or "through an intermediary." Since God commands us to pray, it is apparent that God desires prayer to be the means or "intermediary" which may then be used by

God to carry out the divine purposes. Prayer is the means to the end, or the accomplished purpose of God. Thus God is concerned not only with accomplishing the purpose, but also with using human prayers as a way by which that purpose comes to be carried out. So the prayer is part of the process. Prayer thus becomes the most meaningful of activities, because we simply do not know in what ways God may use our prayers as the means to carry out God's will. The doctrine of providence assures us that prayer is significant and that, in and through our prayers, God is actively at work.

Contemporary Significance

The doctrine of God's providence as understood in the Reformed faith is both an extremely comforting and extremely challenging doctrine. It takes seriously the reality of evil and assures us that in the midst of evil and suffering, God does not abandon us. God is with us.[26] As one Reformed theologian put it:

> Painful and tragic things sometimes happen to us because we live in a
> world that operates according to the natural laws and processes God
> has built into it. But they hurt less when we know that God does not
> will and cause them to happen, but is God with and for us in hard
> times as well as in good times, in failure and sorrow as well as in suc-
> cess and happiness, in sickness and suffering as well as in health and
> prosperity, when death comes as well as when life is spared.[27]

Our comfort is that our world and our lives are held secure in God's hand. God preserves creation and our human existence. God provides for the world, orders the world, and cares for the world. Our lives are entrusted to the God who created us and loves us utterly, as we see in Jesus Christ. This God guides our lives and provides for our needs. As Calvin said in speaking of our knowledge of God's providence, "Gratitude of mind for the favorable outcome of things, patience in adversity, and also incredible freedom from worry about the future all necessarily follow upon this knowledge."[28]

Yet the doctrine of providence is also a challenge for us. It does not relieve us of our human responsibilities. It does not excuse our actions that may be contrary to God's will or purposes for us. But belief in God's providence does challenge us to cooperate with God's purposes in this world, to live according to God's divine will, and to seek that will for our lives above all else. There is no greater motivator for us. We are motivated to action and service in this world because we can trust God's ongoing, sustaining, and guiding power to accompany us. We can fearlessly commit ourselves to God's purposes, believing that God will be with us and lead us in all our ways. Our lives are not left to fate or blind chance; they are guided by the God who created us, who loves us in Jesus Christ, and who calls on us to cooperate with the divine purposes in this world with confidence and joy.

Questions for Reflection

1. In what ways are you aware of God's "providence" in your life?

2. Why is it important that the doctrine of creation lead to the next step, the doctrine of God's providence? What if it didn't?

3. What do you believe accounts for the origin of evil?

4. In the face of human suffering and tragedy, what comfort does the doctrine of God's providence offer?

5. In what ways do you believe God governs or directs our lives?

Humanity: Who Are We?

At some time or other, most thoughtful persons ask themselves this question: Who am I? This is the question of self-identity. It is one of the most basic issues with which we have to deal as human beings. We recognize ourselves as human beings—as being part of the human race along with billions of other people throughout the world. We know we are part of the human family, but we ask ourselves: What does this mean? What does it mean to be part of the human race, to be a human being? What does it mean to be the person I am; the unique individual that I see in the mirror each day? Who am I? This is a basic issue because it directly affects us. We need to know and understand what our nature is, who we are, and—even more broadly—why are we here? What is the purpose of my life?

As Christians, and as Christians in the Reformed tradition, this question is important as well. Our Christian faith supposes certain theological understandings about human beings. In our Reformed tradition, certain emphases have been prominent, and certain theological understandings about human beings have been important. In the Reformed faith, we share some common views with all Christian theologians, as well as some particular perspectives that we believe are consistent with the teachings of the Scriptures.

Biblical Bases

Created by God

The Bible is clear that God is the creator of all things and God is the creator of humankind. The two creation stories in the book of Genesis (Genesis 1 and 2), with varying emphases, both indicate that humans owe their origins to God. The findings of modern science, the theory of evolution, and other contemporary approaches have sought to explain *how* the human species emerged. For some—who have read the opening chapters of Genesis in a literal manner and have assumed that they are intended to tell us the means or methods that God used to create—modern science is made an "enemy."

Yet this does not need to be the case. Scientific theories can present data and hypotheses to explain the "how" of creation. But the Bible's main purpose is to tell us the "why" of creation—to indicate that God *is* the creator, regardless of what methods were used, and to affirm that there is meaning and purpose in God's creation of human beings.

"In the beginning when God created the heavens and the earth . . ." (Gen. 1:1) are the opening words of the Bible. The creation of humanity as "male and female" (Gen. 1:27) is God's "crowning act" in the creation process. The Psalmist praised the creator and the creation in proclaiming, ". . . what are human beings that you are mindful of them, mortals that you care for them? Yet you have made them a little lower than God, and crowned them with glory and honor" (Ps. 8:4, 5). God is the ground of our existence, as humanity in general and of each of us in particular. We gain our "life" from God, just as the biblical story poetically portrays God as forming the first person "from the dust of the ground" and breathing into the nostrils of the person "the breath of life" so that "the man became a living being" (Gen. 2:7).[1] All that we are and all that we can become we owe to our creator who gives us life and breath.

Our meaning and significance as humans is bound up with our creation by our creator. Just as the first humans were to live in a trusting relationship of love and obedience to their creator, so all humans—according to the biblical picture—are intended to live in this same freedom and joy. Our lives and our ultimate destinies are to give praise and glory to the One who has given us life and sustains our life. That is why the book of Psalms is so full of praise: "Praise the LORD!" (Ps. 149:1; cf. other hymns of praise, such as Psalms 24, 29, 145–150). God is the source of life and is to be praised and obeyed as the one who gives us all that we have and makes us all that we are. As the apostle Paul enjoined, ". . . whatever you do, do everything for the glory of God" (1 Cor. 10:31; cf. Rom. 11:36).[2]

The Whole Person

The Bible uses special language to describe human beings. We are familiar with such terms as "body," "soul," and "spirit."[3] Other biblical terms include "flesh," heart," "mind," or "conscience." Sometimes biblical writers use these words in specific ways. At other times, they use them as shorthand ways to describe the whole human person.[4] Both the Hebrew Scriptures and the New Testament use "body" and "soul" not as "ways to speak of different parts of the individual but as different ways to speak of the entire unified, integrated person."[5]

Basically, the Bible sees humans as whole persons who are both "bodily" and "spiritual" beings. The Bible does not seek to be precise in describing the various "parts" of the person in the way that contemporary social scientists would do.[6] The Scriptures are concerned with the "whole person"—both what we call the "physical" and the "spiritual." That is, a person's "body" or physicalness is inextricably bound up with that person's personality or relationships with God and with other persons ("heart," "soul," "spirit").[7] It is the whole person who is related to God and the whole person who interacts in many ways with other persons in the human community. The Psalmist, for example, writes: "Prove me, O LORD, and try me; test my heart and mind" (Ps. 26:2; cf. 7:9); or ". . . my heart is glad, and my soul rejoices; my body also rest secure" (Ps. 16:9). While language designating different "parts" of a person is employed, God relates to the whole person in his or her total existence. This is the effect of Jesus' summary of the law when he says, "You shall love the Lord your God with all your heart, and with all your soul, and with all your strength, and with all your mind; and your neighbor as yourself" (Luke 10:27; cf. Deut. 6:5). We are to love God with all that is within us—with our total selves.[8]

Image of God

A basic conviction shared with all Christians is that as humans we are created by God and created in the image of God.[9] The creation stories in the book of Genesis describe, in differing ways, that God created human beings. And as Genesis 1:26–27 indicates, humans are created in the image and likeness of God. Theologically, this points us to a very significant fact.[10] As Christians we believe we cannot understand who we are as human beings without realizing that we are creatures of God. We are created by God and created in God's image.[11] Our human existence is inextricably connected to God. We live, as human beings, in some kind of relationship with our creator. What this relationship is . . . that is a question.

But, related we are. All other views about human beings—views from the social sciences such as psychology, sociology, or anthropology—look at different dimensions of human beings: their psyches, their social relationships, their cultural customs. None of these disciplines themselves, however, can show us the whole picture of who humans are. As well, none of these disciplines can give us what we as Christians regard as the most important dimension to humanity: the fact that as humans we are related to God. Because God is our creator and because we are created in the image of God, we are related to God. This relationship is, fundamentally, the most important fact of our existence. We cannot think of ourselves—or of humanity as a whole—apart from this basic conviction: We are created by God and created in the image of God. All our "anthropology" must be "theological anthropology." We are related to God in all our "creaturely relationships."[12] From the perspectives of Christian faith, we must view ourselves in light of our fundamental relationship with our creator.[13]

We are created in the "image of God." This phrase, while important in Christian theology, is a phrase that has been interpreted in a number of ways. What does it mean to say that we are created in God's image? In what ways are we like God? In what ways are we different from God?

When we read Genesis 1:27—"So God created humankind in his image, in the image of God he created them . . ."—we encounter the same verb that is used in Genesis 1:1: "In the beginning when God created the heavens and the earth. . . ." This fact points to the indication that the creation of humanity—as male and female—stands as the climax or summit of the divine work of creation. Through all the accounts of God's creative actions—the world, the animals, and all creatures—humans stand as God's consummate activity. Humans have a special status before God, being said to have been created in God's image and likeness, a designation not given to other created beings.

The work that God gives humans to do also points to their special standing. It is their creation in "the image of God" that separates humans from other created beings, and it is humans who are given the responsibility of naming animals (Gen. 2:19f.). This responsibility to tend to the earth and to carry out their God-given tasks is an indication of the value God places on created humans (Ps. 8:6–9).

Christian Tradition

Church theologians have understood the meaning of humans as created in "the image of God" in a variety of ways.[14] These differences in interpretation at some points can be related to background influences on those who wrote.[15] For example, predominant philosophical viewpoints are often significant factors in influencing the way in which one understands the Scriptures.

Image and Likeness

Some early church theologians such as Irenaeus made a distinction between the terms "image" and "likeness" in Genesis 1:26–27. The text says: "Then God said, 'Let us make humankind in our image, according to our likeness. . . .'" These theologians said that the term "image" refers to natural or physical dimensions of humans while "likeness" refers to the spiritual or ethical aspects of human life. In the background is a philosophical distinction, common in Greek philosophy, between "form" and "matter."

Many biblical scholars have pointed out, however, that in other verses in the early chapters of Genesis, the terms "image" and "likeness" are used interchangeably. For example, in Genesis 5:1 the text says: "When God created humankind, he made them in the likeness of God." This is followed by Genesis 5:3, which says that Adam "became the father of a son in his likeness, according to his image." Here, the terms "image" and "likeness" seem completely synonymous and interchangeable. Most contemporary biblical scholars take these verses as an example of Hebrew parallelism—where a term is used and another term is coupled with it as a synonym. If so, then to refer to humans as created in the "image" and "likeness" of God would be to express a single idea.

In the early church, under the influence of Greek philosophy, Christian theologians commonly associated the "image" of God with human rationality and the "likeness" of God with immortality. Some equated the "image" with bodily traits and the "likeness" with spiritual traits. These writers did not believe that humans "lost" the "image" of God after sin entered the world in the fall of Adam and Eve in the Garden of Eden (Genesis 3). The "image" of God—or human rationality—was maintained, even though humans became sinful in God's sight. The "likeness" of God, however—spiritual goodness— was lost by the fall into sin. So, humans stand estranged from God spiritually, but able to function as God originally created them by the use of their human reason or rationality. Only the Holy Spirit can restore the spiritual relationship. But humans can use their minds and rational abilities to comprehend truth without being affected by the power of sin.

In the fifth century, Cyril of Alexandria listed six facts of resemblance to God that humans can share. These six are reflections of God and thus make up the "image of God." They are reason, freedom, dominion, sanctification, incorruptibility, and sonship.

This distinction between the "image" and "likeness" of God continued among theologians in the Middle Ages. In the Roman Catholic tradition, Thomas Aquinas contended that in the fall into sin, humans did not lose the "image" of God, found primarily in the human intellect.[16] Angels, he argued, exhibit the image of God more perfectly than humans because angels are "more perfectly intelligent" than humans. The intellect, for Aquinas, was the most God-like quality humans possess. For Aquinas, the power of reason and human freedom still remain intact for sinful persons. Intellectually, one could come to the belief that a God exists by using forms of arguments ("theistic proofs") to "prove" a God exists on the basis of the world around us. This approach, called "natural theology," is possible because the intellect is capable of knowledge and is unaffected by sin.

Yet for Aquinas, humans did lose the "likeness" of God due to their sinfulness. The "likeness" is the righteousness or right relationship that God created humans to have with God. Thus the "moral image" of God is affected by sin, and it is this moral image that humans no longer possess. For Aquinas, humans recover the moral image as they choose to do good and reject evil in cooperation with God's Spirit. The "original righteousness" of humans is lost because of sin; it can only be restored by God's gift of the Holy Spirit to enable people to cooperate with God's grace. In this view, the "image of God" is intellectual; the "likeness of God" is moral or theological.

Reformed Emphases

Both the major Protestant reformers of the sixteenth century, Martin Luther and John Calvin, rejected the distinction between the "image" and the "likeness" of God. Neither of them claimed that the image of God was lost by humanity's fall into sin. Calvin said that the term "likeness" was used to clarify "image" and was an example of Hebrew parallelism. For Calvin, the primary place where God's image is found is not in the human "soul," as a special part or condition of the human being. Rather, the whole person is created in God's image. As Calvin put it, there was no part of humans, "not even the body itself, in which some sparks did not glow."[17]

The fall into sin has severely affected and distorted the image of God in humanity. The "image" is not totally annihilated, but rather terribly deformed."[18] Human reason and the human volition remain sinful and are affected by being weakened and corrupted by sin.[19]

Yet, for Calvin, it is important to see that the image of God still shines forth in humans. This common characteristic of all human beings created in the image of God should lead us to love and serve others. Paraphrasing Calvin's words: We are not to consider that people merit of themselves but to look upon the image of God in all persons, to which we owe all honor and love. . . . Therefore whatever persons we meet who need our aid, we have no reason to refuse to help the persons. Say, 'that person is contemptible and worthless'; but the Lord shows that one to be one to whom God has deigned to give the beauty of the divine image. Say that the person does not deserve even our least effort for their sake; but the image of God, which recommends that person to you, is worthy of your giving yourself and all your possessions.[20] So, recognizing that humans are created in the image of God had tremendous importance. It forms a basis by which service to other people should be rendered.

Calvin noted in his commentary on Genesis 9:6 that because of the image of God in all people, "no one can be injurious to his brother without wounding God himself."[21] Even if people provoke us by unjust acts, do evil against us, or curse us—even when they are undeserving of our love—there is only one way to achieve the forgiveness and goodness that God requires us to render to those people (Matt. 5:44). That is not to consider people's evil intentions but "to look upon the image of God in them, which cancels and effaces their transgressions, and with its beauty and dignity allures us to love and embrace them."[22]

Renewal of God's Image

Yet humans who are sinful and in whom the image of God is now weakened are not without hope, for the image of God can be renewed in humanity. This renewal happens through faith. Faith is the human response, as a gift of God, given in response to God's Word in Jesus Christ. This response is possible by the work of the Holy Spirit, who, as Calvin said, "creates faith in our hearts." The Spirit carries out the "purpose of the Gospel," which is "the restoration in us of the image of God which had been cancelled by sin." This restoration is "progressive and goes on during our whole life, because God makes His glory to shine in us little by little."[23] When we believe in Jesus Christ by faith, God's Spirit works continually to renew us and to restore the image of God within us. For Calvin, "the end of regeneration is that Christ should reform us to God's image" (Col. 3:10; Eph. 4:24).[24] This process of restoration is not completed in this life, but is only fully completed in the life to come.

Jesus Christ as Model

Our model for what it means to be in the "image of God" is Jesus Christ. The Scriptures refer to Jesus as "the image of God" (2 Cor. 4:4; Col. 1:15). He is the one who shows us most fully what it means to live in the relationship that the divine image implies. He is the one who shows us what humans are created to be like. As Karl Barth put it, "As the man Jesus is himself the revealing Word of God, he is the source of our knowledge of the nature of [humanity] as created by God."[25] Jesus is "the one creaturely being in whose existence we have to do immediately and directly with the being of God also."[26] If we want to see what it means to be "truly human," we look at Jesus Christ.[27] He embodied true humanity and in him the "image of God" shines forth most clearly. He is the "true image" who—in his life, death, and resurrection—has fully actualized authentic humanity.[28] To his image and likeness humans are joyfully conformed (1 Cor. 15:49; Rom. 8:29). We gain our truest, clearest perception of the nature of true humanity, created in the image of God, when we look at Jesus Christ, who is truly the "image and reflection of God" (1 Cor. 11:7).

Contemporary Significance

To Image God

One way of understanding the importance of humans as created in the divine image is to consider humans to be divine "image bearers." In other words, as created by God, humans are to represent God or to bear God's image to others. We are to "image God" to other people. In ancient times, an emperor who ruled over a kingdom could not be present at every place or in every land under the emperor's control. So the emperor would have statues erected in various places. These statues of the emperor would remind everyone who saw them that the emperor was the ruler. They bore the emperor's "image" and thus represented the emperor throughout the whole empire.

To Represent God

In the same way as the emperor's statues, humans created in the image of God are to "represent" God—the ruler—in every place and in every relationship. When people encounter us, they should see God living in us. We are God's representatives throughout the whole world. We were created in the image of God in order to be God's eyes and ears and hands throughout the whole earth. We are created in the image of God in order to "image" God to other people. We "image God . . . if and when and as we stand in a positive (responsive) relationship with God."[29]

God's Image in Others

On the other hand, if we are created in the divine image, then we should recognize that image in every other person. We recognize people at the most basic level, not on the basis of their gender, race, or economic location, but as fellow creatures, created in the image of God. We are united with all others in this world by this most basic of all bonds. We are united on the basis of our common humanity as creatures created in the image of God. This is our most basic conviction about who we are as humans, and who others are: We are all creatures of God who bear the divine image and likeness. Of course, we encounter differences. Humans are unique, distinctive. Each of us is unique, yet we are also all the same. And our "sameness" is that we are all divine image bearers.

Theological Significance

What is the theological significance of being created in the image of God?

1. *Responsibilities.* Theologically, our creation in the image of God means that as humans we have a special standing before God. Humans stand apart from all other aspects of God's creation in that we have received the breath of life from God and have been created for a special relationship with God that no other created creatures have. This relationship brings special responsibilities.[30] Humans are to be stewards of the earth, to manage the resources of the earth, on God's behalf in accordance with God's will, known most fully in Jesus Christ.[31] Humans are God's representatives on earth and are to reflect to the created order the nature of God, the creator of all things. For this reason, contemporary concerns about ecology, the environment, and the responsible use of resources are so important. They are Christian concerns! We recognize the obligations humans have to act justly in caring for the world around us.

2. *Relationship to God.* Theologically, our creation in the image of God means that as humans we are to love God as our Creator.[32] We are to obey God, because God is our Lord, our sovereign, our creator. We are to love and live in the special relationship God intends. We are to obey God and live according to God's will and purposes for our lives. We, as humans created in the image of God, depend on God for all things. We look to God for guidance in our lives. We reflect God's image to others. Being created in the image of God is the most basic thing that can be said about us. For

> Christians believe that this interlocking of the knowledge of God and the self is because human existence is by definition an existence in relationship to God. The being that is human has no existence in itself, but only in its uniuqe relationship to the Creator. In disclosing himself as the God-who-has-made-us-for-himself, the Creator discloses to us that we are the creature-uniquely-related to him.[33]

We love God, we obey God, we depend on God—because God has created us in this relationship. We are created in the image of God.

3. *Created for Community.* But even more, to be created in the image of God is to realize that humans are created for community. We are created for fellowship with God and for community with each other.[34] God creates a human family. God does not create one person and then call it quits. No, the stories in the book of Genesis show how God intends and desires for humans to be in relation with each other. Just as the doctrine of the Trinity points us to the divine interrelationships, so the doctrine of the image of God (Lat. *imago Dei*)

points us to the divine intention that humans live in communal relationships with each other. The love God showed in creating humans is to be shared by humans with each other. All through human history this shared love is the divine intention for human beings.

4. *Created for Relationships*. Most clearly, we see that humans are intended by their creator for relationships.[35] We are created in the image of God, and we are thus dependent on God. Our relatedness to God constitutes the very nature of our being as persons. Jesus is our primary model for this true humanity. What we find in him is not that he was in the image of God by virtue of his intellect or rationality. Rather, he "imaged" God by the way he lived. For "he was the one person who lived completely for God and in thankful obedience to God, and completely for fellow human beings and for their good."[36] To be "renewed" in the image of God is to become more and more like Jesus Christ (2 Cor. 3:18; Rom. 8:29). One writer has put it extremely well:

> What we learn from Jesus, then, is that to be truly human in the image of God is not to possess some intellectual, moral, or spiritual capacity *within* ourselves; it is realized only in relatedness, community, or fellowship with others *outside* ourselves. We cannot be human by ourselves in independent, self-sufficient loneliness. Only as we discover the meaning of our very existence in relatedness to God and fellow human beings can we be truly human. And just then we discover that this means not the sacrifice but the realization of true human selfhood.[37]

Questions for Reflection

1. What difference does it make in your view of humanity if you believe that humans are created by God?

2. If the "whole person" is created in God's image, then should Christians be concerned only with someone's "soul"? Why not?

3. In what ways does seeing humanity as created in God's image radicalize our views of who is our "neighbor"?

4. In what ways did Jesus model the "image of God" that God intends for all humanity?

5. What implications does the belief that humans are created in the image of God have for such issues as the prolonging of human life by medical means, euthanasia, or participation in society?

7

Sin: What Have We Become?

Someone has said that no matter what else is said about humans, we are not what we should be! That's a sweeping claim, but one with which many people would agree. What is wrong with the human race?

From the Christian point of view we've seen that humans are good creations of God and, we believe, are created in God's image. This theological conviction has a number of implications for how humans may live. The sense of dependence on God, thankfulness to God, relationships of care and love for others—all of these emerge from the conviction that humans were created to have a trusting, loving relationship with God as their creator. The best expression of a human who lived out the "image of God" is Jesus Christ. He shows us how to live as a human person who seeks God's will in everything and who, in dependence on God, loves and cares for others in peaceful and just ways. If humans could just "imitate" Jesus, things would be different—we suspect. Or even better, if people could live in the ways Jesus taught, with the attitudes he conveyed, our culture and our world would notice the difference!

What *is* wrong with the human race? The Bible names our basic problem as sin. The human condition is characterized by attitudes, actions, indeed a "human nature" that is a distortion of the image of God in which we are created. In other words, as humans, we do not live in the ways God desires, we treat God and others in ways that are not loving and just, and we hold attitudes in which our own self-interests are primary. We do this because this is *who we are*. We have lost or distorted or perverted or broken the "image of God"; we do not now reflect God in our lives. We no longer "represent" God to others. We have taken hold of our own agendas and we live with our primary intention being to go our own ways instead of seeking God's ways for our lives. Sin takes shape in a wide variety of ways. But if we seek a comprehensive explanation for the way things are—including ourselves—"sin" conveys the biblical perspective.

Biblical Bases

Experiences of Israel as the people of God in the Hebrew Scriptures are marked in part by sin, guilt, and punishment. A variety of terms are used in the Hebrew Bible to express these ideas. They tend to spill over into each other because of what happens when sin occurs. When sin is present, guilt may emerge, and harm and a sense of punishment can happen.[1]

In the New Testament, the writings of the apostle Paul in particular convey the picture of humans as sinners. For Paul, the power of sin is very real.[2] It affects every person (Rom. 3:23). It relates to the origins of the human race (Rom. 5:12ff.), brings alienation and estrangement from God (Eph. 4:18), and leads ultimately to death (Rom. 6:23). The power of sin is so strong that it is ultimately only God's actions in Jesus Christ that can overcome it and break its effects (Rom. 5:15–21).[3]

Images of Sin

Several clusters of terms help us understand what sin is. These terms emerge out of the context of certain aspects or figures of life. For example, we can see sin as it is conveyed in relation to personal, military, religious, economic, and legal images.

1. *Personal.* Personally, sin is alienation from God. Sin ruptures the relationship of love and trust that God seeks to have with humanity. The imaging or reflecting of the "image of God" is broken, and relationships among humans with each other are marked by mistrust, violence, and hatred—to name just a few characteristics. On a human level, this kind of estrangement may mark the relationships of parents with children, or of friends whose bond of friendship is broken because of some action. Jesus' famous parable of the prodigal son shows the effects of a broken personal relationship (Luke 15:11–32). The "younger son" left his home, cut off his relationship with his family, and squandered his property in wild living. His actions showed a complete disregard for his family. When he finally "came to himself" (Luke 15:17), he returned home and found his father welcomed him and treated him as the "son" he had not proven himself to be. In our relationship with God, sin is that separating force which—when we follow our own wishes and desires—leads us away from God and from God's will for our lives. The result is estrangement and separation from God and from other people. Our only hope is that God will overcome our sin and "welcome us back."

2. *Military.* Military images for sin are found in the Scriptures as well. The picture is of those imprisoned—as in a prison camp—who need liberation. More broadly, the Bible portrays the whole human race as enslaved or

imprisoned to the power of sin. In the Old Testament, the story of Israel in slavery in Egypt comes to mind. The nation was in need of help, of liberation (Ex. 6:1ff.). The power of their oppressors was greater than their own. On a broader scale, humanity is enslaved to the powers of evil (Mark 3:22f.; Rom. 6:6; Gal. 4:3). Whatever evil is, it exercises a dominion over the world that is related to human sin. Institutional structures of racism, sexism, injustice, and violence are expressions of these kinds of powers. They are rooted in the human heart and its attitudes; they are expressed in a culture that is bound by them and functions through them. Only a greater power can conquer and overcome them. Our only hope is that God will provide that power.

3. *Religious.* Another set of images for sin emerges from the religious realm. These images are prominent in Old Testament texts that portray humans as sinners to be unclean and thus unworthy to stand in the presence of a holy and pure God (Leviticus 16). The Old Testament sacrificial system was the means by which sin, in this respect, was forgiven and the nation of Israel was purified. Animal sacrifices were offered to God to "atone" for sin, or to make God and humans "at-one" again. God accepted these sacrifices as a sign of the peoples' sorrow and repentance for their sin. In the New Testament, particularly in the book of Hebrews, Jesus Christ is portrayed as being the new and all-sufficient sacrifice for human sin (Hebrews 8 and 9). Humans need purification from their moral uncleanness because they stand in the presence of a God who is holy and righteous. Our only hope is that God will provide the means for purification.

4. *Economic.* Other images of sin are found in the economic realm. If one were a slave who was eager to gain freedom, one would need a "redeemer"— one who would pay a ransom or a price to set the slave free. The power of sin enslaves people to themselves; they live with only their own concerns on their horizons. Their dominant verb is to "get" rather than to "give." In this condition, they need someone who will "pay the price" of their redemption and give the inner freedom they need to be able to live life in a new way. This is the situation in which Jesus Christ becomes a redeemer (Mark 10:45; Rom. 3:24). Our only hope is that God will provide one to secure the freedom we need to be the people God wants us to be.

5. *Legal.* Finally, the Bible uses images from the legal realm to speak of sin that leaves us guilty in God's sight. Here the picture is that humans have sinned by breaking God's law. God's law—given to us in clear form in the Ten Commandments (Exodus 20)—is an expression of God's will for human life. But humans do not obey God's command; we sin. We are thus guilty of breaking God's law. We face God's judgment because we have not rendered the obedience required of us as creatures created by a loving creator. To be forgiven and made "just," we need a savior who can fulfill the law on our behalf and be a righteous one. Jesus Christ has done that. By faith, we accept Christ's

righteousness as being our own. God "justifies" us in that by our faith/identi-fication with Jesus, God sees us as "clothed in the righteousness of Christ" (see Rom. 5:17; Isa. 61:10).

These biblical images of sin and how it is overcome by God's action in Jesus Christ show the variety of ways that human sinfulness is portrayed in the Scriptures. Sin affects the individual and the whole community. The serious-ness of sin is underlined by its connection with God's judgment (Rom. 5:16). The "bad news" about sin is that "all are guilty" (Rom. 3:23; 5:12). The "worse news" is that it leads to death (Rom. 6:23). Yet this is not the final biblical word. There is hope. For "the wages of sin is death, but the free gift of God is eternal life in Christ Jesus our Lord" (Rom. 6:23) and "in hope we were saved" (Rom. 8:24).

Christian Tradition

A number of questions surround sin, and these were dealt with in the emerging Christian tradition of the early church.[4] One question was how sin entered the world.[5] Then, how does it spread in the world? The biblical account of the "fall" into sin by Adam and Eve (Genesis 3) presents how sin became present from the beginnings of life on earth. Adam and Eve are shown to have disobeyed God's divine prohibition not to eat of the tree of the knowl-edge of good and evil in the midst of the garden of Eden (Gen. 2:17). If they did, they would die. They did, and death entered the human story (Gen. 3:6). The opening, trusting relationship that was enjoyed by the first couple prior to this incident was now shattered. Fellowship with the creator was broken. Harmony with the creation was lost.

Early theologians wrestled with how this sin and its effects have become the story of every human life. Many questions were raised: Is sin "transmitted" from generation to generation? Is everyone guilty for one's own sin, or is there an "inherited" sin and guilt from the origins of the human race? What are the effects of sin on a person's mind, heart, and will? What are sin's results?[6]

Original Sin

Varying viewpoints emerged as the church struggled with these issues.[7] The third-century theologian Tertullian used the term "original sin" to express his belief that "sinful souls" have been passed on from humanity's first parents.[8] Tertullian believed that the human soul still possessed a "portion of the good" and that humans are free to choose either good or evil in any situ-ation. This stance led him to oppose the practice of infant baptism since he did not believe that humans inherited the "guilt" of our first parents—just the inclination to choose evil because of our inherited "sinful souls."

Other early church theologians, particularly in the Eastern churches, did not agree with this view. Those known as the "Cappadocian fathers"[9] believed that humans were created in an original state of blessedness and happiness. Sin originates with the misuse of freedom by Adam and Eve. But the Cappadocians did not believe that the guilt of this sin is conveyed from generation to generation. They believed that infants are exempt from sin. Humans are disposed toward sinning but their wills are also free to choose to do good instead of evil. Humanity as a whole does not share in Adam and Eve's guilt. These theologians did not believe it was just for one person to be punished on account of another's sin.

The dominant view of the Western church through Ambrose of Milan (ca. 339–397) and more importantly Augustine was the view that the sin of our first parents has plunged the whole human race into a devastating condition of sinfulness that affects the whole of humanity and the whole human person. Augustine believed that all humanity sinned "in" Adam. All humans bear the punishment for Adam's sin. All humans were potentially present in the first human, and this solidarity of the human race accounts for how sin now infects the whole of humanity. Augustine believed the means of transmitting this sin and guilt was by procreation, the sexual union of men and women (a view rejected today by those who still follow Augustine's main points). Adam is the natural "head" of the race. The actions of the "head" affects all the "parts" (Rom. 5:12ff.). Thus all subsequent humanity shares in the condemnation and results of the sin of the first parents.[10]

Augustine and Pelagius

The swirl of these conflicting views led to a very significant theological conflict between Augustine and a British monk named Pelagius.[11] Pelagius believed that humans have complete freedom of will—to choose either good or evil. Every sin is thus a deliberate act against God. Sin is not inherited from or transmitted by earlier generations. All are born without sin and without fault. While Pelagius did not believe that anyone could remain sinless throughout life, he did believe that turning away from sin could be accomplished by one's own free choices. The "sin of Adam" affected Adam alone. Humans have a history and custom of sinning, and so doing good can be difficult. Continual sinning makes sin an even more difficult habit to shake.[12] But Pelagius believed God gave grace to guide humanity in the form of the law and gives the promise of reward to those who do the right things.

Augustine rejected this view at a number of points. For him, the human will can be free only by the grace of God. "Original sin," for Augustine, meant that humanity is sinful in its "origins." Our first parents had the freedom not to sin if they so chose. They could have obeyed God's word and not eaten of the forbidden fruit from the tree of the knowledge of good and evil. They were "able not to sin" and could have continued in this obedience throughout their lives. But according to Augustine, the biblical accounts show that they used their freedom in a bad way. They ate of the fruit; they sinned. Now the results follow. Freedom is forfeited; death occurs. Those who follow from Adam and Eve have lost their ability not to sin. Sin has now so drastically affected us that we are enslaved to its power. Humans now are "not able not to sin." To Augustine, the first parents sinned from their pride, which led to their disobedience—and to death for us all. The result of "original sin" is sin and guilt transmitted to all posterity. Sin has corrupted the very nature of humans.[13]

The debates between Augustine and Pelagius set the framework for discussions of sin and the questions it raises. Followers who tried to mediate the two views were often called "semi-Augustinians" or, more usually, "semi-Pelagians." The semi-Pelagian view was that the sin of Adam does affect all who are born. Everyone is inclined toward evil. But later humanity does not inherit the guilt of Adam's sin. Human nature is weakened by sin, but humans still have the power freely to choose either good or evil. They can cooperate with divine grace and resist evil.[14]

The "semi-Pelagian" view of sin and human freedom coexisted with the Augustinian view through the period of the Middle Ages. When the Protestant Reformation occurred in the sixteenth century, Martin Luther (who was an Augustinian monk), and later John Calvin, vigorously reasserted the views of Augustine about the nature and effects of sin. They saw sin as more than just "wrong choices" that can be overcome when "right choices" are made later. Instead, they saw sin as permanently affecting the human community and all its members. Sin is a corruption of human nature that can only be restored by the radical action of God.

Reformed Emphases

The influence of Augustine has been strong in the Reformed faith, but the tradition has also developed thought about sin beyond Augustine's own.[15]

John Calvin engaged the issues of his time with an Augustinian emphasis by seeing the first sin as "original sin," which has brought an "inherited corruption" and "depravation of a nature previously good and pure." "Therefore," Calvin continued, "all of us, who have descended from impure seed, are born infected with the contagion of sin."[16] This sin affects both our natures and our actions. The actions that the Scriptures call the "works of the flesh" (Gal. 5:19) spring from our corrupted nature just as, said Calvin, "a burning furnace gives forth flame and sparks, or water ceaselessly bubbles up from a spring.[17]

Total Depravity

Calvin is clear that this sin affects the whole person. The whole person is "overwhelmed—as by a deluge—from head to foot, so that no part is immune from sin." "All that proceeds" from the person "is to be imputed to sin."[18] This condition is what later Reformed theologians called "total depravity." Sin affects the totality of our existence. No part of us—mind, will, or affections—is exempt from the effects of our sinful nature. Thus sin has far-reaching consequences.

Bondage of the Will

A key element in the Reformed view is (echoing Augustine) that sin affects our human wills so drastically that we are unable to choose what is good in God's sight. Our human nature is corrupted by sin, and our actions and choices spring from our nature. The power of sin is such that, on our own, we humans will always choose what we want instead of what God wants; we'll choose what is in our own self-interest, instead of seeking what is God's will. Our natural inclinations will be toward what is contrary to God.[19]

In this sense we have no "freedom of the will" if we understand that phrase to mean the "freedom" to choose the good, or to choose God. We have "freedom of choice" on natural matters such as whether or not to go to the store, whether or not to pick up a pencil, etc. But when it comes to moral and theological choices, to doing God's will instead of our own—our "freedom" is lost. We will act in sinful ways because our human nature is sinful. We have lost what Calvin called the "soundness of will."[20] Citing Bernard of Clairvaux, Calvin wrote: ". . . to will is in us all: but to will good is gain; to will evil, loss. Therefore simply to will is of [humans]; to will ill, of a corrupt nature; to will well, of grace."[21] Our human will is addicted to the power of sin. Only God can change it. Only God's grace can make each person a "new creation" (2 Cor. 5:17).

Imputation of Sin

Since sin is so pervasive in human life, the Reformed faith has had a strong concern to understand its power in both individual and corporate dimensions. Reformed theologians after Calvin proposed different ways of understanding the "imputation" of Adam's sin to humanity.[22] When it became more widely accepted that the Genesis stories need not be read as literal "history," but may be seen as theological stories whose truth does not depend on a literal "Adam and Eve," some theologians continued to affirm the reality of a "fall" into sin, but did not deal with questions about whether or not guilt and corruption were inherited by future generations.[23] In this view, every human being is seen as beginning in innocence as Adam and Eve did, but then as experiencing a "personal fall." "Original sin" is understood to be the human tendency found in all persons to choose wrongly in God's sight. As one writer put it, the fall is "a turning away from God in the life of every person within history."[24]

Social Consequences of Sin

Contemporary Reformed confessions have seen sin as having very strong social consequences.[25] The Confession of 1967 describes human sin as when people "claim mastery of their own lives, turn against God" and against others. They become "exploiters and despoilers of the world. They lose their humanity in futile striving and are left in rebellion, despair, and isolation." Self-interest and hostility infect all human enterprises, even those that are good, such as devotion to "freedom, justice, peace, truth, and beauty." This means, theologically, that all persons, "good and bad alike, are in the wrong before God and helpless" without God's forgiveness. All fall under God's judgment. And no one is more "subject to that judgment" than those who assume that they are "guiltless before God or morally superior to others."[26] This strong expression of sin's social dimensions and its disruption of the human community is continued in A Brief Statement of Faith, which speaks of sin when it says that

> We rebel against God; we hide from our Creator.
>   Ignoring God's commandments,
>   we violate the image of God in others and ourselves,
>   accept lies as truth,
>   exploit neighbor and nature,
>   and threaten death to the planet entrusted to our care.
> We deserve God's condemnation.[27]

While the contemporary confessions do not go into the theological intricacies of the past in terms of what characterizes "original sin" or how sin is transmitted, they confess sin's reality. The "inward" and "outward" effects are real. Sin disrupts our relationship with God, with others, and with our world. Concern for the environment and "ecojustice"—the use and care of Earth's limited resources in ways that are just and will benefit the human community—are eminently Christian concerns.[28]

Similarly, the Reformed faith at its best has also been concerned with economic and political justice because it recognizes that we live in a fallen and sinful world. The oppression of people by political regimes and their deprivation of the resources they need for living are outward manifestations of human sin.

Idolatry

Particularly seductive is idolatry. Idolatry is an obsessive concern or addiction that pulls us away from the right worship and service of God. The biblical prohibition in the Ten Commandments—"You shall not make for yourself an idol" (Ex. 20:4)—has been recognized, in the Reformed faith, as pertaining to more than the fashioning of "graven images" with human hands.[29] Idolatry has been seen to be a fundamental orientation of our sinful existence in which we invest our energies, time, and affections in such a compulsive way that the object of our energies becomes our "god." We thus turn away from the worship and obedience that the true God desires and "worship an idol." The seductiveness of idolatry lies in the fact that what we are focusing upon can, indeed, be a relatively good thing. We can pour our energies into our jobs, our political affiliations, our hobbies, our families, even into the work of the church. But when these become predominant in our minds and hearts, we are in danger of turning away from the true God and worshiping the "idol." The many enticements of American culture to spend money and to spend our hours in entertainment and amusement may make us particularly susceptible.

In Reformed thought, the dangers of idolatry—which can affect Christian believers—are much more real and pervasive than traditional concerns about atheism. Politically, any ideology that is held without being judged in light of the gospel can become an idolatry as well. It becomes an absolute, unchallenged by the prophetic word of God. The church is in danger of idolatry if it compromises the gospel. This was the danger Reformed Christians perceived when they adopted the Theological Declaration of Barmen (1934) in the context of the rise of Nazism. The Declaration warns, "We reject the false doctrine, as though the Church were permitted to abandon the form of its message and order to its own pleasure or to changes in prevailing ideological and political convictions."[30] The temptation to idolatry as a pervasive form of sin is very real.

Contemporary Significance

A theologian once said that the Christian doctrine of original sin is the only empirically verifiable Christian doctrine. What he meant was that we see its truth every time we read the newspaper or watch the news. All around we see signs of the fallen creation. Humans sin; the ozone layer gets a hole in it! Human solidarity and human community are fractured by actions that are both corporate and personal in nature.[31] An individual's actions have a ripple effect on all those around us. What corporate bodies in society do affects the lives of people in society and may serve to perpetuate unjust practices and structures already in place. Our personal and societal lives are intimately intertwined. When they are marked by self-interest, greed, vengeance, or even "benign neglect," the human community—and God's desires for human society—suffer. We all participate in the human failure, rooted deep in our beings and extending back through the generations to some original progenitor.

Sin has many faces in our contemporary world. Traditionally, some theologians have characterized the essence of sin as "pride" or "concupiscence." Today it is realized that while the "will to power," represented by this kind of pride and egocentricity, has been especially prevalent among males in the Western world, females may be more prone to passivity and fear of initiative. In the face of dominating injustice it may be the nature of sin to yield to acquiescence. Neither an inordinate love of self nor a secret hatred of the self are what God intended for human life to be.[32]

The pervasiveness of sin is a mark of this age and every age. There are examples of grossly evil actions in war, violence, abuse, racial and gender discrimination, and widespread injustice. There are examples of the subtle sins, the personal sins that destroy the fabric of human community and relationships together. There are the paradoxical sins, the sins that emerge from absolutizing proximate good or that spring from the evil intentions that masquerade as "doing good."[33]

In the face of all that is destructive, evil, and contrary to God's intentions for our human community, as Christians we can only confess our sins. We confess for ourselves, and we confess on behalf of all humanity. For only in admitting our sin and seeking God's mercy is there hope for forgiveness and new life. Fortunately, the doctrine of sin is not the last word. The last word of the Christian gospel is that God has given us one who will "save his people from their sins" (Matt. 1:21): Jesus Christ.

Questions for Reflection

1. What image of sin seems to be the most accurate one to you?

2. What are some examples of the results of human sin in our culture?

3. Do you believe that we are sinners by "nature" or sinners by "choice"?

4. In what ways do you see the human will as in "bondage" (addicted) to sin?

5. What are examples of corporate sin or sin in communities in our society?

8

Person of Christ:
Who Is Jesus?

The name "Jesus" is familiar to anyone in the Western world. Jesus of Nazareth, called "Jesus Christ," is a figure from history who has had a tremendous influence in our culture. The calendar we use is divided into "B.C." and "A.D."—time "before Christ" and "the year of the Lord," the years after the birth of Christ.[1] Early Christians startled the ancient world by beginning as a small Jerusalem-based sect and within three hundred years seeing Christianity become an official religion of the Roman Empire. The Christian church was devoted to spreading the teachings of Jesus and proclaiming him as God's Messiah, the savior of all humanity. Today, the Christian church is found throughout the whole world. Jesus is regarded as one of the greatest religious leaders. Millions acknowledge him as their "Lord and Savior." Jesus is real as a living, vital person within their own experience. His teachings, comfort, and challenges form the basis for their living. Jesus is alive and can be known. His adherents attest to his living presence and his ongoing power. More than that, they claim that in the encounter with this human person, Jesus, they experience the presence of God. This is what Jesus' first followers found, and his contemporary disciples know the same reality.

Biblical Bases

Jesus of Nazareth is the central figure in the New Testament. The Gospels provide a record or a portrait of Jesus. His birth, life and ministry, crucifixion, and resurrection form the central story or *kerygma* ("message") that was later proclaimed and taught by early Christians to be God's supreme action.

The gospel story of Jesus was seen by his followers to attest to his unique person. Jesus was in every sense a human being, just as all of us are. He experienced joys and sorrows in life (Luke 10:21), human emotions (Mark 1:41; John 11:35), and, at the end, "thirst" (John 19:28).

76

Yet Jesus' followers also proclaimed that he was significantly different, too. In him they experienced the presence of God in an unparalleled way. They believed Jesus was the fulfillment of God's Old Testament promises to Israel to send a "messiah"—an "anointed one" (Gr. *christos*; "Christ") who would be an anticipated king and deliverer. The messiah would establish God's rule on earth. In him, all God's promises to the nation of Israel would be fulfilled. Early Christians proclaimed that Jesus was the Messiah. They preached the "certainty that God has made him both Lord and Messiah, this Jesus whom you crucified" (Acts 2:36; cf. 18:5, 28).

But the man Jesus as "messiah" was not the kind of "messiah" anticipated by his contemporaries. The traditional picture of God's coming deliverer was one who would be from the "lineage of David"—Israel's greatest warrior-king—and who would continue that tradition by driving out the enemies of Israel from its land and establish Israel as the nation to which all other nations would look. The messiah would usher in God's promised kingdom.[2] God's reign would be marked by *shalôm* ("peace") and ultimate harmony among people, nations, and nature. The "messianic age" would be a radical break from "this age" and mark the fullness of God's reign and rule.[3]

Jesus as "messiah" was far different. Through his life and teachings he lived and taught the way of love as a lifestyle (Matt. 5:44; John 15:12). He exemplified "humility" rather than bravado (Matt. 11:29). His emphasis was on ministering in service rather than on military conquests (Luke 22:27). He proclaimed that his death would set people free (Mark 10:45). Yet his death was ignominious. Jews regarded death by crucifixion as a particularly accursed way to die (Deut. 21:23; Gal. 3:13). So those who proclaimed Jesus as Messiah to their fellow Jewish citizens were radically reinterpreting the nature of God's Messiah.[4] They proclaimed that in Jesus God has fulfilled ancient promises in ways that had not been expected or anticipated.

Other names or titles were associated with Jesus, by himself and by his later followers. These include "Son of David" (Mark 10:47, 48); "Son of God" (Mark 1:1); "Servant of God" (Rom. 1:4); "Lord" (Mark 11:3; Acts 2:36); "Son of Man" (Mark 14:62); the "Word" (Gr. *logos*; John 1:1–14; Rev. 19:13). Each of these terms has its own specific history and usage. All of them point to some aspect of who the biblical writers and early church Christians found Jesus of Nazareth to be.[5]

Christian Tradition

The early church wrestled for several centuries with how to express its belief in who Jesus of Nazareth was.[6] The biblical titles and the developing thought of what became the New Testament, especially the writings of the apostle Paul, played significant roles in the church's deliberations.

Theological Language

Part of the church's challenge, however, was to proclaim its message of the gospel—the "good news" of Jesus Christ—in a cultural world that was cosmopolitan and heavily influenced by the language and philosophies of ancient Greece and Rome. While speaking of Jesus as the promised "messiah" who fulfilled the Old Testament Scriptures would be understandable to Jewish audiences, the church from its beginnings after the day of Pentecost (Acts 2) also needed to be able to speak intelligibly to non-Jews as well.

This necessity led to the creation and adaptation of Christian vocabulary, particularly in language about Jesus. This concern was crucial, because with the spread of Christianity, Jesus was talked about and described in many ways. Later, some of these views of Jesus would be considered wrong and misleading by the church.[7] The development of Christian "orthodoxy" or "right teaching" meant that it was necessary for harmful views to be countered and for the church's positive doctrine to be expressed.

Two Natures

What the church wanted to declare and affirm about Jesus during its early centuries centered around two dimensions, his "humanity" and his "divinity." The church also needed to address the issue of how these dimensions were related to each other.[8]

1. *Council of Nicaea (A.D. 325)*. Christological conflict marked the church in the period prior to A.D. 325. In that year, the Roman emperor Constantine—who had been converted to Christianity—assembled church bishops at the town of Nicaea and sought a unified creed of Christian belief. The immediate problem was the presbyter Arius, who taught that Jesus Christ as the divine "logos" of God was a creature formed out of nothing by God the creator. He was not eternal; he was the first being created when God began to create. Arius's slogan was, "There was [a time] when he was not." This meant that Jesus, the Son, could not have a direct knowledge of God and did not share in the same "substance" or "being" as the divine creator.

At Nicaea, the church rejected Arius's views, asserting that the Son (Jesus Christ) is "begotten, not made." This statement indicates that he is eternal, not a creature created by God the Father. The council also asserted that the Son is "of the same substance" (Gr. *homoousios*) as the Father. They share the same being, the same reality—they are divine. The Son is coeternal with the Father. This condition is crucial if salvation is to be a reality. The Son can only be the Savior if he is "truly God." So the theological wranglings had a very practical point: salvation. How can humans be related to God? Our savior must be divine for salvation to be accomplished. As Bishop Athansius put it in the fourth century, "The Word was made human in order that we might be made divine."[9]

2. *Council of Constantinople (A.D. 381)*. This church council did not bring unity to the church's understanding. At Constantinople in A.D. 381, another council met that reaffirmed Nicaea's teachings about the person of Jesus Christ. This was necessary because of the teachings of Apollinarius of Laodicea, who denied that Jesus had a human soul. He believed the divine Logos (reason) took the place of the human mind, will, and energy in the person of Jesus. Jesus was the "flesh-bearing God."[10]

At Constantinople, the church reaffirmed its belief in the true humanity of Jesus. Jesus was truly human. Jesus must have taken on the fullness of human existence, including the human spirit—mind, will, and energy—if he is to be able to redeem the full human person. To think of some aspect of Jesus as being exempt from full humanity again imperils salvation. The theological assumption of the church here was as follows: What the Logos did not assume in the incarnation, the Logos cannot redeem. Without a truly human "soul" or "spirit," Jesus did not have a genuinely human body or share in the completeness of human nature. At Constantinople, the church condemned Apollinarianism and affirmed the full and genuine humanity of Jesus.[11]

The Niceno-Constantinopolitan creed (A.D. 381) is what is commonly today referred to as the Nicene Creed. It confesses Jesus as being "of one substance with the Father," who was also a human person who was crucified, suffered, and was buried—just as any other human being would be.

One Person

Once the "two natures" of Jesus were established, the question came to the fore of how "divine" and "human" can be related in "one person."[12] The Council of Ephesus (A.D. 431) marked the church's confession that Jesus Christ was one integrated person. The immediate problem was the teachings of Nestorius, a monk from Antioch who later became Bishop of Constantinople. In controversy with Bishop Cyril of Alexandria, Nestorius maintained that the two natures of Christ must be held as unaltered and distinct. They are united only by a moral union. Nestorius did not want to say that the divine nature of Christ suffered any pain and to maintain Christ's genuinely human nature, including Jesus' growth, temptations, and sufferings. The divine and human exist alongside each other, each maintaining their own distinct properties.

The impression of Cyril and others in the church was that Nestorius believed Jesus Christ was two persons, and each was conjoined with the other while maintaining its own separate principles of operation. To them, this status denied the unity of Christ and threatened the genuineness of the Word becoming flesh (John 1:14). Cyril spoke of a "hypostatic union," a total union of the person of Christ. The two natures of Christ may be spoken of distinctly, but they are not ultimately separate. One may speak of the "communication of the properties" to say that what can be said of Jesus' "divine nature" can also be said of his "human nature"—and vice versa.[13] The Council of Ephesus affirmed Cyril's interpretation, confessing that Jesus Christ is one person, not two.

The Nature of the Person

The next question became: What is the actual nature of the one person of Jesus? This query was answered at the Council of Chalcedon (A.D. 451), a great landmark in that it set the language and understanding of the "orthodox" view of Jesus Christ. Eutyches, a monk in Constantinople, accused Nestorius of dividing Jesus into two natures. His solution to the christological question was to interpret the church's statement that Jesus was "one person" to mean that Jesus possessed only one nature. This view became known as "Monophysitism" (Gr. *monos,* "one," and *physis,* "nature"). Eutyches saw Jesus as one in whom humanity and divinity commingled so that a new, single nature was formed. In it, the divinity overshadowed the humanity. "After the union, I confess one nature," said Eutyches.

Eutyches was answered by Pope Leo I, who issued a *Tome* ("Letter") that set forth the church's christological understandings. Four main points stand out:

1. The person of Jesus Christ as the God-human is identical with the person of the divine Logos or divine Word.
2. The divine and human coexist in this one person and are not mixed or confused. Each maintains its own properties.
3. Though the natures act separately, they always act in harmony with each other.
4. The oneness of Christ's person means one may speak of the "communication of the properties."[14]

Chalcedonian Formula

More than five hundred bishops came together at Chalcedon and affirmed, against Eutyches, that Jesus Christ had two natures. Further, the "Formula" or "Definition" adopted at Chalcedon became a definitive statement of the church's christological belief. A key statement is that Jesus Christ is acknowledged to be "unconfusedly, unalterably, undividedly, inseparably in two natures." Each of these addressed the issues raised by the four pre-Chalcedonian heresies.[15] The divine and human natures of Christ share a common life. The divine did not merge with the human, and the human was not swallowed into the divine. There was no conversion or adoption of the divine into the human; each maintained its own properties and functions.

The Chalcedonian Formula of who Jesus is became the orthodox view in the Christian church and continues to be so in the Western church. In Eastern churches, the Monophysite position took hold and continues to be held among some Eastern churches today.[16] In the Middle Ages, theologians such as Anselm and Aquinas proposed ways of understanding whether the incarnation—God becoming a person in Jesus Christ—was related to God's nature or God's will.[17] During the sixteenth-century Protestant Reformation, the major reformers including Luther and Calvin upheld the Chalcedonian definition. Their emphases in understanding the person of Jesus varied, but they were united in their adherence to this standard of Christian orthodoxy.

Contemporary Christology

In contemporary times, concerns in Christology have moved into other arenas.[18] Some have critiqued the ancient formulations as being too tied to older philosophical models, as not saying anything about the ministry of Jesus, as separating the person of Jesus from his work, and as being a "Christology from above."[19] This latter phrase describes an approach to describing who Jesus Christ is that begins from his "divinity." An example would be a Christology that takes as its starting point the biblical texts, "In the beginning was the Word, and the Word was with God, and the Word was God. . . . And the Word became flesh and lived among us" (John 1:1, 14). Here Jesus Christ as the divine *logos* who is preexistent with God is the way in which Jesus Christ is initially described. Critics have claimed that this focus on the "origins" of Jesus is not the normal pattern of biblical thinking. In the New Testament, Jesus' disciples came to their understandings and made their claims about Jesus "after Easter" instead of at "Christmas." That is, the primary emphasis of the New Testament writers was on what occurred at the end of Jesus' ministry—his crucifixion and resurrection—rather than on his miraculous beginnings.

Modern theologians have emphasized the "history of Jesus," meaning that they have focused on his life and ministry, death, and resurrection as the focus of learning his identity. This approach has meant a tendency to begin christological thinking with a Christology "from below"—from the "human dimensions" of Jesus' history, as we know these from the New Testament writings. Our understandings of anthropology or who humanity is will assist in understanding who Jesus is according to this approach. A reevaluation of the nature of humanity itself is in order. Contemporary people, they argue, can relate much more readily to a person who has shared all the experiences of life with them rather than to a "divine" figure. Several theologians have used the image of "face" to capture this emphasis. Some speak of Jesus as "the human face of God," or "God with the face of Jesus," or Jesus as the revelation of the ultimate "face of all humanity."[20] Critics of this approach ask whether such a starting point will ever lead us beyond the historic and the human to confess Jesus as "my Lord and my God" (John 20:28) or to enable us to call him "truly divine and truly human," as the church historically has maintained.

Reformed Emphases

The Reformed confessions of the sixteenth century and beyond are strong in their affirmations of the church's historic description of Jesus Christ as "two distinct natures, and one Person forever" who is both "truly human and truly divine." Jesus is the incarnation of God—God "becoming flesh," becoming a human person in Jesus Christ. He is God's promised Messiah. Early church heresies are to be rejected.[21] The Heidelberg Catechism indicates that it is "Our Lord Jesus Christ, who is freely given to us for complete redemption and righteousness" (Q. 18). It asks:

Q. 16   Why must he be a true and righteous man?
A.   Because God's righteousness requires that man who has sinned should make reparation for sin, but the man who is himself a sinner cannot pay for others.
Q. 17   Why must he at the same time be true God?
A.   So that by the power of his divinity he might bear as a man the burden of God's wrath, and recover for us and restore to us righteousness and life.[22]

Crucial for the Reformed confessions, as for the early church, was to confess the fullness of who Jesus Christ is so that human salvation can be secured. Reformed theology, along with the orthodox tradition, has maintained that unless Jesus Christ was "truly human" and "truly God," salvation as a restored relationship with God will be in peril. Unless Jesus is divine, his death on the cross does not have the power to save. It is no different than the death of any other person. Unless Jesus is human, his death on the cross will not bring a complete redemption because he will not have completely identified and entered into the fullness of the human experience. As the early church theologian said, "That which is not assumed cannot be saved." So, the Reformed tradition has affirmed the incarnation, that Jesus Christ is "God become human" as the indispensable basis on which reconciliation with God and salvation occurs.[23]

Two Reformed theologians represent two different approaches to Christology that have been main christological avenues in the last two hundred years.

Christology from Below

Friedrich Schleiermacher (1768–1834) began his Christology "from below"—from the human man Jesus—in trying to make the Christian faith intelligible to his eighteenth-century German contemporaries.[24] In light of the "advances" of the times, Schleiermacher did not believe that traditional christological formulations spoke meaningfully to intellectuals in his day. He believed all persons have a sense of "dependence." They do not all realize it, but this is really a dependence on "God." When one goes outside and gazes into the starry heavens, one has the sense that there is a greatness beyond one's self and that all of life and one's own identity depend on this greater power.

Schleiermacher further believed that the divine can permeate the human and communicate to the human. Jesus of Nazareth was unique because he embodied in an unparalleled way a sense of the divine. He had a "God-consciousness" more real than anyone else has had. He was the perfection and ultimate example of "God-consciousness." In that way, he was set apart from all others. As Schleiermacher put it, Jesus was set off from others, not by his humanity but by "the constant potency of His God-consciousness, which was a veritable existence of God in him."[25] In this sense Jesus can be spoken of as "divine." Schleiermacher felt that language about two "natures" was inappropriate since Jesus was best viewed as a "God filled person." This powerful sense of God made Jesus unique.[26] Schleiermacher's critics, however, asked if he really had explained how Jesus was unique and whether this understanding of Christology truly safeguarded the concerns that the church had spent centuries trying to preserve.

Christology from Above

A major opponent of Schleiermacher's views was Karl Barth (1886–1968). Barth began his christology not "from below" but "from above"—from Jesus Christ as the eternal Word of God.[27] For Barth, all of theology was focused in Jesus Christ as the eternal Word of God. For Barth, all of theology was focused in Christology. It was thus imperative for the church's understandings of Jesus Christ to be congruent with the teachings of Scripture, which themselves present Jesus Christ as the supreme "Word of God." Barth fully defended the definition of Chalcedon, insisting that Jesus Christ was one person with two natures. In Jesus, we find "the one creaturely being in whose existence we have to do immediately and directly with the being of God also."[28] "He alone," said Barth, "can represent God" before humanity and humanity "before God."[29] Jesus Christ shows us what true humanity is like, for Jesus is human as God intended humans to be. Jesus is the "real human." At the same time, "Jesus Christ, the Word of God, meets us as no other than God."[30] Barth reaffirmed the early church's christological teachings.[31]

The Mystery of the Person

Reformed faith recognizes the "mystery" of the person of Jesus Christ. No theological theories can ever explain fully and rationally what "truly human and truly divine" and "one person with two natures" formulations can mean. Christians confess the reality of these convictions by faith. The Scottish theologian Donald Baillie (1887–1954) proposed that we recognize the mystery of the divine and human in Jesus in a way similar to what we recognize about our own Christian experience, the "paradox of grace." That is, we experience on one hand that our salvation comes to us as totally the work of God, who calls us and gives us the gift of faith. At the same time, we recognize our own human role, our freedom to be ourselves. We are most fully human when we are living in response to God's grace. This is the paradox—that both the divine and the human dimensions are real and active in the experience of grace. Baillie suggested that in the person of Jesus Christ, God and humanity find union in a mutual, self-giving love.[32]

Contemporary Significance

The German theologian Dietrich Bonhoeffer (1906–1945) said that the important question is not just "Who is Jesus Christ?" but "Who is Jesus Christ today?"[33] That question was appropriate at his time, in Germany on the brink of World War II, and in our own time, at the beginning of the twenty-first century.

Today the church still is concerned with appropriate theological expressions to affirm the divine mystery of the person of Jesus Christ. But contemporary situations also bring other dimensions of Jesus Christ to the forefront as well.[34]

Liberation Theology

For example, to those who are oppressed, Jesus Christ is the liberator who brings freedom. Latin American theologians as well as African American theologians have stressed the liberating power of Jesus as the Christ to enter into solidarity with the poor and oppressed of the world. Jesus came to the poor and preached to them. Jesus inaugurated the reign of God (Mark 1:15) that revolutionizes all of life, both personally and corporately. Societal structures—social, political, and economic—are infested by sin. Jesus came to bring salvation and justice to the world's structures. Those who truly "know" Jesus will be his disciples and "follow" him into intense involvement with the world on behalf of the reign of God.[35]

Feminist Theology

Some contemporary feminist theologians have raised the question of whether Jesus' "maleness" prevents him from being a savior for women. If Jesus is the protype of "true humanity," and Jesus was a male, does this mean that women must always be less than fully human? In response, other feminist scholars have maintained that in the New Testament, Jesus' "maleness" is not what makes him the "true human." Jesus is "truly human" in that he sought always the will of God, loved others with a radical fullness, spoke words of justice to those in power, and drew in all persons to the emerging reign of God. While the biblical materials were shaped in patriarchal cultures, the words and deeds of Jesus went beyond cultural norms and stereotypes, being critical of them, and opening ways of new life as part of a "new humanity" for all persons—both females and males.[36]

Who Is Jesus Christ Today?

Numerous other issues and concerns relate to contemporary Christology and the question, "Who is Jesus Christ today?" The variety of answers to that question is reflective of the diverse portraits of Jesus found in the New Testament itself.[37] Christians today, and particularly Christians in the Reformed tradition, have the responsibility and the joy of confessing Jesus Christ anew, in whatever cultural situations they find themselves. We do so in continuity with the Jesus who meets us in the New Testament and in dialogue with the experiences of our lives. For all of us, Jesus' question to Peter is our own: "But who do you say that I am?" (Matt. 16:15).

Questions for Reflection

1. A contemporary description of Jesus is "the man for others." Does this seem like a good description? In what ways is it illustrated in the Gospels?

2. Why is it important to affirm that Jesus was both "real God and real human being"?

3. Do you believe Christology should begin from "above" or from "below" (with the "divinity" or with the "humanity" of Jesus)?

4. Do you believe it is important that we fully, rationally understand how Jesus can be "truly God and truly human"? Why or why not?

5. Is there any theological significance to Jesus having appeared on Earth as a male person?

9

Work of Christ:
What Has Jesus Done?

We live in an action age. We're on the move, in motion, always doing . . . something! We admire people of action, too. Those who "just talk," just talk. But those who "do," do, and we like to see what they accomplish. Sometimes we feel we are drowning in a sea of words. What often counts more in our minds is to see the results of "talk." We want to see people enact what they say. They show the genuineness of their convictions by what they do. The old saying holds true: "Actions speak louder than words."

So also with Jesus. The teachings of Jesus are profound. They illumine life; they impart a wisdom that reorients our values and our commitments. But other religious leaders have also made significant statements. The teachings of Buddha, Mohammed, and Confucius have captivated millions. What makes Jesus so "special"? In what ways is Jesus unique? Is there more than just his teachings that set Jesus apart from all others?

The Christian church has answered "yes" to this last question. We believe that not only are the teachings of Jesus important, but so also are his actions. Throughout the gospels Jesus shows care and love and a passionate concern for God's justice. These actions orient our Christian lives in important directions. But Jesus' actions at the end of his life are seen as most important, too. He was crucified on a cross, "dead and buried" as the Apostles' Creed puts it, and "on the third day rose again from the dead": he was resurrected. He "ascended into heaven" where he now reigns until he will come again "to judge the living and the dead." These latter movements in the drama of Jesus' life set him apart from others. And in these actions, Christians through the ages have found God's salvation to be graciously given. From what Jesus did— in his crucifixion, resurrection, and ascension—a whole new reality and a whole new way of living become possible. These actions by Jesus have the most profound effects. They save and redeem, liberate, reconcile, bring peace and forgiveness, and justify sinners before God—in ways that no other person or events can do. Jesus has brought new life!

Biblical Bases

The actions of Jesus Christ (what theologians call the "work of Christ") are portrayed in many ways through the New Testament. What Jesus did was interpreted by his followers as having a significant impact on their lives in every dimension. Jesus' work reoriented and "made new" their understandings of God, their relationship to God, their relationships with others, and their relationship with God's creation and with the cultures in which they lived.

The biblical titles that became designations for Jesus—Messiah, Son of God, Son of Man, Lord, Savior—all of these are ways of saying who Jesus is but also of saying what Jesus does. The core of these understandings were rooted in the Hebrew Scriptures as Jesus came to be seen as the fulfillment of the Old Testament hope that God would send One to announce the end of the present age and to bring divine salvation. Early Christians believed Jesus did both and, even more, that he embodied—in himself—the salvation that God has graciously given to the world. He was God's Messiah, though his rule and reign have taken shape in ways not expected by his contemporaries (see above, chap. 8). God's purposes of calling out a people to serve God in this world, as God did with the nation of Israel according to the Hebrew Scriptures, have now been extended through the mission and ministry of Jesus. Now the whole world is called to be God's people. Jesus announced that the anticipated reign of God (kingdom of God) has now come to be a present reality in his own life and ministry (Isa. 58:6ff.; 61:1–2; Mark 1:15; Luke 4:21).

Jesus' Death

As he moved through his ministry, Jesus' teachings came to include the prediction of his own death (Mark 12:1–8). His recognition that he was a prophet of God led him to see that he would die in the city of Jerusalem (Luke 13:33). Jesus' obedience to the will of God led him to see that his death was a final act of obedience and that, through this act, God would be glorified (John 12:28).

An Old Testament image that Jesus appropriated was the "suffering servant." This image is found in various places in the book of Isaiah.[1] Though it is not clear who the original writer had in mind as the "servant of the Lord," this servant is one who will display God's glory by acting in obedience to

God's will and suffering on behalf of the people (Isa. 53:6). Jesus saw his own suffering and death as giving his life so that others may live (Mark 10:45). Isaiah's suffering servant was a context in which Jesus' self-understanding emerged and which was recognized by early Christian preachers as giving significance to his death (Acts 8:32–35).[2]

The cross of Christ stands at the center of the Christian faith just as it stands at the center of the whole New Testament. Jesus' followers recognized that through his death Jesus had effected a dramatic change, for the world and for all who believe in him. Throughout the New Testament writings, a number of images or metaphors emerged to try to capture what the death of Jesus meant. Each of these draws on other biblical understandings.[3] Central to them is the recognition of the human condition of sinfulness. In some mysterious way, the death of Jesus Christ on the cross has effected a profound change within human beings, between human beings, and in the relationship between human beings and God.[4] Among the ways this is expressed are the following.[5]

1. *Salvation and Redemption.* "Salvation" is a general term meaning "deliverance." It can mean "to save" and "to heal." Jesus came to "seek out and to save the lost" (Luke 19:10). The death of Jesus is the means by which salvation or deliverance from the power of sin and death is accomplished (Rom. 5:1–11; Eph. 2:4–10).

2. *Freedom from Slavery.* The death of Jesus also sets us free from the "slavery" of sin and death (Rom. 6:20–23). Christ's death has the power to free from all forms of addiction and "slavery" (Rom. 7:14; Gal. 5:1).

3. *Liberation through Ransom.* The death of Jesus is the "price paid" ("ransom") that accomplishes liberation and redemption from sin and evil (Eph. 1:7; 1 Pet. 1:18–19).

4. *Reconciliation.* The death of Jesus is the means by which peaceful relationships are restored between God and humanity and between human groups (2 Cor. 5:18–21; Eph. 2:11–22). The cross is a "boundary-shattering event" drawing humanity together with God and breaking down walls of hostility between people in all dimensions.

5. *Peace with God.* The death of Jesus brings peace with God (Rom. 5:1) as God reconciles and brings peace "through the blood of his cross" (Col. 1:20). At his birth, angels proclaimed that Jesus would bring peace (Luke 2:14).

6. *Forgiveness of Sin.* The death of Jesus brings forgiveness of sin (Acts 5:31; Col. 1:13–14; 2:13). Our sin is no longer counted against us; it is forgiven by a pardoning God (Eph. 1:7).

7. *Justification.* The death of Jesus brings justification of the sinner in which a person is set in a new, right relationship with God (Rom. 3:24–26). Justification marks the beginning of the Christian life and anticipates its future consummation (Rom. 8:30–34). The means of justification is by faith (Gal. 2:16), the free gift of God's grace (Eph. 2:8–9).

The death of Jesus Christ is the ultimate expression of God's love, a love that knows no measure and is freely and graciously given (Rom. 5:8). The restored relationships that Jesus' death brings affects the totality of one's existence and is to lead to the same restoration of relationships in human social situations and among all peoples (Eph. 2:14–17). This includes the power to forgive (Eph. 4:32). God's act in the death of Jesus Christ brings "new life" (Rom. 7:6) and a "new creation" (2 Cor. 5:17).

Jesus' Resurrection

The mystery of the death of Christ and its significance went hand in hand with the mystery of Jesus' resurrection.[6] The death and resurrection of Jesus were experienced by early Christians as linked events. The Jesus who died for us was also raised for us (Rom. 8:34).

The message of the cross and resurrection formed the core of the early church's proclamation about Jesus (Acts 1:22; 2:24). The resurrection is the guarantee that Christ's death is effective (1 Cor. 15:14–17, 22). Without the resurrection, there would be no gospel to proclaim. The message of believers was that without God's act of raising Jesus from the dead, "our proclamation has been in vain and your faith has been in vain" (1 Cor. 15:14). The risen Christ is the assurance that believers one day will rise and that evil and death do not have the last word. It is God who gives the "victory through our Lord Jesus Christ" (1 Cor. 15:51–58). This victory is our future hope but is also a present reality as the divine power of Christ's resurrection is experienced in the church and in the lives of Jesus' followers (Phil. 3:10).

The resurrection of Jesus Christ from the dead, the "Easter event," is God's revelation just as Jesus revealed himself to his disciples after he was raised (John 21:1; Acts 1:3). His resurrection means that God vindicated Jesus. Easter was "God's Yes to the ministry of Jesus."[7] In the resurrection, God reversed the injustice done to Jesus in his crucifixion and has made it clear that Jesus is the "righteous one" whose life and teachings and death are now ratified by the power of God who raised Jesus from the dead (Acts 2:23; 10:39ff).

The resurrection also marks God's exalting of Jesus, so he is said to be raised to the "right hand of God" (Col. 3:1; Heb. 10:12). As ancient kings in Israel were enthroned (see Psalm 110), so now Jesus is exalted and raised up to share rule with God over the whole cosmos. As the writer of Ephesians proclaims:

> God put this power to work in Christ when he raised him from the dead and seated him at his right hand in the heavenly places, far above all rule and authority and power and dominion, and above every name

that is named, not only in this age but also in the age to come. And he has put all things under his feet and has made him the head over all things for the church, which is his body, the fullness of him who fills all in all. (Eph. 1:20–23)

Ultimately, it is the resurrection of Jesus Christ that enables our redemption. Just as the fellowship between Jesus and his disciples is restored on that first Easter when Jesus appeared to his followers who had left and deserted him (John 20:19–23), so now Jesus promises restored fellowship—reconciliation—to sinners. For "restored communion with Jesus is reconciliation with God in and through Jesus."[8] Our justification or receiving a right relationship with God is made possible through Jesus' death on the cross and by his resurrection. As Paul writes: "It will be reckoned to us who believe in him who raised Jesus our Lord from the dead, who was handed over to death for our trespasses and was raised for our justification" (Rom. 4:24–25). Believers experience a real union with the living Christ, and thus they are "justified" or "saved"—we receive salvation.[9]

The resurrection of Jesus Christ also reveals the future. Christ has "set us free from the present evil age" (Gal. 1:4) and inaugurated the age to come. The Jewish hope for a messianic age when God's reign will be complete has now been established in the raising of Jesus by God's power (Eph. 1:20). The resurrection of Jesus is the pledge of the future resurrection of all believers, the "first fruits of those who have died" (1 Cor. 15:20). Through the resurrection, believers have a "hope of sharing the glory of God" (Rom. 5:2). In Jesus, "there is the resurrection of the dead" (Acts 4:2; 1 Cor. 6:14; Phil. 3:21). For, "if we have been united with him in a death like his, we will certainly be united with him in a resurrection like his" (Rom. 6:5; 2 Cor. 4:14).

Thus the resurrection of Jesus is central to Christian faith and along with the death of Jesus on the cross provided the major message of the early Christian church. The risen Christ makes "all things new" (Rev. 21:5) for those who know the "power of his resurrection" (Phil. 3:10), enabling us to serve Jesus Christ in the present as we look to the future with a "living hope" (1 Pet. 1:3).

Christian Tradition

C. S. Lewis once remarked, "The central Christian belief is that Christ's death has somehow put us right with God and given us a fresh start. Theories as to how it did this are another matter. A good many different theories have been held as to how it happened."[10] Lewis is right. It was not until Anselm of Canterbury (1033–1109) wrote a work titled *Cur Deus homo?* (*Why Did God Become Human?*) in 1098 that a full-scale technical theory of the meaning of the death of Christ is found. Earlier theologians had used the dynamic imagery of Scripture to explain what became known as the "atonement"—the "bringing together" (making "at-one") of God and humanity.

Theories of Atonement

Many "theories of the atonement" explain the "how" of the cross.[11] The Swedish theologian Gustaf Aulén wrote a significant book translated as *Christus Victor* in which he argued that there have been three main views of the atonement through Christian history.[12]

1. *Christ the Victor.* Sometimes called the "classical theory," this view stresses the victory of Jesus Christ over the powers of evil. Christ defeats them by his cross and provides for human salvation. God in Christ takes on the evil powers that dominate the world and defeats them, thereby effecting a reconciliation between God and humanity. Love is triumphant over wrath and the hostile powers of evil.

2. *Satisfaction Theory.* Anselm's work on the incarnation sought to challenge unbelievers and show that there was no other way to salvation than through the death of Jesus Christ. Anselm reflected the images of feudal society when he argued that the greatness and majesty of almighty God must be preserved. Humans owe God absolute obedience, as a vassal owes to a feudal lord. Sin is the refusal of God's vassals to render God the obedience due. The satisfaction due to God for sin is infinite because God is an infinite being. God cannot forgive this sin or disobedience without punishing (since God is "just"). Creatures need a full "satisfaction" for their sin but are not able to give anything to God to make up for the infinite debt of their past disobedience. Even when we render obedience now, we are just doing what is our duty. Thus, humans cannot meet the demands of God's justice. If redemption is to occur, it must come from God. And God has acted to redeem the world through Jesus Christ. By his obedience and death, Jesus renders to God the honor due to God and thus redeems humanity from the curse of sin and condemnation. Christ fulfills the divine law, pays a debt that is not due from him but pays it on behalf of others. Divine justice is "satisfied," and God accepts the work of Christ as "atonement" for human sin, thus justly granting salvation.

3. *Exemplary or Moral Influence Theory.* In reaction to the "satisfaction" theory of Anselm, Peter Abelard (1079–1142)—whose life was like a tragic medieval romance story—stressed the human response to the death of Christ as the way in which the cross has its power. He took the New Testament theme that the death of Jesus was the great example of God's love and made it the basic meaning of the atonement. Jesus' self-giving love overcomes the alienation within the human heart when humans recognize the suffering love on the cross that Jesus showed. When one recognizes this expression of divine

grace, one's whole life is transformed. A change has occurred—not in God's attitude toward the sinner, but in the sinner's attitude toward God. Now, in response to the amazing, overwhelming love seen in the cross of Christ, the sinner is freed from fear of God's wrath and now has a desire to love God. This love fulfills all God's demands so that God can freely forgive our sin.

A number of other views of the atonement have been variations of these motifs. In the early church, "ransom" was used as an image with some theologians pushing the metaphor to the point of saying that Christ's death was a "ransom" paid to the devil who "owns" the souls of all sinners.

During the Protestant Reformation, the dominant Protestant approach was a modification of Anselm's theory. Luther, who has been claimed as a proponent of the "Christus Victor" or classical theory, has even stronger tendencies toward seeing the cross of Christ as the satisfaction of God's righteousness (instead of God's "honor"). Jesus endured God's "wrath" as a perfect substitute for humanity. Luther wrote: "Since he became a substitute for us all, and took upon himself our sins, that He might bear God's terrible wrath against sin and expiate our guilt, He necessarily felt the sin of the whole world, together with the entire wrath of God, and afterwards the agony of death on account of this sin."[13] This view, with its focus on what Christ has done to change our status before God, stresses the perspective that Christ's death has led God to look at human sinners in a different way—not as "guilty," but as "righteous" by virtue of Christ's death on their behalf. For Luther and other Protestants, faith is the means through which the sinner is "justified" or "set right" with God.

Reformed Emphases

Death of Christ

John Calvin recognized the variety of New Testament images for the death of Christ. In commenting on Galatians 2:21 he wrote: "If the death of Christ is our redemption, then we were captives; if it is payment, then we were debtors; if it is atonement, we were guilty; if it is cleansing, we were unclean. And so, on the other hand, he who ascribes his cleansing, pardon, atonement, righteousness or deliverance to works makes void the death of Christ."[14] Calvin ascribed the validity of the atonement to the work of Christ and, like Luther, saw God as justly condemning humanity for our sin. Christ is our substitute who endures God's wrath for us. This is done, according to Calvin, within the context of sacrifice as Jesus is our great High Priest who offers himself as an atoning sacrifice for us out of his love.[15]

Threefold Office of Christ

An enduring contribution is Calvin's treatment of the work of Christ as mediator between God and humanity as expressed in a threefold office of prophet, priest, and king.[16] This tied the work of Christ to the covenant history of Israel in that prophets, priests, and kings in ancient Israel were all "anointed." Christ as "prophet" is the teacher of perfect doctrine who conveys "perfect wisdom" to us. As king, Christ reigns over the church and enables us to pass through the miseries of the world with the assurance that "our King will never leave us destitute, but will provide for our needs until, our warfare ended, we are called to triumph."[17] As priest, Jesus Christ is our "everlasting intercessor" who through his death has "washed away our sins, sanctifies us and obtains for us that grace from which the uncleanness of our transgressions and vices debars us."[18] Jesus' sacrifice was a willing self-sacrifice—not the demand of a wrathful or vengeful "Father-figure."[19] Jesus Christ was both "priest and sacrifice." These biblical roles of prophet, priest, and king are ways of understanding what Jesus Christ has done. They link his work with God's work in ancient Israel.[20]

The Reformed Confessions convey the same understandings of Christ's death. Some use the prophet, priest, and king images.[21] The French Confession states that "God, in sending his Son, intended to show his love and inestimable goodness towards us, giving him up to die to accomplish all righteousness, and raising him from the dead to secure for us the heavenly life."[22] It is the world that is reconciled to God, not God to the world: "We believe that by the perfect sacrifice that the Lord Jesus offered on the cross, we are reconciled to God."[23] This reconciliation is by Jesus Christ becoming the substitute for sinners in taking on the punishment that human sin deserves from a righteous God. God is merciful, which does not mean that God will not penalize sin (since God is just).[24] But Jesus Christ provides himself as the righteous substitute for the sinner who cannot atone for our sin by our own merits or abilities. As a result, "self-redemption is thus excluded."[25] Instead, Jesus Christ as the perfect mediator between God and humanity—the eternal Word of God who is also a sinless human being—sacrifices himself as the perfect sacrifice, the perfect "atonement" for human sin. It is "through Jesus Christ we are cleansed and made perfect; by his death we are fully justified, and through him only can we be delivered from our iniquities and transgressions" (French Confession).[26] Christ's sacrifice was a "voluntary sacrifice unto his Father for us" (Scots Confession).[27] By "offering up Himself He made satisfaction to God for our sins and the sins of all believers and reconciled us to God, our heavenly Father, and by His death has conquered and overcome the world, death and hell" (First Confession of Basel).[28]

Karl Barth's twentieth-century reinterpretation of the Reformed tradition also uses the threefold office of Christ in the context of Barth's massive treatment of the doctrine of reconciliation.[29] His themes are Jesus Christ, "The Lord as Servant," in which Jesus acts in humility as our priest to redeem from the sin of pride; "The Servant as Lord," where humanity in God's grace is raised to a royal partnership with God and thereby is freed from the sin of sloth; and "The True Witness," in which the union of God and humanity in Jesus Christ conveys prophetic power to counteract the sin of falsehood. For Barth, God has taken on the burden of human guilt in the person of Jesus Christ. The cross is God's triumphant love invading history to counteract human guilt and alienation. "We are forbidden," wrote Barth, "to take sin more seriously than grace, or even as seriously as grace" since God has reconciled the world in Jesus Christ.[30]

Resurrection of Jesus Christ

Reformed faith has also vigorously maintained the power of the resurrection. The Confession of 1967 says of Jesus that "God raised him from the dead, vindicating him as Messiah and Lord. The victim of sin became victor, and won the victory over sin and death for all. . . ."[31] The Brief Statement of Faith puts it this way:

> God raised this Jesus from the dead,
> vindicating his sinless life,
> breaking the power of sin and evil,
> delivering us from death to life eternal.[32]

Reformed Emphases

Two points stand out among the many that could be made about Reformed emphases concerning the work of Christ.

1. *God has taken the initiative to provide salvation for the world by sending Jesus Christ.* The death and the resurrection of Jesus are both divine acts of God's grace to bring "good news" (gospel) to the world. As John 3:16, the most famous verse in the Bible, puts it: "For God so loved the world that he gave his only Son . . ." God sent Jesus to carry out the work of salvation—a mission that Jesus himself freely chose to do. Humans receive the gift of faith to believe in what Jesus has done and to receive the benefits of Christ's reconciling, sacrificial death on our behalf. But it is God who is the provider of salvation. Jesus' death and resurrection are unique, saving events that come to us from God's initiating action.

2. *The work of Jesus Christ is a work of God's grace.* Since humans cannot merit salvation, establish reconciliation, or conquer the power of evil on their own, it takes God's initiating work to reestablish the relationship with humanity that God desires. God freely and lovingly provides the way of salvation through Jesus Christ. God could have chosen not to send Jesus, not to initiate a way of salvation. But God's grace has appeared in the person of Jesus and his work. Grace is God's unmerited favor. Humans receive salvation and forgiveness of sin, which we do not deserve. God's judgment on sin—which we do deserve—is withheld and absorbed by Jesus Christ (Rom. 3:24; Eph. 1:7; Titus 2:11). Reformed theology has stressed God's initiating role in providing salvation and the recognition that salvation comes to us by the sheer gift of God's grace.

Contemporary Significance

The varied forms by which the work of Jesus Christ is presented in the New Testament mean that Christ's work will meet people in the midst of their needs, whatever they are. For some, there is the need to overcome alienation; for others a sense of forgiveness is needed. Some people yearn for a sense of peace with God or for release from the guilt of past misdeeds. In all of these situations and more, Jesus Christ reaches out and by his cross and resurrection provides the "good news" of God's love, power, and grace. The amazing message of the Christian gospel is that God has loved the world and sent Jesus Christ to be our savior. He can "save us from our sins"—whatever they are![33] His actions supplement his words and are to us, the way to become a "new creation" (2 Cor. 5:17).

Questions for Reflection

1. Do you agree with the view that Jesus' teachings are all we need as a guide for living and that his death was unnecessary?

2. In what ways is it significant that the Christian church has never decided that there is only one "right way" to understand the death of Jesus?

3. Why is the resurrection of Jesus Christ sometimes regarded as the "spinal column" of Christian faith?

4. Did Jesus really have to die in order for God to provide salvation?

5. What image of the death of Jesus is the most meaningful to you?

10

Holy Spirit:
Who Is the Holy Spirit?

"God is Father, Son, and Holy Spirit," says the preacher. Holy Spirit? We have a fairly good idea about "Father" and "Son." But what or who is the Holy Spirit?

We wonder. Surely the "Holy Spirit" is the most "elusive" member of the Trinity. How do you define a "Spirit" or recognize a "Spirit"? What would a "Spirit" do? Questions abound.

Biblical Bases

Old Testament

The idea of the "spirit of God" was deeply ingrained in the faith of the people of Israel. The opening words of the Bible introduce us to the spirit: "the earth was a formless void and darkness covered the face of the deep, while a wind from God swept over the face of the waters" (Gen. 1:2). Here the Hebrew term *ru'ah* is a term that means "wind," "breath," or "spirit." The spirit is God's agent in creation. This emphasis is found in the book of Job where we read, "The spirit of God has made me, and the breath of the Almighty gives me life" (Job 33:4), and by the Psalmist who declares, "When you send forth your spirit, they are created; and you renew the face of the ground" (Ps. 104:30). God's spirit brings order into chaos and life into that which has no life. The "spirit of God" is the way by which God acts.

Most prominently in the Hebrew Scriptures, the spirit of God is the way God acts among God's people. God's people recognized God's spirit in their midst. The covenant people of Israel found that God's spirit was a present reality who gave them power and comfort, and who challenged them to do God's will. God's spirit worked among Israel's leaders: prophets, priests, and kings. The phrase "the spirit of God came upon . . ." meant that person would prophesy, or speak God's word (Num. 24:2; 1 Sam. 10:10). The gift of God's spirit was given to Israel's leaders such as Joshua (Num. 27:18), Gideon (Judg. 6:34), and David (1 Sam. 16:13f.). The spirit is the source of the future prophetic ministry of the coming Messiah as in the memorable text (later appropriated by Jesus [Luke 4:16–19]): "The spirit of the LORD God is upon me, because the LORD has anointed me; he has sent me to bring good news to the oppressed, to bind up the brokenhearted, to proclaim liberty to the captives, and release to the prisoners . . ." (Isa. 61:1; cf. 42:1). At the end of the age, in God's ultimate reign or kingdom, God's spirit will be poured out "on all flesh" (Joel 2:28). God's spirit will thus be universalized. God's "new covenant" will be written on human hearts (Jer. 31:31–34), and God's spirit will be present forever (Isa. 59:21).

New Testament

The teachings of the New Testament about God's spirit are rich and deep. They stand in continuity with the Old Testament view that the spirit is the experience of God powerfully present and active in the midst of God's people.[1] The spirit is understood in the context of a relationship to the living and true God. The central focus of this experience of God is Jesus Christ. The decisive event for the Spirit's coming is Pentecost (Acts 2).[2] Three major threads of New Testament writings present complementary understandings of the Spirit. These are the Lukan, the Pauline, and the Johannine writings.[3]

1. *Lukan.* Sometimes Luke is called "the historian of the Holy Spirit," while John and Paul are designated "theologians of the Holy Spirit." Luke uses history as the means for telling how the early Christian church experienced the Holy Spirit of God. He traces God's movement for salvation through history from the birth of Jesus to the spread of Christianity through the Mediterranean world.

In Luke's writings, the Spirit is the source of prophecy (as in the Old Testament) as when Elizabeth (Luke 1:41–45), Mary (1:46–55), Zechariah (1:67–79), Simeon (2:25–27), Anna (2:36–38), and John the Baptizer (3:15ff.) are said to be filled with or guided by the Holy Spirit. God's Spirit was operative in the conception of John the Baptist and Jesus indicating God's new work in salvation-history—God's plan for salvation unfolding in history.

Jesus was endowed ("anointed") by the Spirit at his baptism by John and took up the work of the Messiah ("anointed one"). His ministry will be carried out in the power of the Spirit and with God's divine sanction: "and the Holy Spirit descended upon him in bodily form like a dove. And a voice came from heaven, 'You are my Son, the Beloved; with you I am well pleased'" (Luke

3:22). Jesus carried out God's plan through his ministry, and after his resurrection and ascension to heaven he is the exalted Lord of the Spirit who "pours out" the Holy Spirit to inaugurate a new age to come, the age of the Spirit promised in the Hebrew Scriptures (Joel 2:28–32; Acts 2:16–21).

The Pentecost experience initiates the church as the community of the Spirit, living in the "age to come." Its missionary task is to proclaim the reign of God and teach about the Lord Jesus Christ (Acts 28:31). The dynamic power of the Spirit guides the church (Acts 13:2; 15:28) and speaks to the church (11:12; 21:11). The Spirit "fills" disciples and equips Christians as leaders with the message of the gospel of Jesus Christ (Acts 2:4; see also 1:8; 2:33). The Spirit performs mighty works and enables the church to witness to the gospel as believers are "baptized with the Holy Spirit" (Acts 11:16; cf. 1:5). The Spirit is the active, dynamic power in the church's life.

2. *Pauline.* The writings of Paul provide a rich picture of the Holy Spirit's activities. Paul emphasizes both the age to come and the Spirit's work as well as the present inward renewal of Christian believers by the power of God's Spirit in their lives. To participate in the gift of "salvation" is to live "in the Spirit" (Rom. 8:9).

The dimensions of the Spirit's work in Paul's thought are conveyed in a number of ways. The Spirit is the "first-fruits" of the "glory about to be revealed," the "freedom of the glory of the children of God" (Rom. 8:18, 21). The Spirit is our "guarantee" (2 Cor. 5:5; Eph. 1:14) and we receive the seal of the Spirit (2 Cor. 1:22; Eph. 1:13). The Spirit gives new life shown through the "fruit of the Spirit" (Gal. 5:22) and remakes the Christian into the image of Jesus Christ (Rom. 8:29). The Spirit confers "gifts," (1 Cor. 12:4–11, 28; Eph. 4:11) that are used for ministries and offices in the church. New life and new power are given now by the Spirit, anticipating the fullness of the power still to come in God's future.

For Paul, there is an intimate connection between the Spirit and the historic/risen Jesus who is the exalted Lord. There is no experience of Jesus apart from the Spirit. No "ecstatic experiences" or prophetical words (2 Thess. 2:2) separate from a focus on Jesus are recognized as valid. The Spirit is the "Spirit of Jesus Christ" for Paul (Phil. 1:19) for "no one can say 'Jesus is Lord' except by the Holy Spirit" (1 Cor. 12:3).

Individual experiences of God's Holy Spirit do not take place in isolation from the church as the community of the Spirit. The Spirit unifies the church as the "body of Christ" (Rom. 12:4–8; 1 Cor. 12:17–31; Eph. 4:11–16). While there are "varieties of gifts," it is the "same Spirit" who gives them (1 Cor. 12:4). We are baptized "in the one Spirit" into the "one body" (1 Cor. 12:13). The Spirit calls the church together as the company of those who have faith in Jesus Christ and the "gifts of the Spirit" are given to all who believe. These are not only "special gifts," but also very "ordinary" gifts such as teaching, preaching, and administration (1 Cor. 12:4–11; 27–31).

The whole Christian life is based on the Spirit who lives within and among the Christian community (Gal. 5:25). The Spirit is the source of divine love (Rom. 5:5), joy (1 Thess. 1:6; Rom. 14:17), and hope (Rom. 15:13). The Spirit helps us in prayer (Rom. 8:26–27; Eph. 2:18; 6:18), teaches us (1 Cor. 2:13), frees us from the condemning power of the law (2 Cor. 3:17), and inspires us to worship individually and corporately (Phil. 3:3; Eph. 5:18f.). The Spirit is the powerful dynamic power that leads us in sanctification or growth as Christians (2 Thess. 2:13). For Paul, the Spirit is God's all-encompassing and empowering presence.

3. *Johannine.* The Gospel of John does not so much emphasize the outward expressions of the Spirit (Luke-Acts) or the more inward experiences of the Spirit by Christians (Paul's writings). The writer's focus is on the immediate relation of the individual disciple to Jesus through the Spirit. For John, the Spirit is "another Advocate" or another counselor (Gr. *parakletos*) who comes from the glorified Jesus and takes his place (John 14:16). The Spirit is the guide into "all the truth" (John 16:13). For John there is a balance between the present and dynamic activities of the Spirit (teaching and guiding) and the witness of the Spirit to Jesus himself. The Spirit leads and guides into the remembrance of Jesus and "all that I have said to you" (John 14:26).

John's gospel gives a unique emphasis on the close personal identification of the Holy Spirit as the "*paraclete* with Jesus." The Greek word *parakletos* literally means "one called alongside." As a noun, its connotation is of a "defense attorney," and so some English versions—such as the New Revised Standard version—translate the term as "advocate." As a verb, the term means to "intercede," "comfort," or "console." It can also mean to "exhort" or "encourage." *Paraclete*, then, is a very full and rich word. Jesus said that God will send "another *paraclete*," implying that Jesus himself is a *paraclete*. Both Jesus and the Spirit come from the Father (John 13:3; 14:26); both are sent (5:36f.; 15:26); and both are related to the Truth, as when Jesus said, "I am the truth" (14:6) and when he said that the *paraclete* is "the Spirit of truth" (15:26). Both remain in the disciple (14:17, 20, 23). So Jesus is present to all persons everywhere through the Holy Spirit (17:21).

Christian Tradition

A strong concern of the early church was to understand the ways in which the Holy Spirit is to be understood in relation to God the Father and God the Son. In the development of the doctrine of the Trinity the question of the status of the Spirit was a key one. Is the Spirit equal to the Father and the Son or subordinate?

Divinity of the Spirit

Biblically, there are New Testament passages that link the Spirit to God and Jesus Christ in a triadic pattern. This linkage is found in the announcement of Jesus' birth to Mary (Luke 1:35), in Luke's account of Jesus' baptism (Luke 3:22), in Jesus' temptation experience (Luke 4:1), and in the opening of the book of Acts (Acts 1:1–6). Paul's writings often associate Father, Son, and Holy Spirit together, as in Paul's benediction: "The grace of the Lord Jesus Christ, the love of God, and the communion of the Holy Spirit be with all of you" (2 Cor. 13:13).[4]

The church council at Nicaea (A.D. 325) dealt with the question, "Who is Jesus?" against the Arian view that Jesus was a creature. The creed of Nicaea asserted, "We believe in the Holy Spirit." Through the next half-century, theological debates about the status of the Spirit continued. At the Council of Constantinople (A.D. 381), 186 bishops were present. Thirty-six of the bishops were known as "pneumatomachi," which literally means "spirit-fighters." They denied that the Holy Spirit was fully divine. When they were asked to accept the Nicene faith, they left. So the Niceno-Constantinopolitan creed (A.D. 381), which we know today as the Nicene Creed, expanded the earlier creed of Nicaea. It lengthened the statement on Jesus Christ as the Son, and included a long statement on the Holy Spirit: "And we believe in the Holy Spirit, the Lord and Giver of Life, who proceedeth from the Father, who with the Father and the Son together is worshiped and glorified, who spoke by the prophets." The church maintained that the Holy Spirit is on par with the Father and the Son, that the Spirit is divine, and has a place in the life and worship of the church.

'Filioque' Clause

At the Council of Toledo (A.D. 589), a phrase relating to the Holy Spirit was inserted into the Niceno-Constantinopolitan creed. It is called the "*Filioque* clause" from the Latin term *filioque*, which means "and the Son." The phrase changed the creed to read: "We believe in the Holy Spirit . . . who proceeds from the Father and the Son . . . ," instead of as the original had it: ". . . who proceeds from the Father." Called the "double procession" in the Trinity, the phrase means that the Holy Spirit and Jesus Christ are inseparable and united. They are bound together in mutual love, each sharing the divine essence as fully God.[5] This view became the dominant view of the Western church.

Eastern churches rejected the *filioque* in the interests of a "single procession," as the original Niceno-Constantinopolitan creed had it. Eastern theologians began with the need to affirm the single origin of the Trinity that stresses "God is one." God the Father can be the only source of the divine being (a view called "monarchianism"). Eastern theologians preferred the phrase that the Holy Spirit proceeds "from the Father, through the Son" (making the Father the ultimate source of divinity). They were afraid that the *filioque* subordinates the Spirit to Christ and conceals the uniqueness of God the Father. Western theologians argued that the unity of God must be upheld and that the work of the Spirit should never be separated from the person and work of Jesus Christ.[6]

The *filioque* controversy was never settled. It was part of the reasons that the Eastern and Western churches split in A.D. 1054 and that Orthodox churches in the Eastern world today have a separate independence from Western—Roman Catholic and Protestant—churches.[7]

Person and Work of the Holy Spirit

The person and work of the Holy Spirit took on other important dimensions in the emerging life of the Christian church.

1. *Spirit and Church.* The Spirit is intimately associated with the church itself. Irenaeus, in the third century, formulated it this way: ". . . For where the church is, there is the Spirit of God; and where the Spirit is, there is the church and every kind of grace."[8]

2. *Spirit and Baptism.* The Spirit is associated with baptism (in the New Testament, e.g. Acts 2:38; 1 Cor. 6:11; 12:13; Titus 3:5–7). The early church theologian Tertullian affirmed, "The spirit is in those waters corporally washed, while the flesh is in those same waters spiritually cleansed."[9]

3. *Spirit and Scripture.* The Holy Spirit is also intimately connected with the Word of God in Scripture. The Spirit inspires the Scripture (2 Tim. 3:16) and helps the church interpret Scripture (John 16:13). Martin Luther emphasized that God's Word and God's Spirit were inextricably bound up together. The Spirit of God helps us understand and interpret the Word, and the Word of God guides us into an understanding of what the Spirit of God is moving us toward in the church and in our Christian lives. If Word and Spirit are divorced from each other, the Christian faith can become a pure "intellectualism" (emphasizing the "Word") or a pure "mysticism" (emphasizing the "Spirit").

Reformed Emphases

Those who know the writings of John Calvin recognize that Calvin may rightly be called a "theologian of the Holy Spirit."[10] This is because the Spirit plays such a crucial role in many aspects of Calvin's thought. Several emphases are especially important for Reformed faith.

Spirit and Scripture

Reformed theology has always affirmed that the Holy Spirit inspired the writers of Holy Scripture. While there are different views of how this took place, the Reformed tradition recognizes the reality that it has taken place and that it is a divine mystery.

Calvin, in particular, also laid stress on the role of the Holy Spirit in illuminating the Scriptures. Calvin believed that persons can come to believe that the Scriptures are God's communication and that they have authority for their lives by the actions of the Holy Spirit. The "internal testimony of the Holy Spirit" persuades persons that God is the ultimate author of the Scriptures. Calvin wrote, "We ought to seek our conviction in a higher place than human reasons, judgments, or conjectures, that is, in the secret testimony of the Holy Spirit." The "testimony of the Spirit is more excellent than all reason," Calvin affirmed. He declared:

> The Word will not find acceptance in [our] hearts before it is sealed by the inward testimony of the Spirit. The same Spirit, therefore, who has spoken through the mouths of the prophets must penetrate into our hearts to persuade us that they faithfully proclaimed what had been divinely commanded.[11]

The Holy Spirit "seals" the Scriptures in our heart and produces a certainly that the Bible is God's revelation to us. This conviction by the work of the Spirit is the experience of every believer.[12]

Thus, for Calvin (as for Luther), "Word" and "Spirit" are bound together. Calvin wrote:

> The Word itself is not quite certain for us unless it be confirmed by the testimony of the Spirit. . . . For by a kind of mutual bond the Lord has joined together the certainty of his Word and of his Spirit so that the perfect religion of the Word may abide in our minds when the Spirit, who causes us to contemplate God's face, shines; and that we in turn may embrace the Spirit with no fear of being deceived when we recognize him in his own image, namely, in the Word.[13]

Spirit and Salvation

Calvin also saw that the Holy Spirit plays a major role in salvation. Indeed, "faith is the principal work of the Holy Spirit."[14] Faith in Jesus Christ is a divine gift of grace given by the Holy Spirit, who reveals Jesus' identity to us through faith (Matt. 16:17; Eph. 1:13). For Calvin, as for Paul, the Spirit is "the inner teacher by whose effort the promise of salvation penetrates into our minds, a promise that would otherwise only strike the air or beat upon our ears."[15] The Spirit is the "key that unlocks for us the treasures of the Kingdom of Heaven [cf. Rev. 3:7]." By the Spirit, Christ draws those "given to him by the Father" to himself (John 6:44; 12:32; 17:6). We are baptized "with the Holy Spirit and fire" (Luke 3:16) so that Christ may bring us "into the light of faith in his gospel and so regenerating us that we become new creatures [cf. 2 Cor. 5:17]."[16] "Without the illumination of the Holy Spirit, the Word can do nothing."[17]

Spirit and the Christian Life

The church has always associated the Holy Spirit with the work of sanctification and growth in Christian faith and life. The Spirit initiates faith and is the One who unites us by faith to Jesus Christ. As Calvin wrote, "There is good reason for the repeated mention of the 'testimony of the Spirit,' a testimony we feel engraved like a seal upon our hearts, with the result that it seals the cleansing and sacrifice of Christ."[18] By the Spirit we come to faith in Christ as our Lord and Savior. By the Spirit we are joined in a faith relationship with Christ that brings us salvation. For Calvin, "Paul, in speaking of cleansing and justification, says that we come to possess both, 'in the name of . . . Jesus Christ and in the Spirit of our God' [1 Cor. 6:11]. To sum up, the Holy Spirit is the bond by which Christ effectually unites us to himself."[19] The Spirit "indwells" us as we receive the Spirit (1 Cor. 2:12), leads us as believers (Rom. 8:14), and is "bearing witness with our spirit that we are children of God" (Rom. 8:16).[20] The "sanctification by the Spirit" (2 Thess. 2:13) is the means by which we grow in faith and love as we live as followers and disciples of Jesus Christ. The Spirit is our teacher in prayer (Rom. 8:26) who guides our prayers and intercedes for us with God (Rom. 8:26–27).[21]

Spirit and World

The Holy Spirit works within the church. The Spirit calls the church into being, gives faith, illuminates believers, and works within them to guide the church and strengthen believers in their Christian lives. The Spirit is the "Lord and Giver of life" (Nicene Creed) who brings "new life" through the reconciling death of Jesus Christ and who makes the gospel of forgiveness, repentance, and obedience real within our lives.[22]

But the Holy Spirit is also at work in the world around us. Reformed Christians have recognized that the Spirit of God has a wider work than in just the church. Thus the Brief Statement of Faith says:

> the Spirit gives us courage
> to pray without ceasing,

> to witness among all peoples to Christ as Lord and Savior,
> to unmask idolatries in Church and culture,
> to hear the voices of peoples long silenced,
> and to work with others for justice, freedom, and peace.[23]

God's Spirit is at work in the world as the struggles for peace, liberation, and freedom take place. Christians may and must join with others who are engaged in such struggles. These efforts belong to the nature of the gospel, which Jesus himself proclaimed as he appropriated the text from the prophet Isaiah to describe his own ministry: "'The Spirit of the Lord is upon me, because he has anointed me to bring good news to the poor. He has sent me to proclaim release to the captives and recovery of sight to the blind, to let the oppressed go free, to proclaim the year of the Lord's favor'" (Luke 4:18–19; Isa. 61:1–2; 58:6).[24]

The Reformed tradition has emphasized the multifaceted work of the Holy Spirit. The Spirit is at work in ways we cannot perceive or understand—both in the world and in the church. The Spirit unites believers to Jesus Christ and with one another. The Spirit nurtures faith and guides us into works of love, mercy, peace, and justice.[25]

Contemporary Significance

The Holy Spirit continues to be the "elusive member of the Trinity." As Jesus remarked to Nicodemus, "The wind [spirit] blows where it chooses, and you hear the sound of it, but you do not know where it comes from or where it goes" (John 3:8).[26]

Contemporary theologians deal with the Holy Spirit from a number of perspectives.[27] A significant contemporary church tradition is the Pentecostal tradition. With its origins in the nineteenth century, Pentecostalism has stressed the role of the Holy Spirit as a primary focus of Christian life and experience. It has emphasized the "gifts of the Spirit," including "speaking in tongues" (Gr. *glossolalia*). The "charismatic movement" is a coalition of Christians in various churches who highlight the New Testament descriptions of charismatic gifts bestowed by the Spirit (1 Corinthians 12), the "baptism of the Holy Spirit," and the Spirit's ongoing miraculous work in today's world.[28]

The Reformed tradition has important theological reservations about some aspects of the charismatic movement. These reservations include differing perspectives about the nature of the "baptism of the Holy Spirit," a stress in the Reformed tradition on the communal aspects of the Spirit's work rather than on the "individual-spontaneous" work of the Spirit that often marks the charismatic movement, and the Reformed tradition's stress on the wider aspects of the Spirit's work. Among these aspects are the Spirit's work in creation, concern for the relation of Word and Spirit, the Spirit's work in the church and sacraments, and for the fullness of the Spirit's work in the Christian life and community—elements that go beyond the personal experience emphasis of charismatics.[29]

Yet the Reformed tradition can also learn from "charismatic Christians." Their emphasis on the freedom, joy, and power of the Spirit can be helpful balances to the historic tendencies of the Reformed faith to stress the intellectual, traditional, and institutional aspects of the Christian faith.[30] If we are to be genuinely "biblical Christians," we must always be alert and open to "what the Spirit is saying to the churches" (Rev. 2:7, 11, 17, etc.).

The Holy Spirit is "God among us and within us." The ways and works of the Spirit are mysterious. They cannot be prescribed or predicted. We never know the ways by which God's Spirit may guide and direct us. So our attitude is reflected in the ninth-century hymn by Rabanus Maurus:

> Come, O creator Spirit, come,
> And make within our hearts thy home;
> To us thy grace celestial give,
> Who of thy breathing move and live.[31]

Questions for Reflection

1. In what experiences have you been specially aware of the Holy Spirit?

2. Do you believe contemporary Christians need to become more aware of the "gifts of the Spirit" given to the church and to each Christian? Why or why not?

3. Why is it important that the Holy Spirit be a "full member" of the Trinity and equal in every way to the Father and Son?

4. What is the significance of the Reformed emphasis that only the Holy Spirit can give faith and that we cannot generate faith on our own?

5. Where might we find examples of the wider work of the Holy Spirit in the world, outside the explicit work of the church?

11

Salvation: Receiving God's Gift

We see the occasional bumper sticker announcing "Jesus Saves." One wonders, "Saves what?" Today, we associate "saving" with banks, savings accounts, or retirement annuities. We gather and collect and invest and try to accumulate all the financial resources we can. We are "saving for a rainy day," but even more. We're trying to accrue what we can to protect our futures, to secure stability for the years to come. If Jesus can help us in this effort, then maybe we should take a look at Jesus' "savings plan." How does his plan stack up in the midst of all the cultural voices that clamor for us to cast our lots and our treasures with them so that they can "save us" in the future?

Yet we realize the bumper sticker also has a religious reference. "Jesus Saves" refers to salvation. How are we "saved"? We wonder. Again, many cultural voices vie for our attention. Highway billboards, religious tracts left in restrooms, leaflets left on our windshields in parking lots or by strangers at our doorsteps—all proclaim the "way to salvation." They promote a particular set of "steps to salvation," or invite one to a particular church, or to hear a particular pastor preach. Come to the church, listen to the preacher, follow the "plan," and salvation will be ours. The simplicity of "Jesus Saves" can give way to elaborate processes. Each group has a different slant on how salvation occurs. Each group has a different view of what "salvation" means.

Biblical Bases

A biblical scholar has noted that even if it does not always use formal terms, "the Bible introduces on practically every page the theme of salvation (or its absence)."[1] To express this theme the Bible uses a wide variety of images with different emphases as they appear in diverse contexts.

Old Testament

In the Old Testament, terms for salvation cluster around the needs for safety, deliverance, restoration, and help in times of distress. The people of Israel are given a covenantal relationship with God and receive salvation throughout their history. They are delivered from slavery in Egypt by God's miraculous actions, especially in saving them from the Egyptians at the Red Sea (Ex. 14:1–15:21; cf. Isa. 63:7–14; Hos. 11:1). The people remember this deliverance in the Passover celebrations (Ex. 12:1–28). Through the rest of the Hebrew Scriptures, God continually saves and delivers from enemies (Judges 4–5; 2 Sam. 8:14). A wider salvation for the Gentile nations is pointed toward in the message of the book of Isaiah (2:1–4; 60:1–14).[2]

God is the provider of salvation, the "savior" of the people. God works through leaders such as judges, kings, and prophets. But the Lord is Israel's protector and healer (Ex. 15:26; Pss. 12:7; 103:3; Isa. 31:5). Salvation is a very earthly deliverance—from slavery (Deut. 24:18), enemies (Ps. 108:6), even the threat of death (Ps. 33:18–19).

But salvation is also "spiritual" in the sense that God brings new beginnings (Ezek. 37:1–14) and forgiveness from sin (Ps. 32:1–2), and establishes a new heart and spirit within the covenant people (Ezek. 36:22–32). The Lord loves the people as a spouse or a mother (Isa. 49:14–16; 54:1–8; Hos. 2:14–23; 11:1–9). It is a present reality, as the people experience God's presence in their midst (Isa. 41:10) and a future hope (Joel 2:27).[3] Ultimately, future salvation includes the hopes for resurrection from the dead and God's reign in a transformed world (Isa. 26:19; 66:22; Dan. 12:1–3).

New Testament

Salvation in the New Testament is also expressed in a variety of ways. The Greek term for "save" (*sōzō*) and its related term "salvation" (*sōteria*) have three basic meanings:

1. "To rescue from danger and restore to a former state of safety and well-being";
2. "To cause someone to become well again after having been sick";
3. "To cause someone to experience divine salvation—'to save.'"[4]

Other New Testament terms expressing the idea of salvation include "freedom," "justification," "life," "reconciliation," "redemption," "resurrection," and "rule of God."[5]

Some in the New Testament are "rescued" from physical dangers (2 Cor. 1:10). Some are delivered from sickness (Luke 8:48), possession by demons

(Mark 1:34), or the threat of death (Matt. 14:30). More generally, however, persons need to be "saved" from the power of the "evil one" (Matt. 6:13) and from the power of sin (Mark 1:5) and death (John 12:47).

The emphasis in Paul's writings is on the pervasive nature of human sin (Rom. 3:23) and its alienating, enslaving power (Rom. 5:12–7:25). Yet, for Paul, God has lovingly taken the initiative and out of free, divine grace has given the gift of salvation to humanity in Jesus Christ. This was captured when Paul wrote, "But God proves his love for us in that while we still were sinners Christ died for us. Much more surely then, now that we have been justified by his blood, will we be saved through him from the wrath of God. For if while we were enemies, we were reconciled to God through the death of his Son, much more surely, having been reconciled, will we be saved by his life" (Rom. 5:8–10). This divine deliverance through the cross of Jesus Christ has brought peace (Rom. 5:1), reconciliation (2 Cor. 5:16–21), justification (Rom. 4:25), and a new status as adopted children of God (Gal. 4:5; Eph. 1:5). We are freed from sin (Rom. 6:1–23) and the power of the law (Gal. 2:15–21). Salvation means new life (Rom. 7:6) to all who acknowledge Jesus Christ as their Lord and Savior (Rom. 10:9).

This "new life" is the "eternal life" spoken of throughout the Gospel of John (5:24; 6:54; 10:28, etc.) and especially in John 3:16, the most famous verse in the Bible, which Martin Luther called "the gospel in a nutshell": "'For God so loved the world that he gave his only Son, so that everyone who believes in him may not perish but may have eternal life. Indeed,'" continued Jesus, " 'God did not send the Son into the world to condemn the world, but in order that the world might be saved through him'" (John 3:17). Salvation is being "born from above" (John 3:3; "born again") and sharing in the life of Christ by the power of the Holy Spirit (John 11:25; 14:6, 20).

Through the work of Jesus Christ, human sin is forgiven (Rom. 3:25) and a new covenant, a new relationship between God and humanity is established (Mark 14:24; 1 Cor. 11:25). Jesus Christ is the great "High Priest" who offers himself as the sacrifice for our sins (Heb. 8:1–10:18). He has overcome the cosmic powers that keep humanity in bondage (Gal. 4:8–10; Col. 2:16–23) and has established reconciliation and peace by his cross (Col. 1:20). Salvation now is life "in Christ," united with him by the bond of faith (Rom. 8:1; Gal. 2:20; 1 Cor. 15:22).

The gift of salvation is thus a present reality and a future hope. Jesus spoke of salvation as the reality of entering into the reign (kingdom) of God in which one renounces all claims on self and seeks to do the will of God above all else (Matt. 7:21; 18:3). Jesus also taught his disciples to pray for the coming reign of God, "your kingdom come," "whenever" they pray (Matt. 6:10, 6). To lose one's life for God's purposes will mean ultimately to save one's life in the future (Mark 8:35; 10:29–30). In Paul's language, the coming salvation will mean sharing in Christ's glory (Rom. 8:17; Phil. 3:20–21), obtaining the "hope of salvation" (1 Thess. 5:8). The whole of creation will be freed from decay, and redemption will be full and complete (Rom. 8:18–24). At the return of Christ, he will "save those who are eagerly waiting for him" (Heb. 9:28). Ultimate salvation in Jesus Christ will be "revealed in the last time" (1 Peter 1:5). The glorious vision on which the New Testament ends is in the consummation of salvation when Jesus Christ will reign and God will make "all things new" (Rev. 21:5; cf. 21:1–22:5).

Christian Tradition

God's gift of salvation is given to the world in Jesus Christ who came to "save his people from their sins" (Matt. 1:21) and to be the "savior" (Luke 2:11). The experience of "salvation" is conveyed in the Bible through a number of images and also by terms with their own meanings that relate to God's work of salvation in Christ, including "regeneration," "calling," "conversion," "renewal," and "sanctification." Christian theology has developed various understandings of these themes and how they relate to each other in the whole process of salvation.

Nature of Salvation

Early church theologians advanced views about the nature of salvation by drawing on various biblical images. Each of these images was elaborated upon in order to indicate how the gift of salvation has been received and what God has done in Jesus Christ.

Closely related to each portrait of "salvation" is also a view of human sin. Implicit also are understandings about the nature of God, who Jesus is, and what his death on the cross and his resurrection have accomplished. Thus, one can look at the different theological understandings of salvation as having several components. The first is the "problem": What is the situation of humanity and what is the basic nature of sin in the human condition? Second, what is the "solution"? What has Jesus Christ done to solve this problem? Third, what is God's role? What has God done in providing for Christ's work? Fourth, what is Christ's role? What is the nature of the work of Jesus Christ? Fifth, what are the results of Christ's work? What has salvation achieved? A brief overview will show the ways in which the varieties of New Testament images of "salvation" were developed.[6]

1. *Salvation as Illumination.* Humans live in ignorance, error, and bondage to evil powers. God sends Jesus Christ as the Logos to impart wisdom and

bring enlightenment. Humans receive salvation by following his example and can have a new existence as they live "illuminated" by the life and teachings of Jesus Christ.

2. *Salvation as Restoration.* By the disobedience of our first parents, humans have lost the image of God in which they were created. God has planned for salvation by sending Jesus Christ as the "second Adam" who reverses the sin of Adam and by his obedience regains the image of God for humanity. The Spirit of God unites humanity with God so that humans can be reintegrated into the relationship of love and trust that God initially intended.

3. *Salvation as Satisfaction.* Humans have inherited the guilt of their first parents. Yet God loves the world and sends Jesus Christ to be the sacrifice for sin. This sacrifice, which is acceptable to God because Jesus Christ was fully obedient to God's law, satisfies God who forgives sin and guilt. Salvation is thus a reward made possible by Christ's obedience and death.

4. *Salvation as Victory.* The disobedience of our first parents has plunged the world into captivity to the powers of evil and Satan. God seeks to establish sovereign reign over the earth (a kingdom) and does so by sending Jesus Christ, who in his death defeats the powers of sin and evil; in his resurrection, Jesus triumphs over the "last enemy," the power of death. Humanity is rescued from death by Christ's victory.

5. *Salvation as Deification.* Humans are sinners and thus face death as the consequence of their sins. God provides the way of forgiveness by sending Jesus Christ, truly God and truly human. Christ brings grace to humanity, the forgiveness of sins, and immortality. As believers encounter God, by God's spirit they experience communion with God, an intimate union. This union is made ultimate at death, where immortality is conferred. Salvation is the process of divinization and deification, as believers are progressively united with Christ's divine nature.

6. *Salvation as Justification.* The sin of humanity, inherited from our first parents, has corrupted human nature and alienated humans from God. Yet in God's mercy, God chooses (elects) to save rather than to condemn all sinners. God sends Jesus Christ as the mediator—truly God and truly human—who by his obedience carries out the work of salvation in his death and resurrection so that humans may become a "new creation." The old, corrupt, sinful nature is made new as those who accept Christ's work gain a new status in God's sight as made "righteous."

Augustine

The image of "justification" was stressed by Augustine in his controversy with Pelagius and his followers over the nature of sin and grace (see chap. 7).

For Augustine, justification by God's grace through faith was the only hope humans have for salvation. He rejected Pelagius's view that the human will is "free" to choose whether to sin or not to sin. He also rejected the views of the "semi-Pelagians" who taught that humans could cooperate with God's grace and by the exercise of their wills participate in their salvation through their own choices.

For Augustine, salvation as justification meant that persons become righteous as the Holy Spirit confers the spirit of love in their lives. Through faith, they receive a new will that seeks to do God's will in all things. Their new will is freed—by God's power to obey God. It replaces the corrupt, sinful will that is ours through original sin and is thus a dimension of "human nature." As the Spirit works within them, believers continue to grow in righteousness throughout their Christian lives.

Luther

In the Protestant Reformation of the sixteenth century, Martin Luther challenged the views of salvation held by the Roman Catholic church at his time. During the medieval period, Augustine's views were held in varying forms.[7] As Luther understood it, the contemporary church taught that salvation is achieved when humans choose to accept the divinely revealed teachings of the church. This is "faith." Thereby humans freely cooperate with God's grace, which is being extended to them. This grace comes through the sacraments of the church, beginning with baptism, and continually renewed through participation in the sacraments throughout one's life. This faith combined with good works leads to an increase in justification and ultimately to salvation. Eternal life is given "as a grace mercifully promised" to believers in Christ Jesus and "as a reward promised by God himself, to be faithfully given to their good works and merits (Rom. 6:22)." Since Christ continually gives strength to those who are justified, the works that they do can be considered to have "fully satisfied the divine law according to the state of this life and to have truly merited eternal life, to be obtained in its [due] time, provided they depart [this life] in grace (Rev. 14:13).[8] For Luther, this meant the Roman Catholic formula for salvation was: "Faith + Works = Salvation."

Luther is well-known for two of his famous slogans about salvation: *sola gratia* ("grace alone") and *sola fide* ("faith alone"). Luther was an Augustinian monk before he became a Protestant reformer. His slogans emerged from his study of the New Testament and his understandings of Augustine's teachings. Luther believed, with Augustine, that humans have a corrupt, sinful nature due to original sin. We see our sinfulness revealed in God's law (the Ten Commandments). We know we cannot gain righteousness in God's sight by our human efforts because the law shows us how far short we fall. The law is a "mirror," showing our sinfulness; it is a "hammer," driving us to despair because of our situation. Yet, says Luther, at this point of total helplessness, the law is also a "mask" that hides but now reveals the gospel of Jesus Christ. The good news of the gospel is that out of love, Jesus Christ has died for our sins, that he has obeyed and fulfilled the law on our behalf. By faith we accept his death as being done on our behalf. By faith we receive "justification" in God's sight when God accepts the "righteousness of Jesus Christ" as our own. We are "reckoned righteous" in God's sight by trustfully receiving the gift of Christ's death "for us." Thus, salvation is a restored relationship with God in which as sinners we are accounted as righteous on the basis of Christ's work on the cross.

For Luther, "good works" follow as a result of justification. The forgiven sinner seeks to do God's will and by faith lives as a disciple of Jesus Christ. Luther said that faith is "a lively, diligent, active, powerful thing, which makes it impossible that it shall not unceasingly do good works." Put more simply, he said that "good works do not make a person 'good' (justified), but a 'good person' (justified person) will do good works."[9] "Good works" do not achieve salvation. They follow from salvation. We are saved by "grace alone"—by God's unmerited favor; by "faith alone"—trusting completely in Christ's death on our behalf; and by "Christ alone"—only Jesus Christ can make us righteous before God. Thus, Luther's formula for salvation was: "Faith → Salvation + Works."

Reformed Emphases

Justification

Reformed theology has understood justification in the same way as Luther.[10] The confessions of Reformed churches have recognized the power of original sin and that humans cannot help but sin due to their sinful natures.[11] We cannot perform repentance for our sin or even prepare ourselves to repent because our whole selves are turned away from God and turned in upon ourselves [Luther: *in curvatus in se*]. As humans we cannot work ourselves out of our sinful condition.[12]

Our justification and reception of the gift of salvation spring totally from God's free grace. God relates to humans in love and mercy. The cross of Jesus Christ is the demonstration of that love but even more is also the act through which salvation is made possible and made real.[13] As the Tetrapolitan Confession (1530) put it, our whole justification is to be "ascribed to the good pleasure of God and the merit of Christ, and to be received by faith alone."[14] Faith is the means of our justification, the way by which we receive the grace of God. As Calvin said, "faith is said to justify because it receives and embraces the righteousness offered through the gospel, all consideration of works is excluded."[15] The Heidelberg Catechism asks, "How are you righteous before God?" and answers:

> Only by true faith in Jesus Christ . . . God, without any merit of my own, out of pure grace, grants me the benefits of the perfect expiation of Christ, imputing to me his righteousness and holiness as if I had never committed a single sin or had ever been sinful, having fulfilled myself all the obedience which Christ has carried out for me, if only I accept such favor with a trusting heart.[16]

Here, "faith does not justify as though it were in itself a noble work; it justifies only in that through it the promise of grace is accepted."[17]

Good Works

Our "good works" follow as actions of gratitude and thanksgiving for the wonderful blessings of salvation and the gift of new life in Jesus Christ. Faith is active in love (Gal. 5:6).[18] Good works show the genuineness of faith. But they are not the cause of faith nor do they bring salvation. As the Second Helvetic Confession puts it, "Works necessarily proceed from faith. And salvation is improperly attributed to them, but is most properly ascribed to grace" (see Rom. 11:6).[19] "Why must we do good works?" asks the Heidelberg Catechism. Because

> just as Christ has redeemed us with his blood he also renews us through his Holy Spirit according to his own image, so that with our whole life we may show ourselves grateful to God for his goodness and that he may be glorified through us; and further, so that we ourselves may be assured of our faith by its fruits and by our reverent behavior may win our neighbors to Christ.[20]

Put more simply, we are "justified by faith alone, but not by a faith that is alone"; good works follow.

Faith

"Faith" in the Reformed tradition embraces the whole person—head, heart, and hands. It engages our intellects in terms of what we believe. It embraces our emotions in terms of our love for God in Jesus Christ. It launches our lives in obedience and service to Jesus Christ as Christian people.[21] In Calvin's classic definition, faith is "a firm and certain knowledge of God's benevolence toward us, founded upon the truth of the freely given promise in Christ, both revealed to our minds and sealed upon our hearts through the Holy Spirit."[22] Faith is believing and trusting in Jesus Christ.

Order of Salvation

Reformed theology has sometimes dealt with the question of how the various aspects of salvation relate to each other. Terms such as "faith," "conversion," "regeneration," "election," and "calling" have been distinguished from each other and are all considered to be involved in the overall process of "salvation." In the post-Reformation period, Reformed theologians were concerned with the "order of salvation" (Lat. *ordo salutis*), determining the logical priorities and interconnections among these terms. In what "order" did God act in establishing the plan or way of salvation? What "decree of God" preceded; what followed? What is their "logical order"? Reformed theologians entered into controversies with Lutherans and with Arminians over the order of the divine actions.[23] Reformed theologians also disagreed among themselves.[24]

Receiving Salvation

A major difference between Reformed theology and Arminian theology is over the way in which salvation is received. Arminianism is closer to the semi-Pelagian view. God opens the possibility for salvation to humans, who then have the freedom and the responsibility either to respond in faith or to reject the offer of salvation in Jesus Christ. Humans are sinful, but the human will is perceived still to be able to do that which is spiritually good and thus able to respond in faith to the gospel by its own power. God's grace is given to help the sinful will and sufficient grace is given to all, enabling them to believe the gospel if they so desire. When they respond in faith they are justified and receive forgiveness of sins on the basis of the atonement of Jesus Christ.

In the Reformed theology, against which Arminianism was reacting, the emphases of Augustine on God's divine action and election come to the fore. Humans are sinful by nature, having inherited the guilt of the sin of our first parents. The human will is corrupt and incapable of willing any spiritual good. God's Holy Spirit works to regenerate a person by giving the gift of faith in Jesus Christ as Lord and Savior. The response of faith occurs purely and only by God's gracious initiative in illuminating one's heart and mind by the Spirit and completely changing one's nature from that of "sinner" to that of "believer" in Jesus Christ. The sinner has no power to respond to God by one's "free choice," since our wills are held in bondage to the power of sin. If any change is to occur within us, it must be by God's act and God's act alone. Our sinful, human nature makes it impossible for us to "choose" to accept the gospel of Christ—except by the direct action of the Holy Spirit who gives us faith.[25]

Conversion

"Conversion" is the Spirit's work of "regeneration" made real in one's life so that on the basis of faith in Jesus Christ, we turn away from sin and begin a new life of obedience as we are enabled by the power of the Holy Spirit. Conversion includes "repentance," which is our sorrow for sin and resolve to live a new life, and "faith," in which all trust is put in Jesus Christ. We are "justified by faith" in that faith is the means by which our new relationship with God through Christ is expressed in our lives. We receive "adoption" as children of God, a new status in God's family. As we live the Christian life, we grow in faith (sanctification), we persevere in faith by God's power (perseverence), and we live ultimately in God's reign in the kingdom of heaven (glorification).[26]

Election

Initiating the whole process of salvation, in the Reformed view, is God's eternal election or predestination in Jesus Christ.[27] God has chosen us "in Christ before the foundation of the world" (Eph. 1:4). God has not left humanity to face the full consequences of its sin and its judgment; God has acted to elect or call a people to serve God in this world and to receive the gift of salvation. This is the comfort of the doctrine of election. It is God who saves us, not we ourselves. Our salvation is secured by God's loving power. We are saved by God's grace alone (Lat. *Sola gratia*). We respond and receive God's gracious redemption by the faith given to us through the Holy Spirit. Behind the gift of our salvation is the loving work of the triune God.

Contemporary Emphases

Yes, "Jesus saves"! Jesus saves by bringing us rescue, health, and healing in our relationship with God and with others in this world. Salvation is God's gracious gift given to us through the life, death, and resurrection of Jesus Christ.

An ongoing task for contemporary theologians, for the Christian church, and for individual Christians is to try to understand the significance of "salvation" today. In what ways is life changed, is our existence altered, when we receive the gift of God's love in Jesus Christ? What does God intend for the world and for Christians within the world who have responded by faith to Jesus Christ as their Lord and Savior? Is "salvation" something to be privately preserved, or is it to be shared with others?

Salvation: End or Means?

One way to focus this concern is to ask: "Is salvation a means or an end?" Is it an "end" in itself? Is the goal of God's plan of salvation that I "get saved" and live in a cozy relationship with God so that when I die I will escape eternal death or punishment? Is salvation a "privatized" gift? A number of Christian persons apparently believe it is. In some contexts, "soul-winning" is a major focus of activity and the goal of Christian existence seems only to be to increase the "numbers" of those who are willing to give adherence to a certain set of words or confession.

Or is salvation a "means"? Is the gospel message of God's love in Jesus Christ to be shared with the world in order to bring those who believe into a new, loving, and trusting relationship with God so that they might then be involved with the world by seeking to carry out God's purposes for the world and the kind of world community God desires? Salvation is a "means" to free people to be involved in the issues that count in this world: concerns for the environment, for justice, for peacemaking, and freedom for others.

Give Glory to God!

In the Reformed faith, we seek to do God's work in the world because we have experienced God's free and gracious love in Jesus Christ. God calls us to spread the gospel, to call people to faith in Christ—of course. But God wants us to live out our salvation in the midst of the world right now, by translating God's loving grace in Jesus Christ into meaningful actions that bring glory to God. As we are involved in struggles for peace, justice, and equity, we are showing forth the "love and justice of Jesus Christ," who has made our new relationships with God, with others, and with our world possible. God calls us to respond in gratitude for the "indescribable gift" (2 Cor. 9:15) of salvation in Jesus Christ. And our response in both word and deed is that of the angels at the birth of Jesus: "Glory to God!" (Luke 2:14).

Questions for Reflection

1. In what ways do biblical understandings of "salvation" help to correct some of the language about Christian salvation heard in our society?

2. What image of salvation is most meaningful to you?

3. In what ways does it matter whether we believe salvation is God's "gift" or whether we "earn" it?

4. When you think of your own experience of salvation, do you think primarily of your actions or God's?

5. Do you believe salvation is a "means" or an "end"?

12

Church: The People of God

Christian churches dot our landscapes. Their steeples stretch heavenward in our cities. Sometimes, however, just a storefront announces the "people of God meet here." Suburban sprawl features church buildings strategically located to capture the crest of demography—where the best real estate is located—especially in the "baby boom" communities. Their signs proclaim "seeker services" for those who want to sample the faith, but who are not quite ready for commitment. Our small towns and rural countrysides feature the typical church building that lend solidarity and uprightness to every community. So churches are with us—aplenty!

Of course the varieties bewilder us. The building styles differ and so do the names. Some are "community" churches; others are linked to a "denomination." Still others proclaim they are "nondenominational." Stop in for a visit and the differing worship styles will leave your head spinning as well. Some are "high church"—heavily liturgical. Others are much more "relaxed." Still others can rightly be called "casual." In some services the name of "Jeeesus" is heard repeatedly; in some the "Holy Ghost" gets "loose," and people shout or swoon. In still others, the silence is deep and reverential; the finely tuned choir presents only the "best" in church music. So the diversities jump out at us quickly.

We wonder through all this: What is the church, anyway? What commonalities are there in Christian worship or practice or belief that allow all these different kinds of folks to assemble in all these different kinds of places and do these different kinds of things? We wonder. What is it that unites the "faithful"—whatever they look like, whatever form of Christianity they practice?

Biblical Bases

People of God

The biblical bases for the Christian church are found in the Hebrew Scriptures. The gathering of the Hebrew people at times of great importance in their national life is referred to as an "assembly" (Heb. *qahal*; Deut. 9:10; Jer. 26:17). This assembly is referred to as an "assembly of the LORD" or an "assembly of God" (1 Chron. 28:8; Neh. 13:1; Micah 2:5), indicating that it is God who has called the people together. Israel received the law in a gathered assembly (Deut. 5:22), dedicated Solomon's temple (1 Kings 8:14ff.), and heard the book of the law read by Ezra (Neh. 8:2) while gathered together.[1]

By the end of the second century B.C.E., the Hebrew Scriptures were translated into the Greek language for the benefit of Jews scattered outside their homeland. This translation, called the Septuagint, rendered the Greek term *ekklēsia* to refer to the assembly of God's people.[2] The New Testament writers used *ekklēsia* to describe the congregations of God's people called "Christians" who are united by faith to Jesus Christ as their Lord and Savior. The apostle Paul used the term repeatedly to refer to Christian gatherings both in local places and more generally in a wider area such as a city (1 Cor. 14:4–5; Col. 4:15; 1 Thess. 1:1). He also used the term to describe "all the churches of Christ" (Rom. 16:16). This Greek term referred to the gathering of citizens in a community who were called together to consider issues of importance to the community.

Throughout the New Testament, the character of the church is defined by who it is who has called the community. It is God who has called the church together (1 Cor. 12:28; 2 Thess. 1:4). It is God who has called the churches together "in Christ Jesus" (1 Thess. 2:14).[3] In short, Christians in churches are the "temple of the living God" (2 Cor. 6:16; cf. Heb. 4:9).

Many other images for the church are used in the New Testament.[4] Some are images such as ark, branches of the vine, or God's field. Others are more major images that are full of theological meaning: the nation of God (1 Peter 2:9), the body of Christ (Eph. 1:22–23; 1 Cor. 12:27) with Christ as the head (Col. 1:18), the temple of the Spirit (1 Cor. 3:16; cf. Eph. 2:19–22; 1 Peter 2:5).

To summarize, as one scholar has put it: "The church of Jesus Christ is neither a building nor an organization. Rather, it is a people, a special people, a people who see themselves as standing in relationship to the God who saves them and to each other as those who share in this salvation."[5]

Covenant

The special relationship that marks Christian people to God is rooted in the biblical idea of covenant. The story of salvation, from the Hebrew

Scriptures onward, is the story of God "calling" a "people" to be in a special "relationship" with the Lord. This relationship is a "covenant."

God called Abram and Sarah to go out to a new land, begin a family (which became a nation), and to live as persons who acknowledge God in all they do (Gen. 12; 13; 15; 17:1–7). Through them, all the nations of the world would be blessed (Gen. 18:18; cf. Gal. 3:7–9, 14, 27–29). God's commitment to be their God was marked and sealed by a covenant or a promise to Abraham and Sarah and their offspring (Gen. 15:8–18; 17:1–14). This covenant marked the beginning of the nation of Israel. God "remembered his covenant with Abraham, Isaac, and Jacob" when people of Israel were enslaved in Egypt (Ex. 2:23–25). God liberated and delivered the people and brought them "out of the land of Egypt, out of the house of slavery" (Ex. 20:2).[6]

At Sinai, God again entered into a covenant with the nation of Israel. God reminded the people that God had freed them from slavery and thus was the God of grace who did for them what they could not do for themselves and who has called them together to live as a covenant people (Ex. 20:1–2; Deut. 5:1–3). This covenant was in the form of an agreement with the nation in which God would be their God and they would be God's people (Ex. 19:5). The covenant is marked by the giving of the law of God, to guide the people in the ways God wanted them to live as a nation and as people of the covenant (Exodus 19–24). A ceremony of covenant ratification sealed this covenant as the people proclaimed: "All that the LORD has spoken we will do, and we will be obedient" (Ex. 24:7; cf. 24:3). The sprinkling of blood on the people established the community between God and the people (cf. Matt. 26:28; 1 Cor. 11:25). The covenant relationship was fixed and provided the framework for Israel's self-understanding and for interpreting its history (Judges 2; 2 Kings 17). Israel was the covenant people of God.[7]

The prophets of Israel reminded the people of their covenantal obligations when they sinned (Jer. 11:1–5) and called them back to obedience (Hos. 8:1ff.; cf. Jer. 22:1–8; 34:12–22).[8] The prophet Jeremiah looked forward to a time when God will establish a "new covenant":

> The days are surely coming, says the LORD, when I will make a new covenant with the house of Israel and the house of Judah. It will not be like the covenant that I made with their ancestors when I took them by the hand to bring them out of the land of Egypt—a covenant that they broke, though I was their husband, says the LORD. But this is the covenant that I will make with the house of Israel after those days, says the LORD: I will put my law within them, and I will write it on their hearts; and I will be their God, and they shall be my people. No longer shall they teach one another, or say to each other, "Know the LORD," for they shall all know me, from the least of them to the greatest, says

the LORD; for I will forgive their iniquity, and remember their sin no more. (Jer. 31:31–34; cf. Ezek. 37:24–28)

This new covenant will emerge in the messianic age (Isa. 42:6; 59:21; Ezek. 16:60, 62) when God's eternal promises will find fulfillment. The everlasting covenant of peace between God and the people will be for all nations (Isa. 55:3–5; cf. Zech. 2:11; 8:20–23). God's covenant with David, in which David's descendants will have an everlasting kingdom, will be a reality (2 Sam. 7:12–17; 23:5; Ps. 89:3–4, 26–37; Ps. 132:11–12).

The followers of Jesus found God's covenant promises for Israel to have a deeper and richer meaning in Jesus Christ (Matt. 26:28; Luke 22:20; 1 Cor. 11:25). Through Jesus Christ, God's covenant is now sealed as Jesus links God's covenant people with God's new covenant people, the church (2 Cor. 3:6; Heb. 8–10; 12:24; 13:20). Old Testament Israel and Christian believers are bound together in Christ as the message of the gospel is proclaimed to the Gentiles and in all the world—so that all might receive the blessing (Gal. 3:7–9; cf. Acts 2:39; 7:17).

Jesus evoked covenantal imagery in his last supper with his disciples (Matt. 26:28; cf. Heb. 9:15; 7:22) and anticipates fulfillment of Jeremiah's vision of a new covenant with God's people (Jer. 31:31–34). Jesus has established a new form of the covenant, in continuity with God's ancient promises, and made his followers "ministers of a new covenant" (2 Cor. 3:6). Dividing walls of hostility between people are broken down (Eph. 2:11–21) and through the obedient life and sacrificial death of Jesus Christ a new and better form of the covenant of God's grace becomes real (Heb. 8:6; 9:15; 12:24).[9] The new covenant in Jesus Christ points to eternal life for the covenant people of God (Hebrews 8).

Election

The context in which God's covenant with people is carried out is God's election or calling. The initiative in establishing the covenant—with Abraham and Sarah, the nation of Israel, and with the new people of God, the church— is God's. God "appeared" to Abraham and Sarah and promised to make a covenant (Gen. 17:1–8; cf. 12:1–3). God "chose" Israel to be a blessing to the nations: "For you are a people holy to the LORD your God; the LORD your God has chosen you out of all the peoples on earth to be his people, his treasured possession" (Deut. 7:6–8; cf. 10:15; 14:2; Ps. 105:6). God thus liberated the people from Egypt and gave the law so that they could live in grateful obedience to their Lord. God chooses a people to be in a special, covenantal relationship with God and to carry out God's purposes in this world. The selection or "election" of the people was for service to God and to live as holy people who reflect the divine character of their Lord.

In the New Testament, God's choosing or election is extended beyond Israel to the Gentiles. God has elected the church to be God's covenantal people. Echoes of Israel's election are heard when the church is described as "a chosen race, a royal priesthood, a holy nation, God's own people" (1 Peter 2:9).[10] Those who are part of the church by faith in Jesus Christ are the "called," the "elect" of God (1 Cor. 1:24, 26; Rom. 8:33–39; cf. John 6:37; Mark 13:22, 27). God has chosen them "in Christ before the foundation of the world to be holy and blameless before [God] in love" (Eph. 1:4). The new covenant people of God, the church, are chosen in Jesus Christ (2 Thess. 2:13–14). They are elected eternally by God's divine grace (Rom. 11:5; 2 Tim. 1:9—"before the ages began") and are "chosen and destined by God the Father and sanctified by the Spirit to be obedient to Jesus Christ and to be sprinkled with his blood" (1 Peter 1:2). God's election springs from God's love (Eph. 1:4–5), mercy (Rom. 9:16), wisdom and knowledge (Rom. 11:33). The purpose of God's election of the church and the individuals within it is to carry out God's will and purposes in the world (John 15:16; Eph. 2:10; Col. 3:12; 2 Peter 1:10) and to receive the gift of eternal life and salvation in Jesus Christ (John 6:44; 17:2).

The ways in which election are linked with other dimensions of salvation are captured by Paul in his writing that "those whom [God] foreknew he also predestined to be conformed to the image of his Son, in order that he might be the firstborn within a large family. And those whom he predestined he also called; and those whom he called he also justified; and those whom he justified he also glorified" (Rom. 8:29–30). In summary, "election for Paul means that God, as an act of his love, has eternally chosen a group of individuals in Christ to be holy and without blame. This has brought about their adoption into God's family according to a predetermined plan that included their calling, justification and glorification."[11]

Christian Tradition

The rise of heresies and the experience of persecutions led early Christian theologians to reflect on the nature of the church. Such reflection was crucial if the church was to be able to articulate its Christian faith and resist perversions of it. It was also important in light of the sufferings endured by Christians at the hands of their enemies.[12]

Marks of the Church

The basic unity of the church was one of a number of very practical issues that the early church had to consider. In the Niceno-Constantinopolitan creed

(A.D. 381), the church confessed: "We believe in one holy catholic and apostolic Church."[13] These characteristics are known as the "marks" of the church, yet questions about the meanings of these four marks still persist.

1. In what does the church's *unity* consist: the outward ecclesiastical structures or inward spiritual realities? What is the relationship between local bodies of believers and the "one" church?

2. What makes the church *holy*: the faithfulness of Christian believers in obedience or God's faithfulness and calling of a people to be "set apart" (a meaning of "holy") for God's work in this world? Can a church be composed of "sinners," or must all exhibit a "purity of life" or "perfection" to be considered as Christians?

3. Is the church *catholic* because it is visibly organized throughout the whole world and is thus a "universal" church, or does its catholicity also mean its inclusion of Christian believers in all times and places? Does catholicity also include the conviction that the church through the gospel of Christ should be involved in all dimensions of life—in issues of peacemaking, justice, and economics as well as "spiritual" issues?

4. Is the church *apostolic* because it can trace a direct, historic line back to the earliest apostles of Jesus, or does "apostolicity" refers to the church's fidelity in proclaiming the message and teachings of the apostles as found through Holy Scripture? What aberrant teachings would make a church cease being a church?

As the Christian tradition emerged, different understandings of the four marks of the church also evolved.

Character of the Church

Other dimensions of ecclesiology (the doctrine of the church) also became important through the centuries.

1. *Militant and Triumphant.* A distinction has been made between the church "militant" and the church "triumphant." The church militant is the visible Christian church on Earth. The church triumphant is the church in heaven composed of all who have died and share in the reality of heaven.

2. *Visible and Invisible.* The "visible" church is the outward, organized church on Earth that is apparent and is composed of all who associate themselves with the church as an institution. The "invisible" church is the body of genuine believers in Christ on Earth and in heaven. They may or may not be directly associated with a visible body of believers. As Augustine said of the visible church, "many sheep are without, and many wolves are within."[14] The invisible and the visible church overlap in that those who are true believers in Christ (invisible church) are found in the visible church. Yet, some in the

visible church may not be genuine believers—but may be associated with the church for any number of reasons.[15]

Reformed Emphases

The Reformed tradition has appropriated the basic insights of the doctrine of the church as it developed in the early centuries.[16] But the influence of Augustine's views is strong. In the Reformed confessional writings, "the doctrine of the church is intimately connected with the doctrine of election."[17] The church is the community of faith, elected by God in Jesus Christ. The Heidelberg Catechism strikes this note when it asks:

> Q. 54 What do you believe concerning 'the Holy Catholic Church'?
> A. I believe that, from the beginning to the end of the world, and from among the whole human race, the Son of God, by his Spirit and his Word, gathers, protects, and preserves for himself, in the unity of the true faith, a congregation chosen for eternal life. Moreover, I believe that I am and forever will remain a living member of it.[18]

Election and Predestination

The twin biblical emphases on election and covenant have played important roles in the Reformed faith. Calvin was concerned with very practical considerations when he reflected on why it was that some persons respond in faith to the gospel of Jesus Christ while others do not. He noted that the "covenant of life" does not "gain the same acceptance" among all persons to whom it is preached. Some believe; others do not. The explanation for this is in the eternal election of God. Salvation springs "solely from God's mere generosity" and, said Calvin, Scripture clearly shows that "God once established by his eternal and unchangeable plan those whom he long before determined once for all to receive into salvation, and those whom, on the other hand, he would devote to destruction."[19] This election is from God's "freely given mercy, without regard to human worth." Salvation is by God's sheer grace alone.

Our election to salvation, note Reformed theologians, is an election in Jesus Christ. God has chosen us "in Christ" (Eph. 1:4).[20] Thus, said Calvin, "if we have been chosen in him, we shall not find assurance of our election in ourselves; and not even in God the Father, if we conceive him as severed from his Son. Christ, then, is the mirror wherein we must, and without self-deception may, contemplate our own election."[21] This means, quite simply, that if we ask ourselves, "Am I of the 'elect'?" "Am I called by God?"—our answer is the same as our answer to the question, "Do I believe in Jesus Christ?" For it is in Christ, as the "mirror" of our election, that we know the "inestimable fruit of comfort" that election brings.[22] If we have faith in Jesus Christ, we have been elected or called by God unto salvation. The Second Helvetic Confession in posing the question, "Whether We are Elected," said, "It is to be believed; and it is to be held as beyond doubt that if you believe and are in Christ, you are elected. For the Father has revealed unto us in Christ the eternal purpose of his predestination."[23] It is God's calling to us that is the fruit of our election, its "proof" and solely the work of God's grace. For, by calling the elect, God "receives them into his family and unites them to him so that they may together be one."[24] It is God's "free mercy" that is apparent in our calling, on every side. When we respond to God's call we receive "a pledge of salvation that cannot deceive us."[25] We thus know the truth of our election by virtue of our response, in faith, to God's call to us in Jesus Christ.[26]

Covenant

God's new covenant with the world is found in Jesus Christ. God's "covenant people" are now thus believers in Christ who live in relationship with God as Christ's disciples. The "old covenant" with God's promises to Abraham and Sarah is now extended to the whole of humanity and to all whom God calls or elects to be adopted into the family of God through faith in Jesus Christ. It is through the new covenant in Christ that our sin is forgiven. This marks our "first entry into the church and Kingdom of God," wrote Calvin, and "without it, there is for us no covenant or bond with God."[27] Jesus Christ is God's covenant of grace made with humanity. When, by God's election, we are granted the gift of faith and receive forgiveness of our sins, we become aware of becoming part of God's covenant people, the church. As the Westminster Confession of Faith put it: "the principal acts of saving faith are accepting, receiving, and resting upon Christ alone for justification, sanctification, and eternal life, by virtue of the covenant of grace."[28]

Communion of Saints

The church is the "communion of saints," a "spiritual assembly of believers which is holy and the one bride of Christ, and in which all are citizens who truly confess that Jesus is the Christ, the Lamb of God who takes away the sin of the world, and who also confirm such faith by works of love."[29] The Reformed have stressed a comprehensive view of the church in that the "communion of saints" includes all who have lived and died, the "elect" of God through all ages.[30]

Visible and Invisible

The church is both visible and invisible. As the universal fellowship of believers, the church is "open and known to God's eyes alone."[31] This is the "one, holy, catholic and apostolic church" of the Nicene Creed. It is "the fellowship of those who have enlisted under Christ and committed themselves entirely to his faith; with whom, nevertheless, until the end of the world, those are mingled who feign faith in Christ, but do not truly have it."[32] The outward "visible" church is a "mixed body" of true believers and those who may profess belief in Jesus Christ but do not genuinely enact it.[33] It is important to realize, however, that judgment about who genuinely professes faith in Christ and who does not belongs to God, not to us as humans.[34]

Marks of the Church

There are variations within the Reformed tradition about what constitutes the general marks of the church. Some Reformed theologians spoke of one mark. The church exists where the pure doctrine of the Gospel is preached. Others, including Calvin, said that "wherever we see the Word of God purely preached and heard, and the sacraments administered according to Christ's institution, there, it is not to be doubted, a church of God exists" [cf. Eph. 2:20].[35] Still others, including the Scots Confession, mention three "notes of the true Kirk": preaching, right administration of the sacraments, and ecclesiastical discipline "uprightly ministered."[36]

The accents in these statements on the Word of God "purely preached" and sacraments "rightly administered" point to an enduring Reformed emphasis that the church must be "reformed and always being reformed" according to the Word of God.[37] The touchstone for Christian doctrine and belief, as well as all Christian practice in churches, is conformity to the Word of God in Scripture.

This emphasis was to mark the Reformed (as well as the Lutherans) in contrast to the prevailing Roman Catholic teaching at the time of the Protestant Reformation. Martin Luther reacted against the Roman Catholic view that authority in the church is found in the Scriptures plus the teachings of the Roman church as the authoritative interpretations of Scripture. In that view, Scripture and church tradition—as defined by the Pope and the teaching "magisterium" of the Roman church—is the place where authority is to be found.[38] Luther and later Protestant Reformers insisted that authority in the church is to be found in "Scripture alone" (Lat. *sola Scriptura*). The church is founded on the teachings of the "prophets and the apostles," with Jesus Christ himself as the head of the church (Eph. 2:20). Without these teachings, the church would not exist. Thus the church must listen to the gospel, and the Scriptures must be the supreme authority for the church, under Jesus Christ himself.[39]

Unity of the Church

This commitment to the authority of Scripture and to the lordship of Jesus Christ over the church is what has solidified the commitment of Reformed theology to the unity of the church. Calvin defined the church universal as "a multitude gathered from all nations; it is divided and dispersed in separate places, but agrees on the one truth of divine doctrine, and is bound by the bond of the same religion."[40] From the early days of Calvin and Zwingli, Reformed Christians have been involved in ecumenical dialogues with other communions. Calvin once wrote that he would "cross seven seas" if it would unite the Christian church. In some places, "union" or "united" churches have emerged where churches with Reformed heritages have united with each other or with a church from another tradition.[41]

Yet, the early Reformers also insisted that since the church is founded on God's Word, "there is no church unless it is obedient to the Word of God and is guided by it."[42] Theologically, the unity of the church is given and maintained by God, not accomplished by us. As a contemporary Reformed theologian has well stated: "Recognizing that unity in Christ is God's gift and not a human achievement, Reformed ecumenists concur with all who believe that the goal is the *manifestation* of this God-given unity so that the world may believe. The church is called to be a sign in the world of that ultimate reconciliation of all things to God."[43] Despite all church divisions and schisms, the Reformed impulse is to look to Jesus Christ as the head of the church—and of all churches. It is to confess the affirmation: "I believe in the one, holy, catholic and apostolic church."

Contemporary Significance

The Christian churches that dot our landscapes each have their own theologies and ways of "being church." Their diversities show "outwardly" in what we see, as well as "inwardly" in terms of what they believe about themselves.

Models of the Church

The contemporary theologian Avery Dulles wrote an important book to help us understand and organize the main approaches or "models" of how churches understand themselves theologically. Each of these approaches provides a lens by which churches recognize who they are and what their mission in the world should be.

1. *Church as Institution.* The church is seen as divinely prescribed structures that authorize teaching, governing, traditions, and authority. The church has clear patterns of worship and leadership and unites all members under one organizational form.

2. *Church as Mystical Communion.* The church is the community of the Spirit and consists of all those who have an immediate relationship with God through the Holy Spirit. The interior experience of God's grace unites those "filled with the Spirit."

3. *Church as Sacrament.* The church through its liturgy is the means of God's grace and is a living symbol or sign of the continuing grace of God in Jesus Christ. The church is a visible expression of the presence of God in the world.

4. *Church as Herald.* The church proclaims the Word of God and calls persons to faith in Jesus Christ. Believers are united on the basis of their common confession of Christ as Lord and Savior. The world is challenged to believe, repent, and obey the gospel.

5. *Church as Servant.* The church is to reflect the essential nature of Jesus' life and ministry as one of service. The church gives of itself to the world, as Jesus did in his life and his death on the cross. The church can struggle for justice, peace, and liberation as a servant people of a servant Lord.

6. *Church as Community of Disciples.* The church calls people to be followers of Jesus Christ and to live in the fullness of that discipleship. They worship, learn, serve, and are nurtured and renewed by the living Christ whose life the church appropriates as it lives out his values and concerns.

Each of these models provides positive strengths. There are elements of biblical truth and insight in all of them. But further reflection will also lead us to perceive certain weaknesses in each of them as well. None of them can capture the full essence of what the church is.

Yet through all the diversities, the essential nature of the church remains. The church is one: its *unity* is in God's covenant people's fellowship with God through Jesus Christ in the Holy Spirit. The church is *holy*: God's covenant people are justified by Jesus Christ and participate in carrying out God's purposes in this world. The church is *catholic*: God's covenant people are found in all parts of the world at all times in history, and these people include all races, classes, and economic levels. The church is *apostolic*: God's covenant people are guided by the gospel of Jesus Christ in both word and deed, in what the church believes and how the church lives. What unites all of us as Christians is more much important than whatever particular doctrinal understandings divide us.

The Christian life is a communal life. It is lived in fellowship with others who have confessed faith in Jesus Christ as their Lord and Savior and have been drawn together by the Holy Spirit in the church. There is no "lone ranger" Christianity! The church as a theological community is unlike any other social or civic group. It is perhaps the only organization where one professes to be "unworthy"—a sinner—in order to join! The church is led by the Holy Spirit as it looks to its head, Jesus Christ, in worship and service to God in this world. The church is, as Karl Barth put it, "the earthly-historical form of existence of Jesus Christ Himself."[44]

At times the church disappoints us because it is all too "human." The "not so holy local church" instead of the "holy catholic church" is the church we sometimes know in ways that are too real. The church loses its true focus on Christ, it oppresses people, it becomes captive to cultural powers and allegiances. At those times, we wonder where the Spirit is, where Christ is, and whether God has abandoned the covenant. Yet, through it all, God remains faithful to the church in Jesus Christ. The church can repent. Focus can be regained, liberation can happen, and resistance to cultural captivities can be mounted. Then the church can continue to be the people of God.

Questions for Reflection

1. In what ways would you respond to the argument: "I can be a good Christian all by myself. I don't need the church"?

2. What is the significance of the doctrine of the covenant in relation to the doctrine of the church?

3. If the church is the "elect of God" or the "company of the predestined," then why do we find churches involved in quarreling, injustices, exclusivism, and other sinful practices?

4. In what ways is your local congregation showing what it means to be the "one, holy, catholic, and apostolic church"?

5. What "model" of the church is closest to your understanding of what the church should be?

13

Baptism: Beginning in Faith

One basic question facing a Christian family occurs when children are born. Should the child be baptized? For some families the answer is "yes." For others, "no."

Baptism occurs in Christian churches as a sacrament or an ordinance.[1] Some churches administer "adult baptism" exclusively; others practice "infant baptism" as well as "adult baptism." Still others reject water baptism as an outward act altogether and insist that the only needed baptism is the baptism of the Holy Spirit.[2]

There are also varieties in the modes by which baptism is carried out. The three historic modes have been sprinkling, pouring, and immersion. Some churches do not specify which mode is to be used. Others regard the only valid baptism as being carried out by immersion.

In some church traditions, baptism marks the moment at which faith is considered to be present and salvation occurs. This has been known as "baptismal regeneration."[3] In other traditions, baptism is recognized as a sign of one's new life in Jesus Christ but its effects are only valid for those who have been elected to salvation by God. The time at which the sign of the water is applied may not necessarily be the same instant when one receives the gift of salvation by faith in Jesus Christ.[4]

So there are divergent beliefs and practices about the nature and function of Christian baptism. Churches in Anabaptist and Baptist traditions baptize only adults. The Roman Catholic church, the Orthodox church, and churches emerging from the Protestant Reformation such as Anglicans (Episcopal), Lutherans, and the Reformed practice both adult and infant baptism. Anabaptist and Baptist churches prefer to speak of the "ordinance of baptism" since they do not believe God's grace is conferred through baptism but rather that baptism is a "sign of profession" through which one makes a public acceptance of Christ as Lord and Savior in the midst of a particular church community. When baptism takes place in Baptist churches it must be done by immersion. Persons who unite with Baptist bodies and who have previously had a ceremony of baptism marked by "sprinkling" or "pouring" must be immersed, according to Baptist belief. This is not considered a "rebaptism," because the first "baptism" is not considered to be valid.[5]

So, varieties abound with baptism! Most generally, however, it is possible to say that for all Christian communions: "Baptism is the distinct act, instituted by Christ, by which human beings are incorporated into the community of the church."[6] Baptism is the doorway to the church; it gives us our identity as children of God.[7]

Biblical Bases

Early Christians have baptized since the very beginning. But they were not the first group to do so. The Jews at the time of Jesus baptized Gentile converts. John the Baptist baptized those who responded to his preaching in the river Jordan (Luke 3:3f.). John preached the need for baptism and repentance from sin. Baptism marked a public, social expression of a new life.

Jesus was baptized by John the Baptist (Mark 1:9–11; John 1:32–34). In that act, Jesus was identifying himself fully with sinners, though he himself was sinless. He was choosing to obey God and embracing the mission that God set before him. His suffering love on behalf of others ultimately led to the cross and his death (Luke 12:50).

In the early church, followers of Jesus received the "baptism of the Holy Spirit" and were called to be witnesses to Jesus as the Messiah throughout the whole earth (Acts 1:5; Matt. 28:16–20). Baptism with water was the sign of one's acceptance of Jesus, desire to repent, and commitment to live a new life as a follower of Jesus as the Christ (Acts 2:37–38, 41; 8:12). The Holy Spirit is linked with baptism (Acts 9:17–18; 11:16) and baptism is carried out "in the name of the Lord Jesus" (Acts 8:16; 19:5) or "in the name of Jesus Christ" (Acts 2:38; 10:48).

We are not told in the biblical accounts what mode of baptism was used with adult converts. It was perhaps dipping or pouring or perhaps complete submersion under water. The Greek term *baptizein*, "to baptize," has the sense of "immerse," "sink," or plunge into water. It graphically portrays the death of the "old self" and the rising to a new life—a new creation (2 Cor. 5:17). Sin is forgiven, righteousness in Jesus Christ is given, and the Holy Spirit is received (Acts 2:38). Baptism marks the Christian experience of salvation "through the water of rebirth and renewal by the Holy Spirit" (Titus 3:5).[8]

Union with Christ

The writings of Paul reveal his assumption that all believers in Jesus as the Christ have been baptized. For Paul, being "baptized into Christ Jesus" (Rom. 6:3) is the decisive event that unites a believer with Christ. Paul wrote to the Galatians: "As many of you as were baptized into Christ have clothed your-selves with Christ" (Gal. 3:27). This decisive event unites believers with Christ and with one another, shattering all social distinctions and smashing all artifi-cial barriers. For Paul continues: "There is no longer Jew or Greek, there is no longer slave or free, there is no longer male and female; for all of you are one in Christ Jesus" (Gal. 3:28). It is Jesus Christ who unites all and draws those who believe into union with himself: "for in Christ Jesus you are all children of God through faith" (Gal. 3:26). Baptism means the beginning of a new life in faith as believers are drawn into unity with each other and union with Christ.

Union with Christ in Death and Resurrection

The ultimate importance of this union with Christ for Paul is that baptism means believers are united with Jesus Christ in his own death and resurrec-tion. More than a simple social unity is involved here. The baptism that unites us with Christ and with each other is more that just some cultural cement that binds disparate persons together. The union is a theological unity and is indis-soluble because it is held together by the power of God's Spirit. In Romans 6:1–10, Paul relates Jesus' own death and resurrection to the dying and rising of those who are in union with him. He writes: "Do you not know that all of us who have been baptized into Christ Jesus were baptized into his death?" If this is true, says Paul, then the next step is: "Therefore we have been buried with him by baptism into death, so that, just as Christ was raised from the dead by the glory of the Father, so we too might walk in newness of life" (Rom. 6:3–4).

Baptism has startling ramifications for the everyday life of the Christian. It marks a new beginning, a new existence, a new way of living and a new way of understanding who we are. Now we are the "children of God" (Rom. 8:14, 16), reconciled with God through the death and resurrection of our Lord Jesus Christ (Rom. 5:8–11). Christian baptism is a counterpart to the Jewish rite of circumcision, which is the sign of the covenant made with Abraham (Gen. 17:11; Col. 2:11–13). It is a "spiritual circumcision" in Christ (Col. 2:11; Rom. 2:25–29), a "circumcision of the heart" (Deut. 10:16; Jer. 4:4), which occurs when "you were buried with him in baptism" so that "you were also raised with him through faith in the power of God, who raised him from the dead" (Col. 2:12). The one baptism that all Christians experience unites us with each other and with Jesus Christ in his death and resurrection. For, said Paul: "There is one body and one Spirit, just as you were called to the one hope of your calling, one Lord, one faith, one baptism, one God and Father of all, who is above all and through all and in all" (Eph. 4:4–6). Baptism binds us to Christ and each other in the church—the "body of Christ" (1 Cor. 12:27)—and opens the doors to new life for those whose life is "hidden with Christ in God" (Col. 3:3).[9]

Christian Tradition

The church's understandings of Christian baptism have grown through the centuries. The first theologian to write a special work on baptism was Tertullian in the third century. In *On Baptism* he argued that baptism bestows the gifts of forgiveness of sins, deliverance from death, regeneration, and the gift of the Holy Spirit. He believed that baptism was necessary for salvation. He indicates that church practice is to administer it to children, though he preferred baptism to be postponed until children reach an age of discretion.

In the Eastern church infant baptism was also practiced. Bishop Cyprian urged that children be baptized as soon as possible after birth. He said that the infant "approaches that much more easily to the reception of the forgiveness of sins because the sins remitted to him are not his own, but those of another." By this Cyprian was referring to the sin of Adam, since he believed that from Adam the infant had "contracted the contagion of the ancient death."[10]

Augustine

The influence of Augustine on the doctrine of baptism was also strong. His heavy stress on the inherited guilt of sin from our first parents (see above, chap. 7) led him to advocate infant baptism. Augustine believed that in baptism a person received a spiritual seal—the image of Christ—the Holy Spirit, and the seal of the Spirit, which assure forgiveness of sin and eternal life. He distinguished between the act of baptism itself and its effects. For baptism to be effective, faith must be present.

> Yet how can infants have faith? Augustine's answer was that the sacrament of baptism is one thing, the conversion of the heart is another; but the salvation of [humanity] is effected by these two. If one is missing, we are not bound to suppose that the other is absent: in an infant, baptism can exist without conversion; in the penitent thief, conversion without baptism. . . . [T]here can be conversion of the heart when baptism has not been received, but not when baptism has been rejected.[11]

In Augustine's view, the elect who receive baptism receive its full effects: the grace of God's illumination and justification. They are united with Christ by faith, freed from death and reconciled with God. In the case of infants, the effects of baptism become obvious in later years as the infant appropriates the promises of God in the covenant.

Middle Ages

The Roman Catholic church in the Middle Ages adopted Augustine's basic views about baptism being a "remedy" for original sin. Both infants and adults are to be baptized. Hugo of St. Victor defined baptism as "water made holy by the word of God for washing away sins." Pope Eugene IV indicated that baptism conveys "the remission of all original and actual sin, also of every penalty which is due for that sin."[12] The great theologian Thomas Aquinas went on to assert that through baptism one also "secures grace and powers," which accompany a "character" bestowed in baptism that enables Christians to go beyond their natural, human abilities. These included the power to resist temptation as well as the Christian virtues of faith, hope, and love. These virtues enable Christians to believe in God's revelation, hope for what God has promised to us, and to love God above all things. In baptism also are imparted the "gifts of the Holy Spirit."

Though God bestows these "powers" in baptism, the Roman church taught that humans must cooperate and use them. The use of the powers or virtues is "grace." The more persons resist temptation and cooperate in the use of their powers, the more grace they receive. This process of justification and sanctification must proceed in order to lead to eternal life. All persons begin in the same place—with the sacrament of baptism.[13]

Luther

The preceding approach to baptism was challenged by the Protestant Reformation and the teachings of Martin Luther. Luther believed the Roman view presented a wrong understanding of salvation itself—the issue that he objected to most strongly in his protests against the Roman Catholic church. For Luther, salvation or justification was an occurrence occasioned by faith in Jesus Christ. Sanctification means the growth in faith in which humans have a part. But for Luther, humans do not perform "works"—such as participation in the sacraments—to gain their salvation in the first place. Salvation is a gift bestowed by God.

For Luther, the Holy Spirit uses the water of baptism in conjunction with the Word of God to bring regeneration. The heart is washed clean and one's whole human nature is transformed, bringing forgiveness of sins, deliverance from death and the devil, and "eternal salvation to all who believe as the Word and promise of God declares." The Holy Spirit enters one's life in baptism, and grace is granted to those who have faith and believe in Jesus Christ. Luther goes on to say in his "Small Catechism" that "it is not the water that produces these effects, but the Word of God connected with the water, and our faith which relies on the Word of God connected with the water. For without the Word of God the water is merely water and no Baptism."[14] The Christian struggles throughout life against the recurring power of evil. But the power of the Spirit is the spiritual weapon that enables the "new life" in Jesus Christ to triumph. Luther saw the Christian life as a daily baptism. For, he said, "as we have once obtained forgiveness of sins in Baptism, so forgiveness remains day by day as long as we live."[15]

Reformed Emphases

The Reformed tradition has agreed with the Roman Catholic and the Lutheran traditions in seeing baptism as a distinctive act by which one is incorporated into the body of Christ, the church. It has also seen infant baptism as an appropriate form of baptism, grounded in God's covenant promises made to believers and to their children.

Sign and Seal

The terms "sign" and "seal" have been important in Reformed thought to indicate the nature of what occurs in Christian baptism.[16] Baptism is a sacramental action. A sacrament is, as Augustine put it, an "outward sign of an inward grace." It is an outward expression of a spiritual reality. Reformed theology has seen two sacraments for the church, both commanded by Christ: baptism and the Lord's Supper. Through a sacrament, God graciously communicates the reality of God's redeeming message of love through outward and visible means. They are "visible words" that convey God's promises, as if God had painted a picture. They supplement the proclaimed word of God and are, as one scholar has put it, "gracious concessions to our physical nature and therefore not to be neglected. Word and sacrament, correctly understood, fit naturally together." For "on the one hand, the sacraments make the promises clearer to us; on the other hand, they stand in constant need of the word to make us understand their meaning."[17] Sacraments are called a "means of grace," an "instrument" God uses to convey the gospel of Jesus Christ.

So with baptism. Baptism is defined in the Westminster Confession as "a sign and seal of the covenant of grace, of [one's] ingrafting into Christ, of regeneration, of remission of sins, and of [one's] giving up unto God, through Jesus Christ, to walk in newness of life."[18] Baptism is the symbol of our adoption into the family of God, to be children of God's grace. As Calvin put it, "baptism is the sign of the initiation by which we are received into the society of the church, in order that, engrafted in Christ, we may be reckoned among God's children."[19]

The power of baptism is lifelong. While baptism cleanses us of prebaptismal sins, by God's grace, it also has a continuing effect. It is a "token of cleansing for the whole of life!" Again, said Calvin,

> we must realize that at whatever time we are baptized, we are once for all washed and purged for our whole life. Therefore, as often as we fall away, we ought to recall the memory of our baptism and fortify our mind with it, that we may always be sure and confident of the forgiveness of sins. For, though baptism, administered only once, seemed to have passed, it was still not destroyed by subsequent sins.[20]

This approach has a very practical application for believers since this doctrine of baptism is "only given to sinners who groan, wearied and oppressed by their own sins, in order that they may have something to lift them up and comfort them, so as not to plunge into confusion and despair."[21]

Baptism, as a sacrament, is an outward visible "sign" that attests to God's gracious goodwill toward us. Calvin indicates that sacraments are "testimonies of grace and salvation from the Lord." They are also "signs" of our outward profession of faith, of our loyalty to God. As Calvin continued, "for us in turn they are marks of profession, by which we openly swear allegiance to God, binding ourselves in fealty to him."[22]

Baptism is also a "seal." Royal decrees and government documents were "sealed" in ancient times. When the seal was affixed, the document had authority. In the sacraments—in baptism—the Holy Spirit seals God's promises to those who believe in Jesus Christ so that all the benefits of the gospel are theirs as they enter into the covenant family of faith.[23] The Holy Spirit uses the outward "washing" (or sprinkling) in baptism to establish inwardly the promises of Jesus Christ. The sacrament, or outward action, as a seal does not "confer efficacy upon God's promise as if it were invalid of itself," but the seal of the sacrament serves "only to confirm it [the promise] to us."[24]

Infant Baptism

In Reformed thought, baptism is seen as the New Testament counterpart to circumcision, given as a sign of the covenant to Abraham.[25] Circumcision is a visible expression of one's incorporation into Israel as the covenant community of God's people. So, now, in Jesus Christ, baptism is the outward, visible sign of the "new covenant" (Jer. 31:31–34; 1 Cor. 11:23–26) that God has made with the believers and their children in the community called "church."[26]

This covenant theology of recognizing God's gracious goodness in extending salvation in Jesus Christ has led Reformed believers to stress infant baptism as appropriate since children of believers are also included in the covenant of God's grace in Christ.[27] Heinrich Bullinger wrote:

> When God established the eternal covenant with Abraham, he made it clear that children were to be included in it saying: I shall be your God and the God of your children. It is therefore that children when they are eight days old are to be marked with circumcision as a sign of the covenant. From this it follows that today God is not only the God of adults who are able to come to him in faith and make a confession of faith, but also the God of their children as well. From the standpoint, therefore, of grace and the promise of God they ought to be included in the number of believers.[28]

Bullinger and other Reformed theologians pointed out that Jesus said little children were in God's reign (Mark 10:14), and he indicated that children could have faith (Matt. 18:6). Paul clearly taught that the new sacrament of the covenant was baptism, which replaces circumcision (Col. 2:11–12), and he himself baptized whole households (1 Cor. 1:16; Acts 16:33), in which children must have been included. Baptism, concluded Bullinger, is "a sign of the people of God and the seal of the covenant."[29] Thus emerged the picture of baptism as "a sign of God's gracious promise to the child that the cleansing signified by the sacrament will be accomplished inwardly by the Holy Spirit."[30] Calvin thought that children should be baptized since it follows that

> the children of believers are baptized not in order that they who were previously strangers to the church may then for the first time become children of God, but rather that, because by the blessing of the promise they already belonged to the body of Christ, they are received into the church with this solemn sign.[31]

In sum, the early Reformed theologians who shaped the Reformed tradition saw that "even before the children of believers made a confession of faith, even before they were old enough to make a decision, the Holy Spirit was at work within them applying to them the benefits of redemption in Christ."[32] As John Oecolampadius put it: "Christ washed us from our sins by his blood and in this grace our children also participate."[33]

These Reformed understandings distinguished the Reformed faith from the Anabaptists, who taught only "believer's baptism." They rejected infant baptism because in their view baptism should be administered only to those who profess faith in Christ, and infants are not able to do so.

Yet the Reformed were "quite willing to admit the existence of faith in children before the development of understanding."[34] This view, coupled with a strong theology of the covenant of grace into which children of believers are born, provided a theological justification for the practice of infant baptism. Infant baptism points to the primacy of divine grace in that with the baptism of babies we are reminded that "our salvation rests not on any knowledge or work or experience or decision of our own, but entirely on the grace of God."[35] All persons regardless of age are as helpless as infants before God. Yet God takes the initiative in salvation and draws us by faith into the covenant community. God's promise of grace precedes any human decision to be baptized. For adults as well as children, baptism is a sign of grace and a means of grace. Baptism is a sign that God's grace is being received. The outward action of baptism is an act of God, given by God. The sign is not an "empty sign." It is "the promise of God behind the sign which makes it a true sign."[36] As the Geneva Confession (1536) put it: "Baptism is an external sign by which our Lord testifies that he desires to receive us for his children, as members of his Son Jesus."[37] The Heidelberg Catechism summarizes it well when it asks if infants are to be baptized. The Catechism answers:

> Yes, because they, as well as their parents, are included in the covenant and belong to the people of God. Since both redemption from sin through the blood of Christ and the gift of faith from the Holy Spirit are promised to these children no less than to their parents, infants are also by baptism, as a sign of the covenant, to be incorporated into the Christian church and distinguished from the children of unbelievers. This was done in the old Covenant by circumcision. In the New Covenant baptism has been instituted to take its place.[38]

In the twentieth century, Reformed theologian Karl Barth moved away from the traditional view of the appropriateness of infant baptism. Barth argued that the practice of infant baptism has led to the view that persons can basically be Christians at birth, as one is a citizen of a country by virtue of birth. Barth believed this lessened the effect of divine grace since baptism should be a free, responsible, and obedient act in which there is a human response to God's divine gift in Jesus Christ.[39]

While Reformed churches have not given up infant baptism in response to Barth's critique, his concerns are valid ones and lead to theological reflection in the churches on the nature and practice of baptism. In light of Barth's views, Daniel Migliore has rightly written that

> Common to both infant and adult baptism is the affirmation that we are recipients of the gift of God's love and are claimed for God's service. Just as in the Lord's Supper we are fed by the bread of life and the cup of salvation, so baptism declares that something is done *for* us.

> Whether baptized as children or adults, our baptism signifies primarily what God has graciously done for us, and it is upon this that faith rests.[40]

Together, infant and adult baptism convey a fuller meaning for baptism than either exclusively, alone. The obedient response of faith is highlighted in adult baptism—persons confessing their allegiance to Jesus Christ as Lord and Savior while receiving forgiveness of sins and new life. In infant baptism, God's loving, sovereign initiative in extending the covenant of grace to believers and their children is demonstrated. Infants are loved by God and adopted into God's covenant family—helpless and weak as they are. When parents and the church congregation make vows to nurture the child and raise the child to come to confess Jesus Christ as Lord and Savior, the whole people of God as the Christian community are responsibly binding themselves to the infant as "fellow heirs" and "sharers in the promise in Christ Jesus through the gospel" (Eph. 3:6; cf. Gal. 3:29). Baptism "once received continues for all of life, and is a perpetual sealing of our adoption."[41]

Contemporary Significance

Ecumenical discussions today seek to overcome older barriers among churches about the nature of baptism and its practices. While these efforts have not brought agreements, they have opened new avenues of exploration and have helped Christian communities reflect upon and declare what is essential in their views of baptism.

The 1982 World Council of Churches document, *Baptism, Eucharist and Ministry*, sought to draw an ecumenical consensus on these three important topics. In the section on baptism, the document highlights the clusters of New Testament meaning that are associated with the meaning of baptism. These continue to serve as guiding lights as churches consider the significance of baptism and its meaning today. Baptism is

1. Participation in Christ's Death and Resurrection (Rom. 6:3–5; Col. 2:12).
2. Conversion, Pardoning, and Cleansing (1 Cor. 6:11; Heb. 10:22).
3. The Gift of the Spirit (John 3:5; Acts 2:38).
4. Incorporation into the Body of Christ (Eph. 4:4–6).
5. The Sign of God's Reign (Rom. 8:23).

These images, which vary in their emphases, point to the one reality: that baptism is "the sign of new life through Jesus Christ. It unites the one baptized with Christ and with his people."[42]

Yet this ecumenical document also highlights issues that continue to divide the Christian community among its varying traditions. One dividing issue is the relation of baptism and salvation. In baptism, does God convey the new birth in Christ? One scholar has noted:

> Orthodox, Catholics, and most Reformation churches have histori-cally maintained that baptism is the act in which a woman or man is born again in Christ and is forgiven of past sins. Reformed confessions and Methodist doctrinal statements allow that although this may be generally asserted, the moment of new birth may be separate from the moment when water is applied. Distinctive of many Evangelical churches is the belief that only by affective and explicit faith (conver-sion) is a person born again in Christ.[43]

This distinct theological issue continues to show the divergences among church traditions.

A second issue of dispute is the propriety of the church's practicing infant baptism. Here, Orthodox, Roman Catholics, and most Protestants practice infant baptism while Anabaptists, Baptists, Restorationists, and many others who refer to themselves as "Evangelical" require a person to be able to make a confession of faith as the basis for baptism.

A third area of disagreement is the mode of baptism. Orthodox, most Bap-tists and Restorationists, as well as many other Evangelical and Free-church traditions have maintained that immersion must be the mode for a baptism to be valid. Roman Catholics and many Protestants have permitted sprinkling or pouring as well.[44]

As churches consider their historic traditions and wrestle with what bap-tism means in contemporary contexts, the importance of Christian baptism will become more and more prominent. The meaning and ongoing signifi-cance of the baptismal experience is well captured in The Confession of 1967, which says: "Christian baptism marks the receiving of the same Spirit by all [Christ's] people. Baptism with water represents not only cleansing from sin, but a dying with Christ and a joyful rising with him to new life. It commits all Christians to die each day to sin and to live for righteousness."[45]

Questions for Reflection

1. What does your baptism mean to you?
2. Why is infant baptism important?
3. In what ways is baptism related to the covenant?
4. What ethical obligations does one assume when one is baptized?
5. In what ways might Reformed churches put more emphasis on the mean-ing of baptism for those who are baptized and for the congregation?

14

The Lord's Supper:
Nourishing Our Faith

One of the sad ironies of Christian history is that the Lord's Supper has been one of the most divisive doctrines among Christian churches. The very meal that Jesus shared with his disciples as his last meal and in which they were drawn together in a unity with him has become a source of disunity among his followers.

One indication of this disunity is simply the different names used in churches to describe this meal. In the Roman Catholic tradition, it is called the Eucharist. In Protestant traditions, it tends to be called "the Lord's Supper" or "Communion." Other practices vary as well. The way the elements are received is different. Some receive the bread and dip it into the cup (intinction); others partake of each element separately. In some traditions, people come forward to receive the elements from the priest or minister. In others, the elements are passed through the congregation by church leaders or elders. Some churches use big loaves of bread and real wine. In others, the bread is a tiny square and the "wine" is grape juice. In some churches festive music is played. In others the mood is solemn and somber.

So practices vary, and theological understandings vary. Historically, some of the fiercest battles in the church have been waged over this common meal. Even today, a sure way to arouse the ire of some church members is to suggest a change in the way the Lord's Supper is administered. Sharing in the Supper with those of another Christian tradition is still a stretch for some in our churches. On the ecumenical level, churches are divided and their theologies of the Lord's Supper or Eucharist is still one of the sticking points.

Biblical Bases

During the last night of Jesus' earthly life, he gathered his disciples together to share at meal in an upper room. Scholars differ over whether or not this was an actual Passover meal.[1] Yet all four Gospels record the meal and Paul's description of it in 1 Corinthians 11:23–26 is very familiar to most Christians who have celebrated the "Lord's Supper" (1 Cor. 11:20)—a supper belonging to the Lord. The celebration of the meal is continued because Jesus commanded it (1 Cor. 11:25).

It is often noted that the Lord's Supper gathers together the three tenses of our human existence—past, present, and future. The past comes into the present as God's creative and redemptive work is celebrated by the Christian community around a common meal. Jesus' command to "Do this in remembrance of me" brings the reality of Jesus' life, saving death, and liberating resurrection into the minds and hearts of those who share the Supper. The present tense shares what is happening now, in the Supper, as Jesus' promises that "This is my body that is for you . . ." (11:24) and "This cup is the new covenant in my blood" (11:25) are proclaimed. The future is anticipated in the promise that this Supper is to be celebrated "until he comes"—conveying the Christian hope of Jesus' return and ultimate triumph in the ultimate reign of God. A background image here is the great "messianic banquet" at the end of the age anticipated in the Hebrew Scriptures and by Jesus' teachings.[2]

The New Testament communities who gathered to celebrate the Lord's Supper did so initially in the context of a common, communal meal. Accounts in the book of Acts speak of "the breaking of bread" (Acts 2:42–46). In Troas, when Paul was meeting with believers, this was done in a "room upstairs" (Acts 20:7–11), recalling that Jesus' last meal was also in such a room (Luke 22:12; cf. Mark 14:15).[3] Paul became upset with practices in Corinth where some were being excluded from the Lord's Supper and social divisions were rife. Some went ahead and ate while others went hungry and still others became drunk (1 Cor. 11:21). Paul hotly asks, "Do you show contempt for the church of God and humiliate those who have nothing?" (11:22; see 1 Cor. 8–14; esp. chaps. 10 and 11). For Paul, this violated the essence of the Lord's Supper (1 Cor. 11:27, 33–34), which should celebrate the "oneness" of the body of Christ" (1 Cor. 10:17) and the Christ who "loved us and gave himself up for us" (Eph. 5:2; cf. 5:25; Gal. 2:20).[4] Participating in the Lord's Supper has very strong ethical dimensions.

The experience of Jesus' early disciples, after his resurrection, was that Jesus revealed himself to them at meals. The travelers on the road to Emmaus found that when the stranger—who was really the risen Christ—joined them at their meal, he "took bread, blessed and broke it, and gave it to them." The result was that "their eyes were opened, and they recognized him" (Luke 24:30, 31). In John's Gospel, the risen Christ invites his fishermen disciples to "Come and have breakfast"—and they knew that "it was the Lord" (John 21:12–13).

These post-Easter meals are revelatory events. They compel the disciples to believe that Jesus is no longer dead, but resurrected. He is a living presence to his people who shares with them his own self—as the "bread of life" (John 6:35, 48)—as he is the host at meals. Throughout the Gospels, women and men are found to be eating and drinking with Jesus.[5] As they do, the presence of the Messiah is made known to them. Jesus shared meals with sinners and hated Pharisees (Matt. 9:11; Mark 2:16; Luke 7:36), fed thousands of hungry people (Matt. 14:21; Mark 6:44), celebrated at wedding feasts (John 2:1–11) and banquets (Luke 5:29–39). When Jesus came to dine with Zacchaeus he could proclaim, "Today salvation has come to this house" (Luke 19:9). When early Christians celebrated the Lord's Supper they did so initially in the context of a Christian fellowship meal, called an *agapē* or "love feast." This was a full-fledged meal at which the elements of the Lord's Supper—the bread and the wine—were shared.[6] In this experience, the church found its faith was nourished by the presence of Jesus Christ made real in the Lord's Supper.[7]

Dimensions of the Supper

Among the many dimensions of the Supper, three concepts stand out.

1. *Covenant.* Luke records Jesus as saying that "This cup that is poured out for you is the new covenant in my blood" (Luke 22:20; cf. 1 Cor. 11:25). Jeremiah's prophecy that "The days are surely coming, says the LORD, when I will make a new covenant with the house of Israel and the house of Judah" (Jer. 31:31) is fulfilled here. Jesus' coming death is the "seal" of the covenant, now made in an eternal way with believers. The Supper is the guarantee of God's promise to Jeremiah that, in the new covenant, "I will put my law within them, and I will write it on their hearts; and I will be their God, and they shall be my people" (Jer. 31:33). In the new covenant, the Lord shall be "known" and God promises, "I will forgive their iniquity, and remember their sin no more" (Jer. 31:34). The death of Jesus seals the new covenant promises.

2. *Remembrance.* In the Supper, those who celebrate "remember" Jesus Christ. The body and blood of Jesus nourish his disciples as believers eat and drink and thus receive the benefits of what Jesus has done for them by his death. As reported in John's Gospel,

> So Jesus said to them, "Very truly, I tell you, unless you eat the flesh of the Son of Man and drink his blood, you have no life in you. Those who eat my flesh and drink my blood have eternal life, and I will raise them up on the last day; for my flesh is true food and my blood is true drink. Those who eat my flesh and drink my blood abide in me, and I in them. Just as the living Father sent me, and I live because of the Father, so whoever eats me will live because of me. This is the bread that came down from heaven, not like that which your ancestors ate, and they died. But the one who eats this bread will live forever." (John 6:53–58)

Participation in the Lord's Supper is participation in the nourishment of faith that Jesus Christ himself provides. "Remembering Jesus" is a real and powerful experience. It is not intellectual alone. It means entering into the whole life and death and resurrection of Jesus himself and receiving the blessings of faith that Jesus gives to those who celebrate the Supper.

3. *Reign of God.* By participating in the Supper, Jesus' followers "proclaim the Lord's death until he comes" (1 Cor. 11:26). Jesus said to his disciples that he would not eat the Passover or drink "the fruit of the vine" again "until the kingdom of God comes" (Luke 22:18; cf. 22:16, 29–30; Matt. 26:29; Mark 14:25). The festive messianic banquet is in view. The celebration of the Lord's Supper in the church is a prefiguring of the coming feast (see Isa. 25:6). It is "the continuation and celebration of the administration of salvation directed to the future, which was inaugurated by Christ's coming."[8] By participating in the Supper, the church congregation (the "body of Christ," 1 Cor. 12:27; cf. Eph. 4:12) is "well aware that the Lord's Supper is but a foretaste and pledge of the marriage feast of the Lamb on a new earth and under a new heaven in which righteousness dwells." Then, "we will *see* and *be* what now we only *believe*, namely, that Jesus is the food of eternal life and that we have already passed from death unto life."[9] Eating and drinking with Jesus is an "eternal feasting—as eternal as the life we have in the resurrected body of Christ."[10] The Lord's Supper is thus a "sign and proclamation" that all persons "may and must eat and drink with Jesus in faith, love, and hope."[11]

Christian Tradition

We know of Christian practices of the Lord's Supper from liturgies of the ancient church. The Supper was central to the worshiping life of early Christian communities. For one thing, it was a mark of solidarity among the various churches that were spreading throughout the Mediterranean world. The unity of all believers in Jesus Christ, the "oneness" of the church, is captured in the Lord's Supper celebration.[12] Bishop Cyprian of Carthage (d. 258), a strong proponent of the unity of the church, wrote:

> When the Savior takes the bread that is made from the coming together of many grains, and calls it his body, he shows the unity of our people, which the bread symbolizes. And when he takes the wine that is pressed from many grapes and grains and forms a single liquid, he shows that our block is composed of many who have been brought into unity.[13]

Other early writers, such as Justin Martyr (ca. 100–ca. 165) and Irenaeus (ca. 130–ca. 200) as well as early Christian liturgies saw the Supper as for those who had been baptized and as a celebration of the cohesiveness and unity of the church. An important theme persists: that "because Christ has united us to himself through the eucharistic elements, we are also united to the ecclesial body of Christ and, thus, to one another."[14]

With the separation of the "agape meal" from the celebration of the Supper, a shift in emphasis began to occur. The sense of Christ's presence in the community at the communal meal changed toward emphasizing the elements of ritual with the bread and wine. Two important ways of understanding the nature of the Supper and the relation of Christ to the bread and wine emerged.

1. *Realist Theory*. In this view, the bread and wine undergo a transformation after they are consecrated. When the Holy Spirit is invoked (Gr. *epiklesis*; "invocation"), the elements are changed and become the body and blood of Christ. As Cyril of Alexandria put it:

> For lest we be stunned with horror on seeing flesh and blood set upon the holy tables of the churches, God condescends to our weakness and sends the power of life into the elements and transforms them into the power of His own flesh, that we may have and partake of them as a means of life, and that the body of life may become in us a life-giving seed. And doubt not that this is true, since He clearly says: 'This is my body' and 'This is my blood'; rather, in faith receive the Saviour's word, for He is the Truth and does not lie.[15]

As Jesus turned water into wine at the wedding in Cana (John 2:1–11), "is it incredible that he should change wine into blood?" asked Cyril.

2. *Symbolic View*. An alternative view is also found in the early church. Here, the elements are signs of realities that can only be genuinely apprehended by faith. These theologians interpreted Jesus' words about eating his flesh and drinking his blood (see John 6) in a spiritual sense. The "flesh" and "blood" to be eaten and drunk are Jesus' teachings. The elements in the Eucharist are not changed. Theodoret wrote:

> For even after the consecration the mystic symbols do not depart from their own nature. For they remain in their previous substance and figure and form; and they are visible and tangible as they were before. But they are regarded as being what they have become, and they are believed so to be, and they are worshipped as being those things which they are believed to be.[16]

Augustine's formula, "Believe, and you have already eaten," represents this symbolic tradition.[17]

Middle Ages

By the Middle Ages, these two streams of understanding had become distinct and systematized. Two eucharistic controversies—one between Paschasius

Radbertus and Ratramnus in the ninth century, and one between Berengar and Lanfranc in the eleventh century—aided this development.[18]

The most significant medieval probing of "how" the elements in the Eucharist could be called the "body and blood of Christ" was done by the theologian Peter Lombard. Lombard argued that the "substance" (inner reality) of the bread and wine is changed while the "accidents" (outward appearance) remain the same. This view became known as "transubstantiation." It was made the official view of the Roman Catholic church at the Fourth Lateran Council (1215) and reaffirmed at the Council of Lyons (1274).

The church taught that, when the words of consecration are spoken ("This is my body broken for you"; "This is my blood shed for you"), the body and blood of Christ become "truly contained in the Sacrament of the Altar under the species of bread and wine, transubstantiated by the divine power—the bread into his body and the wine into his blood."[19] The body and blood of Christ are present in a different mode than as a physical object. The bread and wine appear outwardly in the same form ("accidents"); but their inner reality or "substance" (what gives something its identity) is transformed into the body and blood of Jesus Christ.[20] One perceives this change of substance, said Thomas Aquinas, "neither by sense nor by imagination, but only by the mind, which is called 'the eye of the soul.'" The mind is aided by faith and it is faith that makes real recognition possible.[21] The Council of Trent in 1551 further affirmed that "by the consecration of the bread and wine a change is brought about of the whole substance of the bread into the substance of the body of Christ our Lord, and of the whole substance of the wine into the substance of His blood."[22] There is a "real presence" of Jesus Christ in the Eucharist, though "the Saviour himself sits always at the right hand of the Father in heaven according to his natural mode of existence." How Christ can be both in heaven and "present" in the bread and wine of the Eucharist is a mystery. But, said the Council of Trent, "although we can scarcely express it in words, we can conclude [it] is possible for God, and ought most constantly to believe."[23]

Luther

The sixteenth-century Protestant Reformation marked a rejection of the transubstantiation views of the Roman Catholic church. Martin Luther's understandings of the Lord's Supper developed through several stages during the course of his career.[24] Yet through it all, Luther believed that the real presence of the body of Christ was necessary in the Lord's Supper in order for salvation and the forgiveness of sins to occur. Yet Luther considered transubstantiation to be philosophically inadequate and a "monstrous idea" with no biblical support whatsoever. Yet Luther did want to maintain what transubstantiation sought to guarantee: that Jesus Christ is present in the sacrament. Through this presence, forgiveness and salvation can occur.

Over against the Roman view, Luther taught that Christ is bodily present in the Lord's Supper and yet that the elements—the bread and wine—are untransformed. There is a sacramental, spiritual, and real presence of Christ—but not a change of substance. Luther used an analogy from Christology to show this. "What is true in regard to Christ is also true in regard to the sacrament," said Luther. Namely, the church confesses that in Jesus Christ, "the Word became flesh" (John 1:14). The eternal God has become a human being in the man Jesus. So also, in the Lord's Supper, the church proclaims that God dwells "in" and "under" the elements of the bread and wine. Thus, maintained Luther, we may say, "The body of Christ is this bread" or "This bread is the body of Christ." It does not matter that the philosophers cannot grasp this, proclaimed Luther, for "the Holy Spirit is greater than Aristotle"![25]

Reformed Emphases

Luther's views of the presence of Christ in the Supper eventually came to constitute "the major point of difference between the traditions of Lutheran and Reformed theology."[26] Luther had controversies with the Reformed theologian Zwingli of Zurich, whose views were likewise criticized by Calvin. So it is possible to recognize two strands within the Reformed tradition, both of which disagree with Luther's views on the Lord's Supper, especially on the issue of the "real presence of Christ."

Zwingli

While Luther criticized transubstantiation, he did seek to maintain what it focused on—the real presence of Christ in the Supper. Zwingli, however, emphasized the more "subjective" or personal aspect. Zwingli stressed faith and "remembrance." While with Luther, "the emphasis falls on *Christ's* promise and testament to us; with Zwingli, [it is] on *our* remembering of Christ's sacrifice."[27] Zwingli wrote: "Bread and wine are not transubstantiated, and profit nothing, if faith is not present. Faith is the essential thing in the Supper. Faith is the organ of appropriation. The Supper strengthens feeble faith, as the bread sustains the body."[28] Zwingli made a sharp distinction between the "earthly" and the "heavenly," between the "visible" and "material" world and the "spiritual" world. He did not believe that God's Spirit could be tied down to any particular rituals or ceremonies or sacraments. As a result, the physical elements—the bread and the wine in the Lord's Supper (as the water in baptism)—are symbolic and must point beyond themselves to a higher, salvation-giving reality. The elements themselves could never be bearers of the divine salvation.

Zwingli's interpretation of the words of institution—"This is my body"— was that the phrase is a metaphor. The word "is" should be understood as "signifies," Zwingli contended. Jesus often spoke metaphorically, as when he said, "I am the gate" (John 10:7, 10:9), or "I am the good shepherd" (John 10:11, 14). Zwingli made a sharp distinction between the "sign" and the "thing signified" (a distinction also made by Augustine). In the Lord's Supper, believers confess their faith in Christ and make a public testimony to what has happened in Jesus Christ. The sacrament is a "badge" of faith. Yet the elements themselves—the sacrament itself—cannot make Christ "present" and cannot convey salvation. The celebration of the sacrament is the remembrance of that which has already occurred in Jesus Christ. Jesus is spiritually present in the sacrament in "contemplation, faith, hope, and love alone"—not physically so. The elements are signs, but are not themselves what the signs point toward. The Supper is an act of thanksgiving for the gospel; it does not offer the gospel itself.[29] Put in a nutshell: "For Luther, the decisive saying is, 'This is my body.' For Zwingli, it is, 'Do this in remembrance of me.'"[30]

When Zwingli and Luther met with others at Marburg in October 1529 to try to produce an agreement to unify the German and Swiss reform movements, they achieved a unified statement on fourteen of fifteen points. One part of the five parts of the fifteenth article on which no agreement could be reached, however, was "whether the true body and blood of Christ are bodily in the bread and wine." The famous exchange between Luther and Zwingli on this point highlighted the differences between the two theologians. For Luther, flesh and spirit can go together; the elements of bread and wine in the Lord's Supper can be used as a means for salvation. For Zwingli, flesh and spirit are radically different. The Spirit of God needs no material vehicle—such as bread and wine—in order to bring salvation. Christ's presence in the Supper can only be as faith contemplates and "remembers" him. This impasse was so severe that when Zwingli, with tears in his eyes, extended his hand to Luther, Luther withheld his own and said, "You have a different spirit."[31]

Calvin

Yet Zwingli's views were not followed by John Calvin or by the major Reformed confessions that followed. For Calvin, God has ordained the Lord's Supper, as a sacrament, as a means by which Jesus Christ with the benefits of Christ's death are imparted to those who receive the Supper in faith. The sacrament is given "for us" since Jesus said, "This is my body which is given *for you*." "This is my blood which is shed *for you*." Jesus is given for us, and in the elements we have "food for our spiritual life." Calvin put it this way:

> [F]rom the physical things set forth in the Sacrament we are led by a sort of analogy to spiritual things. Thus, when bread is given as a symbol of Christ's body, we must at once grasp this comparison: as bread nourishes, sustains, and keeps the life of our body, so Christ's body is the only food to invigorate and enliven our soul. When we see wine set forth as a symbol of blood, we must reflect on the benefits which wine imparts to the body, and so realize that the same are spiritually imparted to us by Christ's blood. These benefits are to nourish, refresh, strengthen, and gladden.[32]

Thus, for Calvin, not only do the elements in the Supper "represent" Christ's death for us, they also "present" it to us so that by eating and drinking in faith, we gain the benefits of the salvation Christ has accomplished. As Calvin put it:

> It is not, therefore, the chief function of the Sacrament simply and without higher consideration to extend to us the body of Christ. Rather, it is to seal and confirm that promise by which he testifies that his flesh is food indeed and his blood is drink [John 6:56], which feed us unto eternal life [John 6:55]. By this he declares himself to be the bread of life, of which he who eats will live forever [John 6:48, 50]. And to do this, the Sacrament sends us to the cross of Christ, where that promise was indeed performed and in all respects fulfilled.[33]

The Supper, like baptism, is a sacrament that is both a "sign" and a "seal." It is a "badge of faith" or sign to the world that we are believers (as Zwingli maintained). But it is more. It is also a sign that is a "seal"—that communicates to us the benefits of Jesus Christ of which the bread and wine are symbols. Calvin said, "But if it is true that a visible sign is given us to seal the gift of a thing invisible, when we have received the symbol of the body, let us no less surely trust that the body itself is also given to us."[34] This is what distinguished Calvin and many Reformed confessions from the view of Zwingli.[35]

Calvin (like Luther and Zwingli) rejected the Roman Catholic view of transubstantiation. While he recognized that some in the early church had used the term "conversion" to refer to the elements of the Supper, Calvin contended that their purpose was not to speak of the change in the "substance" of the elements, into the body and blood of Christ, but "to teach that the bread dedicated to the mystery is far different from common bread, and is now something else. But they all everywhere clearly proclaim that the Sacred Supper consists of two parts, the earthly and the heavenly; and they interpret the earthly part to be indisputably bread and wine."[36]

For Calvin, Jesus Christ is genuinely present in the Lord's Supper, but he is not physically or substantially present in the elements themselves.[37] Christ is present to the believer through faith, through the work of the Holy Spirit in the sacramental experience, and through the Word of God that is proclaimed in preaching. Like Augustine, Calvin saw a sacrament as a "visible word." It conveys the promises of faith. The Lord's Supper is a means of Christ's self-communication, of Christ's real presence. Christ communicates himself to believers through the signs (the bread and wine). In Calvin's view, "where the sign is, there also is the reality. Since Christ is the content of that reality—the 'substance' of the sacraments—the sign acts as a vehicle for the manifestation of Christ's presence to his people."[38]

This communication is possible by the work of the Holy Spirit, who lifts our "eyes and minds" to heaven to "seek Christ there in the glory of His Kingdom" and who "seals" the full benefits of Christ's death into the lives of believers who eat the bread and drink the cup.[39] Calvin interpreted the words of institution, "This is my body," figuratively and not literally.[40] Thus Christ can be spiritually present, though not physically or locally present ("in" or "around" and "under" the elements—as for the Roman Catholics and Luther). Those who partake of the bread and wine by faith, for Calvin, receive the gift of Jesus Christ himself.[41] By the Holy Spirit, believers receive a union with Christ by faith. This is the fruit of salvation, which "rests on faith in his [Christ's] death and resurrection" so that by "true partaking of him, his life passes into us and is made ours—just as bread when taken as food imparts vigor to the body."[42] Thus Calvin's views of the nature of the sacrament of the Lord's Supper and Christ's presence in the Lord's Supper stand distinct from the Roman Catholic, Lutheran, and Zwinglian positions.[43]

Contemporary Significance

The Lord's Supper is God's gracious gift to be received by faith and is a means by which God in Jesus Christ nourishes and strengthens our faith by the power of the Holy Spirit. Contemporary church traditions continue to reflect historic controversies and viewpoints. In large part this is due to the fact that we can never be rid of history and the fact that whenever theological doctrines are probed in order to be expressed, many of the same questions from the past will inevitably arise and will have a continuing relevance.

Whether any new breakthroughs, ecumenically, between Protestants and Roman Catholics—or between the Reformed and Lutherans, for example—will emerge still remains to be seen. Currently, Protestants are not permitted to share in the Eucharist in a Roman Catholic service. Some Protestant churches continue to "fence the table," meaning that only persons of that denomination or those who meet some particular requirement are invited to commune. All agree that "faith" is necessary for right participation in the sacrament. But disagreements continue about the nature of faith. Is it believing certain doctrines? Is it trust? Is faith possible for children? All these ongoing issues still divide churches.

In the Lord's Supper, liturgical changes adopted through the years have had and may continue to have significant effects in changing some perceptions about what is most central and what is less central to the celebration of the sacrament. In many mainline denominations a shift in emphasis has occurred in the last several decades. This is due in part, it seems, to new emphases in liturgical studies among scholars. In many places where the Lord's Supper is administered, the traditional atmosphere of somberness and sobriety has shifted to more joy and celebration. Some liturgical orders now place a renewed emphasis on the future or eschatological dimension of the Supper, with worshipers invited to the table with the words:

> Friends, this is the joyful feast of the people of God!
> They will come from east and west,
> and from north and south,
> and sit at table in the kingdom of God.[44]

Similarly, hymns used during the Lord's Supper today may include those that likewise strike a more festive note: "I Come with Joy" or "Let Us Talents and Tongues Employ."[45] The Confession of 1967 also strikes this note:

> The Lord's Supper is a celebration of the reconciliation of [people] with God and with one another, in which they joyfully eat and drink together at the table of their Savior. Jesus Christ gave his church this remembrance of his dying for sinful [persons] so that by participation in it they have communion with him and with all who shall be gathered to him. Partaking in him as they eat the bread and drink the wine in accordance with Christ's appointment, they receive from the risen and living Lord the benefits of his death and resurrection. They rejoice in the foretaste of the kingdom which he will bring to consummation at his promised coming, and go out from the Lord's Table with courage and hope for the service to which he has called them.[46]

Jesus prayed for his church "that they may be one" (John 17:22). Contemporary ecumenical discussions have sought to come to some agreements so that a more visible "outward unity" might be achieved. At some points documents have been constructed that seek the widest possible common ground and leave other more secondary questions aside, recognizing the variety of possible answers. This approach implicitly recognizes that there can be significant truth in alternative positions, even if these cannot be fully reconciled.[47] As we participate in communion we can focus on the wider unity sought by Christ, even as we continue our work for greater theological understandings.

The Lord's Supper as the meal commanded and initiated by Jesus is God's gracious provision through the Holy Spirit for Jesus' followers to receive the benefits of his death, be nourished by Christ's presence now, and to anticipate the coming fullness of the reign of God. Our perceptions of what happens at this "spiritual banquet" are important. Yet ultimately what occurs is a mystery and beyond all rational power to explain. Our theological affirmations can never convey the full reality. In the end, we can simply confess with Calvin when he discussed the presence of Christ in the Supper:

> Now, if anyone should ask me how this takes place, I shall not be ashamed to confess that it is a secret too lofty for either my mind to comprehend or my words to declare. And, to speak more plainly, I rather experience than understand it. Therefore, I here embrace without controversy the truth of God in which I may safely rest. He declares his flesh the food of my soul, his blood its drink [John 6:53 ff.]. I offer my soul to him to be fed with such food. In his Sacred Supper he bids me take, eat, and drink his body and blood under the symbols of bread and wine. I do not doubt that he himself truly presents them, and that I receive them.[48]

"Nothing remains," wrote Calvin, "but to break forth in wonder at this mystery, which plainly neither the mind is able to conceive nor the tongue to express."[49]

Questions for Reflection

1. What does it mean to you to "remember Jesus" in the Lord's Supper?

2. What would you tell a friend are the most important aspects of the Lord's Supper?

3. In what ways do you perceive the presence of Jesus Christ at the Lord's Supper?

4. In what ways might Reformed churches make their practice of the Lord's Supper a more joyful celebration?

5. What ethical obligations does one assume when one participates in the Lord's Supper?

15

Christian Life:
Growing in Faith

Someone asked a church deacon if he were a Christian. He replied, "In spots."
All of us must make the same confession. God has graciously come to us in
Jesus Christ, called us, given us faith and means of grace—yet our Christian
faith and Christian life is often "spotty." We have days of faithfulness and days
of failure. We begin in faith, gain nourishment for our faith—yet do not feel
that we grow in faith. On a larger scale, our Christian lives are lived in the context of the Christian church. The church itself is faithful and unfaithful. It
gives us birth, nourishes us, and then lets us down when it too will not grow
in accord with God's Spirit or is downright "un-Christian" in some of its attitudes and practices. The Christian life is a "mixed bag," a path of "zig-zag"
through the pressures and temptations of life. We know that if we are ever to
finish our course and ultimately live in God's reign, it will be solely by God's
loving and forgiving grace alone. We want to grow in our faith, but our frail-
ties and sins are often stumbling blocks along the way.

Biblical Bases

The people of God in the Hebrew Scriptures and the New Testament are
a people of faith. Regardless of what else is said or not said about us, we are
marked by faith.

The great model of faith in the Old Testament is Abraham. He heard
God's call and willingly obeyed (Gen. 12:1–3). He believed God's promise
that his descendants would be blessed and "the LORD reckoned it to him as
righteousness" (Gen. 15:6). When Abraham's faith was tested in the command to offer up his son Isaac, he obeyed (Gen. 22:1–19). Likewise, Moses,
when confronted with God in the burning bush and told to go to Pharaoh to
liberate the people, also believed God and obeyed (Ex. 3:1–12). The covenant

153

relationship of God and the people of Israel was based on faith and obedience. God would be faithful to the people and they were to be faithful to God: "And I will walk among you, and will be your God, and you shall be my people. I am the LORD your God who brought you out of the land of Egypt, to be their slaves no more" (Lev. 26:12–13). The Psalms convey the sense of faith as trust (Ps. 23:3, 4; 78:22; 106:24) since God is the one who "keeps faith forever" (Ps. 146:6). The Old Testament sense of faith is to hold something to be true, to believe, to trust, and fidelity.[1]

When asked, "What must we do to perform the works of God?" Jesus answered, "This is the work of God, that you believe in him whom he has sent" (John 6:28–29). In John's Gospel, the common Greek word for "faith" (*pistis*) does not occur, while the verb "to believe" (from *pisteuō*) occurs nearly one hundred times.[2] "That you may come to believe that Jesus is the Messiah, the Son of God, and that through believing you may have life in his name" is the expressed purpose of John's Gospel being written (20:31). Believing is central to the whole view of salvation in Jesus Christ and is a response to God's revelation (John 14:21) that leads to a knowledge of the truth (John 1:14, 17; 14:6). Since the one who is to be believed in is a person who embodies the truth—Jesus Christ—neither faith or knowledge can be primarily intellectual. The writer of John, as Paul does, speaks of faith as incorporating believers into the body of Christ, so they are "in Christ" (see Rom. 8:1–2; 2 Cor. 5:17–19; John 15:4–10) and thus united with him.

Faith, for Paul, is a new mode of existence. It is a coming to acceptance of the Christian gospel (Gr. *kerygma*; "message"; "proclamation"; see Rom. 10:17; 1 Cor. 1:21; 15:11, 14). Faith is "confessing with your lips that Jesus is Lord" and believing "in your heart that God raised him from the dead. . . . For one believes with the heart and so is justified, and one confesses with the mouth and so is saved" (Rom. 10:9–10).[3] Faith emerges by the work of the Holy Spirit (Gal. 3:14), and those who receive this gift are enabled to walk by the Spirit (Rom. 8:4) and be "guided by the Spirit" (Gal. 5:25). The union with Christ which is effected by the Spirit means that "it is no longer I who live, but it is Christ who lives in me. And the life I now live in the flesh I live by faith in the Son of God, who loved me and gave himself for me" (Gal. 2:20).

Faith must grow (2 Cor. 10:15). Faith is linked with love and hope (1 Cor. 13:13; Gal. 5:5–6; Eph. 1:15–18; Col. 1:4–5). Faith is one of the "fruit(s) of the Spirit" (Gal. 5:22–23), bestowed by God as a gift (Rom. 12:3; Eph. 2:8). It is a shorthand form for the whole Christian life: "For we walk by faith, not by sight" (2 Cor. 5:7). The Christian's growth in faith is a growth in holiness, called "sanctification" in the New Testament (Gr. *hagiasmos*).[4] It is the work of God by the Spirit within the believing community and within the believer (Gal. 5:22–25) and also the activity of individual Christians themselves (Rom.

12:1f.; 2 Cor. 7:1). God has willed for the church and Christian believers to be sanctified "entirely" (1 Thess. 5:23f.) as they "increase and abound in love for one another and for all" (1 Thess. 3:12). Jesus himself incarnates sanctification (1 Cor. 1:30). The ways by which faith, hope, and love increase are the various ways by which Christian discipleship in the church and the world are lived out. While some New Testament texts speak of being "perfect" (Matt. 5:48; Heb. 10:14), the shape of the Christian life is toward a progress in holiness and ultimate attainment of perfection only in glorification, in heaven, after death (Phil. 1:9–11; 1 Cor. 15:42–53).

Christian Tradition

Debates over the nature of the Christian life and the shape of sanctification have been frequent in the history of the church.

Perfection

A number of issues emerged from the early church controversies of Pelagius and Augustine.

1. *Pelagius.* In accord with his view of humanity and sin, the British monk Pelagius preached in Rome (A.D. 384) that Roman society needed to be reformed in the name of Christ. God demands righteousness. Humans can achieve this because they have free will and can renounce the power of sin. God would make no impossible demands. Christian "perfection" should thus be an attainable goal for all Christian believers.

2. *Augustine.* Augustine's central theology and own experience was that God saved the sinner by grace, regenerating the sinful will so that Christians are, indeed, capable of doing good. But Pelagius's perfectionism did not take seriously enough the ongoing effects of sin in the Christian life and the continuing need for divine grace. Neither justification (salvation) nor sanctification—the growth in grace—can be of human efforts. They are both God's gracious work among and within us. No Christian will be perfected until they enter the eternal life of blessedness with God. Thus, Augustine's doctrine "made a distinction between the genuine but limited righteousness of the pilgrim Church on earth and its members, and the perfected righteousness of the heavenly community of the blessed in its enjoyment of the vision of God."[5]

3. *Luther.* The doctrine of "perfection" as an outcome of sanctification on this earth was also opposed by the Protestant Reformers, Luther and Calvin. They rejected the medieval Roman Catholic view that sanctification or holiness is a work of God's grace that enables Christian believers to move steadily toward perfection in this life.[6] Luther's famous formula of Christian existence was that the Christian is "at the same time justified and a sinner" (Lat.; *simul*

justus et peccator).[7] Good works do not earn human salvation; rather they emerge as a result or fruit of the faith by which we are justified by God's grace. The Christian is "saved" in God's sight, but will still "sin" in this life, due to human frailty. Forgiveness of sins is a constant need in the Christian life. Yet, we are to aim toward the goal of our Christian experience, as Luther wrote: "But we constantly strive to attain the goal, under his redemption or remission of sin, until we too shall one day become perfectly holy and no longer stand in need of forgiveness. Everything is directed toward that goal."[8] Good works are important for the Christian life—as the outgrowth of faith. Christian action is required: "Thus we must constantly grow in sanctification and always become new creatures in Christ. This means 'grow' and 'do so more and more.'"[9] Luther and other churches in the Reformation tradition rejected "perfection" as an outcome of the sanctification process. For these Reformation churches, "perfection is associated only with justification, since the righteousness that is given to human beings in justification is the righteousness of God in Christ and therefore perfect. The holiness we acquire in sanctification, however, is always limited by our human inabilities and weakness and so cannot be termed 'perfection.'"[10]

4. *Pietism.* Other groups in the history of the Christian tradition also taught "perfection" was attainable as an outcome of sanctification. Pietism in the eighteenth century stressed that justification should lead to the practice of holiness and a close personal relationship with the Lord. Philipp Spener (1635–1705) and Count Nikolaus von Zinzendorf (1700–1760), the founder of the Moravian Brethren, anticipated that Christians could, in and through the blood of Christ, attain a perfection of faith, love, and personal holiness.

5. *John Wesley.* These pietist and Moravian impulses also influenced John Wesley (1703–1791). Wesley, like other Protestants, saw justification and sanctification as two distinct acts. In justification, the sinner is forgiven of sin, cleansed from guilt, and restored to God's favor. Sanctification is an inward change, genuinely renewing the individual who has experienced a new birth. The love of God is poured so fully into the believer's heart that the Christian will not voluntarily break God's law "either by speaking or acting what he knows God hath forbidden, so long that seed which remaineth in him, that loving, praying thankful faith, compels him to refrain from whatsoever he knows to be an abomination in the sight of God."[11] The believer thus grows in righteousness, will obey God's law, and show love, which is the fulfillment of the law. The Christian may attain full sanctification or the perfection of love, which is the final step of entrance into God's presence in Christ. This purity of motive may not be attained until immediately prior to death. Its evidence is the existence of perfect love in the heart. This perfection is "so entire a love to [God], that you may love nothing but for his sake . . . love the crea-

ture as it leads to the Creator."[12] Christians can come to the point where they will not act "contrary to pure love."[13] This is in regard to consciously willed sins, as involuntary sins will still occur.[14]

6. *Holiness Movements.* Wesley's stress on the development of Christian virtues, the fruits of the Spirit, and holiness in life found later expression in the nineteenth century in various revivalistic and evangelical movements such as Keswick, the "Higher Life," and the "Victorious Life" movements. The Holiness movement grew out of 1840s' revivals in America and began within the Methodist church. It emphasized Wesley's view of full sanctification. New denominations emerged from splits within Methodism.[15]

Holiness churches broke from Methodist churches when it was felt that Methodists had turned away from Wesleyan teachings. In common, they agreed that God intends everyone to love God completely (the Great Commandment—Mark 12:30) and that God is able to do what God intends. Holiness churches, however, differed from the Wesleyan perspective in speaking not only of "Christian perfection" but also of "baptism in the Holy Spirit" (Acts 2) as an experience of this sanctification. Also, Holiness churches typically see the experience of perfection as occurring earlier in life than did Wesley and his followers, who anticipated it occurring near or at the moment of a believer's death. Holiness churches tend to expect believers to be entirely sanctified soon after their conversion. They also differ from Methodist churches in requiring their ministers to have experienced this entire sanctification.[16] Pentecostal churches differ from Holiness churches in seeing the baptism of the Holy Spirit as distinct from full or entire sanctification and that the initial evidence of this baptism is *glossolalia* or the experience of "speaking in tongues."[17]

While there is "no single Christian doctrine of sanctification," the issue of "Christian perfection" is one that has been a decisive divide in theological understandings.[18]

Reformed Emphases

The Reformed tradition, along with the Lutheran and the Roman Catholic traditions, has taught that while Christians are called toward perfection in holiness, they struggle daily with sin and that entire or full sanctification is not possible in this life. Believers are still sinners since for the Christian "sin ceases only to reign; it does not also cease to dwell in them."[19] Sanctification is "the work of God's free grace, whereby we are renewed in the whole [person] after the image of God, and are enabled more and more to die unto sin and live unto righteousness."[20] Yet, as the Heidelberg Catechism indicates, this sanctification can never be perfect.

Q. 114. But can those who are converted to God keep the commandments perfectly?
A. No, for even the holiest of them make only a small beginning in
obedience in this life. Nevertheless, they begin with serious purpose
to conform not only to some, but to all the commandments of God.[21]

Use of the Law

The Christian life, in the Reformed tradition, is marked by a concern for
the commandments, the law of God, as a gift of God's grace to give guidance
for the Christian's walk of discipleship. God's law is an expression of God's
will. It is to be loved and treasured (see Psalm 119). Christians, who have been
justified by faith and who are living lives of sanctification in which the Spirit
is at work, seek to obey God's law because the law gives guidance on how God
wants us to live. The Heidelberg Catechism is divided into three parts: "Of
Man's Misery," "Of Man's Redemption," and "Thankfulness." The progres-
sion is for persons to see the greatness of their sin; how they are freed from
their sins and their "wretched consequences"; and then "what gratitude I
owe to God for such redemption." In the third section on "Thankfulness"—
gratitude—the Ten Commandments as God's law are considered. We keep
the law of God not as a way of "earning" salvation, but as an expression of
gratitude "for" salvation in Jesus Christ. Calvin and the Reformed faith have
spoken of the "third use of the law," which is its "principal use," and that is to
instruct and exhort believers to seek God's will and obey it. Calvin wrote that
"here is the best instrument for them to learn more thoroughly each day the
nature of the Lord's will to which they aspire, and to confirm them in the
understanding of it."[22] God's law is thus a positive help in shaping the Christian life as it shows the concerns of God and the directions God wants human
society and believers to follow.[23]

Good Works

Good works and obedience to God's law are part of sanctification. They
emerge as a response of gratitude to the salvation and redemption we experience in the gospel of Jesus Christ. The doctrine of justification by faith alone
does not mean by a faith that "is alone"—good works will inevitably follow.
The Belgic Confession indicates that

> It is impossible that this holy faith can be unfruitful in [persons]: for
> we do not speak of a vain faith [Titus 3:8; John 15:5; Heb. 11:6; 1 Tim.
> 1:5], but of such a faith as is called in Scripture *a faith that worketh by
> love* [1 Tim. 1:5; Gal. 5:6; Titus 3:8], which excites [a person] to the
> practice of those works which God has commanded in his Word.

Which works, as they proceed from the good root of faith, are good and acceptable in the sight of God, forasmuch as they are all sanctified by [God's] grace: howbeit they are of no account towards our justification [2 Tim. 1:9; Rom. 9:32; Titus 3:5].[24]

Elements of the Christian Life

The Reformed emphasis on good works and response to the law in gratitude has led Reformed Christians into many dimensions of Christian living. Some distinct accents stand out.

1. *Union with Christ.* The Christian life is made possible by the work of the Holy Spirit. Calvin said that the Holy Spirit is the link or "the bond by which Christ effectually unites us to himself."[25] The Spirit unites us with Jesus Christ in a union that is deeply expressed in the first question of the Heidelberg Catechism: "Q. 1. What is your only comfort, in life and in death? A. That I belong—body and soul, in life and in death—not to myself but to my faithful Savior, Jesus Christ. . . ."[26] This declaration has been called "the basic affirmation of the faith of the Reformed Churches."[27] It is sometimes referred to as the "mystical union" or, more generally, "union with Christ." It is not affirming an "absorption" into Christ or a "mystical identification" in which human personality is lost. Instead, it refers to the "indwelling of Christ in our hearts" (the "mystical union") so that "Christ, having been made ours, makes us sharers with him in the gifts with which he has been endowed." By engrafting us into his body, Christ "deigns to make us one with him" so that we share a "fellowship of righteousness with him."[28] Thus, in the words of the Heidelberg Catechism, we "belong" to our "faithful Savior." The results of our union with Christ are that we receive the benefits of Christ's work of redemption. These include regeneration, faith, justification, sanctification, and glorification, which are the theological components of the full Christian life, even to the life everlasting.[29]

2. *Faith.* Our union with Christ is by faith. As Calvin notes, "Christ, when he illumines us into faith by the power of his Spirit, at the same time so engrafts us into his body that we become partakers of every good."[30] Faith is the "principal work of the Holy Spirit."[31] It is grounded in God's Word and in God's promised grace in Jesus Christ, and is defined in Calvin's classic definition as "a firm and certain knowledge of God's benevolence toward us, founded upon the truth of the freely given promise in Christ, both revealed to our minds and sealed upon our hearts through the Holy Spirit."[32] The Christian who is united with Christ by faith has a faith that is comprehensive in scope.

- Faith is *knowledge*—its content is "God's benevolence."
- Faith is *assured* knowledge—"firm and certain," enough for us to trust God fully.

- Faith is *personal* knowledge—"God's benevolence toward us." It is not just intellectual but is also a matter of the heart.
- Faith is a *gift*. God's good will is "freely given" and reaches to us in Christ, even before we are aware of it.
- Faith is a *relationship*. Faith is "revealed to our minds and sealed upon our hearts." The whole person receives God's promise in Christ in personal terms and receives the person of Jesus Christ as Lord and Savior.[33]

Thus, faith in the Christian life is grounded in God's gracious love in Jesus Christ and involves a person's full existence as a follower of Jesus Christ.

3. *Church*. The Christian lives by faith in the context of the church as God's people ("elect"). The Reformed faith is a faith of living persons who express their faith in various cultures and societies with their locus being the whole people of God, the covenant community—the church. The church, where the Word is preached and the sacraments rightly administered, is given by God an outward help—a "means of grace"—to nourish and guide our faith.[34] Our lives of faith in Jesus Christ and our ministries of service to him emerge in an ecclesial context. In the Reformed tradition, the church is not an option for Christian existence; it is an absolute necessity since in and through the church God's Spirit sustains and guides the followers of Jesus Christ.

4. *Mission*. Broadly speaking, the church may be defined as "the association of those who acknowledge God's transformative way with the world in Jesus Christ, and whose purpose it is to increase love of God and neighbor."[35] The church's "purpose" or "mission" has been variously defined within the Reformed tradition. The Confession of 1967, building on 2 Corinthians 5:19, speaks of the mission of the church as the ministry of reconciliation. For "to be reconciled to God is to be sent into the world as [God's] reconciling community.[36] Thus, to increase the love of God and love of neighbor are appropriate ways of seeing the church's mission as the spread of the gospel of Jesus Christ who "came forth to us from the fountain of God's free mercy."[37] The two loves are joined, inseparably, and their increase and promotion is the "purpose of the community and institution called church: in worship and in prayer, in preaching and in sacrament, in training, in building up corporate structures, in mutual service and care, and in going out to all peoples and nations with words and deed of reconciliation and renewal."[38] Reformed Christians participate in all these actions of the church as expressions of their vocations in serving Jesus Christ.

5. *Calling*. The church carries out its mission through the work of Christians. Our efforts in the church's mission find their place in our "vocation" or "calling" as a Christian. Reformed faith recognizes that God calls persons to be followers of Jesus Christ, as Jesus called his first disciples (Matt. 4:21; Mark 1:20). This calling is grounded in God's electing love and its goal is that we be

united with Christ by faith. This union with Christ leads us into the church as Christ's body and God's covenant community. Our "basis for operations" (locus) in the church propels us to mission and to express our faith in all that we do. Our focus in our ministries is the glory and service of God in Jesus Christ. This is our vocation. For

> to be a Christian is to be called to serve, to mission, to be sent into the world, to be a witness, to take up one's cross and to suffer for Christ, to confess by Word and deed, by one's whole existence, what Christ has done, does and will do for all [persons]; in short, it is to be called to be a minister of God's Word and deed.[39]

Reformed faith has emphasized that all Christians have a calling or vocation to serve God in Christ and that we may do so in and through the lives we live and the particular types of work we do. Our "personal callings" exist as ways by which we serve God and serve the common good of society. They serve as a "sentry post" to keep us from wandering around aimlessly, seeking God's will.[40] No one vocation is invested with any more "worth" in God's sight than another—as long as in all of them we exercise two "virtues which the word of God requireth of us in the practice of our callings"—namely, "Faith and Love."[41] All Christians can serve God in Jesus Christ by infusing their lives and work with the intention to be God's people and serve God's reign. Thus, "whether we are physicians, parents, or plumbers, faithful participation means an attempt to glorify God in the midst of our many interrelations with others by joining Christian practice and the practices of particular callings. This is why we should take the time to understand exactly how a particular practice or profession contributes to the public good of God's inclusive commonwealth."[42]

6. *Culture*. To live one's vocation in a society brings up the question of the relation of church and society or church and culture. This is an enduring issue, one that is always present. Through Western history, Christian churches and Reformed churches have found their relationship with culture to vary, according to their contexts and situations. Basically, the Reformed faith has stressed God's good creation, the radicalness of human sin which affects all life and culture, and the transforming power of Jesus Christ for the "present permeation of all life by the gospel."[43] People of Reformed faith have lived out their vocations as ways of serving God in the church and in the world. Reformed history is filled with those who have seen their participation in culture—as a means that Christ may use to transform culture—as significant and meaningful. Reformed Christians have taken leadership roles in arts and sciences, education, medicine, and other fields as their ways of working for the common good and glorifying God.[44] They have not retreated from the world, but have tried to

serve God in the world—through all their vocational activities of service to Jesus Christ. Their trust in God's loving, sovereign, and providential purposes for the world enables them to give their lives in this service, confident in the assurance that it is ultimately God who is "making all things new" (Rev. 21:5).

In what ways does the church relate to culture? At different times and places, in different ways.[45] A realistic view recognizes that no one normative view is valid for all times and situations. For the church is in, with, against, and for the world—depending of the issue and context. At different points, each of these stances comes into play and receives emphasis. The church must be actively involved *in* the world, responding to its changing circumstances and learning from it so that the gospel of Christ might be enacted. The church must be *with* the world, confessing our own sins as well as the world's sins, repenting of all attitudes and actions that betray the gospel. The church is *against* the world at times when it must speak out against political and social injustices in a prophetic role that opposes "principalities and powers" and all climates of oppression. The church must be for the world as it raises the hope for the "new heaven and . . . new earth" (Rev. 21:1), participating as a signpost of God's coming, universal reign. So Reformed Christians in churches will work in the world, love it, and take responsibilities in it.[46] They will interpret the world, suffer with it, and celebrate its goodness, as they also criticize and affirm it as the theater of God's glory. Reformed churches do not "dissociate themselves from God's world; neither do they simply embrace a world of sin, fragmentation, and conflict. They recognize and lament the constricting powers of sin, even as they acknowledge and celebrate regenerating powers of grace."[47]

7. *Worship.* The Christian life as an active life of union with Christ, lived by faith in the context of the church, carrying out mission through our vocations in the midst of culture, is undergirded by worship. Worship is "the reverence, adoration, praise, supplication, and thanksgiving offered by a community of faith to God." It takes place, in Reformed understanding, in response to the "mystery of God's being and to the wonders of God's activity in creation and redemption." The gathered community, in public worship, uses "liturgical language, music and singing, symbolic actions, and silence to communicate with God. God speaks to the worshiping community through scripture, sacraments, sermon, and silence and song." Reformed worship is grounded in Scripture and seeks to carry out this service of God in conformity to God's Word.[48]

Worship supports the life of the Christian in the church community. It enables one to offer praise, supplication, and thanksgiving to the triune God. It is the context in which God's Word is read, proclaimed, and appropriated for the life of service. That Word may come as both comfort and challenge. Worship is the setting in which sin is confessed and forgiveness proclaimed through prayer and declaration. It is where offerings are presented—of the self and the resources given by God—to be used for God's work in the world. Worship is where the sacraments are administered and Christian faith is nurtured. It is where prayers of intercession and supplication are offered—for the world, the church, others, and for one's self. Worship is where God's Word becomes present—in Scripture and preaching and in Jesus Christ himself who is praised and served.[49] In the Reformed tradition, worship is the structure on which our lives are built.

These seven aspects of Christian living cannot give a full picture of the many ways in which Christian experience takes shape and is expressed. The process of sanctification, of growth in holiness and faith, is lifelong, with twists and turns all along the way. The Reformed faith acknowledges the "imperfection of the saints" while trusting in God's sovereign, loving grace to guide and sustain us to our ultimate destinations. At the same time, we seek to "do everything for the glory of God" (1 Cor. 10:31).

Contemporary Significance

The shape our sanctification takes will be different for each Christian. God calls us each along different paths, with different companions, and different vocations in which to serve. In our diversities, there are great commonalities. We all share a common sense of God's initiating grace in our lives, electing and calling us to follow Jesus Christ. We know that at some point, by the work of God's Spirit, we have passed from "death to life" into salvation so that "we too might walk in newness of life" (Rom. 6:4).

If our experience of the Spirit is called "rebirth, this metaphor itself implies 'growth' in faith, in knowledge and in wisdom."[50] This growth is "qualitative," not "quantitative." Our "life in the Spirit" is our discipleship in following Jesus Christ. It is the restoration of the image of God in human beings.[51] In what ways should our sanctification take place today? In what ways do we need to grow in our Christian lives?[52]

One contemporary Reformed theologian, Daniel Migliore, has helpfully targeted five areas of importance.

1. *Growth as Hearers of the Word of God.* We approach Scripture, not as a magical "answer book" but as the church's source of knowing God's sovereign love revealed in Jesus Christ. To grow is to open one's self to the full witness of Scripture and listen to what the Spirit says through the Word.

2. *Growth as Maturing in Prayer.* Calvin called prayer "the chief exercise of faith." It is "conversation with God" in which we place our "desires before God" with confidence.[53] Prayer is our freedom to join with the Spirit of God and be led by that Spirit as we pray for God's name to be hallowed, God's

reign to come, God's will to be done, for our daily bread, for forgiveness, and deliverance from temptation (see the Lord's Prayer, Matt. 6:9–13). To grow in prayer is to be open to listening and learning of God's costly grace, to learning the difference between our "wants" and our "needs" and acknowledging God's all-encompassing grace in every moment of our lives.

3. *Growth as Maturing in Freedom.* Our Christian lives are a liberation from all legalisms and the "power of the law" to condemn us. We are freed in Christ Jesus to "fulfill the law of Christ" (Gal. 6:2) which is the law of love. We love God and love others. To grow in freedom is to leave behind all ideologies that draw us into injustices and cause sufferings. A Brief Statement of Faith confesses that the "Spirit give us courage . . . to unmask idolatries in Church and culture, to hear the voices of peoples long silenced, and to work with others for justice, freedom, and peace."[54] We are freed, in Christ, to give our lives for others.

4. *Growth as Maturing in Solidarity.* As we participate in worship, hear the Word of God, and are nourished by the sacraments, we grow in our union with Christ and in solidarity with other humans. To grow is to be increasingly open to caring for God's good creation, for the plight of those disadvantaged in society—culturally, economically, racially, and by gender divisions. Our active concern and developing action for the "least of these" (Matt. 25:45) is a way of Christian growth.

5. *Growth as Maturing in Thankfulness and Joy.* The Reformed tradition has engendered an "ethic of gratitude." "Grace and gratitude" are two dimensions of Christian experience that go together. "In gratitude to God, empowered by the Spirit, we strive to serve Christ in our daily tasks and to live holy and joyful lives," says A Brief Statement of Faith.[55] Our obedience to God's law emerges out of thankfulness and joy for the gospel, which was proclaimed at Jesus' birth as "good news of great joy for all the people" (Luke 2:10). This is not bleary-eyed idealism or superficial optimism. It is joy and confidence grounded in the actions of God in Jesus Christ. The renewal of our lives and of the whole creation has begun. To grow is to take increasing confidence that as we participate in the means of grace in the church—through Word and Sacraments—we are God's adopted children who are nourished in faith, and grow as we continue to struggle in church, culture, and society, for the coming of God's reign.

Our way will not be easy. We will continually need God's forgiving grace. We are called to self-denial and bearing the cross, as well as to forbearance with patience in the midst of suffering and afflictions.[56] But we grow in faith and we "press on toward the goal for the prize of the heavenly call of God in Christ Jesus" (Phil. 3:14).

Questions for Reflection

1. What does "faith" mean to you?

2. What is the role of "good works" in the Christian life?

3. Have you ever been frustrated because you knew you could never attain "perfection"? If so, how did you handle those feelings?

4. In what areas do you believe you are maturing as a Christian? In what areas do you want further growth?

5. What do you understand your Christian vocation to be? How does this relate to the work you do in a job?

16

Reign of God:
The End toward Which We Move

We often get so busy with our daily lives that we don't take time to stop and contemplate "the big picture." The "big picture" is our personal destiny and the future of the world. What "bigger" questions could we think about than these?

Some things we know for sure. We will die, and so will all other humans. Beyond that, our beliefs are matters of faith. We've had no friends who have come back from the dead recently to tell us what it is like. We die. Others die.

We assume that the world will "die" too, in some sense. We are rightly worried about the threat of nuclear extinction. Now humans have it within their power to obliterate the world as we know it with the flip of a switch, with bombs that can kill the world's population many times over. We worry because it is surely not our human prerogative to be the last generation. What more morally evil act could we do than to wipe out the human race and destroy our planet? Yet we can envision that someday, somehow, the world as we know it may end. We speculate and argue about the world's origins, how it began, and how life emerged. We can equally speculate and contemplate how the world may end. Will life on Earth and the earth itself end with "a bang" or "a whimper"?

We know little about the future. We keep a respectful "tentativeness" to what we say because we only "see in a mirror, dimly" and "know only in part" (1 Cor. 13:12). We're all aware of those preachers and writers and hucksters who think they have the future all figured out. Their sermons and books travel the airwaves and line the bookshelves. Most of these folks believe what they propound is based on the Bible—that it is the Bible's "blueprint" for up-and-coming events that conclude with the end of the world and ultimately God's future judgment. Yet the irony of it is that each writer has it "figured out" a little bit differently! They vary in their predictions, and their blueprints sometimes bear very little resemblance to one another. These people are not shy about their speculations. Yet perhaps they should be! In the last two millennia, people all along the way have predicted the end of the world. Some have set actual dates. Yet these dates have come and gone and the world has continued.

But we doubt that it will continue so forever. The Bible portrays an ultimate end to it all. The book of Revelation concludes with the magnificent vision of a "new heaven and a new earth" (Rev. 21:1). Yet, we have to recognize that the Scriptures do not intend to give us a literal, step-by-step account of what will happen when in history on our way to God's final future. The biblical accounts are written in symbolic and metaphorical language. The experience of history has shown that all proposed schemes for sequencing history's final dramas have failed. Our right recognition should be and is that while we can believe the truth of what the Scriptures proclaim, we cannot impose a ready-made scheme for discerning the "signs of the times," no matter how diligently we try. God's future is on its way. Its coming is secured by God's faithful promises. We can trust and believe that in the end, there is God. We can live in the confident conviction that God's reign will come and that in God's future "all things (are) new" (Rev. 21:5). Our lives will end; history will end. But God is eternal (Ps. 90:2; Rom. 16:26).

Biblical Bases

The "big picture" in the Bible is the reign of God. Our own lives, important as they are to us, are part of God's overarching, sovereign plan in and for history. We are part of the work of God in the human story, and our lives from beginning to end—and on to eternal life—are enveloped in God's loving purposes for us.

Thus when we contemplate the future, we think of the "big picture"—what God is doing in this world, and beyond.[1] We contemplate our own lives as well, and our eternal destiny. In both dimensions, we recognize that we are dealing with the reign of God. God's ultimate purposes will be achieved—for the cosmos and for all therein, including us.

Reign of God

While the phrase "kingdom of heaven" or "kingdom of God" is not common in the Hebrew Scriptures, God is frequently referred to as "king" (Heb. *melek*) or "reigning" (*yimlōk*). These passages lead to the view that "God was imagined as the reigning king over Israel, all peoples, and indeed, nature itself." Thus, even though the exact phrase is not prominent, the idea of God's reign or kingdom is in the Scriptures, and is indeed a widespread idea in the Hebrew Bible.[2] The kingdom of God is not equivalent to the kingdom of Israel. At its best, Israel looked beyond itself to its sovereign Lord. The nation recognized, as the prophet Isaiah put it, "The LORD is our judge, the LORD is our ruler, the LORD is our king; he will save us" (Isa. 33:22).

The Hebrew prophets anticipated the coming kingdom of God to emerge out of history and be ruled by a descendant of King David (Isaiah 9, 11). After the period of Babylonian exile, the people anticipated a kingdom that would break into history, a coming "day of the LORD" when God would judge all the world (Amos 5:18–20; Zeph. 1:14–18). A new and wonderful age would be established, marked by peace (*shalôm*) and justice (*mîshpāt*; see Isa. 2:2–4; Micah 4:1–4). God will be the ultimate ruler whose presence will be the delight of all people who share in the great feast and who find that God will "swallow up death forever" (Isa. 25:6–9).

In Jewish apocalyptic writings, those writings that deal with the end of the world and of human history, some writers look to the earthly dimensions of this kingdom while others point to its suprahistorical (beyond-history) dimensions (Enoch 1–36; 37–71). The figure of a "son of man" is connected with that of a "messiah" or "anointed one" who will rule in the kingdom (Dan. 7:13, 27). God's coming kingdom was prayed for in Jewish prayers, as in the Kaddish prayer, recited in synagogues: "May he establish his Kingdom (*malkûtêh*) in your lifetime and in your days and in your lifetime of all the house of Israel, even speedily and at a near time."[3] The contrast between the "present age" and the "age to come" was as strong as possible. God's reign, marked by the reigning Messiah, will be the final expression of God's sovereign rule.

Many scholars agree that "the central theme of Jesus' message, as it has come down to us in the synoptic gospels, is the coming of the kingdom of God or, as it is usually expressed in Matthew, of the kingdom of heaven."[4] Jesus' ministry began with his proclamation: "The time is fulfilled, and the kingdom of God has come near; repent, and believe in the good news" (Mark 1:15; cf. Matt. 4:17, 23; 9:35; Luke 9:11). Jesus' mission emerged from his understanding of this work: "I must proclaim the good news of the kingdom of God to the other cities also; for I was sent for this purpose" (Luke 4:43). When Jesus proclaimed the "word of God" (Luke 8:11), it is also the "word of the kingdom" (Matt. 13:19). Jesus picked up themes from the book of Isaiah (Isa. 61:1–2; 58:6) when he preached in his hometown synagogue (Luke 4:14) and saw his whole life and mission as being to announce this message: "I must proclaim the good news of the kingdom of God to the other cities also; for I was sent for this purpose" (Luke 4:43). Jesus' message is the reign of God (Luke 8:1; 16:16).[5]

While Jesus' teachings maintained continuity with the Hebrew Scriptures, his proclamation of the reign of God also broke new ground over the prevailing tradition in several ways.

1. *God's reign is dynamic.* The term "kingdom of God" initially sounds geographical in focus. While God's reign does include "all things visible and invisible," Jesus' emphasis is that "God's kingdom is not a place or thing; it is people" who acknowledge God's reigning over them.[6] God's "kingdom" is God's kingship, a "powerful and dynamic reality by which God rules over creation and the nations."[7]

2. *God's reign is universal.* One of the "most distinctive facts that set Jesus' teaching apart from Judaism was the universalizing of the concept. Both in the Old Testament and in Judaism, the Kingdom was always pictured in terms of Israel."[8] By Jesus' time, God's coming reign was thought of as including Israel's sovereign rule over all national and political enemies (see Assumption of Moses 10:8–10). Jesus taught that God's reign is over all and transcends all national affiliations.

3. *God's reign is connected to the person of Jesus.* John the Baptist announced the coming kingdom (Matt. 3:2) and "he who comes after me" (John 1:15; cf. Matt. 11:3; Luke 7:19) and who will "baptize you with the Holy Spirit and fire" (Matt. 3:11; Luke 3:16). Jesus frequently identified himself with the "son of man" and spoke of the "coming of the Son of Man" in a way synonymous with the "coming of the kingdom of God" (see Matt. 16:28; Mark 9:1). The Son of Man rules in a kingdom (Matt. 13:41; 16:28), is "seated on the throne of his glory" (Matt. 19:28), and will come in glory (Matt. 25:31; cf. 26:64; Luke 9:26).[9] These futuristic images join Jesus' self-identification with the coming reign of the "son of man" figure. God's cause will triumph.

4. *God's reign is imminent and demands a response.* Jesus announced in his own actions and ministry that "the kingdom of God has come to you" (Matt. 12:28; Luke 11:20) and that "the kingdom of God is among you" (Luke 17:21). John the Baptist as well as Jesus himself proclaimed that the response to this kingdom is for people to "repent, and believe in the good news" for "the time is fulfilled, and the kingdom of God has come near" (Mark 1:15; cf. Matt. 4:17). One responds in faith and enters God's reign by faith (Matt. 18:3; Mark 10:14). One expresses that faith by being a disciple of Jesus, committing one's self to him, and seeking to do God's will above all else (Matt. 7:21–23; Mark 12:29–30). This entails a whole new life, a life marked by love (Matt. 22:40), and an ethical commitment to faithful discipleship in following Jesus. Throughout the Gospels, "the *norm* for discipleship is defined by the cross. Jesus' own obedience, interpreted as servanthood (Mark 10:45), is the singular pattern for faithfulness."[10] Jesus as the coming "son of man" is also the one who now serves and "gives his life" for his people (Matt. 20:28; Mark 10:45).

Jesus' teaching about the reign of God is often summarized as "already, but not yet." In his own life and ministry, Jesus taught that the reign of God has come near and has already dawned. Now is a new age of salvation—"already." But "not yet." For Jesus also taught his disciples to pray, "your kingdom come" in anticipation of the fulfilled reign of God, which will be "on earth as it is in heaven" (Matt. 6:10; Luke 11:2). The tension between these two dimensions is where we live.

Jewish thought taught that there are two ages: the present age—a time of sinfulness and rebellion against God; and the age to come—the messianic era of justice and peace. Jesus' life, ministry, death, and resurrection signaled the end to the "present age" because in and through him, God's power and rule are now at work in this world—quietly, in new ways. These ways are unexpected (Luke 17:20), for the most part "hidden," and require the eyes of faith to be perceived.[11] Yet while the evil of the present age continues, so does the "mystery" of the kingdom that has been disclosed to human beings in the ministry of Jesus. The future, glorious reign of God is now at work in this world in advance of its open manifestation. God's purposes are at work in history and are the ultimate purpose of history.[12] As the writer of the book of Revelation exclaims: "Hallelujah! For the Lord our God the Almighty reigns" (Rev. 19:6).

Christian Tradition

Earliest Christians anticipated the return of Jesus Christ (Acts 1:11) and the consummation of history that his return would bring. Paul's early letter to the Thessalonians conveyed this interest (see 1 Thess. 4:13–18); the writer of 1 John wrote of living in "the last hour" (1 John 2:18–19). As years passed, the vitality of this hope for the Lord's return was lessened and channeled into other aspects of the church's life and mission. Yet the anticipation of Christ's return to initiate the fullness of God's reign continued and continues to be a part of Christian faith. The Apostles' Creed indicates, "I believe . . . in Jesus Christ . . . who will come again to judge the living and the dead." Along with the establishment of God's reign in the return of Christ are elements relating to personal existence as well: death, resurrection, judgment, heaven, hell. These too are part of the plan and purpose of God and part of God's reign.

Millennialism

A significant passage in the history of Christian thought has been the reference to a "thousand year" reign of Christ in Revelation 20:1–10. "Chiliasm" (from Gr. *chilioi*, "thousand") or "millenarianism" are also terms used to describe thought related to this passage. Three main viewpoints developed.[13]

1. *Premillennialism.* This is the view that Jesus Christ will return to earth prior to his thousand-year reign. His coming is thus "premillennial"—before

the beginning of the thousand years or millennium. Jesus will be physically present on the Earth to carry out his reign over all nations. There is a strong discontinuity between this age and the reign of Christ in the millennium. Usually, premillennialists believe the present age will end with a period of tribulation followed by Christ's return or "parousia" (Gr. *parousia*; "coming"). At Christ's coming, the "antichrist" figure (1 John 2:18, 22; 4:3; 2 John 1:7) will be judged and the righteous will be resurrected. At Christ's second coming, Satan will be bound (Rev. 20:2) and peace will reign on earth. At the end of the millennium, Satan is freed for a short period, gathers nations into rebellion against Christ, but is vanquished by fire from heaven. Then occurs a general resurrection of all people—the "righteous" and the "unrighteous"—judgment, and the eternal destiny of heaven or hell.[14]

2. *Postmillennialism.* In this view, the return of Christ will occur after a period of Christ's special reign on earth for a thousand years. Thus the second coming is "post millennial"—after the millennium. Here there is a stress on the continuity between the present age and Christ's thousand-year reign. The intensification of Christian principles and obedience to God will mark the thousand-year period as the gospel is spread and embraced by peoples. Human efforts help in establishing the millennial period. This view emphasizes the spread of the gospel throughout the earth bringing people to faith in Christ, giving flight to evil (and the "antichrist"—either a literal person or a figurative symbol), and then the millennium arrives. Satan is "bound" for this period (Rev. 20:2) so evil is temporarily thwarted. After the millennium, Satan is loosed, rebels, and comes into final conflict with the righteous (either spiritually or politically). Jesus triumphantly returns and banishes Satan. The second coming leads to a general resurrection, judgment by God, and the eternal destinies of heaven or hell.

3. *Amillennialism.* This view emerged from the thought of Augustine and interprets the "thousand year" reign of Christ figuratively, or nonliterally. The whole period of the church's life could be meant. Various other ways of envisioning the work of the kingdom of God on Earth have been proposed. Amillennialists anticipate the return of Jesus Christ to establish the reign of God and the beginning of eternity in the "new heaven and . . . new earth" (Rev. 21:1). During the time between Christ's first advent in Bethlehem and his final advent in power and glory, the forces of good and evil have struggled through history. The church may anticipate an intensity of persecution, contending always with the spirit of "antichrist" (1 John 4:3) as well as those persons who seem particularly to embody evil. When Christ returns in glory, the fullness of his redemptive work will be completed. Jesus Christ will triumph over evil; a general resurrection, divine judgment, and the transformation of the whole creation will take place. The whole "communion of saints"—all

believers throughout history—will be united to share in God's kingdom. The final judgment articulated by Jesus in his parable of the sheep and the goats will occur (Matt. 25:31–46). The ultimate reign of God will be established for eternity.

Each of the millennial positions have sought to say something important about the end toward which we move: the reign of God. The premillennial view has emphasized the imminence of Christ's return. Jesus could return at any moment. For many premillennialists, this has meant a stress on evangelism and spreading the gospel of Christ. The postmillennialist can emphasize involvement in the world. The church must be active in carrying out its mission socially and culturally as the buildup to the millennial rule of Christ. The amillennialist may combine the emphases of the other two positions. All times are the "end times," and the work of evangelism and social witness must constantly continue. Though the kingdom is not ours to "win" but God's to give, God works through human efforts in history to accomplish divine purposes. Thus all actions on behalf of the gospel of Jesus Christ are significant for God's work.

Reformed Emphases

Adherents to all three millennial views can be found within the Reformed tradition.[15] However, the "majority opinion" has been in favor of the amillennialist view. To a large degree this is due to Reformed emphases in biblical interpretation and the recognition that the eschatological and apocalyptic materials in Scripture are often written symbolically and should not be interpreted literally. Additionally, these materials were composed by persons in very different settings over long periods of time so they should not be expected to be able to be fit into a seamless framework. Jesus himself indicated that "about that day and hour" of his return "no one knows" (Matt. 24:36). So beyond giving us the crucial insight that God's reign will be established and that evil will be defeated, "the biblical documents do not provide dates and detailed sequences. We cannot glean from the Scriptures a group of isolated incidents that together form a series of mileposts from which we can construct an 'end times check list.' Nor can we determine what length of the distance from the first coming to the second the world has traversed. On the contrary, we can only say with the New Testament writers, 'The time is near'" (Rev. 22:10).[16]

Death

Just as "the time is near" for the coming of Christ, so also the time is near for our own death. The transition from "earthly" life to "heavenly" life is part of the reign of God and is a reality that all persons face. Reformed faith takes death seriously. While physical death is associated with sin (Rom. 6:23), death is also part of the natural biological processes (1 Cor. 15:44–49). Yet, while death for the Christian is the "last enemy" (1 Cor. 15:26), it is not the "last word." For Christian faith proclaims that "Jesus is Victor!" and that we are born to the "hope of eternal life" (Titus 1:2; 3:7; John 3:16).[17] To know "Jesus is Victor!" is to "know Him as the living One, the Risen from the dead" and is to "receive and have at once, from the very outset, basic, direct and unconditional certainty of the final victory which is still awaited but which comes relentlessly and irresistibly."[18]

Judgment

The final victory of God in Jesus Christ and the establishment of God's reign unto eternal life also include judgment. The Westminster Confession indicates that "God hath appointed a day, wherein he will judge the world in righteousness by Jesus Christ, to whom all power and judgment is given of the Father." All will be judged to "appear before the tribunal of Christ, to give an account of their thoughts, words, and deed; and to receive according to what they have done in the body, whether good or evil." This confession indicates that the elect will receive eternal salvation; while those who are "wicked and disobedient" ("reprobate") receive damnation.[19]

Yet, this picture of the last judgment may also be read in concert with other Reformed confessional writings such as the Heidelberg Catechism, which speaks of the "comfort" of the return of Christ "to judge the living and the dead" (Q. 52). The comfort is to recognize that judgment will be carried out by Jesus Christ who is also our savior. The catechism answers the question of what hope is here by saying: "That in all affliction and persecution I may await with head held high the very Judge from heaven who has already submitted himself to the judgment of God for me and has removed all the curse from me."[20] In commenting on this answer, Barth said:

> This future *comforts* the church in all affliction and persecution because it *knows* the Judge. . . . The Judge is one who was judged for us. Through him we have been acquitted and from him we can now look forward to joy and glory.[21]

The judgment carried out in biblical passages relating to the last judgment and which the confessions attest to as the "eternal torments," "everlasting destruction," and "everlasting condemnation" is very real.[22] Yet, again, as Barth points out here:

> If we want to understand condemnation correctly, we must hold fast to the fact that all [persons] (we too!) are [God's] enemies—but that we all go to meet the Judge who gave himself for us. It is true that he

is the *Judge*; there can be no doctrine of universal salvation. Nevertheless, he is the Judge whom we Christians may *know*. Would it not be better in the time of grace in which we still live to proclaim to [others] this good news, to tell them who our Judge is, rather than to reflect on whether there is an eternal damnation?[23]

Christians are called to confess that Christ died for "the world" (John 3:16)—that includes us—and for all other "enemies" of God as well. For the elect who await Jesus as judge with "head held high," there can be "no alternative but to proclaim this Judge to those who do not yet know him and thus to remain in solidarity" with all people.[24]

Resurrection of the Body

The Christian hope of eternal life includes the "resurrection of the body" (Apostles' Creed) and the resurrection of the dead. These emerge from the resurrection of Jesus Christ. The resurrection of the dead is God's gracious gift—just as have been the gifts of creation and reconciliation in Jesus Christ. God redeems the whole person—not the "immortal soul"—but the whole existence.[25] Paul asserts that "we will certainly be united with him in a resurrection like his" (Rom. 6:5). This assertion affirms the continuity between Jesus' resurrection and our own. This resurrection is the new life that emerges from the physical death of this earthly existence; it is God's act for us (1 Cor. 15:42ff.).

Our resurrection bodies will be "ours" in that in some mysterious way, our own selves will be raised from the dead—not another human being, but we are the ones who will be "changed" (1 Cor. 15:51–52). This resurrection is total and comprehensive, bringing us a renewed "resurrection body" in which we will be able to communicate with others as Jesus himself did after his resurrection (John 20:19ff.; 21:5ff.). In the book of Revelation, the writer

> heard the voice of many angels surrounding the throne and the living creatures and the elders; they numbered myriads of myriads and thousands of thousands, singing with full voice,
>
> > "Worthy is the Lamb that was slaughtered
> > to receive power and wealth and wisdom and might
> > and honor and glory and blessing!"
>
> Then I heard every creature in heaven and on earth and under the earth and in the sea, and all that is in them, singing,
>
> > "To the one seated on the throne and to the Lamb
> > be blessing and honor and glory and might
> > forever and ever!"
> >
> > (Rev. 5:11–13)

The resurrection of the world will one day join in magnificent praise!

Eternal Life

What are other characteristics of eternal life ("the life everlasting"—Apostles' Creed)? Reformed theology, as all Christian theology, cannot be too precise here. We are given wonderful images and biblical symbols, but beyond these our musings are primarily speculations. Some things do seem clear, however.

1. *Eternal life means the removal of sin.* Sin is forever banished in God's reign (Rev. 21:27). Love is the eternal reality.

2. *Eternal life means God's light is ultimate* (Rev. 22:5). All sadness and sorrow, tears and pain will be no more. Death itself is vanquished (Rev. 21:4). This is the ultimate consummation.

3. *Eternal life means God's presence is all in all* (1 Cor. 15:28; Eph. 1:23). As one writer has put it, "The designation of eternal life, which is a favorite in the Bible and in church history, of course, does not mean a spectator relationship. The point it wants to make is that it is the immediate presence of God and the concomitant certainty and joy that will mark this consummated relationship to God."[26] God dwells in the midst of the peoples; there is no need for a temple since the Lord God is the temple (Rev. 21:3, 22).

4. *Eternal life means perfect oneness with others.* The kingdom of God is eminently social. For "no one possesses, or is given, eternal life for him or herself alone, without fellowship with other people, and without community with the whole creation."[27] God's "saints" are "from every tribe and language and people and nation" (Rev. 5:9). Our fellowship together is blessed and complete. Eternal life brings the redeemed into the fullness of community.

5. *Eternal life means a "new heaven and a new earth"* (Rev. 21:1). The glorified Christ says in the book of Revelation: "See, I am making all things new" (21:5). Thus all things are renewed and transformed by the divine power in eternity. The new creation means that "nothing passes away or is lost, but that everything is brought back again in new form."[28] It is not merely a restoration of the state of nature, but a reformation which, "thanks to the power of Christ . . . presents the entire creation before the face of God, brilliant in unfading splendor."[29] This is cosmic renewal. Creation will ultimately be liberated from bondage and decay to gain the "freedom of the glory of the children of God" (Rom. 8:21). Discord between "nature" and "humanity" is ended. God's justice and righteousness will rule and be at home in the eternal city (2 Peter 3:13) while the "Jerusalem above" comes down to earth (Gal. 4:26; Heb. 11:10, 13–16; Rev. 3:12). All the nations, "bring into the new Jerusalem all they have received from God in the way of glory and honor (Rev. 21:24, 26)."[30]

The vision of eternal life in heaven is awesome and magnificent. None of the biblical images can do it full justice. "Glory," "honor," "praise"—all perfected existence of the saints—is offered to the triune God, forever. The ultimate end toward which we move is the day when "The kingdom of the world has become the kingdom of our Lord and of his Messiah, and he will reign forever and ever" (Rev. 11:15).

Contemporary Significance

Sometimes Christianity has been accused of being a religion of "pie in the sky by and by." The bite of this critique is that Christians can be so focused on the afterlife that they do nothing in this life (an old saying is that Christians are "so heavenly minded that they are no earthly good"). But even worse is when the critique was leveled by those who saw Christians as oppressors—as for example at the time of the United States Civil War, when slave owners taught their faith to slaves promising them eternal bliss in heaven while making their lives hell on earth. The Christian hope of eternal life and the triumph of the reign of God clearly should never be used as justification for inactivity or oppression.

It is easy to relegate "eschatology"—the doctrine of the "last things" or future world—into the background. Since it is still ahead of us, what relevance does it have for today? It is hard enough to see signs of God's reign in the present, perverted world. How do confessions of believing in God's reign impact us now?

In the 1960s, a movement known as the "theology of hope" helped us see the shaping power of our expectations about the future for life in the present.[31] What we believe about the future actually shapes us as much as or more than what we understand about the past. If we have no future to hope in, there is no reason to do anything but despair in the present. If life is not worth living for the days that are ahead, then the present days have no meaning right now.[32]

To believe that we are ultimately moving toward the fulfilled reign of God, even as God's kingdom is taking shape in small ways in the present—that belief brings us hope for the future and meaning in the here and now. We are part of God's plan for history, and beyond. The cosmos around us as well as we ourselves will be renewed and transformed into the eternal praise of God. Because Jesus Christ is raised from the dead, so also will we be raised: because he lives we too shall live (see 1 Cor. 15:20–28).[33] Since Jesus Christ has been raised, as Paul notes to the Corinthians, we know that "in the Lord your labor is not in vain" (1 Cor. 15:58). What we do as part of God's reign here and now is meaningful and significant. We live with the tension of the "already, but not yet." As we do, we can take heart and be "steadfast, immovable, always excelling in the work of the Lord" (1 Cor. 15:58) because we know that someday this tension will be dissolved and the reign of God will come in all its fullness.

The Christian hope gives the church its impetus to continue to contend for God's righteousness, peace, and liberation in the world. The real point of the church is "not to spread the church but to spread the kingdom."[34] If we believe the ultimate future is about God's liberating rule, then the church and all followers of Jesus Christ will do whatever we can to point toward this future reign and to enact God's coming kingdom in history today. The church serves the coming salvation of the world and is "like an arrow sent out into the world to point to the future."[35] Our future Christian hope and expectation shape our present action. We give ourselves totally to the service of God in commitment to Jesus Christ by the power of the Holy Spirit to work for justice, peace, and righteousness because to do so is to seek God's will to be done "on earth as it is in heaven" (Matt. 6:10).[36] Put another way,

> The kingdom of God is both the foundation of the church and the goal of the world. Therefore, we have and we hope; we give thanks and we sigh for more. Living in the tension of such a posture, we cannot be religious dropouts with an idle faith and a passive hope. The hope of the kingdom is an invitation to work while it is day, to be active in love, to sow the seeds of the world and spread the flame of the Spirit.[37]

God's coming reign is a gift to humanity. It is the hope for our future and the world's future. It is also the challenge for us to live as disciples of Jesus Christ, passionately seeking God's will to enact it in our lives and in our culture, while being nurtured by the sustaining power of the Holy Spirit.[38] God's reign is the end toward which we move. Hallelujah!

Questions for Reflection

1. What evidences of the "reign of God" do you see around you?
2. How do you think the world will end?
3. What is the significance of seeing Jesus Christ as our judge?
4. What is the difference between "optimism" and Christian hope?
5. In what ways do our beliefs about God's reign in the future significantly shape our lives in the present?

17

Distinctive Emphases of the Reformed Faith: Comparative Conceptions

A number of ways of defining the distinctive emphases or "essence" of the Reformed faith have been proposed both formally and informally through the centuries. The following are a small sample of the proposals.

- "The distinguishing mark of Calvinism as over against all other systems lies in its doctrines of 'efficacious grace,' which, it teaches, is the undeserved, and therefore gratuitous, and therefore sovereign mercy of God, by which he efficaciously brings whom he will into salvation. Calvinism is specifically the theology of grace; and all are properly Calvinists who confess the absolute sovereignty of God in the distribution of his saving mercy."

    [From A. A. Hodge (1877), revision by B. B. Warfield (1893), "Calvinism," for *Johnson's Universal Encyclopaedia* (1893), in *Selected Shorter Writings of Benjamin B. Warfield*, ed. John E. Meeter (Nutley, N.J.: Presbyterian and Reformed Publishing Co., 1973), 415.]

- *The Ethos of the Reformed Tradition*
    The Majesty and Praise of God
    The Polemic against Idolatry
    The Working Out of the Divine Purposes in History
    Ethics, a Life of Holiness
    The Life of the Mind as the Service of God
    Preaching
    The Organized Church and Pastoral Care
    The Disciplined Life
    Simplicity
    [From John H. Leith, *An Introduction to the Reformed Tradition: A Way of Being the Christian Community*, rev. ed. (Atlanta: John Knox Press, 1981), chap. 3]

- *On Being Reformed*
    God-Centered
    A People of the Word
    The Correlation of Word and Spirit
    The Covenant, the Clue to Scripture
    Church Order
    Doctrine with a Purpose
    A Life and World View
    [From I. John Hesselink, *On Being Reformed: Distinctive Characteristics and Common Misunderstandings* (Ann Arbor, Mich.: Servant Books, 1983), chap. 13]

- *The Reformed Imperative*
    Mystery and Revelation
    The Power of God unto Salvation
    God's Providing, Ordering, and Caring
    Chosen before the Foundation of the World
    A New Heaven and a New Earth
    The Presence and the Power of God
    [From John H. Leith, *The Reformed Imperative: What the Church Has to Say That No One Else Can Say* (Philadelphia: Westminster Press, 1988), chaps. 2–7]

- *The Church and Its Confessions*

    | Trinity | (Church Catholic) |
    | Incarnation | (Church Catholic) |
    | Justification | (Protestant Reformation) |
    | Scripture | (Protestant Reformation) |
    | Sovereignty | (Reformed Tradition) |
    | Election | (Reformed Tradition) |
    | Covenant | (Reformed Tradition) |
    | Stewardship | (Reformed Tradition) |
    | Sin | (Reformed Tradition) |
    | Obedience | (Reformed Tradition) |

    [From Jack Rogers, *Presbyterian Creeds: A Guide to the Book of Confessions* (Louisville, Ky.: Westminster John Knox Press, 1991), from *The Book of Order*, Presbyterian Church (USA), chap. 2]

- "Consider the distinctive: Reformed theology lives from stressing *the prior initiative of God and our grateful response*. This is the Reformed faith's inclination, its bent, its proclivity. This is Reformed theology's tendency and impetus in understanding Scripture and doing Christian theology. It is not a 'central dogma' as such—a single 'Reformed' formulation which in and of itself provides the ordering structural motif for a Reformed 'system of doctrine.' It is rather a Reformed direction throughout doctrines. Each interrelating with others shares this trajectory in common. The Reformed affirmation is toward seeing in all theological declarations that God is prior, God acts; that humans respond, and respond as grateful persons.

Where the Reformed faith has interacted theologically with other traditions and views, it has done so by upholding this contention as the basis for its positive theological statements as well as in its critiques of other positions.

[From Donald K. McKim, "The 'Heart and Center' of the Reformed Faith," *Reformed Review*, 51, no. 3 (spring 1998): 208–9]

18

Some Common Questions

Here are some questions that may arise about some aspects of the Reformed faith.

1. Q. Do we have "free will"?

A. Yes and no. Yes, we have "free will" if that term means being able to make everyday-type choices. We can choose to go to the store or not. We can choose to turn on the computer or not. We have free choice in these matters. We are not puppets. No power on earth can force our wills to choose that which we do not want to do. We may be coerced physically but our wills themselves can never be forced to change.[1] So, in that sense, we have "free will."

But in Reformed thought, we do not have "free will" if that term means the freedom to choose the good, or to choose to do God's will by our own powers of choice. If we are sinful persons, our wills are affected by sin. We make sinful choices and are not able to choose to do God's will. In this sense, our will is in "bondage" to the power of sin. We are sinners by nature. This was how Augustine, Luther, and Calvin understood the human situation in a theological sense.

Theologically, we are sinners and captive to sin. So if there is any change to be made in our condition, it must be God who will make the change. God does so. God chooses to save us (election) and by the power of the Holy Spirit saves us by giving us the gift of faith in Jesus Christ as the means of receiving salvation. We are given a "new nature," we're a "new creation" (2 Cor. 5:17) by the power of God's Spirit with a "free will" now that is freed to be able to resist sin and to do God's will. Only by the work of God in our lives can our wills become "free."

2. Q. *Is there salvation outside the church? Will non-Christians be saved?*

A. Reformed Christians hold various opinions on this question. Some believe that salvation is only possible through an explicit confession of faith in Jesus Christ as one's Lord and Savior. While this is the usual way of professing Christian faith, these Christians believe that unless one has this experience, one cannot be saved.

Others believe that salvation is solely a matter of God's will and that we cannot say what God's decisions about the destinies of those outside the Christian church will be.

Theologically, Reformed Christians should be able to agree in this way. First, God is sovereign and free. God will decide about salvation, not humans, and no one can dictate to God and say that God "must" either (1) save all persons, no matter what (universalism) or (2) save only those persons who make an explicit Christian confession. God is free and God's freedom is ultimate. Otherwise God is not God.

Second, Reformed Christians can agree that we must confess and radically proclaim Jesus Christ as Lord and savior. This is our evangelical mandate (Matt. 28:19), to proclaim the gospel to all people. To honor God's freedom is to make our evangelism and Christian witness more vigorous, because we do not know the ways in which God may use our witness to bring persons to faith in Christ. We believe God has come to us in Jesus Christ and we proclaim that message.

Third, Reformed Christians can agree that the Holy Spirit may be at work in the realm of salvation in more ways than we can know. No one can know the full range of the Spirit's activities. The Spirit is free to work in whatever ways to bring faith—as a means of fulfilling God's election of a people. Thus, we cannot rule out the possibility that God is at work through the Holy Spirit in religious faiths other than Christianity for the purpose of salvation. As Karl Barth put it, "One thing is sure, that there is no theological justification for setting any limits on our side to the friendliness of God towards [humanity] which appeared in Jesus Christ."[2]

So, we do not know who will be saved and who might not be saved. That is not our decision—it is God's. At the same time, we proclaim the gospel in word and deed as vigorously as possible, to be witnesses to Jesus Christ "to the ends of the earth" (Acts 1:8).[3]

3. Q. *What is TULIP?*

A. TULIP is an acronym that comes from the Synod of Dort, held by Reformed church leaders in Dordrecht, the Netherlands, in 1618–1619. It was called to settle the controversy between Arminians (followers of James Arminius) and Calvinists over the issue of predestination.[4] The five "canons" or articles of the Synod on five theological points have been given the famous

TULIP name. They stand for: Total Depravity; Unconditional Election; Limited Atonement; Irresistible Grace; and Perseverance of the Saints. Each of these five points was in answer to the Remonstrance (1610) of the Arminians, which were statements counter to what each of these articles taught. The Calvinist position went this way:

Total Depravity means that humans are totally affected by sin. Every area of our existence is sinful. People are not absolutely "depraved" in the sense of being full embodiments of "evil" but instead our whole selves are governed by our sinful natures. All dimensions of who we are reflect the orientation of our heart and mind as being toward our self and away from God. Put graphically, someone said that "if sin were blue, we would be some shade of blue all over." That is, every aspect of who we are has been affected by our sinfulness. Since we are sinful, we are unable to choose God's ways for our lives (we have no "free will").

Unconditional Election means that if we are to be saved, it must be God who chooses (elects) to save us. God has chosen to do this. God chooses to save us with no "conditions"—we can do nothing to earn our salvation. This is divine predestination. Salvation is all by God's grace. If God has chosen those who will be saved in this way, Christ has died for them.

Limited Atonement means that Christ's death was limited in its effect to the elect. If this were not so, said the Calvinists, then Christ would have died for some persons who are not saved, and the power of his death would thus be limited. But God intended Christ's death to be only for those who will receive the gift of faith and be saved. Christ's death has the power to save all; but not all are saved. The efficacy or effectiveness of Christ's death is for the elect.

Irresistible Grace means that God gives the gift of grace to the elect in an irresistible way; they are not able to refuse it. They are sinful; so God changes their whole lives, including their wills, by the power of the Holy Spirit. God grants them the gift of faith so that they believe in Jesus Christ as Lord and Savior. If they are of the elect, they will be irresistibly drawn into salvation through faith in Christ.

Perseverance of the Saints means that once the elect realize their salvation, they will never lose it. If persons sin and drift away from their apparent faith, they never had genuine faith in Jesus Christ in the first place. The elect, who are saved, are saved by God's grace and power and will never lose their salvation. God's persevering grace endures throughout their lives.

Not all Reformed Christians today subscribe to these "Five Points of Calvinism." Some, in the tradition of Karl Barth, see election in a different way. Some do not believe that "limited atonement" is a proper reading of Scripture, or even of John Calvin's thought. In some Reformed churches, the five points of Calvinism are heavily emphasized; in others they are less so.

4. Q. Why do we emphasize worship?

A. We emphasize worship because it is our joyful response to God's goodness and grace in Jesus Christ. Reformed Christians seek to glorify God in all that we do (1 Cor. 10:31). Worship is the service of God's glory in which we reverence and adore our creator and redeemer through hymns of praise, confess our sins, read and listen to God's word, offer prayers, give of our material blessings to God's service, and are nourished by the sacraments and the fellowship of other believers. Worship is what we do for God; in worship God meets us through the power of the Holy Spirit.

In one sense, worship is the most important thing we do as Christians. It is the free response of our whole selves, engaging our minds and hearts. Worship is participatory, it is the "work of the people" (the meaning of the word "liturgy"). It is not a spectator sport but is what each Christian has the joyful responsibility to do. It is one activity that is absolutely central and crucial for the Christian life. Reformed Christians have always stressed that worship should be intelligible and in the language of the people so that all may enter fully into the worship experience. In worship we freely and joyfully give ourselves to God. As the psalmist proclaims: "Make a joyful noise to the LORD, all the earth. Worship the LORD with gladness; come into [God's] presence with singing" (Ps. 100:1–2).

5. Q. Do Reformed churches have an altar?

A. No. Reformed churches have a communion table instead of an altar. The reason is that an altar is where sacrifices are offered or made. Altars were common in the Hebrew Scriptures. Reformed Christians believe that Jesus Christ is the perfect sacrifice for our sins who has offered himself "once for all" (Heb. 7:27) that our sins may be forgiven. We remember and are nourished by his sacrifice on our behalf in the Lord's Supper, which we celebrate from the communion table, not an altar. In many Reformed churches, the communion table is not elevated above the level of the worshiping congregation, but is on the floor, on the level of the people. This recognizes that the table is our Lord's table in which he shared a common meal with his disciples and is not a high altar where Jesus is re-sacrificed.

6. Q. What's the use of praying?

A. Reformed Christians have always emphasized prayer. Prayer is conversation with God. Prayer is talking to God and listening for God's communication with us through the Holy Spirit.

Reformed Christians also believe that God is sovereign, a loving Lord who carries out divine purposes and also desires fellowship with us. Prayer is the means by which we have a relationship with God in Jesus Christ.

Prayer functions in many ways in the Christian life. One is as our way of seeking and learning God's will. In prayer, God moves us to understand what

God would have us believe and do. God uses our prayers as a means of communicating God's will for us. If we do not pray, we are cutting ourselves off from this channel of grace.

Thus, God works out the divine will in this world and in our lives. Prayer is one of the ways God desires to make God's will known. When we pray we seek to align ourselves with what God wants of us. God uses our prayers as a means of working out the divine will in this world in Jesus Christ. In prayer we seek to cooperate with God's purposes. And one of God's purposes is that we should pray.

7. Q. *What forms of church government are found in Reformed churches?*

A. Historically, the two most important forms of church government (polity) found in Reformed churches are the presbyterian and the congregational. Presbyterian polity places primary governmental responsibilities with the presbytery (or colloquy or classis). This representative body is composed of ordained ministers and elders from churches in a geographical area. It meets periodically to make decisions and oversees local church sessions, which are composed of ordained elders and are responsible for the spiritual oversight of local congregations. A synod is composed of a number of presbyteries, and a General Assembly—which usually meets annually or biannually—is the highest governing body. The correspondence with governmental structures in the United States is: church session (city), presbytery (county), synod (state), General Assembly (national).

Congregational church government places primary governmental responsibilities at the church congregation level. Larger associations of churches may meet, but decisions are made by vote of individual congregations that are considered as part of the universal church.

Some Reformed churches, such as the Hungarian Reformed Church, have provided for the office of bishop. Bishops are important parts of a third major form of church government: the episcopal.

In the United States, Presbyterian churches have been Reformed in their theology. American Congregationalism, which took root in New England in the seventeenth century, was historically Reformed in its orientation. So today's Congregationalist churches as well as the United Church of Christ are congregational in church government. Now, however, many church denominations—such as Baptist, Pentecostal, or Independent churches—have a congregational form of government but are not necessarily Reformed in their theological outlooks.

19

A Catechism
of Christian Faith and Life*

In 1998 the General Assembly of the Presbyterian Church (USA) produced new catechisms for the denomination. These works have great merit and can be beneficial for use by Reformed Christians in many communions.

This catechism seeks to be Reformed and ecumenical. The questions are primarily who, what, where, and how questions. Each answer is one sentence long so that, perhaps, the catechism can be memorized as in the "old days" when youngsters memorized the Westminster Shorter Catechism. My challenge was to be simple and succinct, though I make no claim to felicity of expression. There are fifty-two questions, one for each week of the year.

The order of this catechism roughly follows the order of topics in this book. I have tried to incorporate Reformed emphases in contemporary expression with the hope that this might be a useful way of expressing our faith and passing it along to all who want to learn it.

I offer this catechism for all Christians, everywhere.

1. Q. Who Is God?
A. God is the creator of all things and the sovereign Lord of the universe who loves this world and all people freely and justly in Jesus Christ.

2. Q. What Is God Like?
A. The true and living God is one God who shares a divine life in three persons: Father, Son, and Holy Spirit—each of whom is fully God and who exist together in a unity of a community of persons.

---

*In November 1996 I tagged along with my wife LindaJo on a business trip to Marco Island, Florida. Instead of taking long walks on the beach, I used her laptop computer (while she was in meetings!) to compose a catechism. For some reason I was drawn to this challenge and the results follow.

3. Q. What Did God Create?

A. God created all things good and created people in the divine image to reflect God's goodness and to serve God lovingly.

4. Q. Where Is God's Love Seen?

A. God's powerful love is seen in creation around us and is expressed most clearly, deeply, and fully in the suffering death of Jesus Christ, who is God with us.

5. Q. What Is the Bible?

A. The Bible is God's self-revelation through which we learn who God is and what God desires for this world and for our lives.

6. Q. What Is God's Providence?

A. God's providence is God's governing, sustaining, and directing of the world and all things in it to carry out God's will and purposes for the universe and for human history.

7. Q. How Is God's Providence Known?

A. God's providence is perceived when we are aware of God's presence and loving care through the events, decisions, and persons in our lives and as we are led into opportunities for service.

8. Q. How Does God Enter into Relationships with Us?

A. God desires to enter into relationships with humans and has done so in the covenants described in Scripture with individuals, with the people of Israel, and supremely in the new covenant established in Jesus Christ.

9. Q. What Is Our Nature?

A. As humans we find ourselves to have a sinful nature as part of our solidarity with all other people.

10. Q. How Does Sin Affect Us?

A. Sin affects all of us daily as we turn away from God's will for our lives, act in ways that are contrary to God's intentions, and fail to be all that we can be as God's children.

11. Q. Who Is Jesus Christ?

A. Jesus Christ is both the fullest expression of God and the fullest expression of a human, combining both dimensions in himself in a mysterious way that is completely unique among all who have ever lived.

12. Q. Why Did Jesus Come to This World?

A. Jesus Christ came into this world to embody God's love for humanity and to share fully in human life.

13.Q. What Does the Life of Jesus Do for Us?

A. The life of Jesus Christ is a model for us of a person who was completely dedicated to loving God and doing God's will in all things.

14.Q. What Has the Death of Jesus Done for Us?

A. The death of Jesus Christ on the cross brings possibilities of a new and wonderful relationship between God and humanity in which sin is forgiven and a new life of freedom, love, and joy emerges through God's Spirit at work within us.

15.Q. What Is the Importance of Jesus' Resurrection?

A. The resurrection of Jesus Christ is a completely unique event in which Jesus was raised from death by God's power and brings the reality of a new, eternal life of hope to those who believe in him.

16.Q. What Does the Ascension Mean for Us?

A. The ascension of Jesus Christ means that he is risen to rule the world as its loving Lord and is present with us at all times and places in his loving power.

17.Q. What Is the Christian Gospel?

A. The Christian gospel is the good news that God loves the world and all its people and has made it possible in Jesus Christ for us to live in joyful, just, and loving relationships with God and with others.

18.Q. To What Does the Gospel Commit Us?

A. The Christian gospel as the good news of Jesus Christ leads us to live as people committed to loving and serving God in specific forms of mission and ministry.

19.Q. What Is Salvation?

A. Salvation is God's wonderful gift of a new life and new relationship with God given when we confess by faith that Jesus Christ is our Lord and Savior and resolve to live as followers of Jesus Christ.

20.Q. How Is Salvation Received?

A. Our salvation is a gift of God's grace, given freely to us without our earning or deserving it in any way.

21.Q. From Whom Does Faith Come?

A. God graciously grants us the gift of faith in Jesus Christ, beginning and continuing faith within us by the power and initiative of the Holy Spirit.

22.Q. What Is Faith in Jesus Christ?

A. Faith in Jesus Christ means trusting that by what he has done, our sin is forgiven, and that a new life of freedom and joy in relationship with God and other persons is now a reality.

23.Q. What Is Conversion?

A. Conversion occurs when we recognize that God has loved and forgiven us in Jesus Christ and then begin to live in new ways that bring honor and glory to God.

24.Q. What Is Forgiveness?

A. Forgiveness by God is God's gracious accepting, welcoming, and cleansing of our lives so we can know that our past and present sins are no longer remembered.

25.Q. What Is Forgiveness of Others?

A. Forgiveness of others means accepting and loving persons who have wronged us and remembering the past in a new way—not with anger, but with mercy.

26.Q. When Does Forgiveness Occur?

A. Forgiveness of sins happens when we ask for God's mercy and confess our sorrow for what we have done or failed to do.

27.Q. What Is Repentance?

A. Repentance is our acknowledging that we have done wrong and our living into a new direction for life in which we turn away from sin and seek to do God's will in all things.

28.Q. What Does the Holy Spirit Bring to Us?

A. The Holy Spirit brings new beginnings to life, even when it seems our lives are at a dead end.

29.Q. What Does the Holy Spirit Do?

A. The Holy Spirit breaks into our old ways of life and thinking to bring fresh new ways that give honor and glory to God.

30.Q. What Is God's Election?

A. God's election is God's choosing of persons to receive the gift of faith in Jesus Christ and calling them together by the Holy Spirit into a body of believers—the church—through which they serve God in this world and receive the gift of eternal salvation.

31.Q. Whom Does the Holy Spirit Call Together?

A. The Holy Spirit calls, brings together, and empowers a community of Christian believers who will worship, love, and serve God by being followers of Jesus Christ.

32.Q. What Is the Church?

A. The Christian church is the community of those who believe in Jesus Christ as their Lord and Savior and who desire to live their lives together praising, loving, and serving him in all things.

33.Q. Who Is Part of the Church?

A. The church embraces all persons who desire to be followers of Jesus Christ, yet also recognizes that no one can be a perfect disciple.

34.Q. How Does the Church Live?

A. The church lives from the continual forgiveness of its Lord, Jesus Christ, when it is not a just, loving, and reconciling community.

35.Q. What Does the Church Do?

A. The church's mission and ministries take shape in culture as the church lives out the commands of the gospel and challenges structures, actions, and beliefs that are counter to the will of God and the example of Jesus Christ.

36.Q. What Are the Sacraments?

A. The sacraments of baptism and the Lord's Supper are visible expressions of God's covenant promises, which are signs and seals of God's loving benefits to us in Jesus Christ.

37.Q. What Is Baptism?

A. Baptism is our entrance into the household of faith, either as infants when parents vow to raise their children in the Christian faith, or as adults as we confess our faith in Jesus Christ as our Lord and Savior.

38.Q. What Is the Lord's Supper?

A. The Lord's Supper is a means of nurturing our faith as we experience the presence of Jesus Christ and the benefits of his life, death, and resurrection by means of the symbols of bread and wine.

39.Q. What Is Prayer?

A. Prayer is conversation with God in which we listen to God speaking to us and express to God our adoration and praise, our sins, our thankfulness and needs, as well as our supplications and intercessions on behalf of others.

40.Q. What Is Our Christian Vocation?

A. Our Christian vocation is our calling to follow Jesus Christ in all we do and to enact our love for Jesus Christ by serving God through the specific work and relationships we enjoy in life.

41.Q. Where Does the Christian Life Lead Us?

A. Living as a Christian draws us together with other believers in Jesus

Christ in the church, which is the fellowship and context in which our ministries of service to Christ are carried out.

42.Q. What Are Marks of the Christian Life?

A. The Christian life is marked by worship, learning, and service to God as we are drawn together with others in the church of Jesus Christ.

43.Q. What Are Other Marks of the Christian Life?

A. The Christian life is also marked by works of love, justice, and peace-making through which God's gracious mercy and care for the world are shown.

44.Q. What Does Faith Mean?

A. Faith means continuing to believe and trust God's love and care, even in the most difficult times, and when it seems impossible that God could be with us.

45.Q. What Else May Faith Mean?

A. Faith means letting go of our personal plans and agendas for our lives and following what we perceive to be God's will and directions for us.

46.Q. What Is Christian Hope?

A. Christian hope is a full trust that God's will and work will be done in this world and that God's reign will someday be recognized by all people.

47.Q. On What Is Christian Hope Based?

A. Christian hope emerges from the life, death, and resurrection of Jesus Christ and assures us that because of him, our lives and work for Christ have meaning and significance.

48.Q. What Is Love for God?

A. Love for God is our living every moment joyfully, knowing that God is with us and doing all things with the desire to please God.

49. Q. What Is Love for Others?

A. Love for others is our complete commitment to their well-being and our desire to give ourselves to serving them fully.

50. Q. What Is Christian Worship?

A. Christian worship is our acknowledging with praise and service that the one true God is the gracious Creator of all things who loves us in Jesus Christ and is with us by the Holy Spirit.

51. Q. What Is Eternal Life?

A. Eternal life is the free, joyful, and loving lives we live by faith in Jesus Christ, which begin now and last after death forever, in the heavenly presence of God, angels, and saints.

52. Q. What Is God's Reign?

A. God's reign of peace, justice, and fullness will come in power and glory at the end of time and will be marked by the universal affirmation that Jesus Christ is Lord!

Reformed Churches in Canada and the United States[†]

Canada

Presbyterian Church in America (Canadian Section)
Presbyterian Church in Canada*
Reformed Church in Canada
United Church of Canada*

United States of America

Associate Reformed Presbyterian Church (General Synod)
Christian Reformed Church in North America
Conservative Congregational Christian Conference
Cumberland Presbyterian Church*
Cumberland Presbyterian Church in America*
The Evangelical Congregational Church
Evangelical Presbyterian Church*
Hungarian Reformed Church in America*
Lithuanian Evangelical Reformed Church*
Netherlands Reformed Congregations
Presbyterian Church in America
Presbyterian Church (U.S.A.)*
Protestant Reformed Churches in America
Reformed Church in America*
Reformed Church in the United States
Reformed Presbyterian Church of North America
Second Cumberland Presbyterian Church
The Korean Presbyterian Church in America*
United Church of Christ*

[†]The list is from *HDRC*, 495.
*Indicates membership in the World Alliance of Reformed Churches (WARC).

Comparative Sources

A number of significant theological works have emerged in the history of the Reformed faith. The following is a brief compendium of where to find the topics of this book in some of the established Reformed theology texts, which are listed in the selected bibliography at the end of this chapter. Unless otherwise indicated, the numbers refer to book chapters.

1. Believing in God: Confessing Our Faith
   Guthrie, part 1, chaps. 1, 2; H. Berkhof, 4; Migliore, 1; Rohls, pp. 9–28
2. Scripture: The Word of God
   H. Berkhof, 8–18; L. Berkhof, part 5, chap. 2; Guthrie, part 2, chaps. 3, 4; Heppe, 2; McKim, 6; Migliore, 2, 3; Rohls, pp. 29–34
3. Trinity: Who Is God?
   H. Berkhof, 19–23; L. Berkhof, part 1, chap. 8; Guthrie, part 2, chaps. 5, 6; Heppe, 6; McKim, 1; Migliore, 4; Rohls, pp. 45–54
4. Creation: What Has God Done?
   H. Berkhof, 24–25; L. Berkhof, part 1, chaps. 3–5; Guthrie, part 3, chap. 8; Heppe, 9; Migliore, 5; Rohls, pp. 54–57
5. Providence: What Is God Doing?
   H. Berkhof, 28; L. Berkhof, part 1, chap. 6; Guthrie, part 3, chap. 9; Heppe, 12; Migliore, 6; Rohls, pp. 57–64
6. Humanity: Who Are We?
   H. Berkhof, 26; L. Berkhof, part 2, chaps. 1–4; Guthrie, part 3, chap. 10; Heppe, 11; McKim, 4; Migliore, 7; Rohls, pp. 64–68
7. Sin: What Have We Become?
   H. Berkhof, 27; L. Berkhof, part 2, chaps. 1–5; Guthrie, part 3, chap. 11; Heppe, 15; McKim, 4; Migliore, 7; Rohls, pp. 73–86

8. Person of Christ: Who Is Jesus?
   H. Berkhof, 32–34; L. Berkhof, part 3 (Person of Christ; States of Christ); Guthrie, part 4, chap. 12; Heppe, 17; McKim, 2; Migliore, 8; Rohls, pp. 102–17

9. Work of Christ: What Has Jesus Done?
   H. Berkhof, 35–36; L. Berkhof, part 3 (Offices of Christ); Guthrie, part 4, chaps. 13, 14; Heppe, 18; McKim, 5; Migliore, 8; Rohls, pp. 86–102

10. Holy Spirit: Who Is the Holy Spirit?
    H. Berkhof, 37–38; L. Berkhof, part 4, chaps. 1–2; Guthrie, part 5, chap. 15; Migliore, 9

11. Salvation: Receiving God's Gift
    H. Berkhof, 45–46; L. Berkhof, part 4, chaps. 3–9; Guthrie, part 5, chap. 16; Heppe, 21; Migliore, 9; Rohls, pp. 117–30; 154–66 (election); McKim, 5

12. Church: The People of God
    H. Berkhof, 39–42; L. Berkhof, part 5, chaps. 1–4; Guthrie, part 5, chap. 18; part 2, chap. 7; Heppe, 27; McKim, 3; Migliore, 10; Rohls, pp. 166–77

13. Baptism: Beginning in Faith
    H. Berkhof, 40; L. Berkhof, part 5 (The Means of Grace, chap. 4); Heppe, 25; McKim, 7; Migliore, 11; Rohls, pp. 206–19

14. The Lord's Supper: Nourishing Our Faith
    H. Berkhof, 40; L. Berkhof, part 5 (The Means of Grace, chap. 5); Heppe, 26; McKim, 8; Migliore, 11; Rohls, pp. 219–37

15. Christian Life: Growing in Faith
    H. Berkhof, 47–52; L. Berkhof, part 4, chaps. 10–11; Guthrie, part 5, chap. 17; Heppe, 22; Migliore, 9; Rohls, pp. 130–46

16. Reign of God: The End Toward Which We Move
    H. Berkhof, 53–59; L. Berkhof, part 6; Guthrie, part 5, chap. 19; Heppe, 28; McKim, 9; Migliore, 12; Rohls, pp. 146–48

Selected Bibliography

Berkhof, Hendrikus. *Christian Faith: An Introduction to the Study of the Faith*. Trans. Sierd Woudstra. Rev. ed. Grand Rapids: Wm. B. Eerdmans Publishing Co., 1986.

Berkhof, Louis. *Systematic Theology*. London: Banner of Truth Trust, 1969.

Guthrie, Shirley C. *Christian Doctrine*. Rev. ed. Louisville, Ky.: Westminster/John Knox Press, 1994.

Heppe, Heinrich, ed. *Reformed Dogmatics: Set Out and Illustrated from the Sources*. Revised and edited by Ernst Bizer, trans. G. T. Thompson. Reprint, Grand Rapids: Baker Book House, 1978.

McKim, Donald K. *Theological Turning Points: Major Issues in Christian Thought*. Atlanta: John Knox Press, 1988.

Migliore, Daniel L. *Faith Seeking Understanding: An Introduction to Christian Theology*. Grand Rapids: Wm. B. Eerdmans Publishing Co., 1991.

Rohls, Jan. *Reformed Confessions: Theology from Zurich to Barmen*. Trans. John Hoffmeyer. Columbia Series in Reformed Theology. Louisville, Ky.: Westminster John Knox Press, 1998.

Abbreviations

ABD   *Anchor Bible Dictionary.* Ed. David Noel Freedman. 6 vols. New York: Doubleday, 1992.

AIB   Jack B. Rogers and Donald K. McKim. *The Authority and Interpretation of the Bible: An Historical Approach.* San Francisco: Harper & Row, 1979.

BC   *The Book of Confessions.* Presbyterian Church (USA). Louisville, Ky.: Office of the General Assembly, 1996.

CD   Karl Barth. *Church Dogmatics.* Trans. Geoffrey W. Bromiley. Edinburgh: T. & T. Clark, 1936–1969.

Christian Doctrine   Shirley C. Guthrie. *Christian Doctrine.* Rev. ed. Louisville, Ky.: Westminster John Knox Press, 1994.

Cochrane, ed., *Reformed Confessions*   *Reformed Confessions of the 16th Century.* Ed. Arthur C. Cochrane. Philadelphia: Westminster Press, 1966.

DJG   *Dictionary of Jesus and the Gospels.* Ed. Joel B. Green, Scot McKnight, I. Howard Marshall. Downers Grove, Ill.: InterVarsity Press, 1992.

DPL   *Dictionary of Paul and His Letters.* Ed. Gerald F. Hawthorne, Ralph P. Martin, Daniel G. Reid. Downers Grove, Ill.: InterVarsity Press, 1993.

ERF   Donald K. McKim, ed. *Encyclopedia of the Reformed Faith.* Louisville, Ky.: Westminster John Knox Press, 1992.

HDRC   Robert Benedetto, Darrell L. Guder, and Donald K. McKim. *Historical Dictionary of Reformed Churches.* Historical Dictionaries of Religions, Philosophies, and Movements, No. 24. Lanham, Md.: Scarecrow Press, 1999.

Inst.   John Calvin, *Institutes of the Christian Religion.* Ed. John T. McNeill. Trans. Ford Lewis Battles. Library of Christian Classics. 2 vols. Philadelphia: Westminster Press, 1960.

ISBE   *International Standard Bible Encyclopedia.* Ed. Geoffrey W. Bromiley. Rev. ed. Grand Rapids: Wm. B. Eerdmans Publishing Co., 1979–1988.

Major Themes   Donald K. McKim, ed. *Major Themes in the Reformed Tradition.* Grand Rapids: Wm. B. Eerdmans Publishing Co., 1992. Reprint, Eugene, Oreg.: Wipf & Stock, 1999.

Rohls, *Reformed Confessions*   Jan Rohls. *Reformed Confessions: Theology from Zurich to Barmen.* Trans. John F. Hoffmeyer. Louisville, Ky.: Westminster John Knox Press, 1997.

Turning Points   Donald K. McKim. *Theological Turning Points: Major Issues in the History of Christian Thought.* Atlanta: John Knox Press, 1988.

Notes

Introduction

1. John De Gruchy has noted that "Reformed theologians have never felt that they must slavishly follow Calvin in the way some Lutherans follow Luther. But Calvin remains the 'decisive generating source' for doing Reformed theology. It is therefore essential to remain in dialogue with Calvin throughout the enterprise." See John De Gruchy, "Toward a Reformed Theology of Liberation," in *Toward the Future of Reformed Theology: Tasks, Topics, Traditions*, ed. Davis Willis and Michael Welker (Grand Rapids: Wm. B. Eerdmans Publishing Co., 1999), 108. He cites here James M. Gustafson, *Theology and Ethics* (Chicago: University of Chicago Press, 1981), 163.

2. These include *Readings in Calvin's Theology* (1984); *Major Themes in the Reformed Tradition* (1992); *Encyclopedia of the Reformed Faith* (1992); *Historical Dictionary of Reformed Churches* (1999); and, in part, *Theological Turning Points* (1988). Reformed thought is also dealt with in my work with Jack B. Rogers, *The Authority and Interpretation of the Bible: An Historical Approach* (1979); *How Karl Barth Changed My Mind* (1986); and *The Bible in Theology and Preaching* (1994).

3. I have explored this a bit in "The 'Heart' and 'Center' of the Reformed Faith," *Reformed Review* 51, no. 3 (spring 1998), 206–19.

4. To gain a sense of the breadth of Reformed churches, theology, important figures, and movements, see Robert Benedetto, Darrell L. Guder, and Donald K. McKim, *Historical Dictionary of Reformed Churches* (Lanham, Md.: Scarecrow Press, 1999), and *The Reformed Family Worldwide: A Survey of Reformed Churches, Theological Schools, and International Organizations*, ed. Jean-Jacques Bauswein and Lukas Vischer (Grand Rapids: Wm. B. Eerdmans Publishing Co., 1999). Note especially the "Chronology" in *HDRC*, xxv–xliii. The *HDRC* as well as my *ERF* can profitably be used in conjunction with the present book as these books feature articles on theological terms, historical persons, and main events in the history of the Reformed tradition.

5. See the interesting approach to this topic by I. John Hesselink in his *On Being Reformed: Distinctive Characteristics and Common Misunderstandings* (Ann Arbor, Mich.: Servant Publications, 1983). Hesselink focuses on twelve common misunderstandings of what it means to be "Reformed" before offering some characteristics and distinctive emphases. Hesselink is from the Dutch Reformed tradition in the Reformed Church of America.

6. See, for example, the collection of essays in *Toward the Future of Reformed Theol-*

ogy and the review by Douglas F. Ottati, "Being Reformed," *Christian Century* 117, no. 3 (January 26, 2000), 97–99.

7. Ottati notes that a number of writers in *Toward the Future of Reformed Theology* outline "distinctive emphases of Reformed theology: among them, the word of God attested in scripture; the grace of God in Jesus Christ; the radicality of sin; the law and God's covenant with Israel; and a 'worldly' or participatory ethic." Yet, "the specific emphases mentioned by particular authors often differ and the same emphases are sometimes differently understood," 98.

8. Art. 1 in *BC* 8.04.

9. Jane D. Douglass, "What is 'Reformed Theology'?" *Princeton Seminary Bulletin*, New Series, 11, no. 1 (1990), 8. Jürgen Moltmann writes that "Reformed theology is, as its name testifies, nothing other than *reformatory theology (reformatorische Theologie)*, theology of permanent reformation." See "Theologia Reformata et Semper Reformanda," in *Toward the Future of Reformed Theology*, 120.

10. Calvin, *Inst.* I.5.9. Calvin has also written: ". . . we shall not say that, properly speaking, God is known where there is no religion or piety" (*Inst.* I.2.1).

11. See Questions 28, 32, 36, 43, etc. in *BC* 4.028, 4.032, 4.036, 4.043. Puritan theologians such as William Perkins and William Ames usually divided their teachings into a Doctrine/Use scheme.

12. In the "Preface" to my *ERF*, v.

13. I titled the *Encyclopedia of the Reformed Faith* as I did for the same reasons mentioned in this paragraph.

14. William Perkins, "A Golden Chaine: or, The Description of Theologie" in *The Workes of That Famous and Worthy Minister of Christ In the University of Cambridge, Mr. William Perkins*, 3 vols. (Cambridge: John Legatt, 1616–18), 1:11. Perkins's student, William Ames wrote that "Theology is the doctrine of teaching [*doctrina*] of living to God." See William Ames, *The Marrow of Theology*, ed. and trans. John D. Eusden (Boston: Pilgrim Press, 1968), 77. Ames also wrote that "The two parts of theology are faith and observance," 79. He thus ties together doctrine and life, theology and ethics.

Chapter 1

1. Biographies of Calvin include William J. Bouwsma, *John Calvin: A Sixteenth-Century Portrait* (New York: Oxford University Press, 1988); Alexandre Ganoczy, *The Young Calvin*, trans. David Foxgrover and Wade Provo (Philadelphia: Westminster Press, 1987); Alister McGrath, *A Life of John Calvin* (Oxford: Basil Blackwell, 1990); T. H. L. Parker, *John Calvin: A Biography* (Philadelphia: Westminster Press, 1975); and the old work by Williston Walker, *John Calvin: Organizer of Reformed Protestantism* (reprint, New York: Schocken Books, 1969). Cf. François Wendel, *Calvin: The Origins and Development of His Religious Thought*, trans. Philip Mairet (London: Wm. Collins Sons, 1963).

2. See John H. Leith, *An Introduction to the Reformed Tradition*, rev. ed. (Atlanta: John Knox Press, 1981). Cf. M. Eugene Osterhaven, *The Spirit of the Reformed Tradition* (Grand Rapids: Wm. B. Eerdmans Publishing Co., 1971) and his *The Faith of the Church: A Reformed Perspective on Its Historical Development* (Grand Rapids: Wm. B. Eerdmans Publishing Co., 1982). Cf. John R. DeWitt, *What Is the Reformed Faith?* (Carlisle, Pa.: The Banner of Truth Trust, 1981).

3. In the sixteenth century, the term "reformed" was used as a synonym for "Protestant" and "evangelical." These terms stood in contrast to Roman Catholicism. In England, Queen Elizabeth I once commented in a letter that non-Lutheran churches were "more reformed" in their orientations.

4. See John T. McNeill, *The History and Character of Calvinism* (New York: Oxford University Press, 1954); Andrew Pettegree, Alastair Duke, and Gillian Lewis, eds., *Calvinism in Europe, 1540–1620* (Cambridge: Cambridge University Press, 1994); Menna Prestwich, ed., *International Calvinism, 1541–1715* (Oxford: Oxford University Press, 1985); and W. Stanford Reid, ed., *John Calvin: His Influence in the Western World* (Grand Rapids: Zondervan, 1982). See also Alastair Duke, Gillian Lewis, and Andrew Pettegree, eds., *Calvinism in Europe, 1540–1610: A Collection of Documents* (Manchester: Manchester University Press, 1992).

5. Of importance also are a number of Reformed catechisms. A "catechism" is a means of instruction, often in question/answer form, that conveys the basics of the Christian faith. See David F. Wright, "Catechism," in *ERF*, 59–60. Among important Reformed catechisms are Calvin's Catechism (1538), the Heidelberg Catechism (1561), and the Westminster Larger and Shorter Catechisms (1648). See the collection in *The School of Faith: The Catechisms of the Reformed Church*, ed. and trans. Thomas F. Torrance (New York: Harper & Brothers, 1959). The Presbyterian Church (USA) recently produced "Belonging to God: A First Catechism" and "The Study Catechism" (1998). See Richard R. Osmer, "The Case for Catechism," *Christian Century*, April 23–30, 1997, 408–12. Cf. my "A Catechism of Christian Faith and Life" (pages 186–92, this volume).

6. For more detail see Jack B. Rogers, "Creeds and Confessions," in *ERF*, 89–93.

7. A standard study is J. N. D. Kelly, *Early Christian Creeds*, 3rd ed. (London: Longman, 1972).

8. See "The Confessional Nature of the Church" in *Major Themes*, 20. This document was adopted by the General Assembly of the Presbyterian Church (USA) in 1996 and recently reprinted in the *Book of Confessions: Study Edition* (Louisville, Ky.: Geneva Press, 1999), 353–69. In the following paragraphs, I have modified and supplemented a number of the topics in this document.

9. A helpful resource here is Jack Rogers, *Reading the Bible and the Confessions: The Presbyterian Way* (Louisville, Ky.: Geneva Press, 1999).

10. Among the studies of Reformed confessions, see Edward A. Dowey Jr., *A Commentary on the Confession of 1967 and an Introduction to 'The Book of Confessions'* (Philadelphia: Westminster Press, 1968); Cornelius Plantinga, *A Place to Stand: A Reformed Study of Creeds and Confessions* (Grand Rapids: Board of Publications of the Christian Reformed Church, 1979); Jack B. Rogers, *Presbyterian Creeds: A Guide to the Book of Confessions* (Louisville, Ky.: Westminster John Knox Press, 1991); Rohls, *Reformed Confessions*.

11. These are identified and discussed by Rohls, *Reformed Confessions*, chap. 1.

12. Among principal Reformed Confessional documents are the First Helvetic Confession (1536), French Confession (1559), Scots Confession (1560), Belgic Confession (1561), Heidelberg Catechism (1562), Second Helvetic Confession (1566), Articles of the Synod of Dort (1619), the Westminster Confession (1647), and the Westminster Larger and Shorter Catechisms (1648). See the collection in Cochrane, ed., *Reformed Confessions*. Cf. Ted A. Campbell, *Christian Confessions: A Historical Introduction* (Louisville, Ky.: Westminster John Knox Press, 1996) 123–24. Cochrane's "Introduction" gives a history of attempts to collect Reformed confessions into a single volume.

13. See Rohls, *Reformed Confessions*, 9–10. In contrast, the Lutheran tradition established its *Book of Concord* (1580) which included Luther's Small (1529) and Large (1529) Catechisms, the Augsburg Confession (1530), the Apology of the Augsburg Confession (1531), the Schmalkaldic Articles (1531), Treatise on Power and Primacy of the Pope (1537), and the Formula of Concord (1577) as the only confessional standards for

nearly all Lutheran churches. See Campbell, *Christian Confessions*, 122. Arthur Cochrane noted that "Reformed Confessions . . . are held to be in force only from time to time and in a given historical place. The Lutheran tendency to endow their six-teenth-century Confessions with finality and completeness doubtless accounts for the fact that many Lutherans have been unable to look upon the Barmen Theological Dec-laration of May, 1934, as a genuine Confession," 18. Cf. *Reformed Witness Today: A Col-lection of Confessions and Statements of Faith Issued by Reformed Churches*, ed. Lukas Vischer (Bern: Evangelische Arbeitsstelle Ökumene Schweiz, 1982).

14. The Confession of 1967 states that "confessions and declarations are subordinate standards in the church, subject to the authority of Jesus Christ, the Word of God, as the Scriptures bear witness to him," "Preface" in *BC* 9.03.

15. Jack Rogers indicates that we need to recognize that "the writers of the Confes-sions were persons of their own culture and took for granted many applications of the Christian faith that we would not consider biblical or valid for us. We cannot, there-fore, literally and uncritically cite attitudes or actions recommended in the Confessions without taking into account the assumptions of their sixteenth- or seventeenth-century culture. In general, we want to look for the overarching themes and be careful to understand the sixteenth- or seventeenth-century cultural context when particular issues do not quite ring true to us." *Reading the Bible and the Confessions*, 62.

16. See Arthur Cochrane's chapter, "The Nature of a Confession of Faith, Illustrated from the Theology and History of Barmen," in his *The Church's Confession under Hitler* (Philadelphia: Westminster Press, 1962), 188.

17. Cochrane, *The Church's Confession under Hitler*, 213.

18. Sect. 1 in *BC* 8.01.

19. Theological Declaration of Barmen, Art. 1 in *BC* 8.10.

20. Heidelberg Catechism, Question 1 in *BC* 4.001. Westminster Shorter Catechism, Question 1 in *BC* 7.001.

21. Cochrane, *The Church's Confession under Hitler*, 214.

22. John H. Leith, "A Brief History of the Creedal Task," *To Confess the Faith Today*, ed. Jack L. Stotts and Jane Dempsey Douglass (Louisville, Ky.: Westminster John Knox Press, 1990), 42. See also Leith's listing of representative Reformed confessions of the sixteenth and seventeenth centuries in *An Introduction to the Reformed Tradition*, 136.

23. Karl Barth, *Theology and Church: Shorter Writings, 1920–1928* (New York: Harper & Row, 1962), 112, cited in Leith, "A Brief History," 42–43.

Chapter 2

1. Calvin, Inst. I.1.1.

2. Wolfhart Pannenberg, *Systematic Theology*, trans. Geoffrey W. Bromiley (Grand Rapids: Wm. B. Eerdmans Publishing Co., 1991), 22.

3. See Avery Dulles, *Models of Revelation* (New York: Doubleday and Co., 1983) for a survey of different Christian theological understandings of revelation. Cf. Donald G. Bloesch, *Holy Scripture: Revelation, Inspiration and Interpretation* (Downers Grove, Ill.: InterVarsity Press, 1994), chap. 3.

4. See Dewey M. Beegle, "The Biblical Concept of Revelation," in *The Authoritative Word: Essays on the Nature of Scripture*, ed. Donald K. McKim (Grand Rapids: Wm. B. Eerdmans Publishing Co., 1983; reprint, Eugene, Ore.: Wipf & Stock Publishers, 1998), chap. 6.

5. See Paul J. Achtemeier, *The Inspiration of Scripture: Problems and Proposals* (Philadelphia: Westminster Press, 1980), chap. 3, "How the Scriptures Were Formed," reprinted in McKim, ed., *The Authoritative Word*, chap. 1.

6. Bloesch comments: "The Bible is God-breathed in the sense that it is a production of the creative breath of God. The breath of the Holy Spirit accounts for both the Bible's origin and its viability through the ages," *Holy Scripture*, 120.

7. Bloesch says, "The purpose of the inspiration of writers and writings is to serve God's self-revelation in Jesus Christ," *Holy Scripture*, 120.

8. See G. C. Berkouwer, *Holy Scripture*, ed. and trans. Jack B. Rogers (Grand Rapids: Wm. B. Eerdmans Publishing Co., 1975), 139–42. The New Testament scholar H. N. Ridderbos notes in regard to 2 Timothy 3:15–16 that "the purpose and the nature of Scripture lie thus in that qualified sort of teaching and instruction which is able to make us wise to salvation, which gives God's people this 'completeness' and equips them for every good work." See "The Inspiration and Authority of Holy Scripture" in McKim, ed., *The Authoritative Word*, 185. Cf. I. Howard Marshall, *Biblical Inspiration* (Grand Rapids: Wm. B. Eerdmans Publishing Co., 1982), chap. 3.

9. As G. C. Berkouwer put it: "God's Word has not come to us as a stupendous supernatural miracle that shies away from every link with the human in order thus to be truly divine. Rather, when God speaks, human voices ring in our ears." See Berkouwer, *Holy Scripture*, 145.

10. Bloesch writes that "inspiration does not guarantee that the Bible is inerrant in the sense of being exempt from human misconceptions and limitations—even in the areas of ethics and theology. Nor does it imply that the Bible is free from textual and linguistic errors. It does mean that the prophets and apostles have a basic understanding of the purposes of God grounded in revelation itself. We have in their words a reliable and unfailing witness to God's saving acts but not an infallible record of world history," *Holy Scripture*, 121–22.

11. See John Goldingay, *Models for Scripture* (Grand Rapids: Wm. B. Eerdmans Publishing Co., 1994).

12. A common question is why the number of books in the Roman Catholic and the Protestant "canon" of Scripture is different. At the time of the Protestant Reformation in the sixteenth century in Europe, the Protestant Reformers adopted the Hebrew canon of Scripture, which included thirty-nine books. These, with the twenty-seven New Testament books, gave a canon of sixty-six books. The Roman Catholic church used the Latin translation of the Scriptures made in the fourth century by St. Jerome called the Vulgate as its official canon. The Vulgate was based on the canon of the Septuagint, a Greek translation of the Hebrew Scriptures made for non–Hebrew speaking Jews living away from the Jewish homeland and completed approximately a century before the time of Jesus. This translation includes seven books not included in the Hebrew canon. They are called the "apocrypha" ("hidden") and date from the intertestamental period. These books were accepted by the Roman Catholic church as Holy Scripture, giving its Old Testament canon forty-six books. See F. F. Bruce, "Tradition and the Canon of Scripture," in McKim, ed., *The Authoritative Word*, chap. 5. For a theological treatment, see Berkouwer, *Holy Scripture*, chap. 3.

13. See the various essays in McKim, ed., *The Authoritative Word*.

14. Origen, *On First Principles*, 4.9, cited in Rogers and McKim, *AIB*, 11.

15. Augustine, *The Usefulness of Belief*, 6.13, cited in Rogers and McKim, *AIB*, 25.

16. Cited in Rogers and McKim, *AIB*, 77.

17. Calvin, *Inst.* I.7.4.

18. Ibid.

19. See Henning Graf Reventlow, *The Authority of the Bible and the Rise of the Modern World* (Philadelphia: Fortress Press, 1985).

20. See Rogers and McKim, *AIB*, 147ff., 265ff.

21. There is much literature on this issue now. For a survey of some of it published after the Rogers and McKim *AIB* volume, see the new epilogue in the *AIB* reprint by Wipf & Stock: "A Decade of Discussion of the Authority and Interpretation of the Bible: A Personal Retrospective by Rogers and McKim." Cf. Achtemeier, 50–75, and Goldingay, *Models for Scripture*, chap. 19: "Inspiration and Inerrancy."

22. For a survey see Donald K. McKim, *The Bible in Theology and Preaching* (Nashville: Abingdon Press, 1993; reprint, Eugene, Ore.: Wipf & Stock, 1999), from which the following is drawn.

23. McKim, *The Bible in Theology and Preaching*, chap. 3.

24. See Bradley J. Longfield, *Fundamentalist/Modernist Controversy, ERF*, 148–49.

25. The Scopes trial marked a turning point in the development of Fundamentalist theology, which associated itself with the literal reading of the Genesis creation accounts and biblical inerrancy. See McKim, *The Bible in Theology and Preaching*, 56.

26. See these views of Existential Theology, Process Theology, Narrative Theology, Latin American Liberation Theology, Black Theology, Asian Theology, and Feminist and Womanist Theologies in McKim, *The Bible in Theology and Preaching*, chaps. 8–14.

27. Karl Barth has emphasized the threefold form of the Word of God: incarnate (Jesus Christ), written (Scripture), proclaimed (preaching). Each is inner-connected to the others. See Barth, *CD* I/1, 88–124; McKim, *The Bible in Theology and Preaching*, chap. 6.

28. See Rogers and McKim, *AIB*, 265–379, and McKim, *The Bible in Theology and Preaching*, chap. 5. An important primary source was the article by A. A. Hodge and B. B. Warfield, "Inspiration," *The Presbyterian Review* 2 (April 1881): 225–60. Among Warfield's many contributions to this question are "The Inerrancy of the Original Autographs," *The Independent* 45 (March 23, 1893): 382f., reprinted in *Selected Shorter Writings of Benjamin B. Warfield-II*, ed. John E. Meeter (Nutley, N.J.: Presbyterian and Reformed Publishing Co., 1973), 580–87, and his *The Inspiration and Authority of the Bible* (reprint, Philadelphia: Presbyterian and Reformed Publishing Co., 1970).

29. See Rogers and McKim, *AIB*, 406–26; McKim, *The Bible in Theology and Preaching*, chap. 6.

30. See Rogers and McKim, *AIB*, 380–405; McKim, *The Bible in Theology and Preaching*, chap. 7.

31. An important concept for understanding this view is "accommodation." The term refers to the practice of ancient rhetoricians to adapt their speeches to the capacities of their audiences. Christian theologians trained in the rhetorical condition applied this insight to God's method of communication. Like a parent speaking "baby talk," God uses human beings who use human language to communicate the divine message. God adapts the divine message to limited, human capacities. The supreme example of "accommodation" is the incarnation of Jesus Christ—where God has completely identified with humanity by becoming a human person. See *HDRC*, 2; Donald K. McKim, "Accommodation," in *ERF*, 1; Rogers and McKim, *AIB*; and Ford Lewis Battles, "God Was Accommodating Himself to Human Capacity," in *Readings in Calvin's Theology*, ed. Donald K. McKim (Grand Rapids: Baker Book House, 1984), chap. 2.

32. Though some claim Calvin as supporting the first view mentioned above, my own view is that his approach to Scripture is best exemplified by this model. See my "Calvin's View of Scripture," in *Readings in Calvin's Theology*, ed. Donald K. McKim (Grand Rapids: Baker Book House, 1984), 43–68.

33. This approach was in contrast to Lutheran confessions, which feature no such article. It is sometimes said that the Reformed confessions are built on the "formal principle" of the Reformation—the authority of the Bible—while the Lutheran

confessions are built on the "material principle"—the doctrine of justification by grace through faith. See McKim, *The Bible in Theology and Preaching*, 31–36; Rogers and McKim, *AIB*, 116–25.

34. Reformed confessions seek to establish the Scriptures as authority for the church rather than Scripture plus church tradition, which was the position of the Roman Catholic church. See McKim, *The Bible in Theology and Preaching*, 32–33.

35. See G. C. Berkouwer, "The Testimony of the Spirit," in *Holy Scripture*, chap. 2, reprinted in McKim, *The Authoritative Word*, chap. 9.

36. Rogers and McKim, *AIB*, 125.

37. Heinrich Bullinger, *Summa Christenlicher Religion* (Zurich: Christoffel Fro-schouwer, 1576), cited in Rogers and McKim, *AIB*, 125.

38. For materials on Reformed biblical interpreters, see *Historical Handbook of Major Biblical Interpreters*, ed. Donald K. McKim (Downers Grove, Ill.: InterVarsity Press, 1998), and Rogers and McKim, *AIB*, passim.

39. Westminster Confession of Faith, chap. 1 (*BC* 6.002). This confession calls the Scriptures "the Word of God written." The Theological Declaration of Barmen (written by Karl Barth) says that "Jesus Christ, as he is attested for us in Holy Scripture, is the one Word of God which we have to hear and which we have to trust and obey in life and in death" (*BC* 8.11). Similarly, the Confession of 1967 says, "The one sufficient revelation of God is Jesus Christ, the Word of God incarnate, to whom the Holy Spirit bears unique and authoritative witness through the Holy Scriptures, which are received and obeyed as the word of God written. The Scriptures are not a witness among others, but the witness without parallel" (*BC* 9.27). This confession also recognizes that the Scriptures are human words, "conditioned by the language, thought forms, and literary fashions of the places and times at which they were written" (9.29).

Chapter 3

1. For a discussion of the biblical witness to God, see Edmund J. Fortman, *The Triune God: A Historical Study of the Doctrine of the Trinity* (reprint, Grand Rapids: Baker Book House, 1982), chaps. 1–2.

2. In the New Testament, "the Spirit of God is either presupposed or expressly named as the medium of the communion of Jesus with the Father and the mediator of the participation of believers in Christ" (Rom. 1:4; 8:11, 14–15). See Wolfhart Pannenberg, *Systematic Theology*, trans. Geoffrey W. Bromiley (Grand Rapids: Wm. B. Eerdmans Publishing Co., 1991), 1:266.

3. Pannenberg points out that "the early appearance of the baptismal formula (Matt. 28:19) undoubtedly made an important contribution to the development of a trinitarian understanding of God." Pannenberg, *Systematic Theology*, 1:268.

4. As Pannenberg notes, "The NT statements do not clarify the interrelations of the three but they clearly emphasize the fact that they are interrelated." See *Systematic Theology*, 1:269.

5. For more detail on what follows see my *Theological Turning Points* (Atlanta: John Knox Press, 1988), chap. 1: "Trinitarian Controversy: Who is God?" as well as introductions to church history and the history of doctrine, including now Roger E. Olson, *The Story of Christian Theology: Twenty Centuries of Tradition* (Downers Grove, Ill.: InterVarsity Press, 1999). Cf. Fortman, *The Triune God* and Bertrand de Margerie, *The Christian Trinity in History*, trans. Edmund J. Fortman, Studies in Historical Theology, vol. 1 (Still River, Mass.: St. Bede's Publications, 1982).

6. This is a very practical issue of Christian faith for Athanasius. For "the main interest of this argument was not to prove the monotheistic character of the Christian

understanding of God. It was basically to show how believers themselves could attain to fellowship with God through the Son and Spirit," Pannenberg, *Systematic Theology*, 1:273.

7. See Pannenberg, *Systematic Theology*, 1:279–80.

8. Pannenberg says that Augustine's use of psychological analogies were "simply meant to offer a very general way of linking the unity and trinity and thus creating some plausibility for trinitarian statements," *Systematic Theology*, 1:284.

9. The Roman Catholic theologian Karl Rahner has stressed that the "immanent Trinity" is identical with the "economic Trinity." See Karl Rahner, *Theological Investigations IV: More Recent Writings*, trans. Kevin Smith (New York: Crossroad, 1982), 94–102. Cf. Ted Peters, *God as Trinity: Relationality and Temporality in Divine Life* (Louisville, Ky.: Westminster John Knox Press, 1993), 20–24.

10. See below in the chapter on the Holy Spirit. For a discussion of the Reformation churches' views on the Trinity, see Ted A. Campbell, *Christian Confessions: A Historical Introduction* (Louisville, Ky.: Westminster John Knox Press, 1996), 141–44.

11. Art. VIII in *Reformed Confessions of the 16th Century*, ed. Arthur C. Cochrane (Philadelphia: Westminster Press, 1966), 192–93.

12. Ibid., 193. The Westminster Confession describes God by saying that "in the unity of the Godhead there be three Persons of one substance, power, and eternity: God the Father, God the Son, and God the Holy Ghost. The Father is of none, neither begotten nor proceeding; the Son is eternally begotten of the Father; the Holy Ghost eternally proceeding from the Father and the Son," chap. 2 in *BC* 6.013.

13. Jewett notes that this placement of the doctrine at the end of his work was "something never done before in a treatise on Christian theology." See Paul K. Jewett, *God, Creation, and Revelation: A Neo-Evangelical Theology* (Grand Rapids: Wm. B. Eerdmans Publishing Co., 1991), 266.

14. See Friedrich Schleiermacher, *The Christian Faith*, ed. H. R. MacKintosh and J. S. Stewart, 2 vols. (New York: Harper & Row, 1963), 738. Cf. Hendrikus Berkhof, *Christian Faith: An Introduction to the Study of the Faith*, rev. ed. (Grand Rapids: Wm. B. Eerdmans Publishing Co., 1986), 340.

15. See Barth, *CD*, I/1 (rev. ed.), 295.

16. Cynthia M. Campbell, "Trinity" in *ERF*, 375.

17. Barth, *CD*, I/1, rev. ed., 375.

18. Ibid., 383.

19. Typically, theologians have said that it is the human nature of the Son that suffers and not the divine. Moltmann, however, disagrees and favors the view called "patripassianism"—that the Father actively suffers in Christ's death. This view was rejected as heretical by the early church. See Moltmann's *The Crucified God: The Cross of Christ as the Foundation and Criticism of Christian Theology*, trans. R. A. Wilson and John Bowden (San Francisco: Harper Collins, 1991); and *The Trinity and the Kingdom: The Doctrine of God*, trans. Margaret Kohl (New York: Harper & Row, 1981).

20. Moltmann, *The Trinity and the Kingdom*, 175. Migliore writes that "the Trinity is essentially a *koinonia* [fellowship] of persons in love." See *Faith Seeking Understanding*, 68.

21. Moltmann, *The Trinity and the Kingdom*, 218.

22. Letty Russell, *The Future of Partnership* (Philadelphia: Westminster Press, 1979), 35. Cf. her later work, *Growth in Partnership* (Philadelphia: Westminster Press, 1981).

23. Letty Russell, *Household of Freedom: Authority in Feminist Theology* (Philadelphia: Westminster Press, 1987), 40.

24. For a discussion see Peters, *Trinity*, chap. 2, "A Map of Contemporary Issues," and his chap. 3, "Trinity Talk in the Last Half of the Twentieth Century."

25. Jack Rogers has noted that "for the compilers of the Apostles' Creed, God was Father or parent in two senses. The first and most important, in the setting of the early church, was the affirmation that God was the Father of Jesus Christ. . . . The very next thing of necessity to say is that Jesus Christ is of the same essence with God. . . . It was essential for the early Christians in both the Nicene and the Apostles' creeds to assert that Jesus had an intimate, organic, essential relationship with God. Their way of saying it was that God was the father of Jesus Christ." See *Presbyterian Creeds: A Guide to the Book of Confessions* (Louisville, Ky.: Westminster John Knox Press, 1991), 66–67. Cf. Peters, *Trinity* who refers to "Father," "Son," and "Holy Spirit" as metaphors and as "primarily titles used in address. Titles are typically translated from language to language, whereas proper names are normally transliterated. The trinitarian formula 'Father, Son, and Holy Spirit' is routinely translated, and nobody feels any loss," 53.

26. So Catherine Mowry LaCugna, who wrote that "the trinitarian tradition, like the Bible, is *both* the source of revelatory truth about the mystery of God *and* a powerful resource for patriarchal culture." See Catherine Mowry LaCugna, "The Baptismal Formula, Feminist Objections, and Trinitarian Theology," *Journal of Ecumenical Studies* 26, no. 2 (spring 1989), 238.

27. A common analogy (or children's sermon) for the Trinity has been that God is like H_2O, which can assume three "states" (modes)—as solid (ice), liquid (water), and gas (steam). This is a modalistic model to be avoided!

28. See Peters, *Trinity*, 27–34.

29. See Stanley J. Grenz, *Theology for the Community of God* (Nashville: Broadman & Holman Publishers, 1994), 86. He notes that "each of the three trinitarian members fulfills a specific role in the one divine program. The Father functions as the ground of the world and of the divine program for creation. The Son functions as the revealer of God, the exemplar and herald of the Father's will for creation, and the redeemer of humankind. And the Spirit functions as the personal divine power active in the world, the completer of the divine will and program."

30. See Peters, *Trinity*, 34–37. Peters writes that the "modern view" is of a person as "a unique individual who is a self-initiating and self-determining subject. Each person is a distinct seat of subjectivity and, hence, independent of other persons and things. One's personhood signals one's autonomy," 35.

31. Catherine Mowry LaCugna notes that "to think of a person without thinking of that person in relationship to another person defeats what it means to be a person." See LaCugna's "The Practical Trinity," *The Christian Century* (July 15–22, 1992), 681.

32. Thus Guthrie writes that, "The oneness of God is not the oneness of a distinct, self-contained individual; it is the unity of a *community* of persons who love each other and live together in harmony. And 'personal' means by definition *inter*-personal; one cannot be truly personal alone but only in relation to other persons. Such is the unity and personal character of God the Father, Son, and Holy Spirit. There is a deep, intimate, indissoluble unity between them." See Guthrie, *Christian Doctrine*, 92.

33. Ted Peters, *God—The World's Future: Systematic Theology for a Postmodern Era* (Minneapolis: Fortress, 1992), 104. Peters goes on to note that each of the persons of the Godhead "face inward as well as outward. Each person faces the other two, and hence each is identifiable even within the divine life proper," 105. Cf. his *Trinity*, 69.

34. Peters, *God*, 105, citing the proposal to use "identity" by Robert Jenson, *Triune Identity* (Philadelphia: Fortress Press, 1982), 108. Cf. Peters's discussion of Jenson in *Trinity*, 128–34.

35. See "The Practical Trinity," in which LaCugna writes that instead of focusing on the Trinity as a description of God's "inner life," contemporary theologians are redis-

covering that "by returning to the more concrete images and concepts of the Bible, liturgy and creeds, it has become clear that the original purpose of the doctrine was to explain the place of Christ in our salvation, the place of the Spirit in our sanctification or deification, and in so doing to say something about the mystery of God's eternal being. By concentrating more on the mystery of *God with us*, *God for us*, and less on the nature of God by Godself, it is becoming possible once again for the doctrine of the Trinity to stand at the center of faith—as our rhetoric has always claimed," 678. Cf. her *God for Us: The Trinity and Christian Life* (San Francisco: Harper, 1992).

36. Donald G. Bloesch, *God the Almighty: Power, Wisdom, Holiness, Love* (Downers Grove, Ill.: InterVarsity Press, 1995), 203.

37. Guthrie, *Christian Doctrine*, 85.

38. Grenz, *Theology for the Community of God*, 98.

39. Guthrie, *Christian Doctrine*, 94.

40. Grenz, *Theology for the Community of God*, 98.

41. See Leonardo Boff, *Trinity and Society* (Maryknoll, N.Y.: Orbis Books, 1988), 118–20, cited in Migliore, *Faith Seeking Understanding*, 70.

Chapter 4

1. Cf. Pss. 9, 19, 24, 29, 33, 36, 74, 90, 93, 96–99, 104, 139, 147, 149.

2. See Christoph Barth, *God with Us: A Theological Introduction to the Old Testament*, ed. Geoffrey W. Bromiley (Grand Rapids: Wm. B. Eerdmans Publishing Co., 1991), chap. 1.

3. See Wolfhart Pannenberg, *Systematic Theology*, trans. Geoffrey W. Bromiley, 3 vols. (Grand Rapids: Wm. B. Eerdmans Publishing Co., 1991), 2:20–35.

4. See D. K. McKim, "Creation, Doctrine of" in *Evangelical Dictionary of Theology*, ed. Walter A. Elwell (Grand Rapids: Baker Book House, 1984), 281–83.

5. Basil of Caesarea, "Sermon on Creation" in Ray C. Petry, ed., *A History of Christianity* (Englewood Cliffs, N.J.: Prentice Hall, 1962), 104.

6. Pannenberg, *Systematic Theology*, 2:30.

7. Langdon Gilkey, *Maker of Heaven and Earth: The Christian Doctrine of Creation in the Light of Modern Knowledge* (New York: Doubleday & Co., 1965), 79.

8. The view that God created a good creation out of nothing was made official church teaching at the Fourth Lateran Council (1215) and the Council of Florence (1442).

9. Tertullian, *The Treatise against Hermogenes*, chap. 17, cited in Gilkey, 50.

10. See the discussion below in the chapter on Providence. Cf. Stephen T. Davis, ed., *Encountering Evil: Live Options in Theodicy* (Atlanta: John Knox Press, 1981); John S. Feinberg, *The Many Faces of Evil: Theological Systems and the Problem of Evil* (Grand Rapids: Zondervan Publishing House, 1994); Douglas John Hall, *God and Human Suffering* (Minneapolis: Augsburg, 1986); Gilkey, *Maker of Heaven and Earth*, chap. 7; and Daniel L. Migliore, *Faith Seeking Understanding: An Introduction to Christian Theology* (Grand Rapids: Wm. B. Eerdmans Publishing Co., 1991), chap. 6.

11. Cited in Gilkey, *Maker of Heaven and Earth*, 49. Thus Augustine spoke of evil as the "privation of the good" (Lat. *privatio boni*). See *The City of God*, 12.2–5; *Enchiridion* 11–15.

12. Pannenberg writes that "the faith of Israel and primitive Christianity never entertained the thought of accusing the Creator himself of the evil that had come into his creation," *Systematic Theology*, 2:163. See 161–74.

13. Gilkey, *Maker of Heaven and Earth*, 55. Gilkey went on to write that "the christian understanding of creation as an act of a free and loving divine will is the sole basis

for our confidence that our finite life has a meaning, a purpose, and a destiny which no immediate misfortune can eradicate," 77.

14. Gilkey, *Maker of Heaven and Earth*, 83.

15. For historical attitudes of Christians toward nature see H. Paul Santmire, *The Travail of Nature: The Ambiguous Ecological Promise of Christian Theology* (Philadelphia: Fortress Press, 1985) as well as George S. Hendry, *The Theology of Nature* (Philadelphia: Westminster Press, 1980). Cf. Jürgen Moltmann, *God in Creation: A New Theology of Creation and the Spirit of God*, trans. Margaret Kohl (San Francisco: Harper & Row, 1985).

16. Moltmann writes, "As the image of God on earth, human beings correspond first of all to the relationship of God to themselves and to the whole of creation. But they also correspond to the inner relationships of God to himself—to the eternal, inner love of God which expresses and manifests itself in creation," *God in Creation*, 77.

17. See Scots Confession, Art. 1 in *BC* 3.01, and French Confession, Art. VII in Cochrane, *Reformed Confessions*, 146. More on the Reformed and angels can be found in Heinrich Heppe, ed., *Reformed Dogmatics: Set Out and Illustrated from the Sources*, revised and edited by Ernst Bizer, trans. G. T. Thompson (reprint, Grand Rapids: Baker Book House, 1978), chap. 10, and Barth, *CD* III/3, 369–418.

18. Chap. 4, *BC* 6.022.

19. Art. XII in Cochrane, ed., *Reformed Confessions*, 196. Biblical references cited are Gen. 1:1; Isa. 40:26; Heb. 3:4; Rev. 4:11; 1 Cor. 8:6; John 1:3; Col. 1:16.

20. Moltmann, *God the Creator*, 97–98. Rohls notes that in the principle of Augustine, "the external works of God are undivided." Thus, while the Apostles' Creed ascribes creation to the Father, redemption to the Son, and sanctification to the Spirit, "this ascription cannot mean dissolution of the unity of the triune God in God's externally directed works. All persons of the Trinity participate in each instance of saving action, so that every saving action of *God* is a saving action of the whole *Trinity*. For this reason it is impossible to understand the designation of the Father as creator in an exclusive sense, so that the Son and the Spirit would not have a part in the creation of the world." See Rohls, *Reformed Confessions*, 54–55.

21. Barth, *CD*, III/1, 333.

22. Pannenberg, *Systematic Theology*, 2:22.

23. Karl Barth, *Dogmatics in Outline*, trans. G. T. Thompson (New York: Harper Brothers, 1959), 53.

24. Barth, *Dogmatics in Outline*, 53.

25. Ibid., 53–54.

26. Barth's ways of discussing this are to describe "Creation as the External Basis of the Covenant" and "The Covenant as the Internal Basis of Creation" (*CD*, III, 94–329).

27. Art. 12 in Cochrane, ed., *Reformed Confessions*, 196.

28. Question 1 in *BC* 7.001.

29. Moltmann writes that all stages of evolution in the world are God's "intentional fortuitousness—free creations of God for the purpose of the self-communication of his goodness, with his glorification as their end and goal," *God in Creation*, 207.

30. Barth describes this by saying that "the covenant [in Jesus Christ] is the goal of creation" (*CD* III/1, 231) and that creation is a "benefit" because "it is based upon and attains its end in the divine covenant with [humanity]" (III/1, 363). See Barth, "The Yes of God the Creator" (III/1, §42) in which he writes of Creation as Benefit, Actualization, and Justification (III/1, 330–414).

31. Moltmann, *God in Creation*, 207.

32. See Calvin, *Inst.* I.5.8; I.6.2; II.6.1; III.9.2, etc., for this image of creation as God's "theater."

33. Calvin, *Inst.* I.14.21. For Calvin, the creation shows forth these attributes of God, but cannot give a "saving" knowledge of God because of human sin. See Bk. 2 of the *Institutes.* On this issue see William Klempa, "Knowledge of God" in *ERF,* 206–8.

34. Calvin, *Inst.* I.14.22.

35. See Gilkey's discussions in *Maker of Heaven and Earth,* chap. 2; 148–55; Migliore, *Faith Seeking Understanding,* 95–98; and Moltmann, *God in Creation,* 190ff.

36. Migliore points out that the case of Galileo, the Wilberforce-Huxley debate, the Scopes trial, and current arguments about "creation science" remind us of "how wide-spread the confusion has been and continues to be on both sides about the relationship of science and faith," *Faith Seeking Understanding,* 96. Cf. Conrad Hyers, *The Meaning of Creation: Genesis and Modern Science* (Atlanta: John Knox Press, 1984).

37. See Migliore, *Faith Seeking Understanding,* 96. Wolfhart Pannenberg agrees when he writes that "our evolutionary derivation does not rule out the immediacy of our relation to God." *Systematic Theology,* 2:135.

38. Q. 95, *BC* 4.095, and Q. 94, *BC* 4.094.

39. Part of the seduction of idolatry is that the things we may put our "trust" in can be good or important in and of themselves—it is good and important to achieve certain goals or enjoy certain things. But when these take on the rightful place of God in our lives, they become our "idols" and become a wedge between us and our Creator. Luther called the human mind an "idol factory." Calvin indicates there are four things we owe God: adoration, trust, invocation, and thanksgiving. When we take on other allegiances or find another focus in our lives, we create idols. For "the Lord suffers nothing of these to be transferred to another, so he commands that all be rendered wholly to himself" (*Inst.* II.8.16).

Chapter 5

1. The creator God is also the sustainer God. As Pannenberg points out, "All these works—God's action in preserving and ruling his creatures, and also the bringing forth of new things and God's reconciling and consummating of the world that he has cre-ated—participate in the quality of his action at the creation of the world." Wolfhart Pannenberg, *Systematic Theology,* trans. Geoffrey W. Bromiley, 3 vols. (Grand Rapids: Wm. B. Eerdmans Publishing Co., 1994), 2:41.

2. See G. C. Berkouwer, *The Providence of God,* trans. Lewis B. Smedes (reprint, Grand Rapids: Wm. B. Eerdmans Publishing Co., 1961); Benjamin Wirt Farley, *The Providence of God* (Grand Rapids: Baker Book House, 1988); Pannenberg, *Systematic Theology,* 2:35–59; Paul Helm, *The Providence of God* (Downers Grove, Ill.: InterVarsity Press, 1994); and the 1678 work by the Puritan John Flavel, *The Mystery of Providence* (London: The Banner of Truth Trust, 1963).

3. The Hebrew term *Yahweh jireh* ("God will provide") was translated in the Latin Vulgate version of the Bible as *Deus providebit* and thus is related to the English term "providence." The Greek term is *pronoia,* translated as "forethought," or "provision" from the verb *pronoeō* meaning "to perceive beforehand," "foresee," or "provide for." See Farley, *Providence of God,* 16.

4. Farley points out that "the doctrine of the providence of God is, above all, a doc-trine of faith, based on revelation. It is not a postulate of reason." Our source for believ-ing in God's providence is the Bible and is a "conviction of faith based on revelation." It has to do with "trust, confidence, and hope. It has to do with action, not passivity; it has to do with mighty deeds, valor, and deliverance, not speculation about causal series per se," *Providence of God,* 17, 18.

5. The Latin terms usually used are *conservatio* (preservation), *concursus* (coopera-tion), and *gubernatio* (governance). See Farley, *Providence of God*, chap. 2; Berkouwer, *Providence of God*, chaps. 3–5 and Barth, *CD* III/3,3. A typical definition of providence is from Louis Berkhof who wrote that providence is "that continued exercise of the divine energy whereby the Creator preserves all His creatures, is operative in all that comes to pass in the world, and directs all things to their appointed end," *Systematic Theology* (reprint, London: Banner of Truth Trust, 1969), 166. See his Pt. 1, chap. 6. Barth's three chapters are: "The Divine Preserving," "The Divine Accompanying," and "The Divine Ruling," *CD* III/3, 58–238.

6. See Hendrikus Berkhof, *Christian Faith: An Introduction to the Study of the Faith*, trans. Sierd Woudstra, rev. ed. (Grand Rapids: Wm. B. Eerdmans Publishing Co., 1986), 215–24; Berkouwer, *Providence of God*, chap. 3; and Barth, *CD* III/3, 58–90.

7. Some have seen that the Hebrew language, in which the Old Testament was writ-ten, has "no word for the sustenance of the world, and that sustaining and creating are both indicated by *bara*." As Berkouwer notes, "this does not weaken the distinction between them, but does underscore the Scriptural testimony to the unity of God's word, and the implied dependency of all creation (Isa. 45:7). . . . The word *bara* indi-cates 'Divine origination'; not only the Divine origination of creation out of nothing but also the Divine origination of each moment," *Providence of God*, 65.

8. See Berkouwer, *Providence of God*, chap. 5; Barth, *CD* III/3, 90–154.

9. This human freedom is sometimes called "free agency." Humans are "agents" who can act according to their own willful decisions.

10. Berkouwer, *Providence of God*, 152. Put another way, Berkouwer writes of the providence of God and human responsibility that "they do not exist together in the Scriptures as something problematic. They both reveal the greatness of Divine activ-ity, in that it does not exclude human activity and responsibility but embraces them and in them manifests God on the way to the accomplishment of His purposes," 98.

11. Barth, *CD* III/3, 165.

12. The difference between the Christian doctrine of providence and a belief in blind fate or determinism ("whatever will be, will be") is that with fate or determinism, there is no personality; there is just causality or the beginning of a chain of events that just happens. The Christian affirmation of God's providence sees that "the nature of the personal living God absolutely defines the nature of the determining." God's invinci-ble, sovereign activity is carried out as the work of the personal, loving, and just God—whom we know most clearly and fully in Jesus Christ. God is not "blind fate"; God is the living God of the Scriptures who acts in freedom and love. See Berkouwer, *Provi-dence of God*, 152–53. Barth's emphasis is that Christian providence is unique because the God we know in providence is "the eternal Father of our Lord Jesus Christ." It is not only that God is "over us" in providence, but that God is "with us": "The One who is for us as the Son is over us as the Father." For "we can know of no divine power over us, nor is there any such power, which is not this fatherly hand," *CD* III/3, 28–29.

13. Berkouwer, *Providence of God*, 153. Philosophically, the issues have been well debated and framed in terms of "primary" and "secondary" causes. God is the primary cause; human actions are the secondary causes. God is the "cause" of the law of grav-ity, but if I drop a brick on my foot, I am the "cause" of that action, too. See *Providence of God*, 154–58. Cf. D. A. Carson, *Divine Sovereignty and Human Responsibility: Biblical Perspectives in Tension*, New Foundations Theological Library (Atlanta: John Knox Press, 1981), as well as *Predestination and Free Will: Four Views of Divine Sovereignty and Human Freedom*, ed. David and Randall Basinger (Downers Grove, Ill.: InterVarsity Press, 1986).

14. See Berkouwer, *Providence of God*, chap. 4; Barth, *CD* III/3, 154–238.

15. The danger of trying to read God's purposes from historical facts is tragically highlighted by the "German Christians" who followed Hitler and saw his rise as God's providential plan. Others through history have crusaded with the same zeal and singlemindedness. Berkouwer warns against this tendency to "pluck what for us are the extraordinary events from the entire stream of history" and call them God's "providence." Rather, "the recognition of history as the work of God, directed toward His purpose, His kingdom, does not include a detailed calculation of His intents." We know God's providence in retrospect, as we interpret facts and events from the perspective of faith. *Providence of God*, 174; cf. chap. 5: "Providence and History."

16. An important question is whether there can be a knowledge of "providence" outside the Christian faith? This is related to the issue of "natural theology": can humans come to a knowledge of God apart from God's revelation in Scripture and in Jesus Christ? On the issue of natural theology, Karl Barth and Emil Brunner had a famous clash in the 1930s over whether or not there was a "point of contact" (Ger. *Anknüpfungspunkt*) between God and human sinners and whether humans themselves have a "capacity for revelation" (Ger. *Offenbarungsmächtigkeit*)—both of which Brunner affirmed. Barth denied both. He argued that there is no knowledge of God other than what comes to us in Jesus Christ, and that there is no "general revelation" of God that is knowable from nature. Similarly, there is no knowledge of God's providence that comes to us apart from the knowledge of God in Jesus Christ. See the debate in Emil Brunner and Karl Barth, *Natural Theology*, trans. P. Fraenkel (London: Geoffrey Bles, 1946), and the analysis by J. Bruce McCallum, "Modernity and the Dilemma of Natural Theology: The Barth-Brunner Debate, 1934" (diss., Marquette University, 1994). Cf. Alasdair I. C. Heron, *A Century of Protestant Theology* (Philadelphia: Westminster Press, 1980), 84–91. Cf. I. John Hesselink, "Natural Theology," in *ERF*, 250–53.

17. Pannenberg points out that God's establishment of the "laws of nature" does not mean that God can only bring forth "what is new and unusual" by breaking the laws of nature, because "for all their regularity the laws of nature do not have the character of closed (or, better, isolated) systems," *Systematic Theology*, 2:73. God works in and through the laws of nature to accomplish the divine purposes.

18. Berkouwer, *Providence of God*, 180. The love is the love we find in God incarnate, Jesus Christ. For "Christ has the key to Divine Providence," 48.

19. See Farley's survey in *Providence of God*, chaps. 3–10.

20. Thus the Westminster Confession says: "God, the great Creator of all things, doth uphold, direct, dispose, and govern all creatures, actions, and things, from the greatest even to the least, by his most wise and holy providence, according to his infallible foreknowledge, and the free and immutable counsel of his own will, to the praise of the glory of his wisdom, power, justice, goodness, and mercy," chap. 5 in *BC* 6.024.

21. Barth indicates that Genesis 22:14, where Abraham names the place of sacrifice *Jehovah Jireh*—the "LORD will provide"—shows us that God's providence does not mean only God's foreknowledge, or that God "knows" without "willing" what will happen. Barth says that "in this passage, 'to see' really means 'to see about.' It is an active and selective predetermining, preparing and procuring of a lamb to be offered instead of Isaac. God 'sees to' this burnt offering for Abraham," *CD* III/3, 3. As Bromiley says, "Mere foreseeing does not meet the bill. God also provides," *Introduction to the Theology of Karl Barth* (Grand Rapids: Wm. B. Eerdmans Publishing Co., 1979), 142. For Barth, providence is the execution of God's decree of predestination to save the world in Jesus Christ. See *CD* III/3.

22. Barth put it, "What God knows He wills, and what He wills He does. Not only

does He know all in all but He also works all in all, and He does so as the eternal God," *CD* III/3, 120–21.

23. See Berkouwer, *Providence of God*, chap. 8: "The Problem of Theodicy." Cf. Pannenberg, *Systematic Theology*, 2:161–74, and Jürgen Moltmann, "The Question of Theodicy and the Pain of God," in *History and the Triune God*, trans. John Bowden (New York: Crossroad, 1992).

24. Relatedly, see Berkouwer's discussion of "A Biblical *A Priori*"—that "God is not the Source, or the Cause, or the Author" of human sin, in *Sin*, trans. Philip C. Holtrop (Grand Rapids: Wm. B. Eerdmans Publishing Co., 1971), 27.

25. Calvin, *Inst.* I.17.1.

26. Thus the Heidelberg Catechism asks and answers:

Q. 28 What advantage comes from acknowledging God's creation and providence?

A. We learn that we are to be patient in adversity, grateful in the midst of blessing, and to trust our faith in God and Father for the future, assured that no creature shall separate us from his love, since all creatures are so completely in his hand that without his will they cannot even move (*BC 4.028*).

27. Guthrie, *Christian Doctrine*, 171.

28. Calvin, *Inst.* I.17.7.

Chapter 6

1. The name "Adam" (Heb. *ha'adam*, "the man") means "human being."

2. The Westminster Shorter Catechism, when asking what is the "chief end" or purpose of humanity, gives the answer: "to glorify God, and to enjoy [God] forever." See Q. 1 in *BC* 7.001.

3. See Paul K. Jewett, *Who We Are: Our Dignity as Human* (Grand Rapids: Wm. B. Eerdmans Publishing Co., 1996), 36–44.

4. See G. C. Berkouwer, *Man: The Image of God*, trans. Dirk W. Jellema (Grand Rapids: Wm. B. Eerdmans Publishing Co., 1962), chap. 10: "The Whole Man"; Anthony A. Hoekema, *Created in God's Image*, (Grand Rapids: Wm. B. Eerdmans Publishing Co., 1986) chap. 11.

5. Walter F. Taylor Jr., "Humanity, NT View of" in *ABD*, 3:321.

6. Thus, the biblical scholar J. A. T. Robinson wrote that in the Old Testament, "Any part can stand at any moment for the whole," *The Body* (London: SCM Press, 1953), 16.

7. George Eldon Ladd indicates that in Paul's writings in the New Testament, "recent scholarship has recognized that such terms as body, soul, and spirit are not different, separable faculties of each individual but different ways of viewing the whole person," *A Theology of the New Testament*, rev. ed., ed. Donald A. Hagner (Grand Rapids: Wm. B. Eerdmans Publishing Co., 1993), 499.

8. This is sometimes described as a "psychosomatic unity." See *ABD*, 3:121; Hoekema, *Created in God's Image*, 217.

9. See Douglas John Hall, *Imaging God: Dominion as Stewardship* (Grand Rapids and New York: Wm. B. Eerdmans Publishing Co. and Friendship Press, 1986), chap. 2: "*Imago Dei*: The Scriptural Background"; Hoekema, *Created in God's Image*, chap. 3; Philip Edgcumbe Hughes, *The True Image: The Origin and Destiny of Man in Christ* (Grand Rapids: Wm. B. Eerdmans Publishing Co., 1989), Part 1; and H. D. McDonald, *The Christian View of Man*, Foundations for Faith (reprint, Westchester, Ill.: Crossway Books, 1985), chap. 3.

10. See Marianne H. Micks, *Our Search for Identity: Humanity in the Image of God* (Philadelphia: Fortress Press, 1982).

11. Jewett wrote that "God has created us embodied souls endowed with his image," *Who We Are*, 39. He defines the soul as "the personal self, the 'I,' animating the body and manifest in a bodily way. I am my soul, not my body; yet this soul that is 'I' is the soul of my particular body and of no others," 42.

12. Berkouwer, *Man: The Image of God*, 195. He notes that our "humanness" depends on this relation with God and that the Word of God "never gives us a neutral independent analysis of man in order to inform us as to the components and structure of humanness in itself," 196.

13. This is in accord with the biblical perspective: the person is "always understood in terms of the relationship with God," *ABD*, 3:321.

14. See Hall, *Imaging God*, chap. 3, "Two Historical Conceptions of *Imago Dei*," in which he identifies the first as the "Substantialist," in which to be created in the image of God means that "the human species possesses certain characteristics or qualities that render it similar to the divine being. These characteristics or qualities are built into *anthropos*; they are aspects of human nature as such. They are 'capacities,' 'qualities,' 'original excellencies,' or 'endowments' that inhere in our creaturely substance (hence the 'substantialistic concept' of the 'imago')," 89. The second view is the "Relational," which sees the image of God as "an inclination or proclivity occurring within the relationship . . . between Creator and creature. The image of God is something that 'happens' as a consequence of this relationship. The human creature images (used as verb) its Creator because and insofar as it is 'turned toward' God. To be *imago Dei* does not mean to have something but to be and do something: to image God," 98.

15. See Hoekema, *Created in God's Image*, chap. 4; McDonald, *The Christian View of Man*, Parts II–III.

16. See Jewett, *Who We Are*, 64–65; Hoekema, *Created in God's Image*, 36–42; Hughes, *The True Image*, 195–98.

17. Calvin, *Inst.* I.15.3.

18. Ibid., I.15.4.

19. Ibid., II.2.12.

20. Ibid., III.7.6.

21. John Calvin, *Commentary on the First Book of Moses Called Genesis*, trans. John King (reprint, Grand Rapids: Wm. B. Eerdmans Publishing Co., 1948), 296. Jewett cites this comment in his chapter on "Human Dignity and Racial Prejudice" in *Who We Are*, chap. 3.

22. Calvin, *Inst.* III.7.6.

23. John Calvin, *The Second Epistle of Paul to the Corinthians, and the Epistles to Timothy, Titus and Philemon*, trans. T. A. Smail, Calvin's New Testament Commentaries, ed. David W. Torrance and Thomas F. Torrance (reprint, Grand Rapids: Wm. B. Eerdmans Publishing Co., 1979), *Comm. on 2 Cor. 3:18*.

24. Calvin, *Inst.* I.15.4.

25. Barth, *CD*, III/2, 3. Barth's anthropological approach is christological. As Berkouwer puts it, "Barth arrives at the conclusion that we can not begin with a definition of human nature (as if we already knew what it is!) and then say that Jesus shared in this human nature: it is the other way around. Since Jesus is true man, we must say that 'we possess human nature because Jesus first possessed it,'" *Man: The Image of God*, 92.

26. Barth, *CD*, III/2, 132. For Barth, human sin distorts any knowledge of the true nature of humans. Thus, we must look to Jesus as the "true Man" since he was sinless. Barth wrote that the man Jesus is "the one in whose identity with himself we must rec-

ognize at once the identity of God with Himself. In all other creatures the presence of God is at least problematical, but here it is beyond discussion," *CD* III/2, 68.

27. Barth said that if we wonder where we might find an "authentic revelation" of human nature and true humanity, "we are not led to man in general but to man in particular, and in supreme particularity to the one man Jesus," *CD* III/2, 44. Pilate spoke more truth than he knew when he presented Jesus to the crowd and said, "Here is the man!" (*Ecce homo*; John 19:5).

28. See Berkouwer, *Man: The Image of God*, 107–9; Hughes, *The True Image*, 26–29; Hoekema, 73–75.

29. Hall, *Imaging God*, 107.

30. See Jewett, *Who We Are*, chap. 5: "The Divine Image and the Dominion of Humankind"; McDonald, *The Christian View of Man*, 35.

31. See Hall's call for "dominion redefined Christologically" and seeing Jesus Christ as "the paradigm for our entire understanding of human dominion within creation," *Imaging God*, 185. Dominion will not be "domination," but "service." Cf. his *The Steward: A Biblical Symbol Come of Age* (reprint, New York: Friendship Press, 1985), chap. 7. Stewardship is a biblical concept that means much more than simply raising a church budget for the next year. It is a powerful "symbolic expression for the whole Christian (and human) life." See Douglas John Hall, "Stewardship" in *ERF*, 358–59.

32. Wolfhart Pannenberg uses the "image of God" in "the general sense of a human destination to communion with God." See *Anthropology in Theological Perspective*, trans. Matthew J. O'Connell (Philadelphia: Westminster Press, 1985), 74.

33. Jewett goes on to note that "we are brought to confess that our being is a being-in-relation-to-God, our Creator, only through our knowledge that God is our Redeemer. It is in Christ that we clearly perceive that God is the God-who-has-made-us-for-himself and therefore freely acknowledge that we are the creature-who-is-uniquely-related-to-him," *Who We Are*, 18.

34. This includes genuine equality in gender relationships as well as in social relationships. See Paul K. Jewett, *Man as Male and Female* (Grand Rapids: Wm. B. Eerdmans Publishing Co., 1975), and *Who We Are*, chap. 4, as well as the essays in *The Image of God: Gender Models in Judaeo-Christian Tradition*, ed. Kari Elisabeth Børresen (Minneapolis: Fortress Press, 1991); cf. Molly Marshall, *What It Means to Be Human* (Macon, Ga.: Smith & Helwys Publishing, 1995), chap. 4: "The Duality of Humanity."

35. Hall speaks of the "three dimensions of human relatedness." The human being is "being-with-God, who is source and ground of all being; it is being-with-the-human-counterpart (*Mitmenschen*); and it is being-with-nature," *Imaging God*, 127. Cf. his chaps. 5, 6.

36. Guthrie, *Christian Doctrine*, 198.

37. Ibid.

Chapter 7

1. See Robin C. Cover, "Sin, Sinners (OT)," and E. P. Sanders, "Sin, Sinners (NT)," in *ABD*, 6:31–47, and G. W. Bromiley, "Sin," *ISBE*, 518–25. Among the Hebrew terms used for the idea are words meaning "a missing," "rebellious deeds," "transgression," "perversion," "evil" in disposition, "impiety," and "iniquity."

2. See Herman Ridderbos, *Paul: An Outline of His Theology*, trans. John Richard De Witt (Grand Rapids: Wm. B. Eerdmans Publishing Co., 1975), Part III, "The Life in Sin," and D. E. H. Whiteley, *The Theology of St. Paul* (Philadelphia: Fortress Press, 1966), 45–53.

3. New Testament terms for sin include those that mean "missing the mark," "transgression," "unrighteousness," "impiety," "lawlessness," "depravity," wickedness," "debt," and "evil desire." See *ISBE* 4:518; *ABD* 6:40–41. See also Bernard Ramm, *Offense to Reason: The Theology of Sin* (San Francisco: Harper & Row, 1985), chap. 3, "The Case Against the Human Race," 38.

4. Bernard Ramm said that "no world religion has such an extensive doctrine of sin as Christianity," *Offense to Reason*, 38. See the old study by Julius Müller, *The Christian Doctrine of Sin*, trans. William Urwick, 2 vols. (Edinburgh: T. & T. Clark, 1868).

5. See G. C. Berkouwer, *Sin*, trans. Philip C. Holtrop (Grand Rapids: Wm. B. Eerdmans Publishing Co., 1971), pt. 1. Berkouwer argues that to seek a rational answer for the "origin" of sin is to try to construct an excuse for sin. He was of the opinion that "an explanation for sin is truly impossible," 26. The "riddle of sin" (chap. 5) is that there is "no reason and no sensible motive for [human] sin" (134). It is "senseless," as the Scriptures refer to the "mystery of lawlessness" (2 Thess. 2:7). Sin can only be confessed, not explained. Cf. Philip Edgcumbe Hughes, *The True Image: The Origin and Destiny of Man in Christ* (Grand Rapids: Wm. B. Eerdmans Publishing Co., 1989), chap. 7.

6. See Berkouwer, *Sin*, chaps. 12–17; Anthony A. Hoekema, *Created in God's Image* (Grand Rapids: Wm. B. Eerdmans Publishing Co., 1986), chaps. 7, 8.

7. See McKim, *Turning Points*, 64–70.

8. See backgrounds in F. R. Tennant, *The Sources of the Doctrines of the Fall and Original Sin* (reprint, New York: Schocken Books, 1968).

9. They were from the region known as Cappadocia, modern-day Turkey. The theologians were Basil of Caesarea (ca. 330–379), his brother Gregory of Nyssa (ca. 335–ca. 395), and Gregory of Nazianzus (ca. 329–390).

10. See Ramm, *Offense to Reason*, chap. 5.

11. See McKim, *Turning Points*, 70–73; Hughes, *The True Image*, chap. 14.

12. Bavinck says that for Pelagius and his followers, "sin consists always of unlawfulness, illegitimacy, in the transgression and departure from the law which God laid down for His rational and moral creatures. Such departure from the law can take place in the deeds of men, but it can also come to expression in his dispositions and inclinations, that is, in his nature as he brings it with him from his conception and birth." See Herman Bavinck, *Our Reasonable Faith*, trans. Henry Zylstra (reprint, Grand Rapids: Baker Book House, 1977), 236.

13. Bavinck writes that the original sin in which humanity is "conceived and born is not a dormant, passive quality, but a root, rather, from which all kinds of sin come up, an unholy fountain from which sin continuously wells up, a force which is always impelling the heart of [humans] in the wrong direction—away from God and from communion with Him and towards corruption and decay." Thus "actual sins" spring from this sinful nature. Bavinck, *Our Reasonable Faith*, 246.

14. For Augustine, the essence of sin is "pride." Since "humility" (Lat. *humilitas*) is the basic virtue of the redeemed life, "pride" (Lat. *superbia*) is the basic sin. He cited Sirach 10:13: "Pride is the beginning of all sin." As a result of sin, humanity is infected with "self-love" (*cupiditas*) and "concupiscence," which means "the law of sin in our sinful flesh" (see Calvin, *Inst.* II.1.8 n16). But Augustine went on, however, to narrow original sin to sexuality as he saw the act of procreation as the means by which original sin is transmitted. See Berkhof, *Christian Faith*, 195–97. For Aquinas, "concupiscence" was the love of self or "the inordinate longing for some temporal good." He wrote that "the inordinate love of self is the cause of all sin," *Summa Theologica* I, II, q. 77, art. 4. Calvin wrote that "the whole man is of himself nothing but concupiscence" (*Inst.* II.1.8).

15. In addition to the theologians cited below, important works on sin in the Reformed tradition include Jonathan Edwards, *The Great Christian Doctrine of Original Sin Defended* (1754) in *The Works of President Edwards* (New York: S. Converse, 1829); Emil Brunner, *Man in Revolt: A Christian Anthropology*, trans. Olive Wyon (Philadelphia: Westminster Press, 1947); and Reinhold Niebuhr, *Moral Man and Immoral Society* (New York: Scribner's, 1932); *The Nature and Destiny of Man: A Christian Interpretation*, 2 vols. (New York: Scribner's, 1951). Cf. Merwyn S. Johnson, "Sin," in *ERF*, 350–52.

16. Calvin, *Inst.* II.1.5.

17. Ibid., II.1.8.

18. Ibid., II.1.9.

19. Berkouwer referred to the *"contra*-character of sin"—it is always "against" God. See *Sin*, chap. 8. Cf. Hoekema, *Created in God's Image*, chap. 9. Hendrikus Berkhof saw sin as "the misuse of freedom. We are so made that we need to find the anchoring of our life in the holy love of God by seeking our security in him and by being obedient to him. Sin is the refusal to find our anchoring there," *Christian Faith*, trans. Sierd Woodstra, rev. ed. (Grand Rapids: Wm. B. Eerdmans Publishing Co., 1986), 194. Cf. Ramm, *Offense to Reason*, 140–42, on Berkhof's views.

20. Calvin, *Inst.* II.3.5.

21. Ibid.

22. Two views were called "immediate imputation," by which was meant that God "imputed" or charged the sin and guilt of Adam to all who followed after him. This was done "immediately," without any other considerations being made. A view called "mediate imputation" held that each person inherits a tendency or proclivity to sin as the result and consequence of the first sin of Adam. When they do sin, their sin is "imputed" to them by virtue of their own actions. These views were part of a Reformed emphasis on "Federal Theology." This meant that "Adam" stood as the "federal head" or representative of all humanity. His actions thus held consequences for the rest of the human race. This approach contrasted with the "natural headship" view, which taught that all humanity was incipiently present in "Adam" and thus all acted in Adam's sin so that we are rightly implicated and guilty of his sin, which is also our own.

23. Reinhold Niebuhr spoke of taking the Genesis story seriously but not literally. He saw the story as a "myth" in the sense of its portrayal of a profound spiritual reality that attempts to relate the biblical perspective of life to the meaninglessness of history. Karl Barth used the term "saga" to describe the stories. Donald Bloesch has written: "To affirm that there are mythical and legendary elements in the Scripture is not to detract from its divine inspiration nor from its historical basis but to attest that the Holy Spirit has made use of various kinds of language and imagery to convey divine truth," *Essentials of Evangelical Theology*, 2 vols. (San Francisco: Harper & Row, 1978), 1:104–5.

24. Bloesch, *Essentials of Evangelical Theology* 1:107. He writes that it is "being caught up in a rebellion against our Creator, a rebellion that was "already in effect at the beginning of the race." Cf. Hoekema, *Created in God's Image*, 154–67, and Berkouwer, *Sin*, chaps. 13, 14.

25. Jack L. Stotts notes that "one characteristic of recent *Reformed Confessions* is their specifying of broad issues that the church must address for the sake of its own integrity and for the health of the world." These are issues of social ethics and necessarily include what the church regards as sin. See "Introduction: Confessing After Barmen," in Rohls, *Reformed Confessions*, xviii. This is also true of many understandings of sin by contemporary theologians. See Ramm, *Offense to Reason*, chap. 8, "Sin Among the Theologians."

26. *BC* 9.12–13. This confession echoes an emphasis of Barth, that we see our sin

when we look at Jesus Christ, rather than more abstractly as we consider our actions in light of God's law or the Ten Commandments. For Barth, the sin of humanity is expressed as pride, sloth, and falsehood—each able to be overcome only by God's revelation in Jesus Christ. See *CD*, IV/1, 358–513; IV/2, 378–498; IV/3, pt. 1, 368–480. The Confession of 1967 says: "The reconciling act of God in Jesus Christ exposes the evil" in humanity as "sin in the sight of God" (9.12). Cf. Berkouwer, *Sin*, 276–84, for his analysis of Barth's views.

27. *BC* 10.3.

28. For a contemporary study of the "experiential dynamics of sin and their evil effects" (p. 5) see Ted Peters, *Sin: Radical Evil in Soul and Society* (Grand Rapids: Wm. B. Eerdmans Publishing Co., 1994). See also Cornelius Plantinga Jr., *Not the Way It's Supposed to Be: A Breviary of Sin* (Grand Rapids: Wm. B. Eerdmans Publishing Co., 1995). More technical and philosophical is Christof Gestrich, *The Return of Splendor in the World: The Christian Doctrine of Sin and Forgiveness*, trans. Daniel W. Bloesch (Grand Rapids: Wm. B. Eerdmans Publishing Co., 1989).

29. The early Reformed tradition sought to safeguard worship of the sovereign God from "false worship." See Carlos M. N. Eire, "Idolatry," in *ERF*, 190–92.

30. *BC* 8.18.

31. Hendrikus Berkhof speaks of the consequences of sin as both "interpersonal"—between persons and affecting our daily lives—and "suprapersonal"—based on "the driving force inherent both in the institutions of our established society and in the anonymous powers of current codes of behavior, taboos, traditions, or the dictates of fashion," *Christian Faith*, 213.

32. See the helpful discussion by Daniel Migliore in *Faith Seeking Understanding: An Introduction to Christian Theology* (Grand Rapids: Wm. B. Eerdmans Publishing Co., 1991), 130–35. He quotes Rosemary Ruether who writes that "sin has to be seen both in the capacity to set up prideful, antagonistic relations to others and in the passivity of men and women to acquiesce to the group ego," *Sexism and God-Talk: Toward a Feminist Theology* (Boston: Beacon Press, 1983), 164. Migliore makes it clear that one cannot make a simplistic distribution of sin—saying that certain sins belong to "males" or "females." He notes instead the observation of Mary Potter Engel that sin has many faces and is like a kind of hydra—a monster growing two heads whenever one is severed. See Mary Potter Engel, "Evil, Sin, and Violation of the Vulnerable," in *Lift Every Voice: Constructing Christian Theologies from the Underside*, ed. Susan Brooks Thistlethwaite and Mary Potter Engel (San Francisco: Harper & Row, 1990), 163.

33. Biblically, there is the warning that "Even Satan disguises himself as an angel of light" (2 Cor. 11:14).

Chapter 8

1. It is common today to use "B.C.E."—"before the common era"—to refer to the years prior to the traditional birth of Jesus. The designation "A.D." stands for the Latin *Anno Domini*—"in year of the Lord." Calendar reform was carried out in the sixth century to indicate the years from the supposed year of the birth of Jesus of Nazareth.

2. As one scholar has written, "The whole Jewish literature agrees on only one feature of the Messiah: he will be a political ruler and national hero. His saving power requires that he deliver Israel from its oppressors and restore the authority of the law," O. A. Piper, "Messiah," *ISBE* 3:333.

3. A good summary statement is that the Old Testament prophecies "announce a decisive and lasting change in the plight of the people, brought about by God. War will end, peace and plenty will be restored. Israel and Judah will be reunited, people in Exile

will return; salvation has worldwide dimensions. A new era is inaugurated that will never end; it is absolutely unthinkable that God would allow the earlier situation to return. In these prophecies, the central figure is a descendant of David who represents an ideal of kingship in the name of YHWH; this is also reflected in the books of Samuel and Kings and in the Royal Psalms," Marinus De Jonge, "Messiah," *ABD*, 4:781.

4. Scholars have long pointed out that Jesus does not directly call himself the Messiah. At points he tells his disciples not to say to others that he is the Messiah (Mark 8:30). This is sometimes called the "Messianic Secret." The best understanding is that Jesus was probably afraid of what the people might do if he was associated with this title because of the political connotations it had. At one point a crowd was "about to come and take him by force to make him king" (John 6:15). Instead, Jesus spoke in parables to draw people into God's reign or kingdom (Matt. 13:34; Mark 4:34). See C. M. Tuckett, "Messianic Secret," *ABD*, 4:797–800.

5. The titles approach is used by Oscar Cullmann, *The Christology of the New Testament*, rev. ed. trans. Shirley C. Guthrie and Charles A. M. Hall (Philadelphia: Westminster Press, 1963). Cf. Eduard Schweizer, *Jesus*, trans. David E. Green (Atlanta: John Knox Press, 1971); various dictionary articles on these titles; and Marinus de Jonge, *Christology in Context: The Earliest Christian Response to Jesus* (Philadelphia: Westminster Press, 1988).

6. The most detailed treatment of the development of Christology is the two volumes by Aloys Grillmeier, *Christ in the Christian Tradition* (Atlanta: John Knox Press and Louisville, Ky.: Westminster Press, 1975–1985). Among other numerous studies, see *Turning Points*, chap. 2; David F. Wells, *The Person of Christ: A Biblical and Historical Analysis of the Incarnation* (Westchester, Ill.: Crossway Books, 1984); and J. N. D. Kelly, *Early Christian Doctrines*, rev. ed. (San Francisco: Harper & Row, 1978).

7. This is called "heresy" from the Greek term (*hairesis*) meaning "choice." Heresy usually overemphasizes one aspect of a truth, leading to a distorted view. The church declared some views heretical because it believed they were wrong and posed dangers for the faith of believers.

8. See G. C. Berkouwer, *The Person of Christ*, trans. John Vriend (reprint, Grand Rapids: Wm. B. Eerdmans Publishing Co., 1969), chaps. 8, 9; Wolfhart Pannenberg, *Systematic Theology*, trans. Geoffrey W. Bromiley, 3 vols. (Grand Rapids: Wm. B. Eerdmans Publishing Co., 1991), 2, chap. 10. Cf. Pannenberg's major christological study, *Jesus—God and Man*, 2nd ed., trans. Lewis L. Wilkins and Duane A. Priebe (Philadelphia: Westminster Press, 1977).

9. Adapted from Athanasius, *De Incarnatione*, 54, in *The Early Christian Fathers*, ed. and trans. Henry Bettenson (New York: Oxford University Press, 1969), 293.

10. Cited in J. N. D. Kelly, *Early Christian Doctrines*, 291.

11. Stanley Grenz has written, "Jesus of Nazareth had no predisposing advantages. He traveled no shortcut to maturity, transcended none of the limiting aspects of embodied existence, was spared no difficulty in living in the fallen world. On the contrary, he was truly one with us; he experienced fully our humanness," *Theology for the Community of God* (Nashville: Broadman, 1994), 362.

12. See Berkouwer, *The Person of Christ*, chap. 11.

13. This is technically called the *communicatio idiomata* ("communication of the attributes" or "properties"). It is used as a way of speaking to emphasize the mystery of the incarnation, as in the statement, "the Son of God died on the cross." See Berkouwer, *The Person of Christ*, 272–73.

14. See "Pope Leo I's Letter to Flavian of Constantinople," in *The Christological Controversy*, ed. Richard A. Norris Jr. (Philadelphia: Fortress Press, 1980), 145–55.

15. See the text in Norris, ed., *The Christological Controversy*, 159.

16. For a good discussion of the Council of Chalcedon and its aftermath in terms of Eastern Christianity, see Mark Ellingsen, *Reclaiming Our Roots: An Inclusive Introduction to Church History*, 2 vols. (Harrisburg, Pa.: Trinity Press International, 1999), 1:178ff. Eastern and Western churches split in 1054 over the issue of the status of the Bishop of Rome (Pope) and the procession of the Holy Spirit.

17. If the incarnation is due to God's nature, then because God is love, God had to send Christ to love the world and bring salvation because this would be a result of "who God is." If the incarnation is due to God's will, then God chose to redeem the world as an act of the divine will and could not be "forced" to do so by the divine nature. If God were "forced to do so by the divine nature," the argument goes, then God would not be omnipotent because God would be subject to a power outside God's self.

18. See John Macquarrie, *Jesus Christ in Modern Thought* (Philadelphia: Trinity Press International, 1990), for a survey.

19. See Gerald O'Collins, *Christology: A Biblical, Historical, and Systematic Study of Jesus* (London: Oxford University Press, 1995), chap. 1, "Some Major Challenges"; cf. Berkouwer, *The Person of Christ*, chap. 1, "The Crisis in the Doctrine of the Two Natures"; and Macquarrie, *Jesus Christ in Modern Thought*, chap. 1, "Problems of Christology."

20. See Gerald O'Collins, *What Are They Saying About Jesus?*, (New York: Paulist Press, 1977), 13ff. Cf. Hans Küng, *On Being a Christian*, trans. Edward Quinn (New York: Doubleday, 1976), 447ff.; John A. T. Robinson, *The Human Face of God* (London: SCM Press, 1973); Edward Schillebeeckx, *Jesus: An Experiment in Christology*, trans. Hubert Hoskins (New York: Crossroad, 1981); and Hans Schwarz, *Christology* (Grand Rapids: Wm. B. Eerdmans Publishing Co., 1998), chap. 5.

21. See, for example, the Scots Confession (*BC* 3.06, 3.07); the Second Helvetic Confession, chap. 11 (*BC* 5.062–5.079); the Westminster Confession (*BC* 6.043–6.045); and A Brief Statement of Faith, which says simply: "We trust in Jesus Christ, fully human, fully God" (*BC* 10.2).

22. *BC* 4.018, 4.016, 4.017. Cf. Rohls, *Reformed Confessions*, 102–17, for a discussion of Reformed confessional views of Christology.

23. As the Confession of 1967 puts it, "Jesus Christ is God with man. He is the eternal Son of the Father, who became man and lived among us to fulfill the work of reconciliation" (*BC* 9.07). It begins its christological section by saying that "in Jesus of Nazareth, true humanity was realized once for all. Jesus, a Palestinian Jew, lived among his own people and shared their needs, temptations, joys, and sorrow . . ." (9.08).

24. This was also the approach of the Lutheran Albrecht Ritschl (1822–1889) who believed that "our knowledge of Christ, as of God, moves from below to above." See Pannenberg, *Systematic Theology*, 2:279–80.

25. Friedrich Schleiermacher, *The Christian Faith*, ed. and trans. H. R. MacKintosh and James S. Stewart, 2 vols. (reprint, New York: Harper & Row, 1963), 2:385.

26. On Schleiermacher's thought see Macquarrie, *Jesus Christ in Modern Thought*, 192–211; Pannenberg, *Systematic Theology*, 2:306–10; and Alister E. McGrath, *The Making of Modern German Christology, 1750–1990*, 2nd ed. (Grand Rapids: Zondervan Publishing House, 1994), 41–49.

27. Barth wrote that "no other way whatever exists except the road from above downwards," *Theology and Church: Shorter Writings, 1920–1928*, trans. Louise Pettibone Smith (New York: Harper & Row, 1962), 265.

28. Barth, *CD*, III/2, 132. For Barth it is important to affirm that Jesus embodies God in the "ontological" or true sense of "reality." On Barth's Christology, see Macquarrie, *Jesus Christ in Modern Thought*, 278–88.

29. Barth, *CD*, III/2, 49.

30. Ibid., I/1, 435.

31. See his section on "The Eternal Son" in *CD*, I/1, 414–47. Barth also defended the Virgin Birth of Jesus as "the miracle of Christmas" and saw it as "a single sign that this life is marked off from all the rest of human life." God stands where God's revelation is made flesh (*CD* I/2, 182; cf. the whole section I/2, 172–202). The Reformed theologian Emil Brunner, Barth's early friend, however, believed a literal virgin birth was incompatible with Jesus' incarnation and his true humanity, since it meant that Jesus was not born exactly as are all other humans. See Brunner, *The Christian Doctrine of Creation and Redemption*, trans. Olive Wyon (Philadelphia: Westminster Press, 1952), 353.

32. See Donald M. Baillie, *God Was in Christ* (New York: Charles Scribner's, 1948), 106–32. Baillie appeals to Philippians 2:5–11 and the idea of *kenosis*, which means "self-emptying." Jesus limited or "emptied himself" of divine attributes (such as omniscience) in his incarnation. Cf. Migliore, *Faith Seeking Understanding* (Grand Rapids: Wm. B. Eerdmans Publishing Co., 1991), 149–51, and Macquarrie, *Jesus Christ in Modern Thought*, 327–29, on Baillie's views.

33. Dietrich Bonhoeffer, Letter to Eberhard Bethge, April 30, 1944, *Letters and Papers from Prison*, rev. and enl. ed. (London: SCM Press, 1971), 279; cf. Bonhoeffer, *Christ the Center*, trans. Edwin H. Robertson (New York: Harper & Row, 1978); and Macquarrie, *Jesus Christ in Modern Thought*, 290–92 on Bonhoeffer.

34. See the survey of Christology by John F. O'Grady, *Models of Jesus Revisited* (New York: Paulist Press, 1994), as well as *Encountering Jesus: A Debate on Christology*, ed. Stephen T. Davis (Atlanta: John Knox Press, 1988); cf. the relating of classic Christology to contemporary life by Douglas F. Ottati, *Jesus Christ and Christian Vision* (Minneapolis: Fortress Press, 1989).

35. On Latin American Liberation Christologies see Claus Bussmann, *Who Do You Say? Jesus Christ in Latin American Theology* (Maryknoll, N.Y.: Orbis Books, 1985); Carlos R. Piar, *Jesus and Liberation: A Critical Analysis of the Christology of Latin American Liberation Theology* (New York: Peter Lang, 1994), and the primary work of Jon Sobrino, *Christology at the Crossroads: A Latin American Approach* (reprint, Maryknoll, N.Y.: Orbis Books, 1984). For Black Theology, see James H. Cone, *A Black Theology of Liberation* (Maryknoll, N.Y.: Orbis Books, 1990).

36. See Elizabeth Johnson, *Consider Jesus: Waves of Renewal in Christology* (New York: Crossroad, 1995), chap. 7, "Feminist Christology"; Julie M. Hopkins, *Towards a Feminist Christology* (Grand Rapids: Wm. B. Eerdmans Publishing Co., 1995); Anne E. Carr, *Transforming Grace: Christian Tradition and Women's Experience* (San Francisco: Harper & Row Publishers, 1988), chap. 8, "Feminism and Christology"; and Patricia Wilson-Kastner, *Faith, Feminism and the Christ* (Philadelphia: Fortress Press, 1983).

37. Migliore notes that the plurality of Christologies found in the New Testament include some emphasizing the teachings of Jesus (Matthew), some the passion of Jesus (Mark; Paul's letters), some the glory and triumph of Jesus as the resurrected Lord (John). He writes: "The one unsubstitutable Christ is inexhaustibly rich and gathers the whole range of human need and experience to himself. New situations call for new confessions of Christ, for he wills to be acknowledged as Lord and Savior in every time and place." See Migliore, *Faith Seeking Understanding*, 144.

Chapter 9

1. See the "Servant Songs" of Isaiah 42:1–4; 49:1–6; 50:4–11; 52:13–53:12.

2. The servant image also has strong implications for the lives of Jesus' followers. As

Jesus suffered, so we may suffer, following his example (1 Pet. 2:18–25; cf. Phil. 3:10–11; Col. 1:24). Jesus is "the revelation of God's design for human life." See Grenz, *Theology for the Community of God*, 443.

3. The Confession of 1967 notes: "God's reconciling act in Jesus Christ is a mystery which the Scriptures describe in various ways. It is called the sacrifice of a lamb, a shepherd's life given for his sheep, atonement by a priest; again it is ransom of a slave, payment of debt, vicarious satisfaction of a legal penalty, and victory over the powers of evil. These are expressions of a truth which remains beyond the reach of all theory in the depths of God's love," *BC* 9.09.

4. Many studies in New Testament theology can be consulted. Articles on "Death of Jesus" are found in three dictionaries published by InterVarsity Press: Joel B. Green, Scot McKnight, and I. Howard Marshall, eds., *DJG* (1992); Gerald F. Hawthorne, Ralph P. Martin, and Daniel G. Reid, eds., *DPL* (1993); and Ralph P. Martin and Peter H. Davids, *Dictionary of the Later New Testament and Its Developments* (1997). What is said of the apostle Paul's theology is applicable to the whole New Testament itself: "Paul has no *one* way of explicating the meaning of the cross. Although the crucified Christ lies at the center of his theology, this central truth is capable of multiple interpretations." See J. B. Green, "Death of Christ," in *DPL*, 204.

5. These terms are expanded a bit in my *Turning Points*, 75–78. They are drawn and modified from Edward Schillebeeckx, *Christ: The Experience of Jesus as Lord*, trans. John Bowden (New York: Crossroad, 1981), 477–511.

6. Pannenberg writes that "the crucifixion of Jesus has atoning force only in the light of his resurrection by God." See Wolfhart Pannenberg, *Systematic Theology*, trans. Geoffrey W. Bromiley (Grand Rapids: Wm. B. Eerdmans Publishing Co., 1991), 2:412.

7. John Frederick Jansen, *The Resurrection of Jesus Christ in New Testament Theology* (Philadelphia: Westminster Press, 1980), 46. The discussion here follows the fine treatment given by Jansen. Cf. G. C. Berkouwer, *The Work of Christ*, trans. Cornelius Lambregtse (Grand Rapids: Wm. B. Eerdmans Publishing Co., 1965), chap. 7, "The Resurrection of Christ."

8. Jansen, *The Resurrection of Jesus Christ*, 55.

9. Pannenberg notes that it is the triune God who is the reconciler of the world. Each member of the Trinity participates. See Pannenberg, *Systematic Theology*, 2:437–54.

10. C. S. Lewis, *Mere Christianity* (New York: Macmillan, 1952), 42, cited in William C. Placher, "The Cross of Jesus Christ as Solidarity, Reconciliation, and Redemption," in *Many Voices, One God: Being Faithful in a Pluralistic World*, ed. Walter Brueggemann and George W. Stroup (Louisville, Ky.: Westminster John Knox Press, 1998), chap. 10.

11. Among works that explore these are H. D. McDonald, *The Atonement of the Death of Christ in Faith, Revelation, and History* (Grand Rapids: Baker Book House, 1985), and Robert S. Paul, *The Atonement and the Sacraments* (Nashville: Abingdon, 1960).

12. Not all scholars agree with Aulén's typology but it has been influential. See Gustaf Aulén, *Christus Victor: An Historical Study of the Three Main Types of the Atonement*, trans. A. G. Hebert (London: SPCK, 1930). See Pannenberg, *Systematic Theology*, 2:412 n. 50, on this work.

13. Martin Luther, *Sermons on the Passion of Christ*, trans. E. Smid and J. T. Isensee (Rock Island, Ill.: Augustana Press, 1956), 25, as cited in Donald G. Bloesch, *Essentials of Evangelical Theology*, 2 vols. (San Francisco: Harper & Row, 1978), 1:176.

14. John Calvin, *Galatians, Ephesians, Philippians and Colossians*, trans. T. H. L. Parker,

in Calvin's New Testament Commentaries, ed. David W. and Thomas F. Torrance (Grand Rapids: Wm. B. Eerdmans Publishing Co., 1965), 44.

15. See Calvin, *Inst.* II.16.6.

16. Ibid., II.15. See George W. Stroup, *"Munus triplex,"* in *ERF* 247, and John F. Jansen, *Calvin's Doctrine of the Work of Christ* (London: James Clarke & Co., 1956). Cf. Paul van Buren, *Christ in Our Place: The Substitutionary Character of Calvin's Doctrine of Reconciliation* (London: Oliver & Boyd, 1957); I. John Hesselink, *Calvin's First Catechism: A Commentary Featuring Ford Lewis Battles's Translation of the 1538 Catechism,* Columbia Series in Reformed Theology (Louisville, Ky.: Westminster John Knox Press, 1997), 119–21, and Berkouwer, *The Person of Christ,* chap. 4.

17. Calvin, *Inst.* II.15.4.

18. Ibid., II.15.6.

19. Contemporary critiques of this view of the atonement claim that "it glorifies suffering, pictures God as abusive and vindictive, and sanctions abusive behavior on the part of the powerful." See the January 1999 issue of *Interpretation* devoted to "Atonement and the Church," particularly the essays by William C. Placher, "Christ Takes Our Place: Rethinking Atonement," 5–20, and Nancy J. Duff, "Atonement and the Christian Life: Reformed Doctrine from a Feminist Perspective," 21–33.

20. Migliore has suggestively linked Calvin's use of the threefold office to other atonement theories: "Christ as prophet proclaims the coming reign of God and instructs us in the form of life appropriate to that reign (moral influence); Christ as priest renders to God the perfect sacrifice of love and obedience on our behalf (satisfaction); Christ as designated king rules the world despite the recalcitrance of evil and promises the ultimate victory of God's reign of righteousness and peace (Christ the victor)," *Faith Seeking Understanding* (Grand Rapids: Wm. B. Eerdmans Publishing Co.), 155.

21. See the Heidelberg Catechism, Q. 31 (*BC* 4.031), and the Westminster Confession, chap. 8 (*BC* 6.043).

22. Art. 16 in Cochrane, ed., *Reformed Confessions,* 150.

23. Art. 17 in Cochrane, ed., *Reformed Confessions,* 150. Rohls notes that the "Latin text of the Scottish Confession declares that Christ is the 'fit mediator between God and human beings', who 'by his death has reconciled the Father to us,'" Rohls, *Reformed Confessions,* 91.

24. Rohls writes that "human sin must be expiated, because otherwise God would not be acting justly. The reconciliation that God wills on the basis of the divine mercy can only occur in such a way that it does not offend God's righteousness," *Reformed Confessions,* 91.

25. Rohls, *Reformed Confessions,* 91.

26. Art. 17 in Cochrane, ed., *Reformed Confessions,* 150. The Belgic Confession, after speaking of Christ as the High-Priest who appeased God's "wrath by his full satisfaction, by offering himself on the tree of the cross, and pouring out his precious blood to purge away our sins" goes on to indicate that it is not "necessary to seek or invent any other means of being reconciled to God, than this only sacrifice, once offered, by which believers are made perfect forever," Art. 21 in Cochrane, ed., *Reformed Confessions,* 202–3.

27. Chap. 9 in *BC* 3.09.

28. Art. IV in Cochrane, ed., *Reformed Confessions,* 92.

29. Barth, *CD,* IV/3, pt. 1.

30. Barth, *CD,* III/2, 41. Thus, an appropriate motif in describing Barth's view is "Jesus is Victor!" See *CD* IV/3/1, 165–274, and Donald G. Bloesch, *Jesus Is Victor!: Karl Barth's Doctrine of Salvation* (Nashville: Abingdon Press, 1976).

31. *BC* 9.08.

32. *BC* 10.2.

33. A powerful statement of the contemporary significance of the cross is by Reformed theologian William C. Placher in his "The Cross of Jesus Christ as Solidarity, Reconciliation, and Redemption," *Many Voices, One God*, chap. 10.

Chapter 10

1. D. A. Tappeiner, "Holy Spirit," *ISBE*, 2:732. Cf. George T. Montague, *The Holy Spirit: Growth of a Biblical Tradition* (New York: Paulist Press, 1976); C. F. D. Moule, *The Holy Spirit*, (reprint, London: Mowbray, 1980); and the classic study by H. B. Swete, *The Holy Spirit in the New Testament* (reprint, Grand Rapids: Baker Book House, 1976).

2. The Spirit of God that was experienced in the Pentecost event came to be understood in the post-Pentecost period and through the rest of the New Testament as having a distinct personality and eventually, in the church's understanding, to be a person who is fully God (and thus the capitalization of the term). See James D. G. Dunn, *Jesus and the Spirit: A Study of the Religious and Charismatic Experience of Jesus and the First Christians as Reflected in the New Testament* (Grand Rapids: Wm. B. Eerdmans Publishing Co., 1997).

3. Our discussion here follows Tappeiner, who approaches the material in this way, indicating that the teachings of Matthew and Mark can be drawn into the more developed materials of Luke-Acts (Luke and Acts are both considered to have been written by Luke).

4. Cf. Gal. 4:4–6; Titus 3:4–6; 1 Cor. 12:4–6. Ephesians 4:4–6 emphasizes the oneness of the Spirit, Son, and Father. Christ and the Spirit work in the process of redemption in that God sent Jesus, who was crucified, raised, and ascended, so that "we might receive the promise of the Spirit through faith" (Gal. 3:14). These passages suggested to the early church that the Spirit possesses a distinct personal existence.

5. Augustine spoke of the Spirit as the "bond of love" between the Father and the Son (*On the Trinity*, 6.7).

6. For further discussions see Migliore, *Faith Seeking Understanding* (Grand Rapids: Wm. B. Eerdmans Publishing Co., 1991), 169–71; Barth, *CD* I/1, 448–89.

7. Another major cause for the split of Eastern and Western churches was the power to be accorded the Pope. Ongoing issues that separate the churches are the description of salvation, distinctive liturgies and liturgical calendars (the dates for Christmas and Easter), the authority of the Pope, marriage for priests (permitted in the East), church-state relations, and the *Filioque* clause. See Mark Ellingsen, *Reclaiming Our Roots: An Inclusive Introduction to Church History*, 2 vols. (Harrisburg, Pa.: Trinity Press International, 1999), 1:188–89.

8. *Against Heresies*, 3.24.1, cited in Alasdair I. C. Heron, *Holy Spirit: The Holy Spirit in the Bible, the History of Christian Thought, and Recent Theology* (Philadelphia: Westminster Press, 1983), 95.

9. Tertullian, *On Baptism*, 4, cited in *Dictionary of the Later New Testament and Its Development*, s.v. "Baptism, Baptismal Rites," 122.

10. See I. John Hesselink, *Calvin's First Catechism: A Commentary Featuring Ford Lewis Battles's Translation of the '1538 Catechism,'* Columbia Series in Reformed Theology (Louisville, Ky.: Westminster John Knox Press, 1997), Appendix A, who notes that it was B. B. Warfield who "dubbed Calvin 'the theologian of the Holy Spirit. The doctrine of the Holy Spirit is a gift from Calvin to the church,'" 177, citing B. B. Warfield,

"John Calvin the Theologian" in *Calvin and Augustine* (Philadelphia: Presbyterian and Reformed Publishing Co., 1956), 484–85. Other important treatments of the Holy Spirit by Reformed theologians include the large work (1674) by the Puritan John Owen (1616–1683), *The Works of John Owen*, ed. William H. Goold, 16 vols. (reprint, London: Banner of Truth Trust, 1965–1968); Abraham Kuyper, *Work of the Holy Spirit*, trans. Henri De Vries (Grand Rapids: Wm. B. Eerdmans Publishing Co., 1946); George S. Hendry, *The Holy Spirit in Christian Theology* (Philadelphia: Westminster Press, 1956).

11. *Inst.* I.7.4. Cf. Donald K. McKim, "Calvin's View of Scripture," in *Readings in Calvin's Theology* (Grand Rapids: Baker Book House, 1984), 43–68, and Rogers and McKim, *AIB*, 103–6.

12. *Inst.* I.7.5.

13. Ibid., I.9.3.

14. Ibid., III.1.4.

15. Ibid.

16. Ibid. As Calvin also put it: "It therefore remains for us to understand that the way to the Kingdom of God is open only to him whose mind has been made new by the illumination of the Holy Spirit" (II.2.20; cf. *Inst.* I.7.4–5; II.5.5; III.11.19; III.24.2).

17. *Inst.* III.2.33. The Spirit's illumination is needed because of the sinfulness of humans and their inability to believe on their own power. See *Inst.* III.2.35; II.2.18–21.

18. Calvin, *Inst.* III.1.1.

19. Ibid.

20. Ibid., III.2.39.

21. Ibid., III.20.5.

22. See *BC* 9.21.

23. *BC* 10.4 (lines 66–71).

24. A very rich treatment is given by Jürgen Moltmann, *The Spirit of Life: A Universal Affirmation*, trans. Margaret Kohl (Minneapolis: Fortress Press, 1993).

25. Moltmann defines an "experience" of the Spirit as "an awareness of God in, with and beneath the experience of life, which gives us assurance of God's fellowship, friendship and love," *Spirit of Life*, 17.

26. In the Greek of the New Testament, as with the Hebrew of the Old Testament (as noted above), the same term (Gr. *pneuma*) can mean "wind" and "spirit."

27. See my article, "The Stirring of the Spirit among Contemporary Theologians," *Perspectives: A Journal of Reformed Thought* 13, no. 5 (May 1998), 15–19. See also Michael Welker, *God the Spirit*, trans. John F. Hoffmeyer (Minneapolis: Fortress Press, 1994).

28. A most thorough study of biblical material from a Pentecostal perspective is Gordon D. Fee, *God's Empowering Presence: The Holy Spirit in the Letters of Paul* (Peabody, Mass.: Hendrickson Publishers, 1994). A systematic theology written from a charismatic perspective is J. Rodman Williams, *Renewal Theology: Systematic Theology from a Charismatic Perspective*, 3 volumes in one (Grand Rapids: Zondervan, 1997).

29. See I. John Hesselink, "The Charismatic Movement and the Reformed Tradition," in *Major Themes in the Reformed Tradition*, ed. Donald K. McKim, (reprint, Eugene, Oreg.: Wipf & Stock, 1998), 377–85.

30. See the comments here by the Reformed theologian Hendrikus Berkhof in *The Doctrine of the Holy Spirit* (Richmond: John Knox Press, 1964), 11.

31. Cited in Moltmann, *The Spirit of Life*, 310. Cf. the hymn rendering: "Come, Holy Spirit, Our Souls Inspire," *The Presbyterian Hymnal: Hymns, Psalms, and Spiritual Songs*, ed. LindaJo H. McKim (Louisville, Ky.: Westminster/John Knox Press, 1990), no. 125.

Chapter 11

1. Gerald G. O'Collins, "Salvation," *ABD*, 5:907.

2. See the "salvation" theme throughout Christoph Barth, *God with Us: A Theological Introduction to the Old Testament*, ed. Geoffrey W. Bromiley (Grand Rapids: Wm. B. Eerdmans Publishing Co., 1991), passim.

3. The prophets expressed this future salvation in differing ways: "Amos expected Israel's present existence to end through some new divine action (Amos 7:1–9; 8:1–2). Hosea proclaimed a renewal that would let the people experience a fresh start (Hos. 2:6–7, 14–15; 3:4–5). Isaiah announced the coming of a new Davidic king (Isa. 9:2–7; 11:1–10), Jeremiah a new covenant (Jer. 31:31–34), Ezekiel a new life for the people (Ezek. 37:1–14), and Second Isaiah a new exodus as God comes to restore the people (Isa. 40:1–11), *ABD*, 5:909.

4. Cited in I. Howard Marshall, "Salvation," *DJG*, ed. Joel B. Green, Scot McKnight, I. Howard Marshall (Downers Grove, Ill.: InterVarsity Press, 1992), 720, from J. P. Louw and E. A. Nida, *Greek-English Lexicon of the New Testament Based on Semantic Domains* (New York: United Bible Societies, 1988).

5. See *ABD*, 5:910.

6. For a further discussion, see my *Turning Points*, 79ff. Each of these images is associated with an early church theologian: Illumination—apostolic fathers and apologists; Restoration—Irenaeus; Satisfaction—Tertullian; Victory—Origen; Deification—Athanasius and Eastern theologians.

7. See Heiko Oberman, *Forerunners of the Reformation* (Philadelphia: Fortress Press, 1981).

8. These citations are from the Council of Trent and its "Decree on Justification." This Council (1545–1563) produced the official church dogma of the Roman Catholic church, which stood intact until Vatican Council II (1962–1965).

9. See the discussion in McKim, *Turning Points*, 92.

10. Calvin calls justification by faith "the main hinge on which religion turns" (*Inst.* III.11.1), a phrase similar to that of the Lutheran theologian Philip Melanchthon and found in other Lutheran writings (see *Inst.* III.11.1 n. 3).

11. The Westminster Confession says that "from this original corruption, whereby we are utterly indisposed, disabled, and made opposite to all good, and wholly inclined to all evil, do proceed all actual transgressions," chap. 6 in *BC* 6.034; cf. chap. 11, which states that humanity by the Fall "into a state of sin, hath wholly lost all ability of will to any spiritual good accompanying salvation; so as a natural man, being altogether averse from that good, and dead in sin, is not able, by his own strength, to convert himself, or to prepare himself thereunto," *BC* 6.061.

12. Calvin has a sequence similar to Luther's views of the law as mirror, hammer, and mask. He says that "God lays down for us through the law what we should do," and if we fail we merit eternal death. Then we see that the law is hard and "above our strength and beyond our abilities" to fulfill. So now we see what we deserve and "no trace of good hope will remain." Third, "there is but one means of liberation that can rescue us from such miserable calamity: the appearance of Christ the Redeemer, through whose hand the Heavenly Father, pitying us out of his infinite goodness and mercy, willed to help us; if, indeed, with firm faith we embrace this mercy and rest in it with steadfast hope" (*Inst.* III.1.2).

13. Calvin wrote of the death of Christ: "To declare that by him alone we are accounted righteous, what else is this but to lodge our righteousness in Christ's obedience, because the obedience of Christ is reckoned to us as if it were our own?" See *Inst.* III.11.23.

14. Chapter 3 in Cochrane, ed., *Reformed Confessions,* 57. As Rohls writes: "The fact that God justifies us is the expression of the fact that God is merciful to us. God's grace is the first cause (*causa primaria*)—that is, the sole ground—of justification," *Reformed Confessions,* 120.

15. Calvin, *Inst.* III.11.17.

16. Question 60 in *BC* 4.060. Faith itself is not a "good work" because faith is given as a pure "gift of God" (Eph. 2:8–9). Cf. The Second Helvetic Confession, which says: ". . . because faith receives Christ our righteousness and attributes everything to the grace of God in Christ, on that account justification is attributed to faith, chiefly because of Christ and not therefore because it is our work. For it is the gift of God," chap. 15 in *BC* 5.109.

17. G. C. Berkouwer, *Faith and Justification,* trans. Lewis B. Smedes (reprint, Grand Rapids: Wm. B. Eerdmans Publishing Co., 1968), 52.

18. As Berkouwer notes, while we are saved by faith alone, "love and works are not disqualified; love must follow faith. However, we are not to build our confidence on love, as though for its sake and through it we should expect to receive forgiveness of sins and redemption from God," *Faith and Justification,* 53.

19. Chapter 16 in *BC* 5.119.

20. Question 86 in *BC* 4.086. See the First Confession of Basel (1534): "We confess that there is forgiveness of sins through faith in Jesus Christ the crucified. Although this faith is continually exercised, signalized, and thus confirmed by works of love, yet do we not ascribe to works, which are the fruit of faith, the righteousness and satisfaction for our sins. On the contrary, we ascribe it solely to a genuine trust and faith in the shed blood of the Lamb of God. For we freely confess that all things are granted to us in Christ, Who is our righteousness, holiness, redemption, the way, the truth, the wisdom and the life. Therefore the works of believers are not for the satisfaction of their sins, but solely for the purpose of showing in some degree our gratitude to the Lord God for the great kindness He has shown us in Christ." See Cochrane, ed., *Reformed Confessions,* 94–95.

21. These dimensions can be seen in citations from three confessional documents. The Second Helvetic Confession says: "Christian faith is not an opinion or human conviction, but a most firm trust and a clear and steadfast assent of the mind, and then a most certain apprehension of the truth of God presented in the Scriptures and in the Apostles' Creed, and thus also of God himself, the greatest good, and especially of God's promise and of Christ who is the fulfilment of all promises" (chap. 16 in *BC* 5.112).

The Heidelberg Catechism described true faith as "not only a certain knowledge by which I accept as true all that God has revealed to us in his Word, but also a wholehearted trust which the Holy Spirit creates in me through the gospel, that, not only to others, but to me also God has given the forgiveness of sins, everlasting righteousness and salvation, out of sheer grace solely for the sake of Christ's saving work" (Question 21 in *BC* 4.021).

The Confession of 1967, in describing the ministry of reconciliation made possible by Jesus Christ, says: "To be reconciled to God is to be sent into the world as his reconciling community" (*BC* 9.31).

22. *Inst.* III.2.7.

23. Arminians were the followers of James Arminius (1560–1609), a Dutch theologian who rejected the teachings of Calvinism in the areas of human sinfulness, predestination, and whether or not salvation can be lost. The Wesleyan tradition, stemming from John Wesley (1703–1791), the founder of Methodism, is Arminian in its teachings. See Robert Letham, "Arminianism," in *ERF* 11–12.

24. For a discussion of the various approaches to the "order of the decrees," see the work by Benjamin B. Warfield, *The Plan of Salvation*, rev. ed. (reprint, Grand Rapids: Wm. B. Eerdmans Publishing Co., 1970). Warfield (1851–1921) was a leading nineteenth-century theologian at Princeton Theological Seminary who continued the tradition of Reformed orthodoxy or scholasticism in the "Old Princeton" tradition. See Rogers and McKim, *AIB*, 348–61.

The most significant disagreement among Reformed theologians was between the "supralapsarian" and the "infralapsarian" views. Supralapsarianism teaches that election and reprobation of individual persons occurs logically prior to God's decrees for creation and the fall. God "first" determined to save or not to save individuals "before" God created the world and humans fell into sin. Infralapsarianism is the view that in the order of God's decrees, the decree to permit the fall of humanity into sin is prior to God's decree to save some of humanity ("the elect"). While the "order of the decrees" refers to the logical relationships of the "parts" of God's decrees and not their "chronology," the discussions nevertheless use "chronological language." Yet theologians recognize that there is no "sequence" in the mind of God since God is outside of time and is eternal. All is the "eternal now" in God's sight. See Philip C. Holtrop, "Decree(s) of God," in *ERF*, 97–99. Cf. Louis Berkhof, *Systematic Theology* (reprint, London: Banner of Truth Trust, 1969), 416–22.

25. The differences between the Reformed and the Arminians may be likened to a split in Indian religion over the way by which "salvation" is received. J. S. Whale wrote, "The two parties were known as the monkey school and the cat school respectively. For, on the approach of danger the baby monkey climbs on to its mother's back, holds on and, as the mother leaps away to safety, is saved along with her: primarily through the mother monkey's act of course, but also through the cooperation of her offspring. But when danger threatens a mother cat, she takes her kitten by the scruff of the neck and, willy-nilly, saves it. The kitten does nothing: it contributes nothing at all to the process of its salvation ('not by works, lest any kitten should boast')." Cited in McKim, *Turning Points*, 189 n. 58, from J. S. Whale, *The Protestant Tradition* (reprint, Cambridge University Press, 1959), 140–41.

In this scenario, the Arminian view, which stresses human response, is like the monkey; the Reformed view, which stresses God's power, is like the cat.

26. At the Synod of Dort in the Netherlands (1618–1619) the Reformed rejected Arminian objections to Calvinism and expressed their views on the plan of salvation in the famous TULIP acronym. The letters stand for T=Total Depravity; U=Unconditional Election; L=Limited Atonement; I=Irresistible Grace; and P=Perseverance of the Saints. All flow together in a very tight, logical order.

27. Election or predestination has been an emphasis of the Reformed faith. Presbyterianism and predestination are often associated in the common mind. See G. C. Berkouwer, *Divine Election*, trans. Hugo Bekker (reprint, Grand Rapids: Wm. B. Eerdmans Publishing Co., 1968), and the discussion below in chap. 15.

Chapter 12

1. See Paul D. Hanson, *The People Called: The Growth of Community in the Bible* (San Francisco: Harper & Row, 1987).

2. See *Theological Dictionary of the New Testament*, ed. G. Kittel and G. Friedrich, trans. G. W. Bromiley, 10 vols. (Grand Rapids: William B. Eerdmans Publishing Co., 1964–1976), 3:504. Cf. Hans Schwarz, *The Christian Church* (Minneapolis: Augsburg, 1982), 20, and Eric G. Jay, *The Church: Its Changing Image through Twenty Centuries* (Atlanta: John Knox, 1980), 5ff.

3. Edward Schillebeeckx notes that "the English word 'church' (like the Scottish 'kirk,' German *Kirche*, Dutch *lerl* and so on) comes from the Greek *kyriake*, i.e., 'belonging to the Lord', as does *kyriakon*, the Lord's Day or Sunday. The Greek and Latin term *ekklēsia/ecclēsia* has a different origin"—from the Greek *ekklēsia*. See Edward Schillebeeckx, *Church: The Human Story of God* (New York: Crossroad, 1993), 146.

4. See Paul S. Minear, *Images of the Church in the New Testament* (Philadelphia: Westminster Press, 1960), who lists ninety-six "analogies."

5. Stanley J. Grenz, *Theology for the Community of God* (Nashville: Broadman & Holman, 1994), 605. Grenz goes on to quote the early church theologian Hippolytus who said of the church: "It is not a place that is called church, not a house made of stones and earth. . . . It is the holy assembly of those who live in righteousness." See Hippolytus, *Daniel*, 1.17.6–7, cited in J. G. Davies, *The Secular Use of Church Buildings* (London: SCM Press, 1968), 4.

6. See Christoph Barth, *God with Us: A Theological Introduction to the Old Testament*, ed. Geoffrey W. Bromiley (Grand Rapids: Wm. B. Eerdmans Publishing Co., 1991), chap. 3.

7. Covenant is the concept around which Walther Eichrodt constructed his *Theology of the Old Testament*, trans. J. A. Baker, 2 vols. (Philadelphia: Westminster Press, 1961, 1967).

8. Sometimes Jeremiah and Hosea use a marriage metaphor of husband and wife to describe the covenant (Jer. 3:20; 31:32; Hosea 3), or a parent/child (Hosea 11). Lord and servant images are also used.

9. Notice that because in Jesus salvation is made sure, Jesus is called the "guarantee" of a "better covenant" than that which came from Moses (Heb. 7:22). Also, "there is a direct relationship between Hebrews 7 and 8 and the institution of the Lord's Supper (Matt. 26:28; Luke 22:20) and the sealing of the Sinaitic form of the covenant (Exodus 24). Moses sacrificed an animal and sprinkled its blood on the altar and the people. Christ must have had that in mind when he said his blood was poured out for his people for the forgiveness of their sins." See M. Eugene Osterhaven, "Covenant," in *ERF*, 86.

10. Here, "the connection between God's choice, holiness, and corporate mission is unmistakable." See Gary S. Shogren, "Election," *ABD*, 2:442. Cf. Rom. 8:33; Eph. 1:4; Col. 3:12; 1 Thess. 1:4; 2 Tim. 2:10; Titus 1:1.

11. W. A. Elwell, "Election and Predestination," in *DPL*, 227. On "persons predestined to be like Christ," Elwell writes, "In a related way Paul speaks of God's predestining persons to be conformed to the image of Christ (Rom. 8:29) and adopted into the family of God (Eph. 1:5). This was done in accord with the counsel of his will (Eph. 1:11), and 'in' (Eph. 1:11) or 'through' (Eph. 1:5) Christ. In Ephesians 1:4 Paul parallels this divine ordination with election and defines it as being 'before the foundation of the world.' In Romans 8:29 the act of predestination appears to follow upon that of foreknowing, with calling consequent upon predestining. In Ephesians 1:11 foreknowledge is not mentioned, but calling follows predestination and is in accord with the counsel of God's will (the 'good pleasure of his will,' Eph. 1:5)," 228.

12. One instance that evoked this reflection was the Novatian crisis in the mid-third century. The emperor Decius had decided to stamp out Christianity and to return the Roman Empire to its old gods. He made worship of Roman gods mandatory throughout the empire. Noncompliance meant death. Some Christians refused to offer worship and were killed. These were later called "confessors." Others, however, "lapsed" and capitulated to the Roman authorities.

When the persecution subsided, the question was whether or not the "lapsed" should be readmitted to the Christian church. The "rigorist" party, led by the presbyter Novatian, insisted that they not be readmitted since they had demonstrated apostasy. A church council decided that no one should be barred from readmittance through penance. But the Novatians, arguing that such a church cannot be "holy," set up their own bishops and alternative form of church government.

Bishop Cyprian of Carthage resisted the Novatians and wrote *On the Unity of the Church*. In this book he argued that the church owes its unity to its leadership—the bishops—and is thus one church. Cyprian wrote: "The Church, which is catholic and one, is not cut or divided but is indeed connected and bound together by the cement of priests [*sacerdotes*, i.e., bishops] who cohere with one another." Since God is one, argued Cyprian, so the church must be one. See McKim, *Turning Points*, 50–54.

13. *BC* 1.3.

14. Augustine, *On John's Gospel*, 40.12 (*Nicene and Post-Nicene Fathers*, 7.253f.), cited in Calvin, *Institutes* IV.1.8. Calvin notes that in looking at the church, "those who seemed utterly lost and quite beyond hope are by [God's] goodness called back to the way; while those who more than others seemed to stand firm often fall." Then he quotes Augustine on God's "secret predestination." Calvin continued by saying, "For [God] knows and has marked those who know neither him nor themselves. Of those who openly wear his badge, his eyes alone see the ones who are unfeignedly holy and will persevere to the very end [Matt. 24:13]—the ultimate point of salvation."

15. Augustine spoke of the universal and visible church as being a "mixed body" (Lat. *corpus permixtum*). Today we might say, "The visible church is a 'mixed bag'"!

16. See the Reformed works on ecclesiology by G. C. Berkouwer, *The Church*, trans. James E. Davison (Grand Rapids: Wm. B. Eerdmans Publishing Co., 1976), and Edmund P. Clowney, *The Church* (Downers Grove, Ill.: InterVarsity Press, 1995).

17. Rohls, *Reformed Confessions*, 166. On the doctrine of election, see the survey in Wolfhart Pannenberg, *Systematic Theology*, ed. Geoffrey W. Bromiley (Grand Rapids: Wm. B. Eerdmans Publishing Co., 1998), 3:439ff.

18. *BC* 4.054. Rohls notes that this is the only mention of the doctrine of election in the Heidelberg Catechism.

19. *Inst.* III.21.7. Calvin deals with election in *Inst.* III.21–24. The "mere generosity" citation is from III.21.1. Predestination is God's "eternal decree," (III.21.5).

20. See G. C. Berkouwer, *Divine Election*, trans. Hugo Bekker (Grand Rapids: Wm. B. Eerdmans Publishing Co., 1960), chap. 5.

21. *Inst.* III.24.5. Augustine also referred to Jesus Christ as "the clearest mirror of free election." See *On Rebuke and Grace*, 11.30, cited by Calvin in *Inst.* III.22.1.

22. *Inst.* III.24.4. Cf. Berkouwer, *Divine Election*, passim.

23. Chapter 10 in *BC* 5.059.

24. *Inst.* III.24.1.

25. *Inst.* III.24.2.

26. Calvin movingly writes: "Therefore, if we desire to know whether God cares for our salvation, let us inquire whether he has entrusted us to Christ, whom he has established as the sole Savior of all his people. If we still doubt whether we have been received by Christ into his care and protection, he meets that doubt when he willingly offers himself as shepherd, and declares that we shall be numbered among his flock if we hear his voice [John 10:3]. Let us therefore embrace Christ, who is graciously offered to us, and comes to meet us. He will reckon us in his flock and enclose us within his fold" (*Inst.* III.24.6).

Karl Barth dramatically reinterpreted the Reformed doctrine of election by seeing Jesus Christ as both the "elected" and the "rejected" man. If God has elected the world in Jesus Christ and if in his death Christ bore the rejection of the world in himself, then the message of election is the sum of the gospel. We understand our election as real only in him. See *Church Dogmatics* II/2.

27. *Inst.* IV.1.21. Cf. III.20.45, where Calvin discusses the petition in the Lord's Prayer, "forgive us our debts" (Matt. 6:12) and says that here and in the following petition, "Christ briefly embraces all that makes for the heavenly life, as the spiritual covenant that God has made for the salvation of his church rests on these two members alone: 'I shall write my laws upon their hearts,' and, 'I shall be merciful toward their iniquity'" [Jer. 31:33p; cf. 33:8]. Cf. Rohls, *Reformed Confessions*, 86–90.

28. *BC* 6.079. Reformed theology is sometimes referred to as "Covenant Theology" because of the prominence that the covenant took, especially among some seventeenth-century Reformed theologians. Early Reformed theologians saw the Bible and the church's history as "one long story of God's covenant relationship with humankind" (Dewey D. Wallace Jr., "Federal Theology," in *ERF*, 136). Calvin wrote about the relationship of the "old covenant" to the "new covenant" in Jesus Christ (see *Inst.* II.9–11. This means, in general, the relationship of the Old Testament to the New Testament). While he does not develop the covenant idea as fully as some others have, there are numerous references to it throughout his writings and it is "an important theme which, one suspects, Calvin had ever in mind." See M. Eugene Osterhaven, "Calvin on the Covenant," in McKim, *Readings in Calvin's Theology*, 90.

Some seventeenth-century followers of Calvin developed "Federal Theology," which stressed the "headship of Adam" over the human race and conceived the divine-human relationship as covenantal. Some Reformed theologians, as well as the Westminster Confession, speak of a "covenant of works" made with Adam "wherein life was promised to Adam, and in him to his posterity, upon condition of perfect and personal obedience" (*BC* 6.038). Since Adam sinned, and as the "head" of humanity the guilt of his sin was transmitted to his posterity (see above, chap. 7), Adam became "incapable of life by that covenant," and so God "was pleased to make a second, commonly called the covenant of grace: wherein he freely offered unto sinners life and salvation by Jesus Christ, requiring of them faith in him, that they may be saved, and promising to give unto all those that are ordained unto life, his Holy Spirit, to make them willing and able to believe" (6.039). English and American Puritans stressed the idea of the covenant, linking it to piety and also to national purposes. God's covenant places responsibilities of obedience to God's will upon God's children. The "contractual" dimensions of covenant thought related well to the development of democratic governments. See J. Wayne Baker, *Heinrich Bullinger and the Theology of the Covenant* (Athens, Ohio: Ohio University Press, 1980); John Von Rohr, *The Covenant of Grace in Puritan Thought* (Atlanta: Scholars Press, 1986); William Klempa, "The Concept of the Covenant in Sixteenth- and Seventeenth-Century Continental and British Reformed Theology," in McKim, ed., *Major Themes*, 94–107; and Donald K. McKim, "William Perkins and the Covenant," in *Studies of the Church in History: Essays Honoring Robert S. Paul on his Sixty-Fifth Birthday*, ed. Horton Davies (Pittsburgh: Pickwick Press, 1983), 85–101. Cf. the volume by the World Alliance of Reformed Churches, *A Covenant Challenge to Our Broken World*, ed. Allen O. Miller (Atlanta: Darby, 1982).

29. The First Confession of Basel, chap. V, in Cochrane, *Reformed Confessions*, 92.

30. As the Scots Confession puts it: "This Kirk [church] is invisible, known only to God, who alone knows whom he has chosen, and includes both the chosen who are departed, the Kirk triumphant, those who yet live and fight against sin and Satan, and those who shall live hereafter" (chap. 16 in *BC*, 3.16. Cf. Donald K. McKim, "Communion of Saints," in *ERF*, 76).

31. First Helvetic Confession of 1536, chap. 14, in Cochrane, ed., *Reformed Confessions*, 105.

32. The Tetrapolitan Confession of 1530, chap. 15, in Cochrane, ed., *Reformed Confessions*, 72–73. Cf. Calvin, who says that "in this church are mingled many hypocrites who have nothing of Christ but the name and outward appearance. There are very many ambitious, greedy, envious persons, evil speakers, and some of quite unclean life" (*Inst.* IV.1.7).

33. As Rohls puts it, "the invisible church exists as the communion of the elect only *within* the visible church as the communion of those who externally confess Christ," *Reformed Confessions*, 171.

34. Calvin wrote that while it is of "some value for us to know who were to be counted as [God's] children," God has established for us "a certain charitable judgment whereby we recognize as members of the church those who, by confession of faith, by example of life, and by partaking of the sacraments, profess the same God and Christ with us" (*Inst.* IV.1.8. Cf. IV.1.7).

35. Calvin, *Inst.* IV.1.9.

36. *BC* 3.18. Cf. Louis Berkhof, *Systematic Theology* (reprint, London: Banner of Truth Trust, 1969), 576, who lists those with the various views. Cf. Rohls, *Reformed Confessions*, 174–77.

37. The famous Latin phrase for this slogan is *ecclesia reformata semper reformanda*. See Jack L. Stotts, "Church," in *ERF*, 68–72.

38. The Roman Catholic theologian John Eck maintained that "Scripture is not authentic without the authority of the church." See Donald K. McKim, *The Bible in Theology and Preaching*, (reprint, Eugene, Oreg.: Wipf & Stock, 1999), 32, and chaps. 1 and 2.

39. See Calvin, *Inst.* I.7.2.

40. *Inst.* IV.1.9. Cf. Calvin's views in John T. McNeill, *Unitive Protestantism: The Ecumenical Spirit and Its Persistent Expression* (Richmond: John Knox Press, 1964), chap. V. McNeill writes that "the idea of a catholic unity dominated the church theory of Calvin," 217.

41. See a list of United Churches with Reformed Heritage in *HDRC*, Appendix 4, 503.

42. *Inst.* IV.2.4.

43. Alan P. F. Sell, *A Reformed, Evangelical, Catholic Theology: The Contribution of the World Alliance of Reformed Churches, 1875–1982* (Grand Rapids: Wm. B. Eerdmans Publishing Co., 1991), 112. Sell goes on to write: "Accordingly, the Reformed today typically maintain that the catholicity of the church entails its visible unity, which does not mean uniformity of expression, liturgy, and practice. On the contrary, it is recognized that differences of individual temperament and of cultural heritage are themselves gifts of God to be accepted gladly. But it is keenly felt that the proclamation by a manifestly unreconciled church is inherently incongruous and detrimental to mission. The goal, therefore, is the mutual recognition of ministries and memberships and, above all, the removal of those barriers dividing Christians at the Lord's table when certain doctrines of the ministry and of the sacraments cut across commonly held beliefs concerning the Trinity, the person and work of Christ, the work of the Holy Spirit, and the nature of the church as the people of God," 112–13.

44. Barth, *CD*, 4.1:66.

Chapter 13

1. Churches of the Baptist and other "evangelical" traditions "prefer not to use the term 'sacrament,' because the term itself suggests the idea of a means of grace. Instead, they prefer to speak of Baptism and the Lord's Supper as ordinances, a term that sug-

gests that they are acts that Christ ordained to be followed by Christians. 'Ordinance' does not carry the connotation of an act in which grace is given." See Ted A. Campbell, *Christian Confessions: A Historical Introduction* (Louisville, Ky.: Westminster John Knox Press, 1996), 249.

2. This is true for the Society of Friends (Quakers) and the Salvation Army. As Campbell notes, "as Friends understand it . . . they have not so much rejected Baptism and Holy Communion as they have rejected the 'outward signs' associated with these as being unnecessary, and even dangerous if individuals rely on them in place of the true, inward experience of Christ," *Confessions*, 250.

3. This is characteristic of the Lutheran tradition. See Campbell, *Confessions*, 177.

4. Campbell well writes: "For Reformed Christians, the baptism of an infant brings the child into a covenant relationship with God and the church, which will eventuate in the individual's regeneration [salvation], if the individual is among the elect, but not necessarily at the moment at which water is applied," *Confessions*, 178.

5. "Anabaptism" means "rebaptism" and stems from the sixteenth-century groups that insisted on adult baptism by immersion as the only valid baptism—meaning a "rebaptism" of former Roman Catholics (or other Protestants) who had been baptized as infants by sprinkling or pouring.

6. Campbell, *Confessions*, 176. The Roman Catholic theologian Joseph Martos notes that "as the practice of baptism has varied, Christians' understanding of baptism has varied, and yet through it all there is a continuity which is greater than the differences. For the theology of baptism is always a variation on the theme of salvation played in different modes and different keys in different ages." See Martos, *Doors to the Sacred* (New York: Doubleday Image, 1982), 163.

7. Pannenberg writes that in baptism, "the baptized are related to Jesus Christ and thus to the triune God, so that their person is now constituted by this relation to God and concretely by participation in the filial relation of Jesus to the Father. This takes place by baptizing the candidates in the 'name' of Jesus Christ or in the 'name' of God the Father, the Son, and the Holy Spirit (Matt. 28:19)." See Wolfhart Pannenberg, *Systematic Theology*, trans. Geoffrey W. Bromiley, 3 vols. (Grand Rapids: Wm. B. Eerdmans Publishing Co., 1998), 3:239, and the section on "Baptism as the Constitution of Christian Identity."

8. Günther Bornkamm has written that "baptism is the appropriation of new life, and the new life is the appropriation of baptism," cited in *DPL*, 64.

9. G. R. Beasley-Murray writes that "baptism is a visible act with a spiritual meaning; it is therefore well adapted to be the means of entry into a visible community of God's people *and* the body which transcends any one place or time." See G. R. Beasley-Murray, "Baptism," in *DPL*, 64. Cf. his *Baptism in the New Testament* (reprint, Grand Rapids: Wm. B. Eerdmans Publishing Co., 1981), where he writes that the apostolic writers attribute to baptism and to faith "forgiveness and cleansing, union with Christ in his death and resurrection, and consequently the becoming a new creation in Christ, participation in the sonship of Christ, membership in the Body of Christ, regeneration, deliverance from evil posers and the entry upon the life of the Kingdom of God." He indicates that also on this list can be the gifts of the Spirit (Acts 2:38; 1 Cor. 6:11–13), 276.

10. See Cyprian, *Letters* 70.1; 72.1; 73.6, 21, cited in McKim, *Turning Points*, 127.

11. Augustine, *On the Merits and Remission* 1.25. See McKim, *Turning Points*, 128.

12. Hugo, *On the Sacraments* 2.6.2. Cf. Martos, 184, and Reinhold Seeberg, *A Text-Book of the History of Doctrines*, trans. Charles E. Hay, 2 vols. (reprint, Grand Rapids: Baker Book House, 1966), 2:230.

13. See Martos, 187–90.

14. "The Small Catechism" 4.3, in *The Book of Concord*, ed. Theodore G. Tappert (Philadelphia: Fortress Press, 1959), 349.

15. See Luther's Large Catechism 4:86, in *Book of Concord*, 446, and Seeberg, 2:284.

16. See G. C. Berkouwer, *The Sacraments*, trans. Hugo Bekker (Grand Rapids: Wm. B. Eerdmans Publishing Co., 1969), chap. 7.

17. B. A. Gerrish, *Grace and Gratitude: The Eucharistic Theology of John Calvin* (Minneapolis: Fortress Press, 1993), 107.

18. Chapter 30 in *BC* 6.154. The Belgic Confession says that Christ gives in the sacrament "the gifts and invisible grace; washing, cleansing, and purging our souls of all filth and unrighteousness; renewing our hearts and filling them with all comfort; giving unto us a true assurance of his fatherly goodness; putting on us the new man, and putting off the old man with all his deeds," Art. 24 in Cochrane, ed., *Reformed Confessions*, 214.

19. *Inst.* IV.15.1.

20. Ibid. IV.15.3. Calvin referred to baptism as "the sacrament of penance, since it has been given to those who are intent on repentance as a confirmation of grace and a seal of assurance" (*Inst.* IV.19.17; cf. *Inst.* IV.15.4).

21. *Inst.* IV.15.3. Calvin notes that "if penance is commended to us throughout life, the power of baptism too ought to be extended to the very same limits. Therefore, there is no doubt that all pious folk throughout life, whenever they are troubled by a consciousness of their faults, may venture to remind themselves of their baptism, that from it they may be confirmed in assurance of that sole and perpetual cleansing which we have in Christ's blood" (*Inst.* IV.14.4).

22. *Inst.* IV.14.19. Zwingli emphasized the "sign" aspect. See Gerrish, *Grace and Gratitude*, 105–6. W. P. Stephens, *The Theology of Huldrych Zwingli* (Oxford: Clarendon Press, 1986), chap. 9.

23. Put another way, when preaching occurs and the "word of God" is proclaimed, and the sacrament is carried out (i.e., baptism), then "the word is the pledge of favor, and the sacrament is the seal appended to the word for the sake of ratification," Gerrish, *Grace and Gratitude*, 102. Paul writes that Abraham was reckoned "righteous" in God's sight *before* the sign of circumcision was given and that "he received the sign of circumcision as a seal of the righteousness that he had by faith while he was still uncircumcised" (Rom. 4:11).

24. *Inst.* IV.15.22. The Holy Spirit is our "inward teacher" by whose "power alone hearts are penetrated and affections moved and our souls opened for the sacraments to enter in. If the Spirit be lacking, the sacraments can accomplish nothing more in our minds than the splendor of the sun shining upon blind eyes, or a voice sounding in deaf ears" (*Inst.* IV.14.9). The Spirit conceives, sustains, nourishes, and establishes faith.

25. See Calvin, *Inst.* IV.16.5–6. Cf. Berkouwer, *The Sacraments*, chap. 8.

26. Huldrych Zwingli pointed out that God gives signs to ratify the covenants made with God's people. As H. O. Old summarizes Zwingli's view: "When the eternal covenant which had been revealed to Adam and Eve was renewed to Noah, the rainbow was given as the sign of the covenant. When it was renewed to Abraham, circumcision was given as the sign of the covenant. When the covenant was renewed in Christ, baptism was then given as the sign of the covenant." See Hughes Oliphant Old, *The Shaping of the Reformed Baptismal Rite in the Sixteenth Century* (Grand Rapids: Wm. B. Eerdmans Publishing Co., 1992), 125–26, citing Zwingli's *Refutation of the Tricks of the Catabaptists* in Zwingli's *Selected Works*, ed. Samuel Macauley Jackson (Philadelphia: University of Pennsylvania Press, 1901; 1972), 237. Zwingli went on to note that God

had commanded Abraham to give circumcision to his children (Gen. 17:1–14) and that on Pentecost, Peter specifically said that children of believing Jews and Gentiles are included in the covenant (Acts 2:39).

27. Thus the Belgic Confession says of infants of believers that they "ought to be baptized and sealed with the sign of the covenant, as the children in Israel formerly were circumcised upon the same promises which are made unto our children," Art. 24 in Cochrane, ed., *Reformed Confessions*, 214.

28. Bullinger, *Von dem unverschampten fraefel ergerlichem verwyrren* as cited by Old, 126. Bullinger indicated in his catechism that by baptism the infant was adopted into the family of God, just as the ancient infants were circumcised, for "the children of the faithful are included in the eternal covenant of God." See J. Wayne Baker, *Heinrich Bullinger and the Covenant: The Other Reformed Tradition* (Athens, Ohio: Ohio University Press, 1980), 139. Cf. his discussion of baptism and covenant in Bullinger, 86–88, 144–45.

29. Cited in Baker, 145. Bullinger and the Reformed believed the basic error of Anabaptists—those who rejected infant baptism in favor of adult or believer's baptism—was that they rejected the unity of the covenant. See Calvin's discussion of the similarities and differences of the old and new covenants in *Inst.* II.10–11.

30. Old, *Shaping of the Baptismal Rite*, 126.

31. *Inst.* IV.15.22.

32. Old, *Shaping of the Baptismal Rite*, 135.

33. From Oecolampadius, *Underrichtung*, as cited in Old, *Shaping of the Baptismal Rite*, 135.

34. Old, *Shaping of the Baptismal Rite*, 135.

35. Ibid., 139.

36. Ibid.

37. The Geneva Confession of 1536 in Cochrane, ed., *Reformed Confessions*, 123. To the argument that infants cannot have faith and thus should not be baptized, the Reformed maintained that while it is not assumed that the infant has faith at that point, "the divine promise provides the confession for the person being baptized." In both adult and infant baptism, it is the church that is publicly receiving "those who have already *been adopted* by grace." God's grace has already occurred. It is the divine promise rather than faith in the case of infants that is the "presupposition for administering the sacrament." See Rohls, 211–16. For Calvin, "infants are baptized into future repentance and faith, and even though these have not yet been formed in them, the seed of both lies hidden within them by the secret working of the Spirit," *Inst.* IV.16.20. The Westminster Confession says that "the efficacy of Baptism is not tied to that moment of time where it is administered; yet, notwithstanding, by the right use of this ordinance the grace promised is not only offered, but really exhibited and conferred by the Holy Ghost, to such (whether of age or infants) as that grace belongeth unto, according to the counsel of God's own will, in his appointed time," chap. 30 in *BC* 6.159.

38. Question 74 in *BC* 4.074. For a clear presentation of the Reformed view see Geoffrey W. Bromiley, *Children of Promise: The Case for Baptizing Infants* (Grand Rapids: Wm. B. Eerdmans Publishing Co., 1979). Bromiley writes about children of confessing Christians: "From the very beginning they are in the sphere of the word and Spirit, and the prayer of parents and congregation is made for them. They are not necessarily converted, and baptism itself will not convert them, but the gospel promises are before them and every reason exists to believe that the Holy Spirit has begun his work within them. They thus receive baptism as a sign and seal of the divine election, rec-

onciliation, and regeneration. As they grow older, they may come quickly to individual repentance and faith. On the other hand they may move away for a period, or perhaps forever. But baptism is always there, bearing its witness to the will of the Father, the work of the Son, and the ministry of the Spirit," 80–81.

39. Barth wrote that the meaning of baptism is "to be sought in its character as a true and genuine human action which responds to the divine word and act," *CD* IV/4, 128. In this volume Barth deals with "Baptism with the Holy Spirit" and "Baptism with Water" as the two parts of "The Foundation of the Christian Life." Barth's views shifted over time. Cf. the summary of Barth's views in Geoffrey W. Bromiley, *Introduction to the Theology of Karl Barth* (Grand Rapids: Wm. B. Eerdmans Publishing Co., 1979), 239–43. Another critique of infant baptism from a Reformed theologian is Paul K. Jewett, *Infant Baptism and the Covenant of Grace* (Grand Rapids: Wm. B. Eerdmans Publishing Co., 1978).

40. Daniel L. Migliore, *Faith Seeking Understanding* (Grand Rapids: Wm. B. Eerdmans Publishing Co., 1991), 217.

41. The Second Helvetic Confession, chap. 20, in *BC* 5.186.

42. *Baptism, Eucharist and Ministry* (Geneva: World Council of Churches, 1982), 2. See the discussion of the images, 2–3.

43. Campbell, *Christian Confessions*, 279.

44. These points are drawn from Campbell, *Christian Confessions*, 279–80. The term "Restorationist" as used here refers to a nineteenth-century tradition associated with Alexander Campbell and others that is represented today by the Christian Church, Disciples of Christ, and various churches referred to as Churches of Christ.

45. *BC* 9.51.

Chapter 14

1. For a discussion, see Robert F. O'Toole, "Last Supper" in *ABD*, 4:235–37. O'Toole concludes that "we simply cannot determine whether it was a Passover meal or not; however, a reasonable assumption is that it was celebrated in a Passover atmosphere. If it were not a Passover meal, it may well have been a *tôdâ* meal of praise and proclamation," 240. Cf. Alasdair I. C. Heron, *Table and Tradition: Toward an Ecumenical Understanding of the Eucharist* (Philadelphia: Westminster Press, 1983), chap. 2, "The Last Supper and the Passover."

2. See Isa. 25–26; 65:13; Micah 5:2–4; Zech. 9:17; Ezek. 34:23–24; Matt. 8:11; Luke 6:21; 13:29; 14:15–24; 22:29–30. Cf. Scott McCormick Jr., *The Lord's Supper: A Biblical Interpretation* (Philadelphia: Westminster Press, 1966), chap. V, "The Kingdom and Messianic Feasting"; and the study, Geoffrey Wainwright, *Eucharist and Eschatology* (New York: Oxford University Press, 1981).

3. See also the interesting language pattern Luke used to describe the meal Paul shared when his ship was in danger of shipwreck. He took bread (cf. Luke 9:16; 22:19; 24:30), gave thanks (cf. Luke 9:16; 22:19; 24:30), gave thanks (cf. Luke 22:19—Gr. *eucharistesas*), broke the bread (cf. Luke 9:16; 22:19; 24:30; Acts 2:42, 46; 20:7, 11), and ate it (Acts 27:35), as do others until their hunger has been satisfied. The language is very reminiscent of the language in 1 Cor. 11:23–26. See *ABD*, 4:366.

4. See the discussion by Markus Barth, *Rediscovering the Lord's Supper* (Atlanta: John Knox Press, 1988), who reminds that "the meal to which Christ invites is in essence a festival of love—love for one's neighbor, which has been granted through the love and the Holy Spirit of God and Christ for all people," 70.

5. See Arthur C. Cochrane, *Eating and Drinking with Jesus: An Ethical and Biblical Inquiry* (Philadelphia: Westminster Press, 1974). Markus Barth notes that "in approx-

imately one-fifth of the sentences in Luke's Gospel and in Acts, meals play a conspicuous role. Events in the life of Jesus and of the Apostles, in the time before and after Easter, and a host of brief sayings and extended parables emphasize the relevance of eating," *Rediscovering*, 71.

6. As the Christian church grew, the *agapē* meal and the celebration of the Supper became separate practices. By the end of the fourth century, *agapē* meals were held in Christian homes but the practice eventually became discontinued. See *ABD*, 4:371.

7. O'Toole writes: "During the course of the meal, Jesus, in prophetic manner, identified himself with both the bread and the wine in the cup. At a meal people are fed, and Jesus did identify himself in some way with this nourishment," *ABD*, 4:240.

8. Herman Ridderbos, *The Coming of the Kingdom*, ed. Raymond O. Zorn, trans. H. de Jongste (Philadelphia: The Presbyterian and Reformed Publishing Co., 1962), 416.

9. Cochrane, *Eating and Drinking with Jesus*, 115. Put another way: "The eucharist is the meal at which the messiah feeds His people as a sign of the feasting in the coming kingdom." See Wainwright, *Eucharist and Eschatology*, 94.

10. McCormick, *The Lord's Supper*, 100. David Moessner writes: "Combining the meaning of the sacrifices of the covenant meal, the Passover, and the death of Moses outside the land, this meal is the foretaste of the fulfilled banquet of the new covenant of the Kingdom of God wrought by the death of the Prophet like but greater than Moses. Even as bread and wine embodied the blessings of the land (Deut. 29:6), so now bread and wine are emblematic of the eschatological blessings of the new covenant salvation brought by the breaking and sharing of the body and blood of the Lord of the banquet." See *Lord of the Banquet: The Literary and Theological Significance of the Lukan Travel Narrative* (Minneapolis: Fortress Press, 1989), 275.

11. Cochrane, *Eating and Drinking*, 117. Cochrane's study, following trajectories outlined but never completed by Karl Barth, sees the Lord's Supper as an act of faith—as the Eucharist; an act of love—as the Agape; and as an act of hope—as the Marriage Supper. He sees all eating and drinking generally as "an act of thanksgiving not only for the salvation of the world in the death of Jesus but for the revelation and manifestation of that salvation in his resurrection," 68–69.

12. See Wolfhart Pannenberg, *Systematic Theology*, trans. Geoffrey W. Bromiley, 3 vols. (Grand Rapids: Wm. B. Eerdmans Publishing Co., 1998), 3:283ff., and G. C. Berkouwer, *The Sacraments*, trans. Hugo Bekker (Grand Rapids: Wm. B. Eerdmans Publishing Co., 1969), chap. 9.

13. Cyprian, *Letter 59*, cited in Paul H. Jones, *Christ's Eucharistic Presence: A History of the Doctrine* (New York: Peter Lang Publishing, 1994), 26. Cyprian uses images found in the *Didache* (section 9), a short manual on morals and church practice (written around A.D. 100) and the first document to use the term "eucharist" (Gr. *eucharistia*; "thanksgiving") to describe the Lord's Supper.

14. Jones, *Christ's Eucharistic Presence*, 28. St. Augustine was later to refer to the eucharist as "the sacrament of unity." He wrote, "If, then, you are the body of Christ and his members, then that which is on the altar is the mystery (sacrament) of yourselves; receive the mystery (sacrament) of yourselves. You hear what you are, and you answer 'Amen,' and confirm the truth by your answer; for you hear the words 'The body of Christ,' and you answer 'Amen.' Live as a member of the body of Christ, that your Amen may be truthful." Cited in Jones, *Christ's Eucharistic Presence*, 41–42.

15. Cyril, *Commentary on Luke*, cited in Jones, *Christ's Eucharistic Presence*, 51. John Chrysostom spoke of the "transformation" and "transmutation" of the elements, while Ambrose of Milan said that it is Christ's words that "have power to change the character (*species*) of the elements." Cf. Heron, *Table and Tradition*, 65–66.

16. Theodoret as cited in Jones, *Christ's Eucharistic Presence*, 52.

17. *In Ev. Joh.* Tract. 25.12 [The Latin is *credere, et manducasti*]. Augustine has elements of both "realism" and "symbolism" in his writings. See McKim, *Turning Points*, 138–39. Heron points out that these differing approaches to the Lord's Supper "were by no means mutually exclusive" and that the same writer may exhibit each of them. See *Table and Tradition*, 67–68.

18. The issues in these debates were how the symbolic and the realistic sides of a sacrament are related. Are the two sides barely distinct from each other, or are they closely related? In these controversies, Ratramnus and Berengar emphasized the symbolic side; Radbertus and Lanfranc, the reality side. On these see McKim, *Turning Points*, 139–41. Cf. the discussion in Miri Rubin, *Corpus Christi: The Eucharist in Late Medieval Culture* (Cambridge: University Press, 1991), 14ff.

19. See McKim, *Turning Points*, 141, and Jones, *Christ's Eucharistic Presence*, 91ff.

20. This formulation relies on Aristotelian philosophy in which all things are composed of "substance" and "form." A chair has the "substance" of a chair, but its "form" may be wood, steel, or some other material. Thus "under the influence of Aristotelian thought, theologians gradually came to distinguish between the substance of the Eucharist (the body and blood of the Lord) and the accidents of bread and wine (their weight, texture, color, etc.). These remain, even as the substance of bread and wine changes into the substance of Christ's body and blood." See John J. Strynkowski, "Transubstantiation," in *The HarperCollins Encyclopedia of Catholicism*, ed. Richard P. McBrien (San Francisco: HarperCollins, 1995), 1264.

21. See Aquinas, *Summa Theologia*, III.76.7; McKim, *Turning Points*, 141–42, and Heron, *Table and Tradition*, 96ff. Thus, the transformation of the "substance" is perceived by faith while the "accidents" remain visible to all.

22. *Canons and Decrees of the Council of Trent*, trans. H. J. Schroeder (1941; reprint, St. Louis: Herder, 1955), 73, 75.

23. See Heron, *Table and Tradition*, 101.

24. On these see McKim, *Turning Points*, 143–45, and Ralph W. Quere, "Changes and Constants: Structure in Luther's Understanding of the Real Presence in the 1520s," *The Sixteenth Century Journal*, 16/1 (1985), 45–78.

25. Cited in Heron, *Table and Tradition*, 111. Thus, Luther may be said to affirm "the *intention* of transubstantiation, but rejects it as an inadequate, indeed misconceived *explanation*." See Heron, 113. Luther's views are sometimes referred to as "consubstantiation" (from Lat. *cum* = "with")—that Jesus Christ is present "in" and "under" and "around" the elements of the bread and wine. He used the illustration of a red-hot iron which is, in every part, both iron and fire (hot). Yet Luther never used the term "consubstantiation." See Jones, *Christ's Eucharistic Presence*, 121.

26. Heron, *Table and Tradition*, 112.

27. Ibid., 115.

28. Cited in Jones, *Christ's Eucharistic Presence*, 123.

29. See B. A. Gerrish, "Sign and Reality: The Lord's Supper in the Reformed Confessions," in *The Old Protestantism and the New: Essays on the Reformation Heritage* (Chicago: University of Chicago Press, 1982), 129. Cf. W. P. Stephens, *The Theology of Huldrych Zwingli* (Oxford: Clarendon Press, 1986), 227ff. Gerrish goes on to write that for Zwingli the gift of Christ lies in the past, "as does the gift of faith, and accordingly it is the Christian believer or the Christian community that is the subject of the present sacramental action: *we* give thanks, *we* make confession" before others. "The sacrament is simply a public testimony that you do indeed possess what God has given freely."

30. Heron, *Table and Tradition*, 116.

31. See McKim, *Turning Points*, 146.

32. *Inst.* IV.17.3.

33. Ibid., IV.17.4. Calvin wrote: "Therefore, if the Lord truly represents the participation in his body through the breaking of bread, there ought not to be the least doubt that he truly presents and shows his body. And the godly ought by all means to keep this rule: whenever they see symbols appointed by the Lord, to think and be persuaded that the truth of the thing signified is surely presented there" (IV.17.10).

34. *Inst.* IV.17.10.

35. Gerrish notes that the fundamental difference between the two reformers is that "Zwingli and Calvin held two totally different views of religious symbolism." Zwingli maintained that, " 'if [the sacraments] bestowed the thing or were the thing, they would be things and not a sacrament or sign.' Calvin agreed that the sacraments cannot be both signs and the things signified. But his position is still, in effect, the exact opposite of Zwingli's: *because* a sacrament is a sign, *therefore* it bestows what it signifies. More correctly, because sacraments are divinely appointed signs, and God does not lie, therefore the Spirit uses them to confer what they symbolize," Gerrish, "Sign and Reality," 122–23.

36. *Inst.* IV.17.14. Calvin gave four reasons for rejecting transubstantiation, which he considered a "fiction" because it was not based on Scripture and confused the distinction between the presence of Christ in the sacrament and his local presence in the bread, among other things. To him, early church theologians who spoke of the conversion of the elements did not mean that "the elements have been annihilated, but rather that they now have to be considered of a different class from common foods intended solely to feed the stomach, since in them is set forth the spiritual food and drink of the soul."

37. See Berkouwer, *The Sacraments*, chap. 11.

38. Jones, *Christ's Eucharistic Presence*, 142.

39. *Inst.* IV.17.18. Calvin indicates that on the manner of Christ's presence in the Supper: "For us the manner is spiritual because the secret power of the spirit is the bond of our union with Christ," IV.17.33.

40. They are a "metonymy," a "figure of speech commonly used in Scripture when mysteries are under discussion" (*Inst.* IV.17.21). Cf. Berkouwer, *The Sacraments*, chap. 10.

41. Gerrish has provided six propositions of Calvin's views of the Lord's Supper:
    1. The Lord's Supper is a gift.
    2. The gift is Jesus Christ himself.
    3. The gift is given with the signs.
    4. The gift is given by the Holy Spirit.
    5. The gift is given to all who communicate.
    6. The gift is to be received by faith.
    See *Grace and Gratitude*, 135–39.

42. *Inst.* IV.17.5. Calvin had earlier spoken of the "great assurance and delight" coming from the sacrament that we grow into "one body with Christ such that whatever is his may be called ours." He refers to this as "the wonderful exchange" (the same phrase is used by Luther) in that Jesus Christ has become a human being for our redemption and we become engrafted into his body. He has made us children of God with him, has descended to Earth to "prepare an ascent to heaven for us," and has taken on our mortality, so that we might receive immortality," *Inst.* IV.17.2.

43. B. A. Gerrish has also noted a third stance in the Reformed position, represented

by Heinrich Bullinger and which he calls "symbolic parallelism." When the bread is eaten outwardly, there is "at the same time" an inward feeding on Christ's body. God is offering that which is signified by the elements, just as in preaching the offer of the gospel is given. This view is found in Bullinger's Second Helvetic Confession (1566; see *BC* 5.183; 5.203). This emphasizes the "present tense"—indicating what is happening as believers participate in the Lord's Supper. Gerrish notes: "This, of course, does take us beyond Zwingli, whose characteristic tense is the past, not the present. In Zwingli's view, the elements call to mind something that has happened: Christ's body *was* broken, we *have* turned to him in faith. And yet Bullinger's parallelism is not Calvin's position either, for it lacks the use of instrumental expressions; the outward event does not convey or cause or give rise to the inward event, but merely indicates that it is going on." See Gerrish, "Sign and Reality," 124. Gerrish notes that "where Calvin and Bullinger never agreed was over Calvin's belief that God performs the inward *through* the outward," *Grace and Gratitude*, 167 n. 29. For Calvin, God in sacraments "does not feed our eyes with a mere appearance only, but leads us to the present reality and effectively performs what it symbolizes." See *Inst.* IV.15.14 and IV.17.3. Gerrish coins the following for the three Reformed views: Zwingli—symbolic memorialism; Bullinger—symbolic parallelism; and Calvin—symbolic instrumentalism.

44. From *The Book of Common Worship* (Louisville, Ky.: Westminster/John Knox Press, 1993), 68. This invitation was found in the earlier Presbyterian work, *The Worshipbook: Service and Hymns* (Philadelphia: The Westminster Press, 1970), 34.

45. See *The Presbyterian Hymnal: Hymns, Psalms, and Spiritual Songs*, ed. LindaJo H. McKim (Louisville, Ky.: Westminster/John Knox Press, 1990), no. 507 (by Brian Wren, 1968; rev. 1977), and no. 514 (Fred Kaan, 1975).

46. *BC* 9.52. This description is set in the celebratory, eschatological framework but also refers to the "benefits" of Christ's death and resurrection, the emphases most often accented in other confessions of faith.

47. Heron cites the Leuenberg Concord of 1973 in Europe as an example of this approach. It sought to provide the basis for intercommunion between Lutheran and Reformed churches. See *Table and Tradition*, 150. Heron advocates open discussion of difficult issues, yet with "the conviction that the Lord of the church does not will the sacrament of his body and blood, of himself, to be a cause of disunity," 179.

48. *Inst.* IV.17.32.

49. Ibid., IV.17.7. Having said this, though, Calvin indicated he would go on to "sum up my views"—and did so in good theological fashion!

Chapter 15

1. See Joseph P. Healey, "Faith," *ABD*, 2:744–49. Cf. the full study of the theological understandings of faith by Avery Dulles, *The Assurance of Things Hoped For: A Theology of Christian Faith* (London: Oxford University Press, 1994).

2. See R. T. France, "Faith," *DJG*, 225. Cf. R. Bultmann and A. Weiser, "Πιστεύω," *Theological Dictionary of the New Testament*, ed. G. Friedrich and G. Kittel, trans. Geoffrey Bromiley, 8 vols. (Grand Rapids: Wm. B. Eerdmans Publishing Co., 1968), 6:222–28.

3. See *TDNT*, 6:208–22.

4. Christian believers are often designated in Paul's letters as "the holy" or "saints." See Rom. 1:1, 7; 1 Cor. 1:2; 6:1, 2; Phil. 1:1; 4:21; Philemon 5, 7, etc. Cf. Robert Hodgson Jr., "Holiness (NT)," *ABD*, 3:249–54; Richard A. Muller, "Sanctification," *ISBE*, 321–31; S. E. Porter, "Holiness, Sanctification," *DPL*, 397–402.

5. *ISBE*, 4, 326.

6. The Roman Catholic view of the relation of "justification" and "sanctification" is basically that the two are blended together. In justification, "God's grace continues to lead the baptized person to good works, by which she or he 'merits' eternal life." See Ted A. Campbell, *Christian Confessions: A Historical Introduction* (Louisville, Ky.: Westminster John Knox Press, 1996), 96. God's Spirit infuses Christ's righteousness into the believer and begins a process of renewing human choice that restores original righteousness. This begins one on the process toward perfection by giving a desire for God and infusing spiritual gifts and the Christian virtues of faith, hope, and love into the soul. These "dispositions" (Council of Trent) are the basis toward progressing toward perfection. Good works are thus presupposed since they will be the acts of faith, hope, love, and grace performed by the righteous person who is increasing in holiness. See *ISBE*, 4, 326–27.

7. Luther developed this thought in his 1515–1516 Lectures on Romans at Romans 4:7; 7:25; 12:2. See Hendrikus Berkhof, *Christian Faith: An Introduction to the Study of the Faith*, trans. Sierd Woudstra, rev. ed. (Grand Rapids: Wm. B. Eerdmans Publishing Co., 1986), 474.

8. *D. Martine Luthers Werke: Kristishe Gesamtausgabe* (Weimar: Hermann Boehlau, 1883–1983), 50.642.36, 643.1–2 (hereafter *W.A.*); *Luther's Works*. American edition, ed. Jaroslav Pelikan and Helmut T. Lehman, 54 vols. (St. Louis: Concordia Publishing House; Philadelphia: Fortress Press, 1955–1967), 41:166 (hereafter *L.W.*) cited in Randall C. Zachman, *The Assurance of Faith: Conscience in the Theology of Martin Luther and John Calvin* (Minneapolis: Fortress Press, 1993), 84.

9. *W.A.* 50.643.19–26; *L.W.* 41:166, in Zachman, *Assurance of Faith*, 84.

10. Campbell, *Christian Confessions*, 160. Moltmann writes that "the 'communion of saints' in the Apostles' Creed is not an assembly of people who are saints in the moral sense. It is simply the community of pardoned sinners, reconciled enemies, believers. The person who finds grace in God's sight is also in God's sight good, just and holy. Sanctification as an act of God in a human being signifies a relationship and an affiliation, not a state in itself. What God loves is holy, whatever it may be in itself," *The Spirit of Life: A Universal Affirmation*, trans. Margaret Kohl (Minneapolis: Fortress Press, 1993), 174.

11. John Wesley, *The Works of John Wesley*, ed. T. Jackson, 14 vols. (London, 1831). Cf. Peter Toon, *Justification and Sanctification*. Foundations for Faith (Westchester, Ill.: Crossway Books, 1983), 108.

12. Wesley, *Works*, 11:368. See his *The Plain Account of Christian Perfection* (*Works* 11:366–449).

13. Wesley, *Works* 12:257. Cf. *ISBE*, 4:329, and Berkouwer, *Faith and Sanctification*, 50–53. Toon notes that for Wesley, "justification and regeneration signify a completed act of God. In place of the traditional Protestant idea of growth (from regeneration) *towards* holiness—that is, a process *prior* to its attainment—he substituted a growth *in* holiness, *subsequent to* its attainment (in regeneration). Thus Wesleyan ethics are ethics of realization rather than of aspiration," *Justification and Sanctification*, 109.

14. See *ISBE*, 4:329, citing R. N. Flew, *The Idea of Perfection in Christian Theology* (1934).

15. The Wesleyan Methodists began in 1843; the Free Methodists in 1860. Today, these and other denominations emerging from the Holiness perspective include the Church of God (Anderson, Indiana), founded in 1880, the Pilgrim Holiness Church (1897), and the Church of the Nazarene (1908). In 1968, the Pilgrim Holiness and Wesleyan Methodist churches merged to form the Wesleyan Church.

16. See Campbell, *Christian Confessions*, 236ff.

17. Ibid., 237–39.

18. *ISBE*, 4:330.

19. Calvin, *Inst.* III.3.11. Cf. Rom. 6:6; 8:2.

20. Westminster Shorter Catechism, Q. 35; *BC* 7.035.

21. *BC* 4.114. The next question and answer are: Q. 115. Why, then, does God have the ten commandments preached so strictly since no one can keep them in this life? A. First, that all our life long we may become increasingly aware of our sinfulness, and therefore more eagerly seek forgiveness of sins and righteousness in Christ. Second, that we may constantly and diligently pray to God for the grace of the Holy Spirit, so that more and more we may be renewed in the image of God, until we attain the goal of full perfection after this life," *BC* 4.115. Cf. Calvin, *Inst.* III.17.15.

22. Calvin, *Inst.* II.7.12. Cf. I. John Hesselink, *Calvin's Concept of the Law* (Allison Park, Pa.: Pickwick Publications, 1991). Cf. Q. 97 of the Westminster Larger Catechism (*BC* 7.207). As Berkouwer notes, "Faith and love and law, to Calvin, are allies," *Faith and Sanctification*, 167.

23. In this respect, Luther and Calvin differ on the law. For Luther, the law "generally connotes something negative and hostile; hence his listing the law along with sin, death, and the devil. For Calvin, the law was viewed primarily as a positive expression of the will of God whereby God restores the image of God in humanity and order in the fallen creation," I. John Hesselink, "Law," in *ERF*, 215. Both Luther and Calvin agree on the first two "uses" of the law—that it shows us our sin and convicts us of it.

Karl Barth published *Gospel and Law* in 1935 in which he argued that we must begin with God's promise in the covenant (Gal. 3:17) before we can gain a right understanding of the law. By reversing the traditional Law/Gospel order, Barth was attacking a view that was especially strong in the Lutheran tradition. Barth believed that the law was not a demand, but an expression of God's grace. It is sin that causes us to regard the law as "the law of sin and of death" (Rom. 8:2). As an example, remember that before God gave the Ten Commandments to the people of Israel as the "law" (Exodus 20), God reminded them of God's gracious action as their Lord who "brought you out of the land of Egypt, out of the house of slavery" (Ex. 20:2). The law is given in the prior context of God's act of grace. The nation is to obey the law as an expression of their gracious covenant relationship with God.

24. "The Belgic Confession of Faith, 1561," Art. 24 in *Reformed Confessions of the 16th Century*, ed. Arthur C. Cochrane (Philadelphia: Westminster Press, 1966), 205.

25. Calvin, *Inst.* III.1.1. The Holy Spirit is the Spirit of sanctification (2 Thess. 2:13; 1 Peter 1:2) who "quickens and nourishes us by a general power that is visible both in the human race and in the rest of the living creatures, but [the Spirit] is also the root and seed of heavenly life in us," *Inst.* III.1.2. Calvin may rightly be called "the theologian of the Holy Spirit"—a title initially bestowed by B. B. Warfield (1851–1921). See Hesselink, *Calvin's Catechism*, "Appendix: Calvin, Theologian of the Holy Spirit," 177–87.

26. *BC* 4.001. Cf. the helpful study by Lewis B. Smedes, *Union with Christ*, 2nd rev. ed. (Grand Rapids: Wm. B. Eerdmans Publishing Co., 1983).

27. Wilhelm Niesel, *The Gospel and the Churches: A Comparison of Catholicism, Orthodoxy, and Protestantism*, trans. David Lewis (Philadelphia: Westminster Press, 1962), 181. Hesselink indicates that this statement "may be too strong an assertion, but there is no doubt that this is true for Calvin," *Calvin's Catechism*, 186.

28. Calvin, *Inst.* III.11.10. Other places in Calvin's writings where the idea of union with Christ appears are in our partaking of Christ in the Lord's Supper (*Inst.* IV.17.1,

2, 10). Romans 8:9 shows that "the Spirit alone causes us to possess Christ completely and have him dwelling in us" (*Inst.* IV.17.12). Calvin writes that "Christ is not outside us but dwells within us. Not only does he cleave to us by an indivisible bond of fellowship, but with a wonderful communion, day by day, he grows more and more into one body with us, until he becomes completely one with us," *Inst.* III.2.24.

29. The Reformed theologian Peter von Mastricht (d. 1706) described the union with Christ as: real, not imaginary, total, indissoluble and eternal, and spiritual. See Niesel, *The Gospel and the Churches*, 183–84. For my development of the theme of Reformed Spirituality as lived through the Providence of God, the Presence of Christ, and the Power of the Holy Spirit, see Donald K. McKim, "A Trinitarian, Reformed Spirituality," *Memphis Theological Seminary Journal*, 33, no. 1 (spring 1995), 14–29.

30. *Inst.* III.2.35. Cf. Dennis E. Tamburello, *Union with Christ: John Calvin and the Mysticism of St. Bernard*, Columbia Series in Reformed Theology (Louisville, Ky.: Westminster John Knox Press, 1994), chap. 5, "John Calvin on Mystical Union." Calvin considers our "engrafting" into Christ "to be 'simultaneous' with faith," 85. Cf. Ronald S. Wallace, *Calvin's Doctrine of the Christian Life* (Grand Rapids: Wm. B. Eerdmans Publishing Co., 1959), 17–23.

31. Calvin, *Inst.* III.1.4. Hendrikus Berkhof wrote of faith that "in the New Testament, this faith presents itself as a gift of the Holy Spirit, a fruit of election, a special revelation, an insight which no human heart has conceived," *Christian Faith*, 1.

32. Calvin, *Inst.* III.2.7.

33. These points are modified from Robert McAfee Brown, *Is Faith Obsolete?* (Philadelphia: Westminster Press, 1974), 24–27.

34. See Calvin, *Inst.* IV.1.9. Calvin used maternal and paternal images to describe the church and then said, ". . . for those to whom he is Father the church may also be Mother," an image used also by Cyprian and Augustine. See *Inst.* IV.1.1.

35. Douglas F. Ottati, *Reforming Protestantism: Christian Commitment in Today's World* (Louisville, Ky.: Westminster John Knox Press, 1995), 98. Here Ottati is following H. Richard Niebuhr in *The Purpose of the Church and Its Ministry* (New York: Harper & Row, 1956).

36. *BC* 9.31.

37. This is Calvin's phrase commenting on this central text for the Confession of 1967, in his *Commentary on 1 Corinthians 5:19*.

38. Ottati, *Reforming Protestantism*, 100. For another approach, see Donald K. McKim, "A Reformed Perspective on the Mission of the Church in Society" in *Major Themes in the Reformed Tradition*, 361–71. Cf. the excellent work by Darrell L. Guder, *Be My Witnesses: The Church's Mission, Message, and Messengers* (Grand Rapids: Wm. B. Eerdmans Publishing Co., 1985), who defines the church's task as "to be the witness" to God's reconciliation of the world in Jesus Christ. This means that "the church and the Christian are to *be* the witness, *do* the witness, and *say* the witness," 91.

39. Arthur C. Cochrane, "The Doctrine of the Call in the Constitution of the United Presbyterian Church in the United States of America (1968–1969)," in *Model for Ministry: A Report for Study Issued by the General Assembly Special Committee on the Theology of the Call*, ed. Lewis S. Mudge (Philadelphia: Office of the General Assembly of the United Presbyterian Church in the United States of America, 1970), 43, cited in Donald K. McKim, "The Call in the Reformed Tradition," *Major Themes in the Reformed Tradition*, 342. Cf. the section on "Vocation" in McKim, "A Reformed Perspective on the Mission of the Church in Society," *Major Themes in the Reformed Tradition*, 365–67, and John R. Walchenbach, "Vocation," in *ERF*, 387–88.

40. The term is Calvin's in *Inst.* III.10.6.

41. From the English Puritan theologian William Perkins (1558–1602) in his "A Treatise of the Vocations, or Callings of men, with the sorts and kinds of them, and the right use thereof," in *The Workes of William Perkins*, 3 vols. (London: John Legatt, 1618), 1:722. Perkins spoke of the "general calling" of the Christian and the "particular" (1:752ff.). See Donald K. McKim, *Ramism in William Perkins' Theology* (New York: Peter Lang, 1987), 116. Cf. Ottati, *Reforming Protestantism*, 123–29, for a helpful use of Perkins on "vocation."

42. Ottati, *Reforming Protestantism*, 133. See his whole chapter 6, "The Sanctification of the Ordinary." Migliore cautions: "The vocation of a Christian is not to be confused with having a job by which one earns one's livelihood. Whatever one's job or profession, as a Christian one is called to be a partner in God's mission in the world," *Faith Seeking Understanding* (Grand Rapids: Wm. B. Eerdmans Publishing Co., 1991), 183. Barth says that the Christian's active life of obedience as service for the cause of God is our "direct or indirect co-operation in the fulfilment of the task of the Christian community." See *CD* III/4, 483.

43. H. Richard Niebuhr, *Christ and Culture* (New York: Harper & Row, 1956), 217. Niebuhr's classic study proposes models for the varying views of how Christ (the gospel) relates to culture: Christ against Culture; the Christ of Culture; Christ above Culture; Christ and Culture in Paradox; Christ the Transformer of Culture. He sees the Reformed tradition—through Augustine, Calvin, and Jonathan Edwards—as in the "Christ the Transformer" type.

44. See Abraham Kuyper, *Lectures on Calvinism* (Grand Rapids: Wm. B. Eerdmans Publishing Co., 1931). These were the Stone Lectures delivered at Princeton Theological Seminary in 1898. In them he argued that Calvinism was a "life-system" that affects all arenas of life including religion, politics, science, and art. He appeals to Calvin's notion of God's "general" or "common grace" whereby God restrains human sinfulness and allows arts and sciences to flourish since human competence in art and science derive from the Spirit of God (*Inst* II.2.13–17 and n. 63). This gives the warrant for God's people to devote their efforts to these pursuits. Kuyper himself (1837–1920) embodied this full-orbed commitment to serving God in culture. He was one of the Netherlands' most famous citizens, a leading Reformed theologian, pastor, founder of the Free University of Amsterdam, Prime Minister (1901–1905), leader of a political party, editor of a daily newspaper, and writer of over two thousand devotional meditations and a number of books. See James D. Bratt, "Abraham Kuyper," in *ERF*, 212–13. Cf. the social vision sketched by a contemporary philosopher in Kuyper's Dutch Reformed tradition in Nicholas Wolterstorff, *Until Justice and Peace Embrace*, The Kuyper Lectures for 1981 delivered at the Free University of Amsterdam (Grand Rapids: Wm. B. Eerdmans Publishing Co., 1983).

45. The same may be said about the relation of Reformed churches to governments (the state). In general, the Reformed view has been that the church is to support the state as a God-given institution insofar as governments pursue justice and the aims of the reign of God. When this does not occur, then governments (the "magistrate" in sixteenth-century terms) must be resisted. Thus, Calvinists were involved in the English revolution of the seventeenth century. See Eberhard Busch, "Church and Politics in the Reformed Tradition," McKim, ed., *Major Themes*, 180–95, and David Little, "Reformed Faith and Religious Liberty," McKim, ed., *Major Themes*, 196–213. Cf. *Reformed Faith and Politics*, ed. Ronald H. Stone (Washington, D.C.: The University Press of America, 1983).

46. These are derived from Ottati, *Reforming Protestantism*, chap. 5, "The Church In, With, Against, and For the World." He indicates that "among other things, the ques-

tion of church and world is not fundamentally a matter of choosing or endorsing just one of these prepositions as normative and invariant. It is, rather, a matter of understanding how, in conjunction with the others, each appropriately comes into play, and how now one, now another receives special emphasis," 101. He describes this as a "multivalent relationship," 100.

47. Ottati, *Reforming Protestantism*, 116.

48. These citations are derived from Robert Benedetto, Darrell L. Guder, and Donald K. McKim, *Historical Dictionary of Reformed Churches*, Historical Dictionaries of Religions, Philosophies, and Movements, no. 24 (Lanham, Md.: Scarecrow Press, 1999), 354.

49. On Reformed worship see especially the works of Hughes Oliphant Old, *Patristic Roots of Reformed Worship* (Zurich: TVZ, 1975); *Worship That Is Reformed According to Scripture* (Atlanta: John Knox Press, 1984); "Worship," in *ERF*, 410–12; and *Themes and Variations for a Christian Doxology: Some Thoughts on the Theology of Worship* (Grand Rapids: Wm. B. Eerdmans Publishing Co., 1992), where Old considers five worship perspectives as "doxology," or the praise of God: Epicletic Doxology—calling on God's name for help and salvation; Kerygmatic Doxology—the preaching of the gospel of Jesus Christ; Wisdom Doxology—the study of Scripture to the glory of God; Prophetic Doxology—the reflection of God's holiness among God's people; and Covenantal Doxology—the confessing of covenantal obligations and celebration of God's faithfulness, particularly in the sacraments.

50. Jürgen Moltmann, *The Spirit of Life*, 161.

51. Ibid., 175.

52. Migliore has well written: "It is a mistake to think of sanctification as solely what *we* do in contrast to justification as solely *God's* work. Just as faith is properly understood as a response to the divine justification of human life, so love of God and our fellow creatures is properly understood as a response to the divine sanctification of human life in Jesus Christ. It is first of all the gift of God, and then also a human task," *Faith Seeking Understanding*, 178.

53. See Calvin, *Inst.* III.20 for a full discussion of prayer.

54. *BC* 10.4.

55. Ibid. See my "An Ethic of Gratitude," *The Presbyterian Outlook* (Nov. 20, 2000), 9.

56. Calvin's discussion in *Inst.* III.7.8–10 and III.8. Cf. John H. Leith, *John Calvin's Doctrine of the Christian Life* (Louisville, Ky.: Westminster John Knox, 1989), 74–82, and Wallace, *Calvin's Doctrine of the Christian Life*, part II. Calvin saw our sanctification as being the gradual restoration of the image of God in a person that shows itself in self-denial, cross bearing, and meditation on the future life. The forgiveness of sins received in justification is the first step. Calvin usually referred to the whole process of sanctification as "repentance," which is lifelong (*Inst.* III.3). Repentance has two parts: Mortification—which is the putting to death of the "flesh"—the sinful domination of our natural state by the power of the Holy Spirit; and Vivification—which is the desire to live in holiness through self-denial and is marked by God's Spirit living within us. Cf. Randall C. Gleason, *John Calvin and John Owen on Mortification: A Comparative Study in Reformed Spirituality* (New York: Peter Lang, 1995), chap. 2. Cf. Donald K. McKim, "John Calvin: A Theologian for an Age of Limits," *Readings in Calvin's Theology*, ed. Donald K. McKim (Grand Rapids: Baker Book House, 1984), 291–310.

Chapter 16

1. The term "eschatology" is from the Greek *eschatos*, "last," and *logos*, "study," and means the study of "last things" or the end of the world. For one theological treatment

see Wolfhart Pannenberg, *Systematic Theology*, trans. Geoffrey W. Bromiley, 3 vols. (Grand Rapids: Wm. B. Eerdmans Publishing Co., 1998), chap. 15, "The Consummation of Creation in the Kingdom of God."

2. See Exodus 15:18; Deuteronomy 33:5; Psalm 99:1–4; Isaiah 24:23. The "enthronement psalms" are the fullest expression of God's reign (Psalms 47, 93, 95–99). See Dennis C. Duling, "Kingdom of God, Kingdom of Heaven," in *ABD*, 4:50. Cf. John Bright, *The Kingdom of God* (New York: Abingdon, 1953).

3. See *ABD*, 4:52. As one scholar has noted: "Although the term 'kingdom of God' is rare in Judaism, the idea is almost ubiquitous, either explicitly as the kingdom of the Messiah or implicitly in descriptions of the messianic age." See C. C. Caragounis, "Kingdom of God/Heaven," in *DJG*, 418.

4. Herman Ridderbos, *The Coming of the Kingdom*, trans. H. de Jongste, ed. Raymond O. Zorn (Philadelphia: The Presbyterian and Reformed Publishing Co., 1962), xi. Cf. Joachim Jeremias, *New Testament Theology: The Proclamation of Jesus*, trans. John Bowden (New York: Charles Scribner's Sons, 1971), 96. It has been noted that the synoptic Gospels contain 76 different "kingdom sayings" or 103 including parallels. In John's Gospel, the term does not play a significant role (found twice in the Nicodemus story, 3:3, 5; and the term "kingdom" three times in Jesus' answers to Pilate, 18:36). Concepts of "eternal life" or "life" are equivalent terms (see Mark 9:43–47; 10:17–30 where they are used interchangeably). See *DJG*, 429.

5. Ridderbos writes: "It may be rightly said that the whole of the preaching of Jesus Christ and his apostles is concerned with the kingdom of God, and that in Jesus Christ's proclamation of the kingdom we are face to face with the specific form of expression of the whole of his revelation of God," xi.

6. See Adolf Schlatter, *The History of the Christ: The Foundation of New Testament Theology*, trans. Andreas J. Köstenberger (Grand Rapids: Baker Books, 1997), 125. Jeremias writes that the dynamic concept "denotes the reign of God in action, in the first place as opposed to earthly monarchy, but then in contrast to all rule in heaven and on earth. Its chief characteristic is that God is realizing the ideal of the king of righteousness, constantly longed for, but never fulfilled on earth." See Jeremias, *New Testament Theology*, 98.

7. Frank J. Matera, *New Testament Ethics: The Legacies of Jesus and Paul* (Louisville, Ky.: Westminster John Knox Press, 1996), 18.

8. George Eldon Ladd, *A Theology of the New Testament*, rev. ed. (Grand Rapids: Wm. B. Eerdmans Publishing Co., 1993), 62.

9. Ridderbos says, "'Kingdom of God' and 'the Son of Man' are correlates in Jesus' preaching," *Coming of the Kingdom*, 31.

10. Richard B. Hays, *The Moral Vision of the New Testament: A Contemporary Introduction to New Testament Ethics* (San Francisco: HarperCollins, 1996), 84. Hays notes that in Mark's Gospel "the way of the cross is simply the way of obedience to the will of God, and discipleship requires following that way regardless of cost or consequences," 84–85.

11. Jesus' many "kingdom parables" (see Mark 4; Matt. 13, etc.) convey facets of the "secret" of God's kingdom (Mark 4:11).

12. Much more can be found in McKim, *Turning Points*, 152–55; Ladd, *A Theology of the New Testament*; Jeremias, *New Testament Theology*, 96–108; A. M. Hunter, *The Work and Words of Jesus*, rev. ed. (Philadelphia: Westminster Press, 1973), among other sources.

13. See Millard J. Erickson, *Contemporary Options in Eschatology: A Study of the Millennium* (Grand Rapids: Baker Book House, 1977); Robert G. Clouse, ed., *The Meaning*

of the Millennium: Four Views (Downers Grove, Ill.: InterVarsity Press, 1977); Stanley J. Grenz, *The Millennia Maze: Sorting Out Evangelical Options* (Downers Grove, Ill.: InterVarsity Press, 1992); Anthony A. Hoekema, *The Bible and the Future* (Grand Rapids: Wm. B. Eerdmans Publishing Co., 1979); G. C. Berkouwer, *The Return of Christ*, trans. James Van Oosterom (Grand Rapids: Wm. B. Eerdmans Publishing Co., 1972); and Donald G. Bloesch, *Essentials of Evangelical Theology*, 2 vols. (San Francisco: Harper & Row, 1979), 2:189–204.

14. The movement known as Dispensationalism features a type of premillennialism. Dispensationalism was developed primarily in England by the Plymouth Brethren, John Nelson Darby (1800–1882), and popularized by C. I. Scofield (1843–1921) through his Scofield Reference Bible. Dispensationalism divides all history into various time periods or "dispensations," seen as God's progressive revelation. It has been rejected by Reformed churches and Reformed theologies since it separated God's plans for Israel for God's plan for the church rather than seeing a continuous activity of God. In its view of the future, many Dispensationalists teach a pretribulation rapture of the church. The view gained popularity with the book by Hal Lindsey, *The Late Great Planet Earth* (1970). See Bradley J. Longfield, "Dispensationalism," in *ERF*, 105, and T. P. Weber, "Dispensationalism," in *Dictionary of Christianity in America*, ed. Daniel G. Reid, Robert D. Linder, Bruce L. Shelley, Harry S. Stout (Downers Grove, Ill.: InterVarsity Press, 1990), 358.

15. See I. John Hesselink, "The Millennium in the Reformed Tradition," *Reformed Review*, 52, no. 2 (winter 1998–1999), 97–125.

16. Stanley J. Grenz, *Theology for the Community of God* (Nashville: Broadman and Holman, 1994), 808–9.

17. "Jesus is Victor!" was a phrase associated by Karl Barth with two Pietist figures who influenced him, J. C. Blumhardt (1805–1880) and his son Christoph (1842–1919). It is a capsule of Barth's own theology. See *Church Dogmatics*, IV.3.1, 165–274; *The Christian Life: Church Dogmatics IV,4 Lecture Fragments*, trans. Geoffrey W. Bromiley (Grand Rapids: Wm. B. Eerdmans Publishing Co., 1981), 256–60; and Donald G. Bloesch, *Jesus Is Victor! Karl Barth's Doctrine of Salvation* (Nashville: Abingdon, 1976), 60.

18. Barth, *CD*, IV.3.1, 263.

19. See chapter 35 in *BC* 6.180–82.

20. *BC* 4.052. This was also a note struck by Calvin in his catechisms. In 1538 he wrote: "And from this a remarkable comfort comes to us because we hear that judgment has been transferred to him whose coming could be only for our salvation," Hesselink, *Calvin's Catechism of 1538*, 24. In 1541 to the question (86): "Does the fact that Christ is to come again to judge the world bring us any consolation?" The answer is: "Yes, indeed. For we are certain that He will appear only for our salvation." Question 87: "We should not then fear the last judgment, and have a horror of it?" Answer: "No, since we are not to come before any other Judge than He who is our Advocate, and who has taken our cause in hand to defend us." See *The School of Faith: The Catechisms of the Reformed Church*, ed. and trans. Thomas F. Torrance (New York: Harper & Brothers Publishers, 1959), 18–19.

21. Karl Barth, *The Heidelberg Catechism for Today*, trans. Shirley C. Guthrie Jr. (Richmond: John Knox Press, 1964), 82. Cf. Karl Barth, *Credo* (New York: Charles Scribner's Sons, 1962), 122–26; and Barth, *Dogmatics in Outline*, trans. G. T. Thompson (New York: Harper & Brothers, 1959), 134–36. In these places Barth also criticized Michelangelo's famous painting, as he did when commenting on Calvin's Geneva Catechism answer: "Think of Michelangelo's *Last Judgment*: a Christ coming back and holding out his fist! . . . But this is not the Christian notion of Christ's return, which is

all comfort, because our judge is our advocate at the same time. We have no reason to fear him nor to hold him in horror. To fear the last judgment is a pagan (Persian, for instance), not a Christian idea. There is only one who might be against us: Jesus Christ. And it is he, precisely, who is for us!" See Karl Barth, *The Faith of the Church: A Commentary on the Apostles' Creed According to Calvin's Catechism*, trans. Gabriel Vahanian, ed. Jean-Louis Leuba (London: Collins, 1967), 100–101.

22. In the Westminster Confession (*BC* 6.181) and Heidelberg Catechism (4.052). See Luke 13:25–29; Matthew 22:13; Romans 6:21; Philippians 1:28; 3:19; 1 Thessalonians 5:3; 2 Thess. 1:8f.

23. Barth, *The Heidelberg Catechism for Today*, 82. The doctrine of hell is based on biblical passages such as Matthew 13:42, 49–50; 22:13; 24:51; 25:10–13, 14–30, 46; John 5:29 as well as apostolic writings in 2 Thessalonians 1:9; Hebrews 6:2; Jude 7; Revelation 14:10–14. Its eternality is suggested in Matthew 18:8; 25:41, 46. Jesus' use of *gehenna* (Heb. *ge hinnom*) referred to a valley south of Jerusalem where children were sacrificed in fire to the pagan god Molech (2 Kings 16:3; 21:6; 2 Chron. 28:3; 33:6). To the prophets it symbolized judgment (Jer. 7:31–32; 19:6), final judgment. The area was used as a burial ground for criminals and burning garbage in the time of Jesus, and thus the appropriateness of the image (see Matt. 5:22, 29–30; 10:28; 18:9; 23:33; Mark 9:43–47; Luke 12:5). Yet the term is not used in Paul, who also spoke of God who will "gather up all things" (Eph. 1:10) and "reconcile . . . all things" (Col. 1:20), and the day when "every tongue" will confess that Jesus Christ is Lord (Phil. 2:11f.). God will be "all in all" (1 Cor. 15:28). In his great chapter on the resurrection, Paul does not mention a double-outcome judgment; and his builds an Adam-Christ typology—"life for all" (Rom. 5:18). For "as all die in Adam, so all will be made alive in Christ" (1 Cor. 15:22) and God will "be merciful to all" (Rom. 11:32). Among many sources see Jürgen Moltmann, *The Coming of God: Christian Eschatology*, trans. Margaret Kohl (Minneapolis: Fortress Press, 1996), 240ff.; Hendrikus Berkhof, *Christian Faith: An Introduction to the Study of the Faith*, rev. ed., trans. Sierd Woudstra (Grand Rapids: Wm. B. Eerdmans Publishing Co., 1986), 534–37.

24. Barth, *The Heidelberg Catechism for Today*, 82. Guthrie puts it this way: "If we know that while we ourselves were 'helpless,' 'ungodly' sinners and enemies of God, Christ died for us (Rom. 5:6–11), how can we not do what we can by our attitudes, words, and actions to let those other sinners and enemies know that the same good news is for them too? If we do not believe it for them, how can we believe it for ourselves? If we know that the hope any of us has is that all of us will one day stand before the Judge who is the 'friend of sinners' (Luke 7:34), must we not hope *for* rather than *against* the wicked. . . ?" *Christian Doctrine*, rev. ed., 389.

25. An important book has been Oscar Cullmann, *Immortality of the Soul or Resurrection of the Dead?* (New York: Macmillan, 1958). To speak of an "immortal soul" is reminiscent of Greek philosophical ideas and assumes that there is a part of the person—the "soul"—that has always existed and will always exist. The "soul" is separate from the corruptible "body" that it is temporarily inhabiting and is itself indestructible. The resurrection of the body affirms that God gives life to the whole person. Migliore notes that "even if we cannot adequately conceive of a resurrection body, the symbol stands as a bold and even defiant affirmation of God's total, inclusive, holistic redemption." See *Faith Seeking Understanding* (Grand Rapids: Wm. B. Eerdmans Publishing Co., 1991), 244.

26. Berkhof, *Christian Faith*, 538.

27. Moltmann, *The Coming of God*, 131. He goes to conclude that because of this "*the kingdom of God* is a more integral symbol of the eschatological hope than eternal life."

Herman Bavinck indicates that "the great diversity that exists among people in all sorts of ways is not destroyed in eternity but is cleansed from all that is sinful and made serviceable to fellowship with God and each other," *The Last Things: Hope for This World and the Next*, ed. John Bold, trans. John Vriend (Grand Rapids: Baker Books, 1996), 167.

28. Moltmann, *The Coming of God*, 265. He goes on to say that "the *creatio ex nihilo*, the creation out of nothing, is completed in the eschatological *creatio ex vetere*, the creation out of the old." See his part 4, "New Heaven—New Earth: Cosmic Eschatology."

29. Bavinck, *The Last Things*, 160.

30. Ibid.

31. See Jürgen Moltmann, *The Theology of Hope*, trans. James W. Leitch (New York: Harper & Row, 1967).

32. As G. C. Berkouwer put it, "Eschatology is not a projection into the distant future; it bursts forth into our present existence, and structures life today in the light of the last days," *The Return of Christ*, trans. James Van Oosterom (Grand Rapids: Wm. B. Eerdmans Publishing Co., 1972), 19. An excellent book to show ways in which differing views of the nature of God's reign lead to very practical consequences is Howard A. Snyder, *Models of the Kingdom* (Nashville: Abingdon, 1991).

33. Moltmann says, "The Christian hope for the future comes of observing a specific, unique event—that of the resurrection and appearing of Jesus Christ," *Theology of Hope*, 194.

34. Jürgen Moltmann, *The Church in the Power of the Spirit*, trans. Margaret Kohl (New York: Harper & Row, 1977), 11. Likewise, "Christianity does not exist for its own sake; it exists for the sake of the coming kingdom," 164. The Roman Catholic Hans Küng wrote that the church is "not the bringer or the bearer of the reign of God which is to come and is at the same time already present, but its voice, its announcer, its herald. God alone can bring his reign; the Church is devoted entirely to its service," *The Church*, trans. Ray and Rosaleen Ockenden (New York: Sheed and Ward, 1967), 96.

35. Moltmann, *Theology of Hope*, 328.

36. As Moltmann puts it, "the Spirit of God works in history as the creator of a new future and as the new creator of what is transient for this future. The Spirit of God makes the impossible possible; he creates faith where there is nothing else to believe in; he creates love where there is nothing lovable; he creates hope where there is nothing to hope for," *The Church in the Power of the Spirit*, 191.

37. Carl E. Braaten, *The Flaming Center: A Theology of Christian Mission* (Philadelphia: Fortress Press, 1977), 43.

38. See Mortimer Arias, *Announcing the Reign of God: Evangelization and the Subversive Memory of Jesus* (Philadelphia: Fortress Press, 1984), chaps. 6–8.

Chapter 18

1. This freedom to make choices is sometimes called "free agency."

2. Karl Barth, "The Humanity of God," in *God, Grace and Gospel*, trans. James Strathearn McNab, Scottish Journal of Theology Occasional Papers No. 8 (Edinburgh: Oliver and Boyd, 1959), 50.

3. For a more detailed discussion, see my essay, "Reformed Convictions and Religious Pluralism," in *Many Voices, One God: Being Faithful in a Pluralistic World* (Louisville, Ky.: Westminster John Knox Press, 1998), 78–92.

4. See Alan P. F. Sell, *The Great Debate: Calvinism, Arminianism and Salvation* (West Sussex, England: H. E. Walter, 1982).

Index of Non-English Terms

Index of Names

Subject Index